BLIND SPOTS

BLIND SPOTS

THE MEMOIRS OF
A BABY BOOMER
ON THE ROCKY ROAD
TOWARDS
SPIRITUAL
AWAKENING

JOHN
DOMENICO

Outskirts Press, Inc.
Denver, Colorado

Outskirts Press, Inc.
http://www.outskirtspress.com

ISBN: 978-1-4327-4737-4

Outskirts Press and the "OP" logo are trademarks belonging to Outskirts Press, Inc.

PRINTED IN THE UNITED STATES OF AMERICA

This book is lovingly dedicated to all who are mentioned in its pages, and especially to Julianne. We haven't seen eye to eye on many issues, but through the good times and the bad, we've managed to stick it out.

Thanks to Tanya Clusener and Ronnie Gavarian for their unending encouragement and the many hours they spent editing the stories of my life.

John Domenico

Contents

BEFORE I BEGIN

When I first set out on this undertaking, to tell my story, the first thought that occurred to me was, "Who are you and who cares about what you have to say about life, religion, politics or anything for that matter?"

I'm not and have never been a rock star, an actor, a politician, a sports figure, a serial killer, or a self-made millionaire. I'm just an average family guy who happened to be born in the 1950's and was part of the most interesting, influential generations in history. I had a lot of questions...and still do. I came out of the "Don't trust anybody over thirty" crowd, and here I am in my mid-fifties still wondering, "Who can you trust?"

I finally decided that there are more people out there in the world who could relate to me and my story, rather than the success stories of Hollywood celebrities, front-page criminals and the like. So with the baby-boomers in mind, folks who have lived through the emergence of The Beatles, the magnitude of Woodstock, the tragedy of Viet Nam, the assassination of political heroes and the turbulent sixties...folks who have been appalled by our government, the 9-11 disaster and who continue to question authority...and especially folks who have been indoctrinated into some form of organized religion and are having doubts about issues of faith, I present my story.

OPENING REMARKS

A long time ago when I was around seventeen years old, when I started to realize missing church on Sunday wasn't really a sin, I held onto the notion that I didn't want to be categorized in any way, shape or form. I had this very idealistic mindset there should be no separation among men. The fact we are all born into this world without any say of our own made me see the truth in the expression "All men are created equal," the earth is our home, and it should be nurtured and cared for by all who live upon it. I believed every human being had the same obligation to love their planet and our survival depended upon it. I was born into this world a free spirit and without a choice I was labeled American, Italian, Catholic, Democrat... At this rebellious time of life I preferred to be identified simply as a free being, designed to live in harmony with the rest of creation, "A Universal Child of God" who happened to live on Planet Earth. As time moved on, somehow in my quest for love and success, whatever that may be, and my search for truth, whatever that may be, my idealism took a backseat as life sucked me in to its crazy rat race. All these years later as I slowly coast into retirement, I went full circle.

There's something about the teenage spirit that is truly amazing. For a few precious years we really believe we've got all the time in the world ahead of us. The span of time between birthdays, summers or Christmases seems eternal. I know when I was at that indestructible time of my life, if someone approached me and asked questions that had to do with life and death and where I thought I was going to spend eternity, I'd laugh and say he was some sort of a religious kook. It's funny the kind of things I started thinking about when I realized there was more life behind me than there was ahead of me...

PREFACE

It was late August 2006 when I had to attend one of those obligatory parties, the kind of affair people show up at only because they don't want to hurt the feelings of the host and hostess and not because they're looking forward to mingling with the other guests! Practically all in attendance were old friends and acquaintances who at one time or another were members of the local Full Gospel Christian Church, a place of worship I chose to leave several years prior to this event. My wife on the other hand remained a loyal and dedicated member of the congregation, so occasionally I found myself in social situations connected to her church.

I don't know if most guys will readily admit this or not, but I'm not the least bit reluctant to say I never forget a pretty face. I may not be very good at remembering the name attached to that face, but nevertheless the eyes, the smile, the hair and the lips get permanently stored deep into the recesses of my memory banks.

At many of these Christian gatherings it was rare that alcoholic beverages were served, so I had to settle for a paper cup of fruit punch to wash down the homemade baked ziti, instead of my customary glass of a red California varietal. As I stood up to go pour myself another cup, I saw a woman walk into the room. "I know that face," I thought to myself, but for the life of me couldn't remember her name or even when I last saw her. I turned to my wife for help, and she not only reminded me where I knew her from, but told me her name was Angela. It was all coming back to me. Angela used to attend the same church as we did and always sat in the third or fourth pew on the left. I remembered she was married to this guy who I met once at a non-church function. He never came with her to church and my first and only impression of him was that of a would-be mobster. One day I just never saw her in church anymore; but that's the way it is with church congregations, people come and go and a familiar face becomes a distant memory.

Angela certainly remembered me. After making eye contact we made our way towards one another. We gave each other the customary hug and kiss hello.

"It's been a long time," I said, then without any prodding from me she explained why she had disappeared. Being submissive to a controlling husband, she had left church, friends and family and moved Upstate for several years. But then, fed up with her life in the wilderness, she made the decision to become a weekend wife and move back to her hometown in suburban Long Island. With hopes of avoiding the endless questions about her mysterious life, she chose to attend a church a few towns away.

"So!" she said, "Enough about me! What's this I hear about you leaving the church? What happened?"

It was incredible to me how word traveled. I told her that the past few years of my life had taken me through many changes. I probably shouldn't have gone into it, but I've always been one for telling it like it is. I gently tried to explain to her how my spiritual views had changed and how I wasn't sold on the soul-saving business of Christianity anymore. I thought she was going to cry right then and there.

"Are you telling me you don't believe the Bible is the inspired Word of God?" she sadly questioned.

I tried to be tactful by telling her I believed many great books have been and will be Spirit-inspired. Then she hit me with the next question.

"Are you telling me you don't believe Jesus is the Son of God?" she asked hesitantly.

I knew I said way too much already and I began wishing I had never said a word.

"I believe we are all sons of God, Jesus just realized it more than we do!" I responded diplomatically.

"Oh my God!" she cried, as if she were suddenly afraid of me.

Then inching back as to leave a safe distance between us she said, "John, I'm going to pray for you!"

She then gave me a mini-sermon about too much knowledge being spiritually fatal, told me it was good seeing me, and then disappeared into the crowd. To tell the truth, our short conversation left me feeling quite disturbed. I was sincerely hoping she was secure enough in her faith, because as much as I take pleasure in getting people to think, I don't ever want to rock someone's boat so badly they fall overboard. The other thing that rattled me for a moment was realizing something I held so dear throughout my youth and most of my adult life was gone. A belief I once thought shaped the very fabric of who I was, no longer existed. Seeing mainstream Christianity in a whole new light, I was no longer comfortable identifying myself as a Born Again Christian. Who knows, maybe I *was* really, finally born again. And then again?

INTRODUCTION

Many years ago I heard a televangelist relate a story about a man who embarked on a journey. The story goes that after long hours on the road and covering countless miles, the traveler realized he should have already reached his destination. He traveled a little further before he made the decision to stop at a roadside information booth. When he asked the attendant there for directions, he was told he journeyed way past the spot at which he should have exited the highway. He was instructed to turn around and travel back to the place where he was supposed to exit and from that point he could continue his trip. The traveler became very frustrated and annoyed and even questioned the travel guide's knowledge. He complained about how far he had come and how much time he had spent going in the wrong direction that he decided to ignore the attendant's advice and stubbornly continue on his way, convinced at some point he would indeed arrive at the place he set out for.

Obviously, not following the instructions of the attendant was going to take this sorry soul even further out of his way. How many of us behave in a similar fashion, ignoring signs and good advice, traveling aimlessly down life's highway missing our exits and driving unnecessarily in the wrong direction? Whether it's stubborn pride, our mistrust, the inability to read life's road maps, or our loyalty to those who unknowingly give us incorrect guidance, there comes a time when we have to ask ourselves, "Do I turn around or do I blindly continue on?"

Many times it's all too easy to get lost. We have to be able to recognize it when we do and then have the sense enough to continue on the right road even if it requires backtracking. We need to watch for the signs. Missing one could lead us way off course.

What you are about to read is an account of my journey. Writing this book was an attempt to finally find out just who the heck I am. This exercise in putting my thoughts down in words was a way of trying to figure out exactly what I believe about God, about myself and why.

Throughout the pages that follow, I have taken the liberty of expressing my feelings about the many people who have at one time or another entered the microcosm of time I call "my life." In some way everyone we interact with on our journey through life has an influence on who we are whether we know it or not. If we should meet someone who we admire, it's only natural we would try to emulate that person's good qualities. The opposite is also true, when we encounter someone who is a complete asshole, we try our very best to avoid becoming like that person. Each one of us has the awesome ability to make a lasting impression on someone, good or bad.

In order for me to regard this collection of thoughts, memories and opinions as a successful undertaking, I had to approach it with the intent of being totally honest. It has never been my intention for anyone to be offended by anything I've said, but as the saying goes: The way to divide a room is to talk about religion and politics. If anyone is upset about my perception of occurrences, or the way he or she has been portrayed, or behaviors, and attitudes…what can I say? It's my book and I told things the way I saw them. But should anyone want to add to the stories or have totally different perceptions of the same events, please feel free to accept my invitation to blog me on my website, www.outskirtspress.com/blindspots.

PART I

BACKGROUND CHECK

I must admit for the most part I've lived a pretty good and full life. I am the oldest of four children. (After me came my sister Virginia, and then my mom had a miscarriage, followed by my two brothers, Bill and Jim.) I've been blessed with warm, loving and giving parents, good extended family, numerous friends, a great sense of humor, a curious mind and a little rebellious streak. Mom and Dad tended to most of my needs and I can honestly say I never wanted for anything. To this very day, God bless them, they are still there to lend a hand no matter what the need be. Sometimes I want to blame their unrelenting love for possibly holding us back a bit and creating an unintentional yet abnormal dependency on them. But maybe I'm confusing love with protection, because truthfully, no one can ever get enough love. Nevertheless, there was never need to fear because mom and dad were our superheroes, always accessible, always ready to save the day! Whether or not this safety net held me back from achieving some of my dreams, I'll never know.

I was born in 1952 in the Bronx (home of the N.Y. Yankees) where my mom and dad lived with my dad's parents. For as long as I remember my grandma and grandpa always seemed old. She didn't speak much English and from what I can recall from behind the clouds of Italian cigar smoke, he rarely spoke at all. "Johnny!" he would call out to me saying the one word I could understand, "Mangia!"

What I gathered from the stories I'd heard throughout the years, my grandparents were Italian immigrants who settled on a farm in Pennsylvania somewhere. (Come to think of it, being a farmer may not have been such a bad life after all.) When my dad's older brother Cosmo, who everybody called Jack, got taken ill, my grandfather sold the farm and moved to New York City so Jack could get the proper medical care. Back in those days there weren't many doctors in close proximity of the Pennsylvania cornfields.

My mom and dad met in New York Hospital where they were both involved in an X-ray technician-training program. Mom became an X-ray tech and dad sold X-ray equipment for Ansco, which later became known as GAF. They fell in love, got married in December 1951, and then moved in with my grandparents. Ten months later in late September, I was born. From the tales my mom had told me about the constant intrusions by her new in-laws, it's a wonder how she ever became pregnant. I imagine the living quarters were situated in a way that didn't allow for much privacy. My dad's oldest sister Jean (whose real name was Josephine), according to legend, would actually barge into my parents' bedroom, sit on their bed and have bedtime conversations with them.

I'm not very certain if what I consider to be memories of my short stay in the Bronx are genuine, or am I simply remembering the old eight-millimeter movies and photographs I'd seen over the years. There is however one authentic Bronx memory that definitely stands out in my mind and it's the night my mom had a miscarriage. I can still see her standing beside the chrome legged kitchen table preparing a graham cracker crust cheesecake. Next thing I knew, my Aunt Jean was on hand to watch my sister Virginia and me while my dad was trying to rush my mom out of the house and off to the hospital. I was sitting on the living room couch engrossed in my pirate puzzle books. As she was leaving, I looked up to see mom smile as if to reassure me everything was fine. She never seemed to show signs of worry or fear. It's just the way she was.

Besides that recollection, I have only a few other vivid early childhood memories. One involves me climbing into my sister's crib and cutting off all of her hair with a very large seamstress' shears. Fortunately she still has both her ears!

Another one features my mom giving my sister and me a bath together and suddenly realizing that she (my sister) must have pooped in the tub. When I noticed floating brown lumps, I immediately brought them to my mom's attention, at which point she swiftly pulled us from the sewage. (Come to think of it, I don't recall if we ever got re-bathed?)

Then there was the time when my dad brought home a puppy. Being the brave youngster I was, I stood upon a kitchen chair, trembled with fear and cried as if I were about to be thrown to the lions.

One incident I probably shouldn't even own up to is running scared when the neighborhood utilities man pointed to the gas flame emblem on his car door and accused me of setting his vehicle on fire. Most likely, he was just trying to be funny, so I could only imagine what he thought when he saw me run for my life! Why I remember these things is something I'd probably have to discuss while lying on a psychiatrist's couch.

On the other hand, there were also a couple of instances that demonstrated my budding creative energies. There was the time I created heart designs on the arms of my grandfather's leather recliner by puncturing dozens of tiny holes with a pushpin. Each and every time the pinhead pierced the chair, I had a sneaking suspicion I may have been doing something wrong, but hoping my artwork might be appreciated, I continued. Oh! My folks were "proud" of me for that one, but not half as proud as the time I drew abstracts all over the living room lampshades with my mom's red lipstick. I'm sure given some time they would have grown to love their potential Picasso's designs, leaving them on display for all to see. I guess I could have considered myself lucky to have not gotten my ass kicked.

In 1956 we moved from the Bronx to Jackson Heights in Queens to live with my other set of grandparents (my mom's folks). My grandmother on my mom's side spoke fluent English so for that reason alone I felt closer to her than my dad's mom. My mother's dad was a rather large man, also an Italian immigrant, whose broken English was slightly better than my other grandfather's. Naturally, being of Italian descent I was raised Roman Catholic and it was there in Jackson Heights at Saint Gabriel's where I began the first day of a twelve-year run in the Catholic school system. I only attended St. Gabriel's for a few months before we moved, but during that short time made many attempts at escaping. Maybe I knew even way back then, I should have gotten out while I had the chance.

After the morning bell sounded and all the school buses were gone, and all the mothers who had dropped off their kids were attending to their household chores, only one person stood alone at the schoolyard gate... my mom! She had to wait around for the inevitable. It would only be a matter of minutes before I came crashing through the school building's exit doors like a thoroughbred racehorse busting through the starting gate, screaming as if my very life were in danger. Mom had to grab hold of me, reassure me everything was all right and drag me back into the penitentiary and into the hands of the nuns.

Before I was even halfway through first grade at St. G's, my family packed up and moved again. My grandparents sold their house in Jackson Heights and bought a parcel of land in what was a completely untouched wooded area in a wilderness known as College Point, and built a rather large house. The only way grandma and grandpa could have taken on this project was if my mom and dad had agreed to move in with them, which they did. It was at the time of my parents' move to College Point when they enrolled me in my second Catholic grade school…St. Fidelis, whoever he was!

WELCOME TO THE NEIGHBORHOOD

A kid is supposed to feel secure in knowing that the adults have things somewhat in control. A kid should be able to go to bed each night with a satisfied smile on his face, dream sweet dreams, and wake up the next morning confident that all is well. It should be okay to be silly and a little naïve because it's only a matter of time before he'll have to face up to the responsibilities that come with adulthood.

For most school kids, early dismissal was a cool thing. At this delicate time in my life, when St. Fidelis, the neighborhood and all of its surroundings were completely new to me, leaving school before the three o'clock bell was good enough reason to be alarmed. I really didn't know my way around at all. I boarded the school bus on my corner every morning and Frank, the friendly driver, would drop me off at the schoolyard. Every afternoon Frank picked me up in front of the school and returned me safely to my corner. Although the familiar smell of the school bus fumes that seemed to infuse the air were probably harmful, they were comforting. Anything deviating from the security of this simple routine could easily have become a nerve-racking situation, not only for me, but also for any young impressionable kid. One morning, not even an hour after school was in session, we were informed there was going to be an early dismissal. I don't recall what the reason was. It may have been the death of a pope, a bishop or an electrical problem, I don't know. All I knew was there would be no school bus service available and I was faced with having to take public transportation in order to get home. Across the street from my grammar school was St. Agnes, the all-girl high school. For the very same reason we were dismissed early on that day, so were they. I never had to ride the city bus on my own before and so needless to say, I was bewildered. Why there were no adults around to supervise all these kids, or even just me for that matter, I had no idea! I nervously tried to call my mom but no one answered the phone. Answering machines hadn't been invented yet so I couldn't even leave a message. I then followed the crowd to the bus stop on this damp misty morning and stood among what seemed like hundreds of teenage girls who were waiting for a bus I only hoped was headed for my house. All of this commotion was doing quite a job of stressing me out, and of all things, what could have possibly happened next? There have been many times when I'd looked back at certain situations in my life and it seemed as though I was watching a scene from a movie. Well this was one of those situations and I can picture myself as the central character in the scene. There I was, squashed among all these older female strangers anxiously waiting for the bus to arrive, when from out of nowhere I heard the horrifying screams of a girl and the screeching of tires. The camera locked in on a close-up of my terrified face and then cut away to the body of a young woman being dragged along the street from under the chassis of an out of control automobile. I quickly became a few degrees shy of a total basket case! All around me St. Agnes girls were screaming and sobbing. My silent trembling had to be a dead giveaway of how frightened I was, yet no one was the least bit concerned about me! The bus finally arrived and when I stepped up to face the driver, I realized I had no money and no bus pass. He must have seen the look of dread on my face and asked me where I lived. With a frantic stutter I did my best to explain the location of my house. The bus driver was compassionate enough to let me ride for free, and later saw to it I got off at the right stop. The bus was filled to capacity with kids who had just witnessed a classmate get run down by a car. I pushed my way through the hysteria and found a seat where I sat frozen with fright. I stared directly at the wet fur of the coat on the girl who stood before me, and in my over-active imagination it appeared to be blood-soaked. As soon as I exited the bus I ran home screaming for dear life. Under the impression I was still safe at school, my mom couldn't imagine who it might have been when she heard the blood-curdling cries of a child running around the house banging on every door and window. Curious as to what she was hearing, my mom finally stepped outside and much to her surprise found yours truly shaking uncontrollably as if death itself was stalking me. I could only wonder as to what she was thinking! She probably figured I was reverting back to my "elementary school escape artist" ways. When she saw the tears of terror streaming from my eyes, she had to presume something was terribly amiss.

I couldn't get the frightening image of a young girl's head protruding from below the bumper of the runaway automobile out of my mind. I became a nervous wreck, couldn't sleep at night and was scared of my own shadow. It took months, lots of attention from mom and dad, and a prescription of tranquilizers before I returned to being a semi-normal functioning child. After making some inquiries with the police and the local hospital, we learned the girl was going to be all right...and for whatever reason, after knowing that, so was I.

CATHOLIC ITALIANS

As a kid I thought if someone wasn't Catholic and Italian, they were really missing out. They were not just missing out on ever entering the pearly gates of heaven; they were missing out on eating the best food in the universe. I truly felt sorry for non-Italians, especially the Irish and the Jews. I couldn't imagine life without lasagna or grandma's rice balls. A home just wasn't a home without a fig tree in the backyard or a garage full of grapes waiting for Grandpa to make his homemade wine. The Jews had pastrami and the Irish had corned beef and potatoes, but it couldn't compare to the large pot of tomato sauce and meatballs simmering on the stove every Sunday.

Saint Fidelis provided me with an elementary education surrounded by nuns, statues, Jesus nailed to a cross with His eyes painfully looking up towards the heavens, catechism, saints, priests, confession, Lent, Ash Wednesday, sacraments, candles, purgatory, rosary beads, limbo and endless other holy rituals, traditions, artifacts and teachings designed to pave our path to heaven. The nuns walked about in outfits, which to a six year old, made them appear as if they were celestial beings. As for the students, we had to set ourselves apart from the public school "masses" with our neatly creased military style uniforms. Then of course, Catholic school curriculum included "Catechism" or religion class, the first steps in the process of molding young minds to believe they were soldiers in the army of the one true church.

When I was about 8 years old I was fascinated with the whole idea of

Mass. My grandmother, who was an excellent seamstress, custom made me my very own priest vestments. I set up an altar in the boiler room of my house complete with candles, tabernacle and linens. I used one of my mom's fancy wine glasses as a chalice and Nabisco vanilla wafers as the Communion host. For anyone who had the patience and kindness to sit through it, I would perform to the very best of my ability, the home version of the Mass. I wonder now whether my family and relatives were amused or tortured. Sometimes I even tried to recruit my sister Virginia to play the role of altar boy. To all those who had the patience to tolerate my enactments of a Sunday morning Mass, I deeply apologize. Sitting through the real one was more than enough for anyone to have to endure.

My house had statues of saints all over the place. My mom prayed to dead people. She thought (and may still think) St. Anthony helps her to find things that are lost. St. Jude helps with anything that may seem impossible. Rosary beads hung on our bedposts like good luck charms. Priests smeared ashes on our foreheads on Ash Wednesday and blessed our throats with magic candles on St. Blaze day. We dipped our dirty fingers into small bowl shaped containers of stagnant holy water and then touched our brows with it after hundreds of other dirty fingers were in the same sludge. Like conditioned robots, we sat, we knelt, and we stood to the sound of a clicker (a sound very similar to that of a cricket) and the ringing of bells. Most of us had no clue whatsoever as to why we believed what we believed. The only reason any of us ever picked up a Bible was because we heard the word "ass" was in there and we had to see it for ourselves. We just went along with whatever they taught us and were made to feel guilty if we didn't. I used to think God spoke Latin, Jesus really sat on a big chair next to His father, and the Holy Ghost just hovered above the two of them on its heavenly perch. This was enough to make any thinking person become an atheist.

Catechism was also a form of preparation or training intended to make us spiritually ready to receive the sacraments such as confession, Holy Communion, and confirmation. These sacraments we "received" as kids were usually just excuses for our parents to throw parties. We got money and the grownups got drunk. Catholic kids who went to the local public schools usually had to go to weekly religious instructions at our school to receive what certainly seemed like a much milder dose of indoctrination and sacramental preparation. For some reason this always occurred on a Wednesday but all it meant to me was I had a half-day of school. Catholic School kids loved Wednesdays!

BUYING INTO HEAVEN

From the day I was able to comprehend the meaning of yes and no, I was taught to believe, both at home and in religion class, that being a Catholic made me a member of the "privileged" faith, that we were the only souls bound for heaven. It was instilled in me at this early age to have an understanding that God did indeed exist, that he knew my every move, and fearing Him was considered normal, rational behavior. In school we also learned the basics. They were, "God loves you," and "God is everywhere" (although His main residence is heaven). We were taught there was a heaven (a place of eternal joy) and a hell (a place of eternal torment). We were also taught that two other dwelling places existed in the hereafter as well. One was known as purgatory and the other as limbo. The souls still blemished by the stain of small sins were sentenced to purgatory, and the amount of prayers that were recited or candles that were lit for them, depending on the severity of the offense, determined the length of the stay. In order to light a candle for someone suffering in purgatory it was first required to purchase that candle. Small votive candles were twenty-five cents and the large ones that usually stayed lit for a month were one dollar. Of course candle lighting was all done on the honor system since one could have easily just lit a candle without paying for it. But let's face it, would God really honor such a candle? I don't think so. (Today I understand the candles are electric and unless they are paid for, they don't ignite... so much for trust!) So what I got out of all of this was God could be bought. History teaches how the church once sold indulgences, making people believe they could actually buy their way out of purgatory. A comforting thought for the wealthy. Make no mistake, vows of poverty aren't what made the Catholic Church the power it is today…capitalism is alive and well within its confines. (If God were indeed EVERYWHERE, wouldn't it mean there could not be a place where God wasn't, totally negating the concept of hell, limbo and purgatory!)

I learned that sin was broken down into two categories: mortal and venial. If somebody died with mortal sin on his or her soul it was a ticket straight to hell. Venial sin sent one to purgatory. In case we were having difficulty in getting the idea, our Catechism provided us with the following visual of the three milk bottles: The first bottle was all white, illustrating a pure soul headed for heaven. The second had a few scattered black dots, indicating a stopover in purgatory. The third bottle was completely black, representing a soul damned to hell and its eternal fires. So naturally our teachers had to help us draw up some kind of list as to determine what a mortal sin was and what a venial sin was. We had to have some idea of where we were headed if we just so happened to sin before our next confession! Murder was definitely mortal. Telling a lie was venial, unless of course the lie resulted in someone's murder. Stealing was probably venial, unless the amount stolen exceeded the fifty thousand dollar limit or if the theft resulted in someone's murder.

I will never forget sitting in a church pew reading a "missalette," a tiny prayer book filled with tiny prayers that were supposed to be repeated over and over again. These holy mantras were called ejaculations. (No kidding! They were really called that!) In parenthesis alongside each of these ejaculations was a number. Some read 50, some 100 some 500, some even 1,000. Should anyone had the misfortune of being sent to purgatory, these represented the number of years their sentence would decrease for each time someone recited the prayer and struck their breast with their right hand. As soon as I learned this little trick, I jumped down to my knees and began beating my hand to my heart repeating those holy ejaculations like crazy, as if I were making contributions to my Soul Insurance Policy. In my head I was adding up the years and hoping they were being stored away in heaven's penance storehouse so my inevitable stay in purgatory would be very short.

BLESS ME FATHER

The nuns making us go to weekly confession, or "the sacrament of penance," was really an anxiety-laden trip for us grade-schoolers. They would line us up during our school day and march us over to the church where we stood in fear to wait for a turn to confess our sins to a priest. He would then look on his holy charts to see exactly how much penance we had to do in order for our souls to be wiped clean. If we were lucky enough to die immediately after stepping out of confession (provided we didn't lie in the confessional), we had a ticket granting us entrance right into heaven...pass "go" collect $200.00.

We would enter a small cubicle by passing through a dark curtain, and behind a wall inside the ominous closet sat the priest looking forward to hearing us confess our nasty little sins. I don't think there was anything that made me as nervous as going to confession. The priest put his ear up against the tiny screened window that separated us and closely listened as I timidly whispered, "Bless me father for I have sinned..." trying desperately to remember exactly what I did to unleash God's wrath during the past week. Theoretically, confessions were supposed to be anonymous. The confessional was designed so the priest could not recognize the confessor through the mesh covered opening. Trusting soul I was, every week I recited my usual spiel; "I lied, I disobeyed my parents, I said bad words, had impure thoughts...and oh yes, and I just lied again!"

At Saint Fidelis, there were four confessionals and each priest of the parish was assigned his very own station. Most parishioners, especially us kids, had a preference as to which priest we wanted to confess our sins to. There was this one priest named Father Conway and he was one crazy character. He was loud and he was mean and no one liked having to get on his line. The other priests were very laid back and they seemed to take our confessions pretty lightly. They probably thought, "Just how bad could a kid possibly be?" The penance they doled out was usually very light...a Hail Mary or two and the offenders would be on their way to hopefully sin no more! Penance, the action whereby the sinner could pay for his sins, actually made absolutely no sense at all... weren't we told Jesus paid the full price for our sins? A standard penance consisted of saying a few prayers or lighting a couple of candles. I was pretty sure this system of justice had God's stamp of approval all over it. I guess penance for a Catholic could be compared to doing a little community service or paying a small fine. It wiped the sinner's slate clean for the time being. Father Conway, however, never let us off the hook that easily.

One afternoon Sister Richard Lawrence, one of my dear sweet teachers, instructed me to get on Conway's line. I couldn't believe my luck! Anything but Father Conway! Having no choice in the matter, I obediently took my place in line and when it was my turn, I unwillingly slipped behind the curtain and proceeded to do my "sins of the week shtick".

When I whispered that I had disobeyed my parents, he roared, "How many times?"

There was silence and then I stuttered, "About two or three times father," to which he replied ferociously, "What is it, son...two or three?"

I was kneeling in that dark persecution chamber for what seemed like forever. I knew everyone in the entire church could hear his loud reprimanding voice echo through the rafters as his demeaning words struck me like a cracking whip. All I could hear resonating in my head was the evil tone of his voice demanding to know, "How many times, how many times, how many times?" After what felt like several lifetimes, he pardoned my sins and I saw the shadow of his hands bless me with the sign of the cross. Sweating profusely and embarrassed beyond description, I slowly slithered off back to my seat, feeling as if even the statues were staring me down, pointing and making judgments.

After my class returned to the school and I was sitting safely at my desk, there was a knock on our classroom door. An older student from a higher grade entered the room and approached my teacher. While looking directly at me I heard him say to her, "Father Conway wants to see that boy who just made his confession."

Sister Richard, fortunately not remembering which line she put me on, asked me if I had been in Father Conway's confessional. As I trembled with the possibility of having to face that madman again, I looked her right in the eye and denied it.

"No sister," I sighed like a coward, "I went to Father Harrison." There I went and lied again.

HOLY MISCOMMUNICATION, BATMAN!

"Holy Communion," also known as the Eucharist, was another one of those supernatural occurrences of the Catholic faith that took place during Mass. It made absolutely no sense to any rationally thinking human being, yet week after week children and adults alike would line up to take part in this ritual. Holy Communion is the sacrament wherein a thin white wafer (the host) melts in your mouth, not in your hand and is believed by Catholics, to be the actual, not symbolic, body of Jesus. Most of the Mass is a reenactment of the crucifixion (Christ's death on the cross), and it is during this Mass when a miracle supposedly takes place. After a priest makes some magician-like hand motions and chants some standardized prayers, the wafer miraculously becomes flesh. In retrospect, it's amazing to me how as kids we weren't grossed out at the thought we were eating Jesus. But that's what they taught us. When participating in this magical mystery ritual, a Catholic was strictly forbidden to eat any solid food for three hours or consume any liquid for one hour prior to partaking. Many a time ushers had to deal with parishioners fainting from low blood sugar! We were also told the wafer was sacred and instructed never to chew it. And heaven forbid should it accidentally drop on the floor! If and when that ever happened, the host was covered with a white linen napkin as not to disrupt the service. Later it was scooped up with a gold plate and disposed of with the sacred garbage (a drain leading directly into the earth instead of the sewer system). This didn't really make sense, because when we digested the sacred wafer, it would eventually become part of our own body waste and end up in the public sewer system anyway.

The priest would place the wafer firmly on the tongue of each receiving believer. Where his fingers had been was anybody's guess. His hand would go from one person's mouth to the next, feeding the procession of believers the "Body of Christ." Then the parishioner would return to his pew, place his head in his hands and meditate about the miracle that just took place, the very body of the Lord becoming one with his! I would have thought we should have been praying we didn't contract some communicable disease.

Part two of this magic act was the changing of ordinary table wine into the alleged blood of Jesus. "This is my body, and this is my blood, do this in remembrance of me," is a line from the Bible that the Catholics stretched way beyond the imagination. The priest stood before the congregation, held up his chalice for all to see, then consumed all of the wine (the blood of Christ).

After sucking down the very last drop of blood wine, the priest wiped out his gold chalice and then tucked it safely away into the tabernacle until the next happy hour. The tabernacle located on the center of the altar, was a miniature closet with a gold plated door, a curtain that was color co-coordinated with the priests' vestments. At the end of the Mass, the consecrated holy wheat thins and the gold chalices were stored away inside. I could understand the gold chalice, but why they found it necessary to keep the Lord's body locked up, I don't know. Maybe they feared someone would kidnap it and hold it for ransom! Although it's most embarrassing to admit, I fell for it hook, line, and sinker. I thought I was actually swallowing God's body. What I was swallowing was just one big load of false doctrine.

Even more confusing than a wafer becoming flesh was the idea of limbo. Limbo was a place where the souls of dead babies went if they were not baptized into the Catholic faith prior to their early passing. Since we were taught we were born into this world with the stain of original sin (the first sin committed by Adam and Eve), an innocent baby didn't even have a chance of making heaven if he or she should have choked on the umbilical cord and died before having had his or her first thought. Who would want a whole bunch of un-baptized babies hanging around in heaven anyway?

Didn't anybody ever conclude, maybe all this supernatural information was way too much to be dumping on a child? Maybe that was the trick...

since kids will usually believe anything, drum it into their heads when they're young and there's a good chance they will carry it with them into their adulthood. It must have worked because my parents never tried to teach us any differently, only proving they must have fallen for all the same religious mumbo jumbo as we did. As kids, we had an excuse, what the heck did we know? But as for thinking adults, I would assume somebody somewhere had to realize most of the stuff we were swallowing was no more real than the tooth fairy. (By the way, Pope Benedict had recently decreed Limbo no longer exists!)

ALTAR BOY

I think it's safe to assume anyone who has ever been an altar boy could tell some interesting tales from the sacristy (the church green room for Mass performers). I was an altar boy for a short time, and my partner (altar boys worked in pairs) John Frank was a bad influence, to say the least. It was the job of the altar boy to fill the cruets with water and wine before each Mass. One morning I saw John taking some pretty large swigs from a Gallo bottle while preparing the cruets. I couldn't believe he could be so brazen as to drink the liquid that would soon be transubstantiated into the blood of our Lord! Naturally he didn't want to act alone, so he generously offered some to me. I, as the weak-willed thrill seeker, obliged him. I looked upon it as something rather risky; we were too young to be interested in sex, so we would drink the church wine to get our kicks. We each watched out for the priest and when the coast was clear, we would take a slug! Of course what did I know about good or bad wine, but I do remember how it warmed my insides.

Before assisting in his first Mass, every new recruit had to take a training class to learn the holy choreography and the sacred language. Just like a Broadway show, there were stage directions that had to be adhered to. When a priest and his altar boys were synchronized, the Mass had more of an impact on the crowd. The altar boy who fumbled and stumbled about was a major distraction and could easily cause someone to question the credibility of the ritual. If an altar boy was lucky enough to be teamed up with the same priest often enough, he'd get to know his signs and signals making for a smooth performance. It was imperative that the altar boys were alert at all times, ready to ring those bells, pour the wine, and catch those falling wafers.

Not ringing the bells at the correct moment was the most obvious mistake an altar boy could make. Just to emphasize how naïve I was, it wasn't until I became an altar boy, when I realized the sound of bells didn't come directly from heavenly sources. When I attended Mass and heard the bells ring at crucial stages, (such as the moment when the bread supposedly became flesh), I never saw anybody physically ring bells, so I just assumed it was a supernatural occurrence. Nevertheless, when I discovered it was the altar boys' responsibility to jingle-jangle those bells, I saw to it that it was me who assumed that lofty position. There was something so gratifying in knowing that at given moments during the Mass, the clang from the bells that I rang would cause people to pay attention, stand, kneel, strike their breasts and genuflect. I had the power!

To be an effective altar boy, I was required to recite from memory certain prayers completely in Latin (probably the world's deadest language). Don't ask me how I ever passed the "altar boy entrance exam," because aside from a few catch phrases, I couldn't speak a word of it. Mass after Mass, just like John Frank and most of our cronies, we faked it. All we had to do was bow our heads pretending to be as devout as a grade school kid could possibly be, and "speed mumble." "Speed mumbling" was an art by which at a level just above a whisper, altar boys would spew out gibberish as fast as they could, and then at key points during the incoherent chatter, we would slightly raise our voices and correctly pronounce a few choice and recognizable words such as "Dominus Vobiscum," "Et cum spiritu tu tuo," and "Kyrie Eleison." If we were able to fool the priests, just imagine how we fooled the congregation. The one very important thing that never occurred to me back then was this: "Where did God fit into this messy charade? What kind of shallow God did we serve anyway? How did we even think this forty-five minute farce could be acceptable to Him?" Nevertheless, my short-lived career as an altar boy gave me my first taste of show business. Being up on the stage in full costume before the crowd was a cool feeling for an un-cool kid like me.

GROWING PAINS

The early 1960's were my wonder years and they brought along with them some emotional and confusing moments. Even at the ripe old age of eight, I perceived my classmate Mel Miller to be a little old man walking around in a kid's body. He was like the child version of George Burns. He always shrugged his shoulders, had his hands in his pockets and seemed to have that, "I'll tell you what I'm gonna do for you," type of attitude. He was so different from the other kids. He took things at a leisurely pace, and was not in any way an excitable guy. I remember him occasionally having some difficulty breathing, so that probably explained his nonchalance. One morning our teacher walked solemnly into the classroom, and with her eyes noticeably red from crying, explained to us in the gentlest way she could, Mel had passed away. It was very strange to look at Mel's empty seat and know he was never coming back. He died from post-operative complications of a tonsillectomy. I thought kids weren't supposed to die. Most of us attended the funeral and a lot of us cried as we watched the tiny white casket being carried down the center aisle of the church. This was probably the first time in my life I had to confront death and it wasn't the death of a grandparent or elderly person. It was the end of the short life of a friend. Mel was someone who I hung out with, someone whom I traded baseball cards with, someone who told me jokes. Just like that, Mel was out of our lives and what was funny was how we all seemed to get over it rather quickly. We just took it for granted Mel was in heaven scaling baseball cards with the angels. That's what they told us so we believed it. But they also told us about Purgatory. How did anybody know for sure what condition Mel's soul was in? If Purgatory was indeed real, and if Mel slipped up a few times after last confessing his sins to a priest, the possibility he wasn't going straight to heaven certainly existed.

"*Now I lay me down to sleep I pray the Lord my soul to keep, and if I die before I awake I pray the Lord my soul to take.*" My mom taught me that prayer when I was a toddler and every night as she tucked me in she would coach me along as I tried to recite it from memory. Never gave much thought to what it meant until Mel's premature passing.

DEVELOPING CHARACTER

I remember wholesome entertainment such as Sky King, the Lone Ranger, Crusader Rabbit, Rocky and Bullwinkle, Sandy Becker, Sonny Fox, Claude Kirschner and Clowny, Soupy Sales, Chuck McCann, Officer Joe Bolton, Ted Mack, "Mr. Ed," "My Mother the Car," "I'm Dickens He's Fenster," "My Favorite Martian," and all the wonderful shows and personalities that were part of an age of innocence or at least a time when no one knew any better. Dad went to work every morning and mom took care of getting the kids off to school, tidying up the house and preparing the meals. On Saturdays Dad cut the lawn, mom went shopping and on Sundays, when all the stores were closed, we went to church as a family. After church, dad and I would take a number and wait on line at the local bakery, then bring home an assortment of crumb buns and jelly donuts. Everybody was happy, or at least it seemed that way through my young and innocent eyes.

It was on one of those routine weekdays in November of 1963 when something happened that not only shook our nation but the entire world. I was at my desk when I heard the school P.A. system hum. There was a slight hesitation followed by the voice of our principal. "Excuse me for the interruption," she said, "but President Kennedy has just been assassinated!"

My teacher began to cry. She turned her head away from the class, pulled a tissue from under her sleeve and wiped the tears before they rolled past her cheeks. I sat there behind my textbook in a state of bewilderment. I don't think I fully understood the impact of this situation; after all I was just a silly naïve kid. Indeed I was confused but that was a state I seemed to be in frequently. I fully understood the assassination of our president was a terrible tragedy, but it also meant no school! I remember the reaction of my parents when my friends called me up to see if I wanted to go to the movies. "How could you? The president died! Have some respect! How in the world could you want to go to the movies?" I just wasn't upset, so I went to the movies anyway. Mom and dad quietly moped about the house as if they were in a funeral parlor. They stopped in front of the television and stared into it like they were gazing into a coffin. They mourned the death of Kennedy as if he were a close relative.

For the next few weeks we watched nothing on television except for the news. This completely disrupted my regular TV viewing because all of my favorite aforementioned shows were cancelled. It was bizarre. The repetitive newsreel footage of JFK's funeral and of Jack Ruby shooting that fatal bullet into Lee Harvey Oswald made those images permanently etched into my memory bank whether I liked it or not. Suddenly we all became a little less naïve to the evil in the world. For many of those in my parent's circle of friends, Kennedy was not just our president, he was a Catholic, and so they considered the loss even greater. At a time before CNN, no one knew he was sleeping with Marilyn Monroe. How would things have turned out if we had known?

THE GUY WITH THE POINTED HAT

Not every event of the era was tragic for the Catholic community. There were joyous occasions as well, (joyous for me was defined as getting a day off from school). In 1965, our city had the honor of being visited by Pope Paul VI, also known as The Holy Father, the Vicar of Christ on Earth, the Pontiff, and the Big Ragu. Every student from every Catholic school from within a hundred mile radius was there for this historical moment. We boarded buses and drove to our appointed location. Miles and miles of students, all decked out in their green, blue or plaid uniforms, lined every inch of highway traveled by the Pope's limousine. Kids held flowers and banners and waited patiently just to get a glimpse of the mysterious figure. In the distance we could see the procession of long black automobiles approaching as the Holy entourage cruised along the major thoroughfares of Forest Hills. Hands waved and voices cheered as the visitor from Rome extended his arms and blessed the crowds. Finally the moment we'd all been waiting for arrived. For no more than a fleeting thirty seconds, we got the opportunity to see the face of the leader of the Roman Catholic Church. "I think I see him!" excited young voices cried out. He smiled, he waved, and made a few signs of the cross as his car slowly disappeared from view.

The entire spectacle was in fact rather disappointing. I personally didn't get it. We'd spent an entire day driving and walking and waiting to see the holiest man on the planet, the successor of the apostle Peter, God's infallible earthly representative, our Lord's right hand guy, right here in Queens. And there he was, just a regular guy wearing robes and a funny hat, waving from a window as he was being driven along Queens Blvd. At least there was no homework that day.

JUST THE FACTS, PLEASE!

The strangest story I've ever heard regarding the question, "Where do babies come from?" had to be the one my grandmother told me long after I had started a family. Right up until the time she was to be married, she believed in the following fascinating explanation: First the woman urinates in a bucket. The man then urinates into the same bucket. The bucket is covered with a blanket and nine months later a baby is born! Imagine her surprise when my grandfather set her straight.

In comparison to the fables my grandmother was fed, my education two generations later was not much more sophisticated. As far as I can remember I'd always been fascinated by girls. The problem was I'd never been taught anything in school or at home relating to the opposite sex. I was well aware of our biological differences, I was intrigued and confused, but no adult took the time to clarify things. Around the time I was twelve years old, I was throwing snowballs with my friend and neighbor Johnny Costopolis, and he told me a joke I didn't quite understand. Because I didn't even have a clue about the birds and the bees, he looked at me and wondered why I wasn't laughing hysterically.

Johnny questioned me with a befuddled look on his face, "Don't you know where babies come from?" he asked.

I looked right back at him and with an even more befuddled look replied, "Well yeah, sort of!"

It was on that very afternoon when my friend John (who was a little older than me) gave me a biology lesson I never would forget. Once I got the disturbing mental picture out of my head of what my dad actually had to do to my mom to make a baby, I started feeling pretty cool that I finally knew! It was like a hidden mystery had been revealed to me; I was onto a secret of the universe. Somehow or other, I let the cat out of the bag one evening while talking to my mom. From the silly grin on my face, she knew that I knew, and when I innocently asked her, "Did dad ever get stuck?" she laughed a little embarrassingly. The few words she spoke to me later that night seared into my consciousness like a sizzling red-hot branding iron meeting raw flesh, "You ever get a girl pregnant," she chuckled half seriously, "and I'll cut it off!"

So from that brief conversation I knew one thing… sex was wrong! Being taught by nuns and raised in a devout Catholic household put a different slant on sex for us Catholic kids. Since the clergy was celibate, and Jesus was born of the Blessed Mother Mary who was a virgin, abstinence from sex was looked upon us a good and noble thing. We weren't told what was really going on with our bodies and it was drilled into our heads that sex was dirty. I was somehow under the impression girls didn't like it and they would think more of me if I didn't expect it of them. I wish someone could have at least clued us in to the idea that sex was a healthy and normal function intended for couples in love ("the two shall become one"). I was always fighting a battle between raging hormones and a confused conscience. I was in the bewildered state of sexual confusion and fantasy. Where was the voice of experience to clue me in to those awkward changes my body and emotions would be going through? I could only imagine what protective, archaic thoughts my parents may have put into my sister's impressionable mind that has kept her from actively seeking a sexual companion at any time in her life.

My first official girlfriend was an eighth-grader named Cathy. She was a cute blonde who rolled up her plaid uniform skirt so it would fall several inches above her knees. Why she was interested in me, I had no idea because I was a pre-pubescent fifth-grader who had no clue as to what an eighth grade girl even thought about. All I knew was that she told her friend she liked me and her friend told my friend, then my friend told me. The next thing I knew I was asking her to go "steady" and found myself in Woolworth's buying her a friendship ring for forty-nine cents. How I ever came up with the forty-nine cents is another mystery. (Okay, I found it just lying at the bottom of my mother's pocketbook!) Even if I had spent a whole two dollars on the ring, Cathy wouldn't have been able to tell the difference. She wore my ring proudly. We lived on opposite ends of town so it was difficult having anything more than a schoolyard relationship. I'm not even sure if we even held hands! It was late spring towards the end of the school year and I had just returned home from an afternoon dentist appointment. No sooner did I step foot out of my mom's car when I saw my friend and neighbor Bob Connelly waddling up the block, waving his arms and calling my name. Bob was overweight and because kids are naturally cruel, he had to work a little harder to prove he was cool and gain acceptance among my "in crowd." Occasionally his efforts resulted in winning him some. Sometimes, however, those efforts were extremely annoying, so much so, my friends and I made an art form out of trying to avoid him. One day when we saw him coming our way we actually paid money by hopping on a bus to escape him. Years later when I realized what a dysfunctional family he came from, I felt bad for all of the times I ditched him. His mom was a tough as nails Italian who was never without a Parliament dangling from her lips. His dad worked a second job moonlighting as a bartender where he led a double life as a closet homosexual. Bob's younger sister was an early developer who had quite the reputation solely due to rumors that spread based upon how she flaunted her incredible figure. Bob also had two uncles on his mother's side who were known mobsters, one being the infamous Tony "Ducks." So with all that on his plate I guess Bob deserved a lot more slack than we allowed him.

"I got to tell you something man!" he shouted from a half block away. "You ain't gonna believe who was here looking for you!" I couldn't imagine whom he was talking about until he stretched out his arm and sitting right there in the palm of his hand was the forty-nine cent friendship ring I gave to Cathy. The only thing different about it was that it was completely flattened. "Cathy told me to give this to you," he said as he handed me the ring. "She said she's breaking up with you because she can't be a girlfriend to a mama's boy." If ever there was a time when Bob got on my nerves, this was it. I took the stomped upon "symbol of my love" from Bob, placed it in my pocket and made a lame attempt in telling him (just to protect my pride) I was going to break up with her anyway. I never spoke to her again. She graduated from the eighth grade and went on to high school, and I leaped ahead to sixth grade.

One of the very first scuffles I had with my conscious occurred simply because I still didn't have ALL the facts. Because things related to sex, such as the menstrual cycle and nocturnal emissions, were considered strictly taboo by the "one true religion," many of us spent a good part of our adolescence all screwed up. Upon waking up the morning after having my very first wet dream and discovering a wad of nasty goop in my pajama bottoms, I freaked out. Nobody ever briefed me on something like this ever happening. All I could go on was the notion that anything related to the penis (except urinating) was dirty and wrong. I was pretty certain God was quite disappointed in me for doing whatever it was I did that caused me to waste perfectly good sperm. Not only did I have to contend with cleaning my soiled pajama bottoms so my mom wouldn't unearth my filthy secret, I had to clean my soiled soul and get myself right with my Maker. I could remember walking along the neighborhood streets on the way to my friend Gino's house feeling like I had the weight of the world on my sorry shoulders. I was having a one-way apologetic conversation with God over something I was sure put me on His shit list! I felt so burdened not having anyone with whom I could share my shameful secret. With every step I took I repented, just begging for God's forgiveness and prayed I would never have to face such a disturbing experience again. Eventually the guilt dissipated and life went on. Looking back I have to sadly admit my Catholic upbringing certainly did a number on me. But I was not alone. I knew a Catholic girl who was never told all the details about her monthly period. No one ever clued the poor kid in to the fact that the bleeding stops after a few days. Until her mom solved the mystery of the disappearing sanitary napkins, she wore protection 365 days a year.

OLDER NO WISER

One afternoon during a gathering of the grammar school bowling league gang, a couple of the guys got involved in what was known as a "rank out" session. The slurs were flying back and forth, lightweight stuff like, "Your mother wears army boots!" My friend Gino thought he had a good one when he fired the words "You were born in a test tube" at his attacker. Immediately his rival retaliated with, "Yeah, well you came out of your mother's ass!"

Gino thought he had him good. He was laughing with such victorious satisfaction. Totally convinced he did indeed spring forth into this world from his mom's back door, he shouted out hysterically, "I know I did! Where did you come out of?"

Those of us who were wise to where babies really came from started cracking up. Trying my best to make Gino settle down from his victory dance and what he thought was a triumphal comeback, I took him aside and clued him in to the truth. He gave me a look of total disbelief and said, "No way!" I later discovered how Gino was able to have such a misconception. When explaining to him how babies were born, his dad compared the way a woman's muscles push an infant through the birth canal to the way muscles are used to push when having a bowel movement. Putting two and two together, Gino came up with three.

Believe it or not, in spite of being a tad nerdy and a whole lot confused, I was a pretty popular kid. Because I always managed to get good grades I was friendly with the smart kids. On the other hand, because I couldn't resist being a class clown and because I had a tendency to be a little rebellious, I was chummy with the troublemakers. It seemed like I was always attending parties. At the smart kids' houses we played charades, pin the tail on the donkey, ate chips, had cake and mingled with the parents and relatives. At the not so smart kids' parties, the parents were usually out for the night or upstairs away from all the "action." These parties began with kissing games like "spin the bottle" and usually ended up in make-out marathons. It was in these dark basements where the battle of my flesh and conscience began. One side of me was crying out for the hot sweaty physical contact I'd fantasized so much about, while the other side saw my mom's penis guillotine waiting to come sweeping down on me. It was a very awkward being in the arms of my ready and willing little female classmates and not having a clue as to what to do or not to do. Growing up sure wasn't easy.

Gino and I hit it off from the very first day I entered Sister Joan Mary's first grade class at St. Fidelis. Maybe it was because I was so tall that he befriended me, but nevertheless, throughout the eight years of grammar school we were like family. It was when we were in the seventh grade when Gino and I hooked up with Denise and Christine, two best friends who had happened to transfer to our school. They were extremely friendly and fun loving and somehow, someway, they became our girlfriends. What better arrangements could one ask for, two best friends going steady with two best friends? We all had the perfect alibi for our concerned parents as to our whereabouts. At that time in our lives "girlfriends" were kept very secret from our families. I was with Gino and Gino was with me and that was all our folks had to know. The fact we were all hanging out at Paula Braumeister's every afternoon after school was strictly confidential, classified information they certainly did not need to be aware of. Paula lived in the heart of town in the factory district. Her mom and dad both worked and according to Paula, they didn't seem to mind we were all hanging around in their living room, watching television, eating junk food and making out. I would meet Christine there almost every day during the time we were "going steady" and she would take her place beside me on the sofa where we would kiss until it was time to go home for supper. Paula had an older sister who was married and every now and then she and her husband would stop by just to see what was going on. Paula's brother-in-law was a real character. He was a tall thin fellow with long sideburns and slicked back greasy black hair. Whenever we saw him he had a beer in his hand and would always be sure to offer some to us! He usually wore a muscle tee shirt with a box of cigarettes tucked under a sleeve. He was definitely a certified member of the "Greaser" generation. Occasionally his behavior became a little rowdy, which was probably due to his drinking, and I found it to be somewhat uncomfortable. My conscience was nudging me to leave, but I was so addicted to my make-out sessions with Christine, I subjected myself to the perverse sideshow put on by this idiot and his wife. I wonder if he realized we were all just seventh-graders when he stood in front of the television, placed his hands on his young wife's breasts and said, "Hey kids, I don't like what's on, do you mind if I change the channel?" So for the next few minutes this moron carried on before a roomful of children pretending that his wife's boobs were television knobs. They seemed to get a real kick out of themselves thinking their antics were hysterical. I laughed nervously and just wished they would leave. Eventually they did, leaving me a few more precious minutes of make-out time!

Another classmate was having yet another party and as usual I was looking forward to spending some special time together with my girlfriend. When I arrived at the party, however, Christine didn't come running over to greet me like she usually did. Instead, she stood in a corner in a huddle with her girlfriends trying her very best to ignore me. As young and as inexperienced I was in boy-girl relationships, I could feel the tension mounting and the tremendous heartache I was about to encounter. When I finally approached her she turned to me and said, "We have to talk!" She must have seen my face fill with dismay as she spoke the words that delivered the painful blow to my heart and my ego, "I don't want to go steady anymore!"

Up to that point in my life no one had ever broken up with me face to face. I had my crushed ring handed back to me by a third party, but never did I have to go through the kind of humiliation I suffered that evening. A complete embarrassment to every male in the room including myself, I reached out to her and pleaded, "Please change your mind, and give me another chance, I'll do whatever it is you want me to do please!!!" Then not being able to hide my agony any longer, I burst into tears and cried uncontrollably. Was I just a fragile, sensitive boy unable to contain his emotions, or was I just a pathetic wimp showing a pitiful display of weakness? I felt like the latter.

It just so happened, a kid named Joe Maggiola was attending the party and he was the coolest guy in the school, kind of like the Fonzie of St. Fidelis. By no means was he threatening in appearance, yet no one ever messed with him. If you had any connection to Joe you could be certain no one would mess with you either. He was like the "Godfather" of the seventh grade. When the "Madge" (as he was called) saw me sobbing like a baby, he grabbed me by the arm and took me outside where he tried his very best to console and encourage me. "Come on man!" he said assertively, "no chick is worth it. You're much too good for her!"

He thought enough of me to leave the party and walk the neighborhood streets with me until my supply of tears was completely exhausted. I felt like such an idiot but I really couldn't control myself. I finally calmed down enough to return to the party and nobody even dared to comment because I was in the company of Joe Maggiola. The following morning when I woke up my eyes just didn't feel right. I looked in the mirror and discovered a scab on the surface of each of my eyelids. I couldn't imagine what could have caused these blemishes, until I suddenly realized that from the hours I spent the previous night rubbing the tears from my eyes, I actually burned off two small patches of skin. Naturally, my observant mom took notice of the new additions to my face and questioned me as to what happened. Of course I wouldn't dare tell her the truth of what a wimp her son was, crying hysterically over some very average, flat-chested, stick-leg Catholic schoolgirl. Never in my whole life, before and since, have I cried like I did that night. Uncontrollable sobbing I really didn't understand, and still don't. So I did what I had to do, I lied. I told my mom for some reason my eyes had been extremely itchy, and I couldn't stop from rubbing them. She believed me. She always did.

Two weeks later at yet another grammar school, soda-pop, kissing party, something coincidental happened that was too weird to believe and may have even taught me a lesson in love and life. Helen Mazzarelli somehow found the nerve to break up with her boyfriend Joe Maggiola. Right there in front of my own now scab-less eyes, I witnessed the King of Cool have a total breakdown. He cried unstoppable tears where at one point I was afraid he wasn't going to be able to continue breathing. Now it was only right that I do my best to console Joe, after all, one good turn deserves another. It was so strange watching the same scene unfold before me, only this time Joe and I had switched roles. I grabbed him by the arm, took him outside, and while we walked the streets together, I repeated the same words he spoke to me just a short time ago, "Come on man, no chick is worth it! You're too good for her!"

I must admit, seeing someone as cool as Joe so broken and helpless was a little unsettling for me. It was like I was given the opportunity to see what I looked like when I bawled over Christine and I promised myself to never cry over a girl again. Over and over again he poured out his heart telling me how much he loved Helen. I knew he didn't love Helen any more than I loved Christine, but he was going to have to find out for himself. I was already over Christine and quickly learned the difference between a broken heart and hurt pride. Besides, time heals all wounds! I was sure Joe would bounce back. The only other reason I could see that Joe might have possibly been upset was because he loved bowling and it just so happened that Helen's father was the owner of the local bowling establishment where Joe and Helen got to bowl for free. That was definitely something worth getting upset over. I'd heard it said from a guy's point of view that girls are a dime a dozen, but a girl whose dad who owned a bowling alley were few and far between!

I was in eighth grade, my last year of grammar school. The morning bell had just rung. The class sat quietly, sensing that something big was about to happen. Monsignor Osborne, the parish pastor, was walking the school's corridors with Sister Rose Marie, our principal. They entered our classroom and whispered some words to our teacher, Sister Kevin Mary. She appeared to be very upset and then ordered us to remain in our seats and keep quiet. She quickly left the room with the principal and the pastor and closed the door behind her. Immediately the room buzzed with the wondering whispers of curious students. There were just a handful of us who were wise to what was going on and we were sworn to secrecy. Somehow it looked like the secret was out.

The preceding afternoon Brian Wolf invited a select few of his classmates over to his house after school for what he promised was going to be something spectacular. We all paraded along the streets of our blue-collar factory town following closely behind Brian and Charlene, a very pretty, well-developed seventh grade girl, who walked closely by his side. Although we thought we were quite the bunch, still decked out in our green school uniforms, we posed no threats to anyone. As we all entered the foyer of his house single file, he ordered us to lay our coats on the floor. Brian was the class bully so everyone usually did whatever he asked, and strangely enough, we considered it an honor to be included in anything he might be scheming. When all the coats were spread evenly about the hardwood floor, Brian ordered the crowd to move into the adjacent room where, if we so desired, we could watch from a window. At that moment he and Charlene lied down on top of the pile of coats, and at the very tender ages of twelve and thirteen, proceeded to engage in a very awkward attempt at sexual intercourse. To tell you the truth, I didn't know what to think. In the very next room on top of our coats two classmates were doing the unthinkable, taking part in the most forbidden deed we could imagine! Although I personally didn't see anything, I felt as if I was involved with something that was tremendously sinful, dirty and wrong.

Before we knew it, the whole escapade was over and every one of us was on the way back home to our families with some of our innocence bruised. Well, Charlene ended up telling her parents. Her parents obviously contacted the school. The powers that be really weren't prepared to handle a situation of this magnitude. Before long the entire school knew. Charlene's mom took her by bus to and from school every day. I used to take the same bus and I would think how embarrassing it had to be for both of them. Thank God Charlene didn't get pregnant. When we asked Brian how it was, he told us in no uncertain terms, "It wasn't so good, I'll probably never do that again!"

THE PRESIDENT IS POWERLESS

Don't ask me why it was necessary for an eighth grade grammar school class to have elected officials, but for whatever reason, we did! Perhaps our teacher was trying to educate us as to how our political system worked. Just like it was done in our government, the class voted by secret ballot. After all the votes were counted, it was announced that I was unanimously nominated class president and Gino, vice-president. We had no platforms and we did no campaigning. We were simply the two most popular kids in the class, so we won!

I must admit, being class president gave my ego a little boost. Now that the prestigious title belonged to me, the honor was bestowed upon me to sit in a front row desk right beside my friend and second in command, Gino. My duties as the class's high-ranking officer, however, were zilch. I was assigned no special tasks and I had no additional responsibilities until one day Sister Kevin Mary, who we nicknamed "Bucky" because of her protruding front teeth, made this announcement: "Listen up, class! I have to leave the classroom for a short while, so while I'm gone, John, your class president will be in charge! Listen to him as you would listen to me!" She positioned a television that sat atop a large rolling stand in the front of the classroom and tuned it into an educational program. She looked at me sternly and said, "John, if anyone misbehaves, I want you to write their names on the blackboard and I will deal with them when I return." With what appeared to be a sense of urgency, she clutched her brief case, hurriedly left the room, swinging the door closed behind her.

I don't know about my fellow classmates, but I seemed to forget, or not even realize, that nuns were human beings. It never even occurred to me the reason she may have had to leave the room in the middle of a lesson was because she may have had to visit the restroom. In my mind, nuns didn't get stomachaches, get their periods, or even get headaches. A nun's habit was comprised of so many layers, including belts, ropes and miles of rosary beads, if they did have to use the bathroom, it would have had to take them hours.

No sooner than the teacher was out the door the mischief began. Carolyn Polanski and Patricia Becker seemed a lot older and a lot more experienced than your average 1960's Catholic grade-school girls. They folded their green plaid skirts high above their knees and kept the buttons of their white cotton blouses opened just enough to show they were a little further developed than most of the other girls in the class. Carolyn lit up a cigarette and Patricia kept changing the channels on the television until the class collectively requested she kept it tuned to "Popeye" cartoons. Everyone was up and away from their desks. Spitballs were rocketing across the room, more cigarettes were being lit and I knew I was in deep shit! Gino looked over at me and started laughing uncontrollably when Patricia and Carolyn, the two ringleaders, approached the desk of the president. Carolyn put her arms around me and was making a bold attempt to make out with me while Patricia watched. "Kiss me!" she commanded, "Patricia bet me a dollar I wouldn't make out with you!" "Get away!" I yelped, "You're going to get us all in big trouble!"

My classmates knew I wasn't the kind of guy who would rat them out, so they continued to revel in the pandemonium. I just prayed things would settle down before "Bucky" returned. They didn't! The door of the classroom flew open and as the students scrambled back to their seats, Carolyn waved a textbook through the air trying to diminish the smell of smoke. "Bucky" stood furiously in front of the classroom. Her hands were planted firmly on her hips, her habit draped over her arms, making it appear as though she possessed wings. She quickly lunged at the television, bringing an episode of Popeye to an abrupt end, just as he was about to down a can of spinach. There was silence for a moment. She stared at me. She stared at Gino. "You both have greatly disappointed me!" she sighed as her upper front teeth covered her bottom lip, "What do you have to say for yourselves?" Looking down at the floor I mumbled, "Sorry, Sister!" "Who's responsible for this, Mr. Domenico?" she continued, "I don't see any names on the blackboard, so I am assuming this is your doing!" Totally exasperated, she stared down the entire class, and choosing what was probably the most appropriate and inappropriate word possible, she reprimanded us by stomping her foot and hollering, "Why do you children 'buck' me?" She reiterated, "Why, I said, why do you children want to 'buck' me." I couldn't understand why someone with the teeth of Bugs Bunny could so carelessly select a word like "buck" (conveniently rhyming with "fuck") to convey her feelings to a roomful of cruel insensitive kids who were just waiting to make the connection. My career in politics was over. Gino and I were dishonorably stripped of our dignified positions!

THE POOL

One of the simple pleasures of growing up in our house was the family pool. I always remember summers being incredibly hot right up until mid-September. My sister Virginia and I usually had our fair share of household chores to do before spending the remainder of the day relaxing in the pool. While we were still young, mom always acted responsibly and wouldn't allow us in the water unless there was adult supervision. As we grew older, mom became less rigid and eased up on the restrictions, which at times may have not been such a good idea. One hot summer afternoon Virginia and I were splashing about and I got the bright idea to play "Houdini the Escape Artist." Virginia got to be Houdini first. Clear-headed lunatic I was, I got a piece of clothesline and tied her hands and her feet together behind her back and then let her drop down into the water. As she struggled to set herself free, I nonchalantly swam about not paying too much attention to what was going on below the surface. It was then and there in that very pool, I swear to this very day, I heard a heavenly voice order me to reach down and pull Virginia up from under the water. As soon as I did, she gasped for air and pleaded with me not to let her go. While I was untying her she told me how she had just about given up and accepted the fact she was going to die and as her short life flashed before her eyes, she prayed frantically. I am so thankful I obeyed that voice. If 'Ginia would have drowned as a result of my being an idiot, I know I would have become a totally functionless human being.

Our backyard and the Candella's were adjacent to each other. On a hot July Saturday afternoon while we were keeping cool in the sparkling clear water of our pool, Debbie Candella, who was a couple of years older than me, would walk along the fence that separated our property. From there she would smile and wave hello trying to get the attention of my dad, or me, which really wasn't too hard to do. My dad was always a softhearted guy, especially with cute young girls in two-piece bathing suits, so he extended an open invitation to Debbie to join us for a swim, which she did. The very next day, there was Debbie standing by the fence in her bathing suit, only this time standing right beside her was her friend Sharon McCain. Sharon was a beautiful full figured thirteen-year-old blond. Debbie asked if the open invitation stood for her friend also. I was around eleven years old at the time, so I had absolutely no idea my dad was probably thinking the same thoughts as Lester Burnham in the film "American Beauty." "Sure Deb," he called out, "any friend of yours is a friend of ours!"

So there I was, a gawky eleven year old with slightly bucked teeth, swimming around in my pool with two very desirable teenage girls. At first I thought it was my imagination, but as I was swimming about, I would have bet my life Sharon was chasing me and trying to pull off my bathing trunks. The more she chased after me, the quicker I tried to get away. I didn't really know what to make of the situation so I would get out of the pool. This same scenario happened every time Sharon was in our pool. Then one day she actually admitted to me she had been trying to take off my pants. "You know the way I chase you and try to pull off your pants," she shamelessly said, "well how about you chase me and try to take off mine!"

At the time I declined her challenge, but down the road I'd ask myself from time to time, "Why did I get the opportunity of a lifetime when I was so young and so stupid? Why didn't those opportunities present themselves when I knew better?"

BISHOP EDMUND J. REILLY HIGH

Back in my day, most Catholic high schools were either all boys or all girls. Even though Bishop Reilly High was co-educational, they managed to separate the genders by having a boys' wing and a girls' wing, which were joined by a communal library and cafeteria. Only seniors enjoyed the privilege of having lunch with the opposite sex. Once again, nuns were on the scene, only now they were restricted to associating solely with the girls. The guys, however, had to contend with a new breed of clergyman, the Brothers. Brothers were not quite priests. Comparing a brother to a priest would be like comparing an emergency medical technician and a surgeon. Another way of classifying a brother would be to call him a male nun. Brothers wore long robes, rosary beads, and practiced celibacy. (I never saw celibacy as something that needed practice because how do you get better at it?) Unlike priests, brothers were not certified to perform the mysterious stuff like Mass or administer the sacraments. Theirs was basically a teaching ministry. Why a man would want to give up women, wear a robe, live with a group of men, and hang out with teenage boys all day without any inclination of ever becoming a priest is, well…?

The reason why our parents paid good money to send us to private Catholic school was because they were under the impression there was a higher standard of education than what was available in the public school system. Whether or not I received a better education is debatable, but needless to say, there was no getting around the fact that for four more years, unlike in the public schools, religion class was mandatory. I could never understand why parents left the religious training of their children to others such as priests, nuns, brothers, rabbis, and ministers rather than discussing spiritual matters in their own homes. I mean if adults didn't believe in a certain belief system, why send their children off to learn about what they themselves didn't take seriously? In the same way, if the adults did believe in a particular belief system, why then couldn't they instruct their own children? Why are the clergy any better qualified than parents? By attending a Catholic high school I developed some great relationships, but throughout the four years, however, I can't say I'd ever experienced anything that enabled or encouraged me to have a closer relationship with God. If anything, I drifted a little further away. I would say that defeated the very purpose of going to a religious school. If only I knew then what I know now and if only I knew now what I will know five years from now. Life is a learning process. Only an ignorant man will claim he knows it all. The only way to learn is to question and move on.

From the day my parents gave me a phonograph and my first two forty-fives as a birthday gift in 1962, I fell in love with rock and roll. "Venus in Blue Jeans" by Jimmy Clanton and "Teenage Idol" by Ricky Nelson infected me with an incurable bug. Collecting forty-five's became a passion for me. Any song that made the charts I had to own whether I liked the song or not. I would venture over to the neighborhood Woolworth's Five and Dime store on a weekly basis to check out the pop charts and shell out my sixty-nine cents to purchase whatever new forty-five entered the top ten. Every Tuesday night when Scot Muni, the DJ on WABC radio, played the top seven, I tried to synchronize my record player to play my forty-five's along with the radio simultaneously. It never worked; it was always a slight bit off. I was sure my parents must have thought I was nuts! As I developed into a teenager, however, my musical tastes were also developing. My spirit took on a touch of rebelliousness and I no longer cared for what was mainstream top forty radio. I became proud of the fact my likings were different from others and gradually some of my classmates became interested in what I was listening to. In 1967, I tuned into WNEW FM 102.7 and it was as if I'd discovered a new world. It was an oasis away from the top forty AM radio play lists we'd become so accustomed to listening to. I found my salvation!

High school was certainly quite different from grammar school. Our parents and teachers no longer looked upon us as children and expected us to behave like the young adults we had become. Little did they know what lay ahead? Times were changing. The British had already invaded our shores with the likes of the Beatles and the Stones and we were about to enter the psychedelic era.

A year or so before I began high school, I was already playing the drums and even had a rock group. The energy that radiated from our black and white television the night we watched the Beatles perform on the Ed Sullivan show caused me to have an epiphany. I remember sitting cross-legged on the living room floor, being mesmerized by the band and thinking, "This is what I need to do!" The Christmas that followed those three memorable television performances in 1964, mom and dad sprung for a full set of Gretsch champagne sparkle drums, cymbals and hardware included. That very same Christmas Gino got an electric guitar, complete with amplifier, and within a few weeks we recruited Henry Emig to play Zimgar electric bass. (For those of you who may not know, a Zimgar instrument was as low end as you can go and still be considered as a musical instrument.) We rehearsed at my house and before long had a repertoire with enough songs to play a gig. Bobby Cook's birthday party was the first and only gig for this band of thirteen year olds, but we were a sensation. As we struggled our way through hits like "Satisfaction" and "Mr. Tambourine Man," with me singing lead vocals, our classmates thought we were the coolest. Henry had a little trouble doing that slide thing on "Mr. Tambourine Man" but I was sure nobody caught on! After rave reviews, the band broke up and graduation sent us on our separate ways.

I began high school in 1966, and around that time, albums or "long-players" were getting very popular, so my record collection and my hair began to grow. My dad would always encourage me in all my endeavors and support me when and wherever he could. He always seemed to make connections through his line of work. It just so happened he befriended a fellow who worked for Columbia Records. Every other week without fail, a box of all the latest albums would arrive at our house via US mail from my dad's new pal. I was getting the newest music before it even hit the stores. I was so cool!

The Mariano's lived across the street from us. Frank Sr., a balding burly man with bushy sideburns, was a brilliant musician and a masterful guitarist who played for the NBC orchestra and was often featured on the "Tonight Show" with Jack Paar. The entire Mariano family was musically inclined. Four of the five kids, including my friend Rick, played semi-professionally in a folk rock band. I had such an admiration for Rick, who with his long black hair and sideburns had the look of a pop star. At one point in their not so huge career, they even had a hit record in the Billboard Top Forty. Rick and I had a good but rather strange friendship. I think he enjoyed my company because it was an escape from the business of his family. Through me he was able to experience the non-professional side of music and the "normalcy" of my family life. I, on the other hand, enjoyed his companionship because I was so enthralled with the professional side of music and the idea of being involved with his older brother and sisters fulfilled my dream of possibly becoming a rock star. I loved hanging out at Rick's house. The Mariano home was unlike anybody else's I knew. In the center of their living room was a baby grand piano surrounded by amplifiers and guitars. There was a full set of drums and a PA system and microphones always ready and waiting for the next rehearsal. Because of my friendship with Rick, I was at their house so often that it just worked out I became their drummer for a year or so. I thought I was so cool (and so privileged) to be in their band, especially when the group was on the same bill with "The Vagrants" (Leslie West's band prior to "Mountain"). I think I was more excited about this gig than the Mariano's were. I spent most of the day in the head shops of New York City's West Village with Rick and his older brother Frank hunting for something really groovy to wear for the occasion. I finally bought this hand-painted yellowish, Indian cotton Nehru shirt. Frankie purchased a bunch of massive slow-burning candles when he came up with the brainstorm of playing by candlelight. On the night of the show the stage was so dark no one in the audience was able to see the band or my cool shirt. I wasted twenty bucks, probably more than I got paid.

Rick and I were the youngest members of the group, so it was inevitable that the influence of his brother and sisters would eventually lead me to places I probably wasn't ready for. I can remember going for joyrides with Rick and his siblings, always with Frankie at the wheel. I never knew where we were going but almost every trip was an adventure. Whether we wound up in a Greenwich Village flat, a street corner in Spanish Harlem, or the deepest, darkest recesses of Central Park, each journey resulted in meeting up with the weirdest characters, a handshake exchange of money for drugs and then a quick exit. This was a whole other world for me. Most of the time, I was scared out of my wits. It was always way later than my curfew and many times I would ask myself, "What in God's name am I doing here? I want to go home!" Being cool, however, meant taking some risks, so I would just go with the flow. It was Rick Mariano who introduced me to "psychedelia," turned me on to my first joint and opened up what for me was a whole new approach of listening to music. Rick had the coolest room…black light, lava lamps, incense burners, strobe light, day-glow posters and a stereo that could really crank! I would bring over some of my newest records, Rick would roll a couple of joints, and before long I'd feel as immobile as a piece of his furniture, totally fixated on the sound waves that seemed to engulf me as they came rushing out from his immense speaker columns. Later it was just a matter of getting back home without mom and dad finding out where I was or what I was doing. I had a couple of close calls when my father, suspecting I may have been drinking, asked to smell my breath. I always managed to pass inspection!

Rick got a little carried away with himself when it came to drug experimentation. He would walk through vacant lots and backyards picking a variety of weeds then tried to smoke them. He was thoroughly convinced there had to be other plants besides marijuana that could get him high. He never thought twice about popping a pill, dropping acid or taking speed. One afternoon he and I were in a local market where he purchased a box of rat poison because belladonna was among its ingredients. He had heard ingesting belladonna could result in a high, so against my advice, he ate some rat poison. I guess since he wasn't a rodent he didn't die, but he didn't get high either. Another time he miscalculated the amount of speed he was taking and remained wide-awake for days. He came ringing my doorbell at six o'clock that Sunday morning carrying a copy of the Sunday Times in which he colored in all the O's with a ball point pen throughout the entire paper. It's totally amazing how Rick not only functioned, but how he remained alive.

Throughout a span of several years, Rick and I played in quite a few different bands together. Whether it was during the psychedelic stage of our teens, the country rock sound of our early adulthood, or the attempts we made in the studio recording our original music, I considered Rick a genius and a perfectionist. I just wanted to play, but Rick wouldn't settle for anything shy of excellence. He had a remarkable ear and every note he played or sang was from his soul. He also knew all the ins and outs of the studio; so needless to say, I was in awe of his talent.

In one of the very first bands we were in together, we were given the opportunity to audition for a paying gig. It was a teenage dance that was to take place at an exclusive country club. First of all, we did not play dance music. Second of all, if we had auditioned live, because of our volume, we would have never gotten the job. Rick came up with the idea of bringing part of our sound system and a pre-recorded tape to the audition. We explained to the fellow who was in charge of booking the band for the dance, that we had too much equipment to transport, so he agreed to listen to "our tape." Rick had doctored up an obscure recording by the "Byrds," and as it came blasting out from the speakers we had rigged up, the guy looked at the two of us and asked skeptically, "That's you guys?"

We answered proudly and deceptively, "Yep, that's us!"

We got the gig and let me say those kids, who were expecting to hear top ten radio, were shocked when they heard the most non-danceable, excruciatingly loud music coming from our little power trio. Towards the end of our last song, Jimmy Hayman, our bass guitarist, suddenly got the strangest gleam in his eye, and like a man possessed, charged his wall of amplifiers with his instrument, using it as if it were a battering ram. The speakers shrieked with the deafening shrill of uncontrolled feedback. Rick strummed a few last power chords and I smashed my cymbals with a fury. It was so cool being a rebel.

The same artistic flair that inspired me to destroy my mom's lampshades with lipstick when I was a child also caused me to nearly set our garage on fire one afternoon by spelling out the name of one of my rock and roll bands on the garage floor with gasoline, then setting a match to it. I thought it would have been neat to see the name "Electric Dust" written in flames, not realizing the flames would reach the ceiling! Boy genius I was, I ran to the swimming pool with a bucket, filled it with water, and then doused the flames with the water. I didn't recall ever learning that gasoline and water do not mix. With the help of nearby sand, dirt and an old blanket, I was able to extinguish the inferno. What I did for the sake of art!

Coming from a family who was artistic and out of the ordinary, Rick could never handle the dress codes and the discipline of a Catholic school, so he decided to go the public school route. By the time I entered junior year I had established relationships with a lot schoolmates, some of which became life-long friendships. Because we went to different schools, sadly Rick and I didn't get to hang out as frequently, and my new friends began to take up more and more of my time. It's funny how things work out in life. For some reason, there always seems to be that fork in the road.

The biggest drag about high school, especially with us "hippie types," was the dress code. We weren't required to wear uniforms, but nevertheless, there were many restrictions. We weren't allowed to grow our hair too long, which was sort of ironic for a religion that followed Jesus! There were statues, paintings and pictures all over the place that depicted Jesus having long, waving-in-the-wind kind of hair! Some Bible scholars, I came to learn many years later, tell of how Jesus took some kind of vow that forbade Him to cut his hair. He certainly didn't don the military look Bishop Reilly demanded. Besides the hair regulation that always presented problems for me, shoes couldn't have heels or points, pants couldn't be flared and jackets had to have collars. Definitely no Beatle-wear was permitted. Our principal was a short, stocky, obnoxious fellow whose name was Brother Thomas. The entire student body knew him by the endearing nickname, "Stinky." The truth of the matter was you could smell him from miles away. If by some chance you were somewhere you weren't supposed to be, such as cutting class or smoking in the boys' room, the terrible stench exuding from his armpits sent a warning and thus ample time to safely get away. Stinky never cracked a smile unless he was assigning you detention. He seemed to take pleasure in our misery. Brother Thomas didn't work alone. He had a sidekick named Brother Ernest whose official title was "dean of discipline." Ernie, as we un-affectionately called him, made Rocky Balboa seem like a high society intellectual. His Brooklyn accent (dees, doze, and tirty tree) made him sound like an illiterate when he spoke. He sported a flat top style crew cut, was slightly cross-eyed and was forever pushing the sleeves of his robe up to his elbows as if he was threatening to throw a punch. He used the sleeve thing as a scare tactic and it worked because everybody feared Ernie. He was a psycho! He thought nothing of punching out a student and when he did, he had every intention of making it hurt.

George Everley was one of the coolest guys in my class. He always tried his best to make a fashion statement by pushing the dress regulations to the limit. Sometimes he succeeded, sometimes he didn't. One memorable afternoon right in the middle of an English class, Ernie came crashing through the classroom door. Interrupting a class meant nothing to Brother Ernest. He pointed his finger at George and with a demented almost sadistic smile, motioned for him to get up from his desk then forcefully escorted him out of the room. George wore his long red hair strategically slicked back behind his ears as not to attract attention to himself. When he rose from his desk I could see by the look in his face he was all too aware of his fate. We could hear the tapping of his Cuban heels against the hard finish of the classroom floor as Ernie dragged him out into the hallway. Mr. Calderone, our slightly effeminate English teacher and a pretty nice guy, let out a long "Charles Nelson Reilly type-sigh," then tried to continue with his lesson when suddenly we heard the unmistakable sound of George's head getting slammed into the metal locker doors. Not once, but at least five times, the thuds shook the walls as we sat silently at our desks in anger and frustration. Seconds later, when George returned to the classroom, his face was as red as an over-ripened tomato. While trying to maintain his coolness, he tended to the task of adjusting his paisley tie. That was the price some of us had to pay for trying to look cool. Even then I couldn't understand why we all didn't revolt. What possibly could have happened if two hundred teenage boys got up and beat the life out of that maniac hiding behind a cross and a cloak? Fortunately I never had to face that kind of extreme punishment. I've gotten my hair pulled a few times and was always threatened with suspension if I didn't cut it, but I got really good at ducking both Stinky and Ernie. It's ironic how men who presumably dedicated their lives to serving Jesus Christ took such pleasure in tormenting boys. This behavior reeked of hypocrisy, something I could never stomach.

Gym class was yet another unpleasant chapter in the memory book of high school. It's not that gym couldn't be fun, but for me it was always scheduled just before lunch and the Nazi gym teacher, Mr. Cosmo, forced us to take showers after class. First of all, I wasn't too fond of standing stark naked in the very, very close quarters of what they considered a locker room with forty other guys. Secondly, I hated getting to lunch late because the lines were endless and all the good food choices would be gone. As soon as the bell sounded and we were dismissed from gym, we would make mad dashes towards the locker room. The first thing many of us would do was to grab a towel, run over to a sink and splash a little water on our faces, then scoot back over to our locker where we would stand while pretending to dry ourselves for shower inspections from Cosmo. Nine times out of ten we would fool him. It was on that tenth time when he knew he had us. He would humiliate us by making us strip down and march right into the shower. Whenever I heard him order us about with his German accent, it brought to mind the concentration camps of Auschwitz. It gave me the creeps. On one such day he came sneaking up behind me and insisted I had not showered. I assured him that indeed I did. He ordered me to present him with my wet towel, which I could not. Then with his evil little smile he commanded me to make my way to the showers. I had no choice but to surrender and marched unwillingly into the steamy shower without removing my black nylon socks. For the remainder of the day my feet swished about inside my shoes. With every step I took I wanted to beat that little Kraut on his flat head.

In spite of the torment I had to undergo by spending many of my high school days ducking in and out of classrooms, stairways, and hallways trying to avoid Stinky, Ernie and Cosmo, I survived! It was only because of the great friends I made that I can say I came away from it a better person. Together we created wonderful memories and grew a tiny bit wiser as to what this life was all about. I can't speak for everyone, but I was still somewhat spiritually and sexually confused during those bittersweet years. The trick was to not let anybody catch on.

One morning on the bus ride to school, Mark, who liked to consider himself as one of the guys but wasn't really one of the guys, pulls an "x-rated" romance novel out from his book bag. Mark always had to come up with something out of the ordinary to get recognition from the guys he looked upon as his buddies. He was a little obnoxious, a little overweight and had this annoying mole on his face. Just like my old friend Bob Connelly, Mark had to work a little harder for the "in crowd" acceptance, and on this day he struck gold. He snuck this book of sexually explicit stories out of his house, and for a couple of weeks he was basking in the pleasure of being the most popular guy in the back of the bus as the book made its rounds. One morning the book found its way into my hands. Unaware as to the images my spongy brain was about to soak up, I started to read. Before long I was feeling almost breathless as strange waves of excitement seemed to electrify me. The book vividly described acts of lovemaking I'd never imagined were possible. I couldn't believe there were so many pleasurable things men and women could perform on each other! It was the first time I'd ever read anything of the kind and I'm not certain if it was the anonymous author's talent or my imagination that caused my heart to race and pump blood to places where my blood's never been before. I got quite an education on that bus ride. All I could remember was reaching the moment when something told me I had better close the book. If I read any more, the possibility existed I would have risked embarrassment. I guess that was one of the drawbacks of an overactive imagination and being repressed. That thirty-minute trip to school added a whole other dimension to my sexual awareness. Someday, somewhere, some girl was going to benefit from me reading the exploits in that novel.

One of the most wonderful things about my parents was the way they accepted all of my friends and made their home available to them. In our house my friends were always made to feel welcome and comfortable. When I was in high school I belonged to the drama society. Not only did great friendships develop among this group of young actors, actresses, and stagehands, but also, dramatics as an extracurricular activity was a great place for meeting girls. At the end of each school year there would always be a customary cast party.

During my senior year, my mom and dad allowed me to volunteer them to host the party at our house. Everything was done first class. There was plenty of good food and drink, music and of course, should anyone feel so inclined, the pool. At this particular time in my life I was dating Regina. Although Regina and I both participated in dramatics and performed in the same productions, I never got to really talk to her until we met one Saturday evening at a mutual friend's party right after I had returned with a blind date from a Ten Years After concert in Central Park. My friend Tim had set me up with Maria, a friend of a friend, a manic-depressive who had attempted suicide prior to meeting me. Maria wasn't much of a conversationalist and although I felt sorry for her, I felt sorrier for myself having to pretend I was having a good time. I knew my disinterested attitude towards her was probably very detrimental to her self-confidence, self-esteem and general mental health, but I was never good at faking my feelings. I could only imagine what Maria thought of me when we arrived at this party and I totally ignored her once I saw Regina. In my teenage mind, Regina looked absolutely incredible that night and from the moment I laid eyes on her I wasn't aware of anyone else in the room besides us. I stuck to her like glue. Tim and his date were well aware of the situation and helped me out by offering to drive Maria home. It was strange how we just seemed to hit it off, and from that evening on, Regina and I enjoyed a short stretch of time as boyfriend and girlfriend.

Here's where the pool comes in. We were all having a really good time at the cast party. It was a warm summer night and it was just a matter of time before someone was going to get thrown into the water. The time did arrive and Regina was the victim. When she came out from the pool in the white tee shirt that clung to her wet body, she obviously caught a chill and everyone knew it, including my dad. She must have made some impression on my father because to this very day he'll still ask, "Hey John, how's Regina doing?" I have to remind him I haven't seen her in thirty-seven years. After Regina and I spent a wonderful season together of summer concerts in Central Park, our relationship ended almost as mysteriously as it began. One September evening as we were walking along Second Avenue on our way to the Fillmore East to see Crosby, Stills, Nash and Young, she tripped on a crack in the sidewalk. Suddenly my entire image of Regina changed. I must have thought I was just so cool that it was embarrassing to be seen in the company of a girl who had the nerve to be so clumsy in my wonderful presence. That night it was over and I can't even say why, except for the fact that I was an immature idiot. I kissed her goodnight in the backseat of my friend's big black jalopy and decided I wasn't going to call her again. Man, was I an asshole or what? And NO! I never got to try any of the moves I read about in that steamy book! (Regina, I think about you often and if you ever happen to read this, I'm terribly sorry!)

One girl who stood out among the few I dated was Gloria. I also met Gloria in the drama society and I found something about her to be very seductive. Although she had a pretty good body for a high school girl (not that I knew what to do with it), it was her lips that did it for me. I took her to the movies one evening. I didn't have my driver's license yet, so my dad gave me a lift to her house. She invited me in and offered me a soft drink. I was a little nervous about possibly having to meet her parents but they didn't appear to be around. From her house we took the bus to the theater, and I was gentleman enough to pay her fare! The featured movie was "Yellow Submarine." We sat in the balcony and from the first frame to the final credit we made out. (Today I am reminded of the Jerry Seinfeld episode when he and his girlfriend made out during "Schindler's List".) Although I really had every intention of watching the movie, it turned out I didn't have a clue as to what it was about. Gloria had the softest moistest lips and I couldn't pull my mouth away. For two hours our faces melded as we exchanged pools of saliva. I literally thought I was going to burst. After the movie I took her back to her house and found it extremely strange that her parents were still nowhere in sight. In my useless imagination I had her sprawled out on the couch running my inexperienced fingers all about her lovely body. In my pathetic reality, my fingers reached for the phone and I called my dad to come pick me up. I still wonder what would have happened if I found the nerve to have made a clumsy move!

Many years later at a twenty-fifth high school reunion, I ran into Gloria. She still looked great and she surprised the life out of me when she mentioned the night we made out in the balcony. After introducing me to her husband, she remarked about how she never did get to see "Yellow Submarine." I laughed and told her I would buy her the video, to which her husband sarcastically replied, "It seems to me it just wouldn't be the same unless you're watching it with her!" I thought to myself, "Damn! She remembers!"

High school religion classes didn't explore any unfamiliar territory. It was all pretty much the same catholic propaganda, we're the one true faith blah, blah, blah...The Brothers entertained our never-ending questions about evolution, other faiths, Bible stories as fact or myth, and even tried to answer them as best they could. I don't think any of us (students or teachers) were convinced about anything. Matters concerning God were always presented and discussed in a textbook format. Book knowledge seemed a lot less threatening than heart knowledge and much easier to grade.

In junior and senior year a little sex education was slowly incorporated into our religion classes. I guess someone in authority must have finally surmised that teenage boys with curious minds and crazed hormones should be given a little guidance. There are certain "old wives' tales" that have stuck with us throughout our lives even though we know they're not true... "Don't go swimming after lunch or you'll get cramps and drown!" To this day I don't know of a single soul who drowned after eating lunch. I still have yet to meet someone who went blind from masturbating. Now there was a favorite topic in Brother Ed's class, masturbation! I don't think I'll ever forget the reason he gave to discourage us boys from masturbating. He said, and I quote, "The act of masturbation is sinful because it is wasting the sacred seeds designed by God for the procreation of human life. They were not to be absorbed by tissues and flushed down a toilet as a result of this self-gratifying act!" Somehow he managed to keep a straight face and expected us to buy this load of nonsense in the same way we believed eating meat on Friday was displeasing to God! We were older now. No way could anyone have ever convinced me that priests and brothers didn't take matters into their own hands from time to time.

Towards the end of junior year, the school organized a three-day retreat for the guys. Most of my friends and I decided to go because we'd be missing a day or two of school and what the heck, it may have even done us some good. It was at this very retreat where I was warned not to eat the mashed potatoes because they contained a chemical known as saltpeter. Consumption of saltpeter, we learned, killed the male's sexual desire. Not in a million years did a bunch of teenage boys want anyone or anything messing with their sexual desires, no less kill them…not even for three days, and not even if there wasn't a female anywhere in the vicinity. Sure enough, mashed potatoes were served with every meal, and needless to say, we avoided them like the plague. The funny thing was, even though I abstained from the chemically spiked spuds, I couldn't recall thinking about sex even once!

I know for sure that during those three days we spent living in the company of the Jesuit clergy, we had several religious discussions and a fair amount of meditation time. I'm certain the purpose of this retreat was to make us more spiritually aware, but no matter how hard I try, I just can't seem to remember anything of any spiritual significance. The one and only thing that attached itself to my memory from that three-day diversion from everyday life was the image of all those untouched stinking potatoes!

The older I got, the further I slipped into a spiritual limbo. I started to pick and choose; developed my own doctrines, followed my own principles and made up my own rules. I wanted to believe in the traditions of my family even though I started to doubt many of things associated with the

Catholic religion. Towards the end of High School I stopped attending church regularly, showing up only at Christmas and Easter. Although I never stopped believing in God or doubting His goodness, I started to wonder whether or not the wafer we were told was the body of Christ was actually what they claimed it to be or was it nothing more than a wafer. Were millions of Catholics just blindly following some badly misinterpreted verses of scripture? I quit going to confession and could justify there was no sin terrible enough to condemn somebody to hell except for cold-blooded murder. Even in the case of murder, I reasoned that anyone who could kill a fellow human being must be insane and therefore excused of having to suffer any consequences, throwing the theory of a "hell" right out the window. I started assessing similar issues more and more, thus becoming a bit rebellious towards my religion. The problem was, these traditions had been so instilled in me, it was going to take many years to shake completely free of them. I didn't understand why priests, nuns and brothers couldn't marry. The clergy in other Christian faiths had wives and families, why did Catholics have a different set of rules? Why did it seem like we were trained to go against the very basic nature in which we were created?

So there I was in my comfortable little corner of the planet trying to figure out the meaning of life before graduating high school. Meanwhile, in other parts of the world, we put men on the moon (or so they told us), our country was fighting a senseless war in a tiny country called Viet Nam, and a half a million people joined together in upstate New York for three days of peace, love and music. I regret not going to Woodstock, but I have no qualms about not going to Viet Nam. It was the summer of 1969 and three of my best friends decided to drive to Yasgur's farm to be part of history. I chose not to join them and to this day could kick myself for it. I really can't say why I didn't go, except for the fact that my folks were against it, and because I was a spoiled kid from the suburbs who enjoyed the comfort and security of his own bed. As I watched every news report that was broadcast from the festival, I felt I was at least there in spirit. Years later I learned that Joni Mitchell, who wrote the song "Woodstock," wasn't there either. She in fact, watched it on television as well, so I was in good company so to speak. It was the beginning of the sexual revolution...sex, drugs and rock and roll. I experienced the drugs and the rock and roll, but was still waiting for the sex.

OH BUMMER

If it weren't for "The Bummers," I can't even imagine how life would have turned out. Pat, Wesley, Jack, Joe, Mike, Tall Mike and I all met in high school. As circumstance would have it, all of our paths crossed and a friendship was born that for most of us has lasted over thirty-five years. High school was over. The second we shed our caps and gowns and escaped the prison walls of Bishop Reilly, we all transformed into the bunch of longhaired hippies we all longed to be. If I remember correctly, it was Jack and I who came up with the idea of calling ourselves "The Bummers." Jack Kelly, one hundred percent Irish American, was a very handsome lad who had one great head of straight thick long black hair and an infectious laugh. One day we were both a little depressed because of girlfriend trouble, and feeling sorry for ourselves decided to cruise around the neighborhood all night. In our travels we composed this unending sing-a-long type of anthem about teenage depression, which we titled "Oh Bummer." Hence, "The Bummers" were formed and shortly after came the first and only Bummer recording, available on eight-track cassette tape exclusively. Even though there were just seven of us, we were always able to recruit people to do whatever we wanted to do. We formed The Bummer Bowling League that was officially sanctioned by the American Bowling Congress. I'll never forget the expressions on the faces of the beer-bellied, cigar- chomping older men who bowled on the league beside us. I don't think they knew what to make of us. We were a bunch of shaggy freaks with really cute girlfriends who just happened to enjoy bowling. They couldn't keep their eyes off of the girls and couldn't get over the fact that guys with hair down to their shoulders could actually bowl. We got a kick out of amusing them.

We hosted annual Halloween parties that always had a theme. One year we all came dressed as the characters from the "Wizard of Oz," which surely would have won us first prize if we were competing somewhere. New Years' Eve parties were always something we looked forward to even if it meant having to wake up the next morning to the stench of pigs' feet in vinegar. I guess that's what we had to expect when we asked Pat to cater the party from his family's Italian specialty store. Whatever possessed him to bring pig's feet appetizers along with the baked ziti and six-foot heroes, we'll never know.

During some of our think tank sessions we even concocted plans to build a Bummer's shopping mall. Unfortunately, the plans never found their way to the drawing board. Tall Mike totally took over his family's basement and turned it into The Bummers' clubhouse. Mike was a lanky, blond fellow who all of us looked upon as the "strange" one of the group. He pretty much knew how to fake his way through anything. No matter what the field, whether it was music, mechanics, poetry, carpentry, medicine or even religion, Mike considered himself an authority. He totally believed in himself and his ability to succeed at anything he tried. The problem was he was the only one who believed it. The floor of Mike's basement was covered with thick mats of foam rubber so anywhere you happened to plop yourself it was fairly comfortable. There were amplifiers, musical instruments and makeshift recording equipment all about so we could record our spontaneous shenanigans. On the "clubhouse" walls were montages of photos we had taken. Written in construction paper cut outs were the words, "These are Those Days" displayed atop them. We recruited musicians in order to perform a Bummer concert, a live performance of our cassette. We were also responsible for creating our very own winter sport; we called it panel riding. Crocheron Park was our home away from home. With its many rolling hills, every winter it was a haven for sleigh riders. Pat was the one who came up with the brainstorm of tying a four foot by eight foot wooden panel to the top of his car and bringing it to the park. All decked out in our parkas, hats and gloves, we carried the panel to the top of the highest hill. One by one we climbed aboard until with one good push we went sailing with reckless abandon down the icy paths screaming at anyone who was in our way to run for their lives. We found it challenging to see how many people we could pile on top of the panel at one time, and in how many different positions, including a pyramid. Like with any new experience, the thrill eventually wore off, and so from those four-foot by eight-foot panels, we graduated to our cars. We were borderline lunatics and actually found a way to use our own cars as sleigh mobiles. Somebody up there was definitely watching over us when Joe's lemon yellow Pontiac Lemans slid uncontrollably down the icy slopes of the park. None of us ever lacked company or something to do. Little by little, friends of friends wanted to be part of the Bummers. Bummer fever was spreading.

It was around this time in my pathetically inexperienced life when I was sort of "going out" with Hannah. Hannah lived down the block from Mike's Bummer clubhouse and after she saw me playing drums at a local club with my band called Justice, she told Mike she wanted to meet me. Mike delivered the message and of course I started to wonder who the heck this girl Hannah was. After interrogating him over and over again, in my mind I tried to conjure up an idea of what she looked like. I told Mike I was interested in meeting her. Then one night as we were all hanging out at the local Carvel, Hannah showed up and introduced herself to me while I was sipping a Chocolate Thick Shake. She seemed sweet. She had long blond hair and bangs and to me she looked very similar to Joni Mitchell. I absolutely loved Joni Mitchell. How couples became couples I had no idea, but the next thing I knew, Hannah and I were a couple, meaning when we all hung around together, she was there with me. When the night's festivities were over I would drive her home and we would sit in the car in front of her house and make out. Hannah remained very mysterious during our short "romance" never revealing too much about herself. After weeks and weeks of holding hands and making out, I finally decided to make my move, a big deal for a repressed Catholic boy. There we were, parked in our usual spot, our arms around each other and our faces joined in what felt like an endless kiss. I thought to myself, "It's now or never!" I clumsily reached my hand down and around up and under Hannah's shirt. To my surprise she wasn't wearing a bra and also to my surprise she didn't resist! "Now what do I do?" I asked myself. There I was with my hand on her breast; I leaned back, looked her in the eye and said, "You know what? You're alright!!" I removed my hand from under her shirt and we called it a night. God did I feel like a jerk! There was no resistance and I stopped at first base. I never got the chance to reach second.

The next time we were together, Hannah was crying and she gently told me that maybe we shouldn't be seeing each other anymore. "You're much too good for me," she said, "You deserve somebody much better!" I couldn't believe she was handing me that old standard break-up line. At first I thought she was breaking up with me because of my awkward and inept sexual advance, but as the light from the corner streetlamp created an eerie glow inside my car, I watched her wipe the teardrops as they trickled down her face and knew it was deeper than that! We sat in the car for what felt like hours and she began to open up the doors to her deep dark past. Like a priest who was hearing a confession, I sat in the shadows of the streetlight and listened to her tell the story of drug abuse and a steamy relationship with an ex-boyfriend. How I found myself in these situations I just didn't know. "You're much too nice a person!" she sobbed, "to be involved with the likes of me!"

Why did I have to be the good-natured soul, listening attentively as she poured her heart out, instead of being the reckless lover going to town in the back seat? I was really getting annoyed with my conscience. Years later, Hannah married her neighbor and fellow Bummer Tall Mike. Two decades and one child later, they divorced!

The Bummers lived to laugh, have fun and enjoy youth to its fullest. None of us were very politically minded, except for the fact that we were all opposed to the Viet Nam war, the draft and violence in general. The patriotism of the generations that preceded ours seemed to fade as reports of war casualties invaded the comfort of our living rooms daily. We spent many hours marching in local anti-war demonstrations. Our government instituted a draft lottery and The Bummers were all candidates. This was a lottery where the winners were losers and the losers were winners. If our number (which was our birth date-month and day) was selected, we could be called to serve in the military. Some guys would go to any extreme to avoid getting drafted. There were stories about fellows who would amputate toes, overdose on pills, act insane or claim to be gay. There was a tale going around at the time of a desperate fellow who actually ate peanut butter out of his own ass to try and convince the draft board he was nuts! Fortunately for all of us, we had high numbers. There was no need to have to remove any body parts, date other guys or eat sandwich spread from out of our behinds. Getting drafted was not yet something we needed to concern ourselves with. The day the lottery numbers came in we all went down to the park and celebrated with a couple of gallons of our favorite cheap wine. The Bummers would not in any way be serving in the armed forces. The country was safe for the time being.

HIGHER LEARNING

College was an interesting place to be in the late sixties and early seventies. All of my friends and I stayed home and went to local schools. Unlike the exorbitant amounts of money a college education costs today, because I went to a city college, I think my entire education cost less than six hundred dollars. Thank God, because in those days we spent more time in moratoriums and marches protesting the war than we did in class. Although it was drummed into our heads by our parents and ex-teachers how important it was to obtain a degree, girls were highest on our priority list of why we attended college. My friend Joe and I not only decided to attend the same school, but we even registered for a lot of the same classes. We must have been some sight. I was tall and thin standing about six foot two with long brown shoulder length hair, while Joe was much shorter with thick shoulder length blond hair. We looked like the Mutt and Jeff of the Woodstock generation. For two semesters we went from class to class surveying the entire campus daily and were unable to find or attract any suitable female companions.

During my first semester as a college student, a professor of mine dedicated an entire period to conducting a behavioral experiment regarding mob mentality. Although I don't remember the exact details of the experiment, I do remember that none of her students, including me, had any inkling as to what she was up to. As she gave directions to the class to perform certain actions, I remained in my seat ignoring her instructions simply because I found her commands to be ridiculous. One by one the entire class obeyed her every order, except for yours truly. I don't know why, but I just sat there looking at everybody and I thought to myself, "Why are they subjecting themselves to these stupid and lame requests?" When the professor told them all to return to their seats, which of course they did, she explained the purpose of her experiment. She told us that she just proved people are basically like sheep and will usually go along with almost anything if they are prodded enough. She then lectured us on the importance of being able to think on our own. She singled me out and commended me for sticking to my convictions and not joining the rest of the class. I'd always been proud of that moment and have tried to live my life not being a follower. Sometimes it's been easy. Sometimes the peer pressure has been overwhelming.

The first semester of my second year at Queens College, scheduling was a real headache. Who would have thought this inconvenience was to change the course of my life? Trying to find a class that would fit into our weekly schedules without conflicting with another class was next to impossible because of the extremely large student body. So it was common practice to register for any class that just so happened to give us the necessary credits and fit into our weekly schedules. We learned how to settle and not select, so Joe and I settled for Linguistics One. I had no clue as to what Linguistics One was and had absolutely no interest in finding out, but I needed to accumulate some credits. It was in that awful and boring class where I met my future wife, Julianne. Having scoped out all of my classes and once again failing to spot any potential main squeeze, I arrived in Linguistics. I gave the room the once-over and still saw no one who even sparked an interest. Then all of a sudden, as if God sensed my frustration, into the classroom strolled Julianne and her girlfriend Roseanne. They were attempting to get permission to join a class that was already closed out. The strangest thing was that Jule and Ro looked like the female counterparts to Joe and I. Julianne, the taller of the two, had straight long brown hair and Roseanne, always right by her side, was a dirty blond. The professor took the over-tally requests from the girls and motioned for them to find seats. As luck would have it, there were two vacant seats directly in front of Joe and I, and Julianne and Roseanne fit in them just perfectly. I knew it was time for me to be sharpening up my class clown skills. From the minute I saw Julianne I knew I had to get busy and make this girl take notice of me.

All throughout my college years the book I valued the most was my unlined spiral notebook. By the time I graduated, every page was filled with pen, pencil, and full color cartoon drawings, poems, song lyrics, and the random thoughts of my slightly deranged mind. My notebook was most certainly a conversation piece and was instrumental in helping to strike up a conversation with Jule and Ro. Once I got their attention, I invited them to a Bummer party that was to take place on the following weekend at the home of Tom Cello, lead guitarist in my band. Tom's parents were conveniently away. The girls graciously accepted. I was very attracted to Julianne and figured that bringing her to this party would be a good way of getting to know her. Julianne insisted upon meeting me at the party and bringing along a couple of her friends. After all, she really didn't know anything about my friends or me, so her caution was understandable. This was also around the time I met Roxanne. Roxie was a very cool fun loving girl, who I hit it off with from the moment we met, but always thought of her as a buddy and not a girlfriend. I invited her to the same party not even realizing she may have thought I was asking her as my date. As it turned out, both Julianne and Roxie showed up at the party, and what could have been a sticky uncomfortable situation, worked out just fine. No matter what the Bummers did or where the Bummers went, we always made sure we had fun and this night was no different. The party was in full swing and all the guests were having a great time. Everyone loved Roxie and she immediately became an official Bummer. Julianne seemed to genuinely like all my friends and they all liked her. When she took me by surprise by sitting on my lap and making out with me, I figured she must have liked me too. Whether or not it was the wine, I didn't know, but somehow I knew this was going to be the start of a wonderful relationship. I didn't realize it at the time, but years later I found out that when we first met, Julianne was not the least bit attracted to me and never even considered me as a possible boyfriend. Ironically, Jack advised me not to date Julianne because we lived too far away from each other! Our first formal date was two weeks later to a concert at Carnegie Hall to see Frank Zappa and the Mothers of Invention. What better way to start out?

MEET THE FAMILY

When we officially became a couple we were both nineteen, the age when you know nothing and think you know everything. She was beautiful, and we shared a common background; us both being of Italian decent and raised in the Catholic faith, we clicked almost immediately. Having these two important issues in common saved each of us the burden of having to explain a whole lot of craziness. On the other hand, the homes in which we were raised were very different. Julianne was the oldest of nine. Her mother was one of nine and her father was one of nine. If I added up all the aunts and uncles, cousins and second cousins, I would have had a number larger than the population of some states. Trying to remember all the names and faces was a difficult task.

The first time I met Jule's dad was on the day a bunch of us decided to take off from school and head Upstate to our favorite country getaway where we frolicked, and communed with Mother Nature. Later on that evening, Julianne joined my family and me for dinner at my house, followed by a night of Bummer bowling. I told her to call her folks several times during the day, but being the stubborn rebellious girl she was, she refused. I finally got Julianne home and just as I was about to kiss her goodnight, her father came barreling through their front door. He obviously couldn't sleep from knowing his daughter was not yet home and jumped right out of bed when he heard us pull up. He was a short man so naturally he had to look up to me. Wearing a white guinea tee shirt and holding his khaki trousers up with one hand, he pointed his finger at me with the other. He reprimanded his daughter, told her to get in the house and scolded me for keeping her out so late on a weeknight. Julianne was embarrassed and I was totally taken by surprise. She tried to give her father an explanation of where we were and why we were so late, but he refused to listen and just kept on ranting like a madman. She apologized to me, told me to go and she would call me tomorrow. I could only imagine what he thought when his eyes met the likes of me. There I stood, towering over him with hair down way past my shoulders, my jeans all faded and torn and my army jacket decorated with peace signs. The craziest thing was that everything he was probably thinking couldn't have been further from the truth. I guess it was hard for her dad to believe we could spend an entire day together without getting high or having sex. We were having a better time in his imagination than we actually did. What made this event strangely amusing was the fact that my dad joined us for the ride to Jule's house that evening. Since it was late and the trip was forty minutes, he thought I might want company for the ride home. He had parked down the block to give us privacy and had no idea of what was going on. When I got back to the car, he asked me if everything was all right. I said, "Everything's just great!"

In the beginning, I had a lot of respect for Julianne's dad, Ray. To me he was a mechanical wizard. It seemed like he could build anything and fix anything, and he was always hard at work for his family. After putting in an exhausting day at the maintenance shop of the New York City Transit Authority, he'd return home to tackle the things that needed to be done around the house. Having such a large family to support, money was always tight. So when anything needed repairs, whether it was the cars, the appliances or the electronics, he did them. He even took on the enormous task of extending their miniscule house into one that could fit eleven people more comfortably. He always amazed me with his mechanical ability and his know-how. There was barely a time when Ray wasn't working, but in those few instances, he'd be standing in front of the full sized mirror he had in his backyard so he could practice his golf swing. If he could have had things his way, he would have practically lived at the golf course. It was many years later that I started to see the sometimes-extreme effects his "work ethic" had on his kids.

My first impression of Marie, Ray's wife, was that of a sweet, hospitable, hard working mom, who in her own way, tried to make me feel comfortable in her home. One afternoon, while Julianne and I were relaxing on the couch in her parents' den, a quarrel broke out between her mom and Julianne's younger brother, Gregory, who had to be around thirteen at the time. Gregory was sort of like the runt of the litter. He was hard of hearing in one ear, which caused him to say "what?" so often that he couldn't help but get on one's nerves. Whatever Gregory and his mother were quarreling about I couldn't say. Most likely it was over something trivial such as a chore that was overlooked. I watched in amazement as Gregory kept successfully ducking the broomstick his mom was swinging at him. Marie tried locking him out of the house but it was only a matter of minutes before we could hear the sound of his key slowly slipping into the lock of the rear door and he came sneaking back in.

"I thought I told you to get out of the house and to stay out!" his mom screamed frantically and frustratingly.

"I have to take out the trash!" he responded pathetically.

Gregory just didn't know enough to lay low for a while. Once again the broomstick went swinging; Gregory performed his survival acrobatics, grabbed the garbage and was out the door unscathed. Without missing a beat, Marie turned to me and in the most pleasant tone asked, "John would you like a cup of tea?" To Julianne this was just another normal day. Her mom was a full-time household manager. Not only was she supposed to be raising nine children, she also had to cook, clean, shop, manage the money and along with all that, try to keep her sanity.

When I met Ray and Marie I asked myself why a couple would want to have so many kids if they really couldn't afford them. Well in their case and those of many other practicing Roman Catholics, the answer was because the Church didn't believe in birth control. What better way to build an empire by dictating to its followers that birth control was wrong in the eyes of the Church and therefore in the eyes of God! A simple equation: More Catholics, more money…more money, more power! Somewhere in the Bible I knew it mentioned something about being fruitful and multiplying, but I didn't think there was any mention anywhere about not pulling out or using protection. I never felt a woman was meant to keep spitting out children until her insides collapse. For the better part of their life together, Marie was pregnant and Ray was working one way or another trying to provide for his family. Since I grew up under completely different circumstances, I saw it as being quite unfair that all parties were deprived of many of the joys of childhood and parenthood.

Gino was also one of nine children. Because we attended different high schools he missed out on the Bummer years, but nevertheless, we remained the greatest of friends. I'd always loved Gino's family as if they were my very own. Like Jule's dad, Gino's dad was a very devout Catholic. The difference was that Gino's dad was a dentist and because he was much better off financially, he was able to provide not only in things, but also in the time he had to spend with his kids. I can remember hearing Dr. D's voice cheering Gino on from the stands at our little league games. Julianne's brothers sadly admitted they'd never had that kind of relationship with their dad; it was all work and no play. It was the control of the Church that manipulated the lives of people like Ray.

As to how devout my parents were as Catholics, what can I say? They never missed Mass, didn't eat meat on Fridays, and fasted during Lent. As to their position on birth control, I was never too sure. When I talk to my dad these days, he claims he'd always been selective as to what he found acceptable in Catholic doctrine. He feels that because he'd always been a fairly intelligent man, he was able to form his own opinions and didn't need Rome to make his decisions for him. How he actually felt fifty years ago is questionable and I'm sure if I asked him, I wouldn't get a totally honest answer. Dad's always kept most of what went on in the bedroom, in the bedroom.

My folks had four children and one miscarriage and while she was still in her childbearing years, my mom had a hysterectomy. I never saw my dad as one of those "keep them barefoot and pregnant" type of guys, so her hysterectomy was in no way a result of that kind of primitive thinking. It was just one of those things. My mom loved kids, so who knows, I could have very well been the oldest of eight or nine, and things may have turned out totally different for me. My mom chose to put aside her career as an x-ray technician to raise us kids while my dad worked in sales. When I was living at home I never had any idea as to how much or how little money my dad made. I knew we weren't rich. My mom had to keep a budget and make the money stretch, but because there weren't that many mouths to feed and because my dad always drove a company car, they were able to afford some of the extras. We enjoyed some of the luxuries that Julianne's family couldn't, such as drive-to overnight getaways to places like Lake George or Gettysburg in Virginia. We occasionally went out for dinner at a nice restaurant, and we all took private music lessons. I took drum lessons while Virginia studied the accordion. In years to come Bill was given guitar lessons while Jim learned to play piano. We lived with my grandparents in a brand new house so this low maintenance situation allowed for us to enjoy the many hours of free time my dad had. When dad got home from the office he didn't have to work on the house or repair things so he had the time and energy to get involved in the lives of his children.

I should probably thank my grandparents for my love of music. My grandfather played the guitar and mandolin and my grandmother sang. There was always plucking and strumming and the singing of Italian songs. As cool as I thought it was to hear my grandfather play, it drove my dad just as nuts as my band practices drove my grandparents.

Compared to Julianne's dad, my dad wasn't the least bit mechanically inclined. But he was a good talker. He's always had the gift of gab and was able to charm the socks off of almost anyone. When I was seventeen, one of the major New York radio stations ran an on-the-air Battle of the Bands contest. Local bands would submit tapes and if selected would get to play on the air right from the station's studio. The listeners would then call the station casting votes for their favorite band. The top ten bands would then get to play and compete before a panel of judges at Carnegie Hall. My band, Justice, entered the contest and was given the opportunity to be heard on New York radio. Once again, my dad was there to drive us into the city, help with our equipment and act as our spokesman. After we were done playing, while we were packing up our instruments, I saw my dad talking, laughing and shaking hands with Bruce Morrow, a/k/a Cousin Brucie, the major D.J. at the station. Cousin Brucie and a couple of the other disc jockeys told us how good we sounded, congratulated us on our performance and wished us luck as we left the studio. A few nights later, while my family and I were having dinner, the telephone rang. I picked it up, said hello, and a familiar voice asked for my dad. I asked who was calling to which the voice replied, "It's Bruce Morrow from WABC!" I wondered why he would be calling my father. Well as it turned out, while we were playing, my smooth-talking dad discovered that Cousin Brucie was a photography buff and had offered to send him free film. Mr. Morrow took him up on the offer and the next thing I knew, Cousin Brucie and my dad were phone pals and my band just so happened to make it to the finals at Carnegie Hall. When I think back now on how we sounded then, it had to be the free film that got us there.

Nobody wanted me to be a success in the music business more than my father. He'd always loved music but lacked the patience to learn an instrument, so until this day he remains a frustrated musician. Always trying to make a connection for my benefit, I never forgot the time he thought we may have struck gold. He knew a fellow whose brother allegedly had some big ties in the entertainment business. At the time, I was writing and performing my own material in my band "The Convertibles." We had just released our first record on a very independent label. This acquaintance of my dad instructed us to put together a press kit containing the record, pictures and a bio, all of which I quickly threw together. We were to meet him one evening at a nightclub in Brooklyn near the Verrazano Bridge. As usual, my pop drove and as we made our way down to Brooklyn, I thought to myself, "Why Brooklyn? Usually anything related to music takes place in Manhattan!" We arrived at the address we were told to report to and parked the car among the limos and Cadillacs that lined the ominous street. When we entered the bar I looked around and thought, "Oh my God, what are we doing here in the midst of all these mobsters?" My dad's friend greeted us, sat us at the bar and instructed the bartender to treat us to whatever drinks we wanted. He took the press kit from my reluctant hands and informed me that the gentleman he wanted me to meet would be arriving shortly.

My pop leaned over and whispered in my ear, "John," he said, "don't turn around but the guy in the corner is a convicted killer. I've seen his picture in the paper."

I said "Dad, I think we'd better excuse ourselves and get the hell out of here!"

By then the Jack Daniels was getting to my head so the evening started to take on a different perspective for me, from one of skepticism to one of amusement. My dad's connection finally re-entered the room, only this time standing beside him was the real connection, my golden opportunity, and my link to the entertainment business. He approached me, firmly shook my hand and in a voice straight out of a Sopranos' episode said to me, "So, you're an entertainer?"

I told him about my band's record and as he glanced over my press kit I had the feeling he had absolutely no idea of what rock and roll was about. Then he asked me to follow him to an adjoining room in which there was a very typical Italian wedding band playing Sinatra, Jerry Vale and other Goodfella favorites. He looked at me, and with the most serious but clueless expression on his gangster face, suggested I go take the microphone and entertain the crowd by singing a few numbers! I told him he didn't exactly understand my style of entertainment and as I politely bowed out of an extremely uncomfortable and embarrassing situation, he told me he'd listen to the record and see what he could do. I turned to my dad and said, "Let's get the fuck outta here!" Sometimes it's not who you know!

Although I received a tremendous amount of support and attention from my parents and although I'd never been in need of friends, the one thing I felt was lacking in my life was a relationship with cousins. One thing Julianne had for sure were cousins...a load of cousins. When they were kids, they lived in the same community and experienced growing up together. They hung out, played and made memories they all still share to this day. There is only one cousin of mine I had anything in common with and he'd always lived too far away for us to really have any kind of a close relationship. Most of my aunts and uncles were spread about all over the country so I probably have cousins I'd never even seen. One of my father's sisters, Jean, is the one relative who didn't move away. Aunt Jean did something so revolutionary for our family that it must have sent them all buzzing. She married Hank Schwartz...a Jew. It was just something that had been instilled in us since birth, Catholics were supposed to marry Catholics, period. In our family, if he or she were Italian, all the better!

Aunt Jean and Uncle Hank never had any children, but when I was a kid, I always looked forward to their visits. Aunt Jean reminded me of the character of Lois Lane from the old black and white adventures of Superman. Whenever I saw her she'd be wearing a conservative skirt, a little hat and high heels. She was a short energetic woman, who for many years was a New York City executive's secretary, and she could type faster than anyone I knew. She had typed many a term paper for me. She also ran a small mail order business from her apartment. She sold knick knacks and novelties and every holiday season, paid my sister and me a commission when we would go door to door selling the items from her catalog. With the money we earned, Aunt Jean took us to the department stores so we could do some holiday shopping of our own.

My Uncle Hank worked as a mailman and was a very funny guy, always quipped with a wisecrack or witty comeback line. Sometimes he tried to come across as strict and stern, like whenever he would make us stop banging on Aunt Jean's piano. Underneath, however, was a soft, kind-hearted, pussycat of a man. He reminded me of a cross between Bud Abbott and Shemp from the Three Stooges. He had a long strand of black hair that would always fall in front of his face and he would forever be pushing it back. He would do anything for Aunt Jean and because she didn't drive, he drove her wherever she wanted to go. He shared all the Christian holidays with our family and even attended the Catholic Church with Aunt Jean on many Sundays. He was there so often they made him an usher where he assisted in collecting the offerings. With the "us and them" mentality of Catholicism, it was quite comical how my Jewish uncle made himself fit right in.

For a few years, while I was still in late grammar school and early high school, Jean and Hank threw an annual holiday dinner party at their apartment and this was probably the only time I got to meet my Uncle Hank's side of the family. They all were so very nice and so friendly but in my immature and misdirected mind I couldn't get past the fact they were also Jewish. Every year as we all crowded into Jean and Hank's apartment, I could just sense this unspoken prejudice, not so much from them, but from us. As Catholics, we seemed to have had this arrogant attitude that God favored us and us alone. Jews, on the other hand, had always been known to be God's Chosen People, but I never sensed an attitude from them. It just didn't seem that big of an issue. My awareness that there was such an obvious difference between the Schwartz's and my immediate family didn't come from the Schwartz's; it probably came from the anti-Semitic environment that surrounded me. Maybe subconsciously I thought, "Hey, you're nice people, don't you guys want to get to heaven one day?" When I looked at my Uncle Hank I never saw him as my Jewish uncle and I'm sure he never looked at me as his Christian nephew. Who was right and who was wrong was never even a matter of discussion. At the time, the only thing I knew about Jewish people was that they didn't believe in Jesus. I also wasn't the least bit aware of the fact that Jesus Himself was a Jew. As to what Hank believed, I didn't know. Differences in our religions never came up in conversation. I guess Uncle Hank figured, why take chances, so he played both sides of the fence. I suppose he thought that was one way of guaranteeing getting into heaven. I could see him passing through the Pearly Gates wearing his usher pin proudly and hoping nobody would blow his cover!

COULD THIS BE LOVE?

I majored in Communication Arts and Sciences at Queens College. In other words, since I had no idea whatsoever of what I wanted to do with myself once I graduated this higher institute of learning, I took the easiest Liberal Arts courses I could find. How hard could studying about television and radio be? My plan was to be a rock and roll star and never have to join the real world. Sometimes I think one of the major stumbling blocks that kept me from succeeding in the music business was the same reason I didn't go to Woodstock, that is, I didn't want to rough it. What I mean by "roughing it" comes from the stories I'd read about most of my favorite rock stars who left their homes, took to the streets, slept in their cars, and scraped together whatever money they could for food, until eventually, they were discovered. Maybe I just didn't want it that bad. I lived in a nice house with a loving family in a good community and everyone I hung out with lived the same cushy circumstances. I wasn't willing to give up the creature comforts for a life on the road. Life was relatively safe and I guess I liked it that way. I was waiting for someone to come knocking on my front door and say, "John, I think you've got what it takes to be a rock star. Sign on the dotted line!"

One morning as I sat daydreaming in an English writing class, the guy who sat behind me kept whispering lyrics to Buffalo Springfield songs in my ear. I never understood how he knew I was a huge Neil Young fan or why he thought I'd appreciate his familiarity with Young's music. I finally acknowledged his poetic chattering by letting him know I approved of his good taste and from that moment on, Richie Soriano and I became good friends and song writing partners. Rich looked like a cross between Fidel Castro and Jerry Garcia. He was a big guy with a hairy face and a receding hairline. He too was a guitar picker and most definitely a poet. We started hanging out a lot together and within weeks wrote hundreds of songs. Between his knack for writing the most controversially clever lyrics and my ear for melodic hooks, we were certain our success was inevitable. Eventually we recruited a couple of friends and formed a band. We started playing around in some small clubs and if nothing else, we had a great time.

My college years were a time of immense fun. Because we went to local colleges, all of my high school friends were still around. I made some new college friends, I had my very own rock'n roll band and I was in love. Julianne had always been such a serious minded student and I was probably the reason why she didn't follow her plans to do something more with her education. I would try anything to get her to cut class and hang out with me. I even went as far as to place a notice on the door of her classroom announcing the cancellation of the class due to the professor being ill. It worked, most of the students left. Some days Richie and I would stroll past her classroom windows trying to create a panic by screaming as loudly as we could, "Evacuate! Radiation! Radiation!" Don't ask me how, but she fell in love with me too, got attached to all my friends and jumped onto the party train. It was a wild and wonderful period in my life.

I was crazy about Julianne. We tried to spend as much time together as we possibly could. The only drag was she lived out on Long Island, which was about a thirty-five minute drive from my house. It was a little different than dating the girl next door. We would spend lots of time in the car driving to and from each other's houses, which gave us the opportunity to talk about a lot of things. Among the many topics that came up, we often discussed our belief in God, our Catholic upbringing, our views on going to church and superficial spiritual stuff like that. We seemed to agree on a lot of things, but most importantly was the fact that we believed in God, that somehow He brought us together and no couple on this planet could possibly, in any way whatsoever, love each other as much as we did. Julianne once told me that when she was a young girl, she was greatly impressed by the stories she read about kids who had visions of saints. She laughed while admitting how she used to think that someday a saint was actually going to appear to her. I was definitely no saint, so I was sure it wasn't me.

At around the time Julianne and I had been going out for nine months, one of her girlfriends was getting married. Julianne was to be in the wedding party and I, of course, was invited as her guest. The best part of all was that the wedding was to take place in Florida. Both of us convinced our parents we undoubtedly could be trusted and that the accommodations would certainly meet their approval. I would be staying in a local motel and Jule would be staying with her friend's family. Instead, we saved up our money, went to a travel agent and booked ourselves a room at a luxury hotel. We had the time of our lives acting as if we were a couple on their honeymoon. The beach, the sun, the meals, the room service and being able to spend the night together every night for an entire week, was more fun than either of us had ever imagined.

At the same time we were living it up in Florida, Julianne's parents were also away experiencing the rejuvenation of their love for each other at a "marriage encounter." "Marriage Encounters" were retreats sponsored by the church to help couples restore their hurting or troubled marriages. When we returned home, Ray and Marie were on such a high from their little getaway, they never asked us even one question about our trip, which meant we didn't have to fabricate any more lies. At the time, they were so into each other, they were oblivious to anything else that was going on around them, including us. Things, however, didn't go quite as smoothly at my house. One afternoon my mom gave me this serious look of disapproval and I knew something was really wrong. No matter how much I prodded her, she refused to say anything except, "Wait until your father gets home!" Well I waited, and eventually my father did come home and he didn't appear to be too happy either. He reached up and took hold of an envelope that had been sitting on top of the refrigerator. He threw it down in front of me onto the kitchen table and said, "Can you explain this?" I picked up the envelope and could not believe my eyes when I saw the return address was from the very hotel that Julianne and I stayed at. What made it even worse was the letter addressed to Mr. And Mrs. John Domenico, thanking them for staying at their establishment and welcomed them to come back again soon. I had to assume my parents knew it was us and not them to whom the letter was referring. I tried my very best to come up with an alibi but I knew we were busted. I used whatever acting skills I had to make it appear I was ashamed and genuinely sorry. The truth of the matter was that I didn't know what I was pretending to be sorry for, lying, or sleeping with my girlfriend. My dad was disappointed in me for lying and pulling a fast one. My mom, for having to face the possibility her son wasn't a virgin anymore! That evening before going to bed, I went to say good night to my mom as I normally did. She stood motionless and with an expression of disgust, disappointment and hurt on her face, she looked me right in the eye and said, "I can't believe you let Julianne see you in your underwear!" I should have responded by saying, "Mom, I wasn't wearing any underwear," but I let her think what she wanted to think.

On a rare night, when Julianne slept over our house for matters of convenience only, my mom wouldn't retire to her bedroom until after she patrolled the halls like a prison guard, making certain that Jules and I were confined to our sleeping quarters, inopportunely far apart from each other. How times have changed.

DENIAL?

I'm not quite sure how our parents could have been so blind to many of the antics we pulled off in our crazy youth. We were two hot-blooded kids madly in love with each other who anxiously waited for the weekends just so we could be alone together. Whenever we made our way out of Julianne's front door on a Friday or Saturday night, we answered her mom's question the same way every time, "To the movies…!" We must have told Jule's parents we saw "A Clockwork Orange" at least six times. If they had any idea we were spending those evenings fogging up the windows of my Datsun 1200 or checking into "The Golden Meadowbrook Motel" under the alias of John Colletti, they would have killed us.

One of the most difficult tasks I ever had to face, during those years when we lived double lives, was trying to behave normally around my family while I was stoned. On a late Saturday afternoon, one of my fellow employees at the home center just so happened to have in his possession a chunk of killer hash-hish, which he so generously decided to share with us. After taking a few hits out in the parking lot, I became so incapacitated I couldn't think. I couldn't count change; I could hardly walk and could definitely not help customers.

The buzz got more intense as the day went on and while driving home from work, in that condition no less, I told God I would never get high again if He would allow me to come down before pulling into my driveway. God didn't come through; the prayers went unanswered. I seemed to just float into my house and somehow managed to find my way to the table where I joined my family for dinner. I sat quietly and tried to remain as inconspicuous as possible. This wasn't easy, because in my slightly altered state, my family members all took on those exaggerated and colorful cartoon-like qualities, which forced me to totally focus on my mashed potatoes in order to thwart completely freaking out. By the time dinner was over I had straightened out considerably and nobody even had a clue. Could they have been so oblivious or was it just another case of parents seeing only what they want to see? By the way, God probably knew I wasn't going to keep my part of the bargain so He made me suffer through it!

Another evening at the same dinner table we were having a family discussion about the dangers of drugs. One member of my family made the statement that smoking pot led directly to heroin use. I strongly disagreed and was immediately placed in front of the firing squad.

"How do you know? What makes you such an expert? Did you ever smoke pot?" they inquired.

"Yeah" I answered, "for your information I've smoked a lot of pot and have never tried heroin, so I guess I am an expert!"

That very second my sister Virginia called me a jerk while my brother Bill and my mom began to cry simultaneously. My dad dropped his fork and as it crashed onto his plate, he shook his head in disapproval, and then I got the speech about how disappointed he was in me. I sat there totally bewildered by my family's reaction and regretted what I'd just said because I hated to see my mom cry. My siblings on the other hand had to get a life.

In the years that followed, there were so many occurrences in our lives and the lives of our siblings that led me to believe our parents were either clueless, in the comfortable state of denial, or too tired to even give a shit about what we were doing! Whatever it was we were trying to hide from them, whether it was the sex, the drugs, or the booze, it sure seemed as though we succeeded. It wasn't because we were so clever; it was because they were just so damn unaware!

My youngest brother Jim was a master of deception. Nobody knows for sure how Jim turned out to be such a peculiar guy, but the time he fell on his head from my upper bunk when he was eighteen months old may offer a clue. While my folks believed he was out playing basketball at the park, he was actually taking public transportation to a neighborhood which was uncharted territory to me, but was home to the nearest x-rated movie theater. This may be what contributed to his early teen promiscuity and his many nights of sneaking about with who knows who. Mom always waited up for Jimmy and would greet her little boy with freshly made chocolate pudding even if it was two o'clock in the morning. Where in the world did she think he was anyway?

I never had the heart to tell my folks that while on the evenings they were sitting comfortably on their sofa, fixated on some made for TV movie, my brother was upstairs in his bedroom with his girlfriend and they weren't playing Scrabble! Jim really had them fooled even though he was too stupid to hide the evidence. Luckily for him, my sister found his discarded condoms in the kitchen garbage before my parents did.

Julianne had a cousin who I had a feeling was a closet homosexual from the very first day I met him. He was engaged to a very beautiful girl, but the fact that he wore woman's Huckapoo blouses clued me in. Before he came out of the closet and broke off the engagement, the news spread like wildfire throughout Jule's family about the cousin's visit to the proctologist. Jule's mom, who'd always had a flare for gossip, couldn't help but share with us the latest news. As we sat around the conference table, sipping Shop-Rite tea and snacking on Stella D'Oro biscuit treats, she made the announcement, "...and Francis had to see the doctor because he'd been having problems with his rectum..." While I asked myself, "You call THAT news?" Marie, with the most naïve facial expression, continued with her own slant on the story, "I'll bet that's because he wears his pants too tight!" Did their conclusions come from being clueless or was it denial? Eventually everyone found out the truth. Doesn't the truth always come out? "Not that there's anything wrong with that!"

HYPOCRISY?

Since the day I met him, Julianne's father had always been quite an interesting character. He professed to be a moral, righteous and God-fearing man. He would not tolerate profanity, which he demonstrated one Christmas day by storming into the living room where Julianne and I and our friends Wesley and Toni-Ann were listening and laughing hysterically to a George Carlin album. As he clutched the arm of the phonograph with his angry fingers, we heard the scratching of the needle as it skated across the vinyl. "Don't be playing this garbage in my house," he hollered, and the laughter came to an abrupt halt. The Christmas present Julianne had bought me now had a nice scratch clear across side A.

He also wouldn't stand for anything he perceived to be sacrilegious. In college I was required to take courses in basic filmmaking. At the time, my friend Jack Kelly had transferred to Queens College. Conveniently, he had the same course requirements I did, so the two of us became filmmaking partners. Jack was always full of great ideas. I have always said he was ahead of his time. He came up with the concept of music videos long before MTV even existed and people were not yet conned into thinking cable was a necessity. It was right there in Professor Turner's "Introduction to Filmmaking" when "Kel-Dom Productions" began. Together, Jack and I made a series of films, but the one we entitled, "Thanks but No Thanks," was the one that made Julianne's dad pull the plug on his family's private screening of the "Kel-Dom" film festival. In this movie I portrayed Jesus desperately trying to convince two fishermen He was who He claimed to be. After performing a number of miracles, which we achieved through the primitive technique of in-camera editing, the fishermen were bored and unimpressed. Jesus then vanished into thin air. In the next scene, one of the fishermen felt something tugging on his line and he reeled in, of all things, a condom. (In those days condoms were sold behind the counter, so it was quite comical when Jack and I walked into a local drugstore to purchase only one, trying to convince the pharmacist it was a prop for a movie.) The camera then zoomed in on the condom only to find the bearded miracle worker inside it, attempting once more to win the two non-believers. It was that very scene that caused the plug to be pulled on my super-8 projector and made Jule's dad lose respect for me as a filmmaker and a Catholic.

I was twenty years old and still held the same job I'd had since high school at a local home center. I was still somewhat immature, so I had a way of justifying some of the things I did that I was very well aware of being wrong. I knew Jule's dad was doing some home improvements, so in an attempt to redeem myself, I offered him the opportunity to come by the store on a night when the boss was away and help himself to some lumber. I figured it was a way to not only win some points with him, but a chance to see Julianne during the week while I had to work. Surprisingly, he took me up on the offer and with his daughter along for the ride, made a visit to my place of employment. Like a kid let loose in a candy store, he stacked up 2x3's and 2x4's as if they were going out of style and together we marched them out into the street and into his van. He seemed a bit self-conscious as he laughed a Barney Rubble laugh that was uniquely his own, and walked out of the store with one last armload of eight-foot boards. Somehow he was able to head home with a van-load of stolen merchandise and a clear conscience. If keeping his daughter out "unreasonably" late on a weeknight, listening to a comedian use four-letter words, and taking part in the making of a film he considered blasphemous were incidents that definitely did not meet his approval, how then did stealing hundreds of dollars worth of building supplies? He put a new twist on the eighth Commandment; "Thou shall not steal, unless thou thinks thou cannot afford not to." Although now I am ashamed to admit I had anything to do with stealing, I was unquestionably an accomplice. It was my tempting offer that put Jule's dad in this irresistible situation. I led him to the forbidden fruit so to speak.

There is one other fellow who deserves dishonorable mention for his contribution to the "Great Lumber Heist of 1972." Jimmy Petrocelli was really a very nice guy. J.P. was in charge of the store on the evening of the robbery and not only did he close his eyes to it, he assisted in it. Marty and Morty were two brothers-in-law who owned the small operation and played the good cop-bad cop game. Marty was the rugged hard ass who always made it known how hard he worked for his money. Morty was the gentler of the two, the comedian-type, never taking anything too seriously, looking more like the kind of guy who belonged in the nightclubs in the Borscht Belt. They were flexible with the scheduling of our hours so we could work around our school and social calendars. The pay was nothing to get excited over but who's ever satisfied with their salaries? Jimmy certainly wasn't! J.P. started working for them since the day they opened. Jimmy was a schmoozer! He knew just what to say and do and it wasn't very long before his full round face, with the ever-present smile and trimmed moustache, won him their trust and respect. Marty and Morty were very family-oriented and once they felt secure in knowing they could leave their business in the capable hands of Jimmy, they made it a practice to quit early a couple of nights a week. Trusting souls they were, they would also take off on occasional weekends to get away with their wives and kids, while leaving Jimmy to manage the store! After months of working together with Jim, I learned about the two things that drove him: the love of sex and the love of money! It was on one of those absentee-owner Saturdays, when Jimmy, after his usual discourse of explicitly describing his latest sexual conquest, confided in me about how he'd been ripping off Marty and Morty to earn himself some extra bonus money. I guess he felt that if he got me involved in his scam, he wouldn't have had to worry about me ratting him out. He showed me how easy it was to double my salary with his foolproof system on how not to ring up certain sales and keeping the cash for ourselves. At the day's end, when he handed me my share of the loot, I was hooked. There were some days I feared we were going to get caught because we would net more than the bosses. Jim sensed my nervousness and reassured me there was nothing to worry about, that he had all of the bases covered. One of the advantages of the computer-less age was that when the time of the year rolled around to take inventory, it was our job to do the counting. Jimmy figured if we fudged the numbers, it would make it appear as if they had more stock than they actually did. Our method of counting inaccurately was our way of keeping their losses to a minimum and not arousing any suspicion. In our minds, our actions were justifiable. We thought we deserved raises, so in our own way, we got them.

One day I was telling my friend Joe about the little income-producing scheme we had going on at the home center, never giving a thought to the possibility it would turn him to a thief as well! Joe worked as part-time manager at a local dairy/convenience store where just for kicks we would open jars of peanut butter, mayonnaise and the like, and put little notes on the insides, with the hopes of freaking out the customers once they got home and opened them. Every Saturday morning he would call me up from work and I could almost see him grinning through the phone as he announced the grand total that went into his pocket during his shift. I created a monster! Not only was I a bad influence on my future father-in-law, I introduced my best friend into a life of crime!

It was nice always having some extra spending money in my pocket, but when Jim showed up for work one day in a brand spanking new car, I got the feeling he'd been pocketing a lot more than I knew about. My stolen bonus dollars afforded me a bit more fun on a weekend maybe, but never enough for a major purchase like an automobile. I was a little late for work one Saturday morning and as I pulled into the parking lot I noticed Jim's shiny new metallic blue Volkswagen Beetle was not in its usual spot. I walked into the store and said my "good mornings" to the crew and before I even asked, Marty told me that J.P. didn't work for him anymore. He didn't offer an explanation as to whether Jimmy quit or was fired, but he did let it be known he was aware he'd been ripped off. "That son of a bitch took me for a new car," he said, and never mentioned another word about it.

It wasn't until almost a year later when out of the blue I got a call from Jim. He was also a musician and the call had something to do with the possibility of the two of us putting together a club date band. We got together just this one time to play a few songs and to see if we'd click. Musically, however, we were on different wavelengths so the band never materialized. To say Jimmy had changed would be an understatement. He didn't refer to sex or money even once, and his eyes were wide open with the excitement of a kid on Christmas morning. His almost maniacal smile never left his face for even a moment and his Bible never left his hand.

He put his face close up enough to mine I could smell his wintergreen breath, and with a tone of such sincere concern, he asked if I knew Jesus. He rapidly flipped through the pages of his Bible and quoted scripture with the expertise of a televangelist. He explained to me how he found Jesus and I replied with a joke by saying, "I never knew He was lost!" The man who I knew to once have an insatiable appetite for sex and money stood before me with what certainly seemed like a sincere hunger and thirst for God. Jimmy preached to me until he was almost breathless. He practically pleaded with me to surrender my life to Christ and gave me an open invitation to join his Bible study group. In my mind, I was cool with God and Jimmy simply went off the deep end. His enthusiasm was wearing thin and I couldn't wait for him to pack his Bible, his guitar and leave. I don't think his intentions were ever to start a band, he just saw it as an opportunity to get to me. That was the last I'd ever heard from Jimmy Petrocelli, never knowing this was a foreshadowing of what I was to become. And then un-become.

SAUSAGE MAN

I first met Pat in Room 207, homeroom, freshman year high school. We hit it off right from the start and have shared what will soon be a forty-year friendship. Pasquale, his given name, was always very proud of his Italian heritage. A red pepper hung from the rear-view mirror of his 1969 Mustang and an Italian flag graced the rear bumper. Today, Pat is the brain behind a local chain of Italian gourmet food stores that had its humble beginnings in his grandfather's pork store in what was once the Italian immigrant section of Brooklyn, New York. On every corner there were Italian social clubs, bread bakeries and pastry shops. I couldn't understand how all those bakeries could survive by just selling bread and cannolis. The characters that hung out there seemed to do nothing all day but stand around, read the Racing Form and drink espresso.

How I know that to be true is because one summer I had the experience of working for Pat's dad at the pork store. Every morning like clockwork, Manny from the pastry shop across the street would bring over freshly made cannolis and the daily numbers. Each workday began with an Italian pastry sugar rush and a caffeine blast from the high-octane coffee readily available throughout the workday. My first daily assignment at the pork store was to untangle and wash the casings that were used for stuffing sausage. I never gave a thought to what sausage meat was actually wrapped in, that is, the intestinal linings of the animal. What was once stuffed with shit was now being used to house chopped meat. So there I stood before a large sink filled with the miles and miles of tangled intestinal lining that had to be prepared for my next task, stuffing the chopped pork into those slimy skins. Making the sausage was almost as nauseating as handling the blobs of knotted casings. The chopped pork was plopped into this gadget that sort of resembled a wine press. Near the top of the press was a metal tube approximately one foot long with a three-quarter inch opening. I had to slide the casing onto the tube, sliding as much casing onto it as possible. Near the bottom of this contraption was a lever, that when pressed with my knee, caused the meat to eject from the tube and into the casings I gently guided along. I guess it could have been worse; I could have been cleaning cesspools. Nevertheless, there I was day after day, decked out in a long white butcher's jacket and a white hardhat, which they made me wear because of my long hair. Although Pat's dad liked me, he wasn't too fond of longhaired hippies and probably got a little kick out of making me look like a jerk with my hair shoved up inside the helmet.

Those summer days were long and torturous and as I cleaned casings, stuffed sausage, trimmed fat and performed all the other low-end janitorial jobs of the meat business, I kept one eye on the clock and one on the cast of characters who made their way in and out of the shop. At least once a week one of the neighborhood hookers would enter the store then disappear into the back room with one of the butchers for a quick little business transaction. I heard the unmistakable sound of bodies pounding up against the walk-in box wall and soon after saw the giggling working girl exiting the store with her goody bag full of cold cuts and assorted meats, while her satisfied customer tied his apron and returned to work. It seemed as if it was just a normal part of life, another routine day on the streets of Brooklyn. It was an interesting summer to say the least, and more often than not, Pat and I didn't talk much to each other on the ride home from work.

Before our days of working at the pork store together, Pat was attending Business College in Manhattan. It was on the subway ride to school where he met Erica. Erica was a pretty girl with ghost-white skin, wavy dark hair and deep dark eyes. From the moment I met her I liked her. She was different from most of our friends. She was deep and enjoyed conversations that stimulated her intellect. She liked to discuss religion, life and death and other such topics, rather than the typical adolescent small talk. I found Erica to be very refreshing and it was easy to see why Pat was so attracted to her. At the same time I knew, as long as he remained under the controlling influence of his conventional, conservative, Catholic family, the relationship could never work.

Her dad was an artist who escaped the hustle and bustle of the city and relocated to a rustic old farmhouse in the Massachusetts countryside. Pat and Erica would make regular trips to Massachusetts to visit her dad and on a couple of those getaways Julianne and I had the opportunity to join them. A small-framed man whose thinning hair and receding hairline made him appear older than he was, Fred ranked among one of the most interesting individuals I'd ever had the pleasure of meeting. He had his very own vegetable garden from which we harvested some of the best tasting carrots I'd ever eaten. He was able to walk around in the neighboring woods, swim in the local lake and commune with Mother Nature wearing nothing but the outfit he wore when he first entered this world. In my mind he was a rebel who found a way to successfully drop out of the daily rat race.

Erica's dad made a living as an artist, with what I thought was little compromise. He painted designs for textiles. Some of the floral or geometric prints seen on various tablecloths, curtains, wallpaper, and towels may just be his. He was even spared the inconvenience of having to bring his artwork to the city because the corporations he designed for would send messengers to his home to pick it up. As far as I was concerned, having a set-up like Fred's, working from home and doing what I loved to do, would be a dream come true, but Fred was unhappy about it. He felt as if he was prostituting his talent. He wanted to paint what he wanted and when he wanted. I could easily understand his frustration by comparing him to the accomplished classical musician who wants to be respected for his talents yet has to resort to writing elementary pop songs and jingles as a means of achieving any commercial success. But since I had never been one who saw myself becoming trapped in that structured nine to five approach of making a living, from what I could tell, Fred had it made in the shade. Despite these sentiments, I would later become that "nine to five guy", everything Erica's dad wasn't. (Actually eight to seven is more accurate.)

But at the time, being kids from rigid suburban homes, Julianne and I were captivated by Fred's out of the ordinary lifestyle. His very liberal thinking impressed me and I thought he was the coolest. The fact he wasn't opposed to Jule and I sleeping together, even though we weren't married, made him even cooler in my eyes. He had candles and incense burning throughout the house and I was sure he must have gotten high, only he wasn't quite liberated enough to smoke with his daughter and her friends. From the vast amount of books that filled the shelves and tabletops, I readily assumed Fred was a wealth of information. In the evenings we all sat around the table and listened to Fred voice his opinions about organized religion, life, death, and politics. He dabbled in astrology, astronomy; he read tea leaves, tarot cards, and palms. He even attempted to tell us about our past lives and predict our future. I never forgot when he told me that someday I was going to meet a short, stout man with a wide neck who was going to make me wealthy. In my life I'd come across a few people who fit that description and none of them had helped to increase my wealth by even a nickel. Either Fred was wrong or I just haven't met Mr. Midas yet. After spending some interesting evenings listening to Fred lecture very convincingly about everything from Adam to Zeus, I was able to walk away with my own beliefs unscathed. I had ideas of my own about religion and even though I wasn't really grounded in my own faith, at that point, I wasn't too willing to give it up or start experimenting. I was in the prime of my life, I was in love with a beautiful girl, we were both away from home and we were sleeping together in the same bed. Buddha, Jesus, Krishna, Allah, if it didn't have to do with rock and roll, sex or getting high, at that time in my life, I didn't care! The one thing Julianne and I did know was when we got married we were going to live in the country in a house just like Fred's. I'd have a career as a hit songwriter and she was going to tend to the garden. It sounded like a great idea at the time…still does.

Pat and Erica were the first of my friends to announce they were going to get married. We were all very excited for them, and also for ourselves, because we knew that soon we'd have friends with a place of their very own where we could hang out. Pat quit college and started working full time for his dad at the sausage store. They found themselves a nice apartment not far from where I was going to college, making it very convenient for me to drop in from time to time. Pat was a creative, energetic, hard working guy who had a pretty good idea of what he wanted in life. The wedding took place as scheduled, October 1972. I had the honor of being in the wedding party and everyone had a wonderful time.

Not long after the newlyweds settled into their new home, I would drop in on Erica now and then on my way from school. We had wonderful conversations that covered many topics, but all too often Pat's family, the business, and their strong-headed Italian traditions would be the focal point of our afternoon chats. I could tell she was uncomfortable with some of their cultural differences. Knowing Pat's family so well and after spending a few weekends with Fred, it became more and more apparent that Pat and Erica's worlds were incompatible. Sometimes when I looked into Erica's eyes, she would turn away because she must have felt I could read her thoughts. Five months after their wedding day, Pat called me to say he and Erica were getting separated.

During the short five months Pat and Erica were married, my friends and I shared quite a few good moments with them in their cozy second floor apartment. Just above the archway separating their kitchen from the dining room hung a decorative plaque that read "Eat, Drink, and be Merry." That was basically what we succeeded in doing. Erica prepared some excellent dinners, we drank what we thought was the finest wine, even though it was usually "Matteus" or Lancer's Rose, and we had lots of laughs, much of which were under the influence of one stimulant or another. The thing I couldn't quite grasp was that from the day Erica said, "I do," she knew that one day she'd be saying "I can't do this anymore." Pat had very strong family ties and for as long as he remained married to Erica, his family would have considered her an outsider. Deep down inside she knew from the start the marriage was doomed because Pat's parents never really gave her their blessing. How could they, she wasn't Italian! For five months she put on a good show. I think I may have been the only one who had a clue.

Pat didn't take the separation very well and because I loved the two of them, I became a middleman. First I would talk to Pat, and then I would talk to Erica, trying desperately to help them find some common ground or at least trying to get them to talk things over. Finally Erica wouldn't even take my phone calls anymore. It was over. Pat was emotionally shattered and before long his emotional state started to manifest itself physically. His body broke out in a rash and blisters appeared on his neck and face. Sometimes the blisters would ooze and I'd find myself giving Pat signals so he knew to take a tissue to his face. We were all really feeling bad for Pat, so for as long as he needed, we tried our best to always be around to help keep his troubled mind occupied.

Pasquale had always been one for looking ahead and not looking back. He didn't let unpleasant things linger, so it wasn't long after his separation that he forged ahead with filing for an annulment. According to the rules of Rome, if someone was married in the Catholic Church and then got divorced, in order to get married again in the Catholic Church, he or she was required to have the marriage "annulled." An annulment is the Catholic way of pretending the marriage never happened. If an annulment were not granted, in the eyes of the Church, they were still considered married. In other words, just like with any political system, it was all about knowing or buying the right people. It just so happened that I knew Father Roland Ghirlando. Rollie, as we affectionately called him, was a priest from our family's neighborhood parish. He took a liking to my folks and found his way into becoming a part of our family. He performed all of our religious functions such as weddings, baptisms, funerals, and exorcisms. He was often the guest of honor when attending our family parties, barbeques and occasional Sunday dinners. Rollie worked his way up the Catholic corporate ladder of success from a local parish priest to a judge on the Tribunal at the diocese headquarters in Brooklyn. Rollie was in the position to grant or deny annulments. Since we considered both Pat and Father "G" part of our extended family, Pat's annulment was a sure thing. Although Rollie probably could have just granted him the damn thing, he did have to go through all the legalities, which included collecting seven hundred dollars from Pat and having two witnesses write an extensive character report on both Pat and Erica. Julianne and I were elected. We painstakingly did what we had to do, even though it wasn't easy having to make judgments about two people we regarded as dear friends.

After carefully reviewing their case, the Holy Roman Catholic Empire granted Pat and Erica an annulment. Pat was free. Erica was free. The annulment was seven hundred smackers. I never saw or heard from Erica again and from time to time I think about her and wonder just what kind of hand life dealt her.

FOR BETTER OR WORSE...IS THAT A QUESTION?

In the early nineteen-seventies the wedding bug bit and one by one most of my friends decided to follow each other's footsteps and get hitched. It seemed as if every other week Julianne and I were attending a wedding either as a guest or as a member of a wedding party. Although Pat's was the first official "Bummer" wedding, his bachelor party was a result of inexperience, poor planning, and the involvement of his meddling mother and brother. Instead of the traditional topless bar, Pat found himself among all of his friends at a Hawaiian luau style smorgasbord at the Astoria Manor, a well-known catering establishment in Astoria, Queens. I wasn't quite sure of what we were thinking when we agreed to go along with this rather dull idea for a bachelor party, and for that matter, what Pat must have thought when he gazed around the room and didn't see anyone who even remotely looked like a topless dancer. It was truly bizarre to see all of us guys joining the crowd of hungry, middle-aged and senior citizen couples, who were filling their plates with roast pork, pineapple, sipping tropical drinks and listening to pre-recorded Don Ho music. All I can remember thinking, as I kept an eye on a motionless clock, was "When are they going to serve coffee so we can get the hell out of here?" All Pat must have been thinking was, "My friends are idiots! I packed condoms in my wallet for this?"

If the bachelor party was any indication of how the marriage would turn out, it's no wonder why Pat's marriage failed. When the Hawaiian festivities were finally winding down, someone suggested we all go into the city to a strip club. By this time it was too late because most of us spent whatever cash we had by chipping in on dinner and decorative cocktails. Live and learn, Aloha.

The next couple to walk down the aisle was Wesley and Toni-Ann. Wesley was truly a sight. His long bushy hair was an absolute nightmare for anyone who might have been sitting behind him in a movie theater or concert hall. Wesley is probably one of the nicest human beings on the planet but Pat's mom could never take a liking to him just because she couldn't get past the hair. He met Toni-Ann at the meat counter of the Big Apple Supermarket, the grocery store where they both worked. Toni was only fifteen years old at the time. Her long black hair was parted in the middle, outlined her cute baby face and fell just below her very full sized breasts. No way did any of us think she could only be fifteen. Wesley was eighteen and from the very first day he started dating Toni-Ann, we teased the life out of him by making accusations he was robbing the cradle. From the day they met, Wesley and Toni were literally inseparable and finally on the eleventh of November of nineteen hundred seventy-three they were married.

A few days before their wedding, we threw Wesley the customary bachelor party. This time, however, we planned it out a little better with intentions of having a lot more fun than we did at the previous disaster. Being we were all new to organizing a party of this nature, we were open to any suggestions. None of us had the slightest idea as to how and where one would go about hiring a stripper. I believe it was Toni-Ann herself who suggested a topless bar named "The Salem Inn" that was located on the north shore of Long Island in a small town called Port Washington. Her cousin lived in that town and according to the rumors that were going around, if you just so happened to be there on a good night, the strippers bared all and anything could happen. For all a bunch of inexperienced city boys knew, Port Washington could have been Montana, but who cared, we were going to see naked girls! We piled into our cars and with high hopes made our way out to Long Island for our first genuine bachelor party!

"I can't believe that shit comes out of that asshole!" I don't think I will ever forget those immortal words or the look on my friend Tom's face, as he bravely stood up with a beer in his hand and expressed such great admiration for the barmaid's bottom. The club's ceiling and walls were flat black with tacky neon "Budweiser" and "Miller" signs providing the only room light, except for the spotlight that lit the mirror-backed platform stage. The barmaids were very attractive and their outfits left very little for the imagination, which seduced newcomers like us into ordering a continuous flow of bottled beer. It's amazing how alcohol could alter a man's rationality so much so he could believe an almost naked barmaid is attracted to him and that the huge tips he tucks into her g-string has absolutely nothing to do with the attention he's getting from her!

I drank a ridiculous amount of beer that evening and in the hours that followed, paid the consequences dearly. The first stupid thing I did that resulted from all my drinking was to actually use the line "I'm a songwriter" on our barmaid, then tell her I was going to write a song about her and come back one night to play it for her. She told me she couldn't wait to hear it and of course I believed her. She was the same girl whose ass Tom was fascinated by, and the drunken asshole I was that night, had no doubt she was fascinated by me!

The second stupid thing to result after consuming even more beer, was my transformation into one very loud obnoxious philosopher who was trying desperately to rationalize how we could all be spending our time and our money gawking at "tits and ass" while our fellow Americans were dying over in Viet Nam! Standing on my seat and using a beer bottle as a prop to represent the planet, I pointed very dramatically to our approximate Long Island location. Then in a sweeping motion, my finger landed on another part of the bottle to where I thought Viet Nam should be. I must have really been messed up because my friends kept telling me to "Shut the fuck up" as they tried their best to hold me down in my seat and make me behave.

The evening's headliner was a tall thin brunette with firm large breasts who proudly took her place upon the stage wearing not much more than a top hat. She did a few memorable contortions; she gyrated, danced, bounced, wiggled, teased and then walked among her crowd of admirers as they filled her top hat with monetary tokens of their appreciation. The third stupid thing to result from my overindulgence of alcohol was when I stood up, reached out, grabbed the dancer's top hat and sent her hard-earned money scattering all over the place. I think she may have called me a "fuckin' asshole" and I never figured out why the bouncers didn't beat the living crap out of me and throw me out the door. My friends decided, while I was still alive, it was time to leave, so we bid our waitress farewell, stumbled past the bouncers and exited the smoky club. The fresh cool night air hit me like a ton of bricks. I took a few deep breaths but knew I was going to be very sick. They threw me in the rear seat of Joe's Lemans, made me hang my head out the window, and witnessed as I left a twenty-mile trail of vomit all the way from Port Washington to Queens. I didn't recall ever feeling so sick in my entire life. After my friends got me safely home, I spent most of the wee hours of the morning staring into the bottom of the toilet, heaving the last drops of anything that dared to remain in my spasmodic guts. My parents insisted on taking me to the emergency room but I didn't have the strength to even crawl. I swore to God I would never drink again. Oh how we lie in times of trouble! The entire next day was a total wash out. I didn't wander too far from my bed as I tried desperately to recuperate. Miraculously, I joined the living later that evening and made it on time to the rehearsal dinner. Wesley and Toni got married as planned and in June of the following year Julianne and I would do the same.

I never formerly proposed to Jule. I think we just had a mutual understanding that one day we were going to get married. All the same, I decided I should make it official, so I went diamond shopping. My Aunt Jean introduced me to Henry, a friend of hers who was a jeweler in Manhattan's diamond district (thank God for connections). Using a little bit of craftiness, I managed to finagle a way of getting Julianne's ring size. One day, unbeknownst to what my intentions were, I tried on all of her rings, making a mental note that my pinky was the same size as her ring finger. With whatever money I had stashed away in my very modest savings account, and with Henry's assistance and generosity, I bought Julianne an engagement ring, a big move for someone who's never been too fond of jewelry.

One evening while we were parked at our favorite little make-out hideaway, I reached for her hand. She put her hand in mine and as I held it, began to remove her everyday ring from her finger. She was probably wondering what the heck I was up to but her inquisitiveness turned to astonishment when she noticed I had made a switch, replacing her ring with the diamond ring. Not expecting I would be the type to ever pull off something like that, Julianne was extremely excited and pleasantly surprised. She couldn't wait to get home to tell her mother the good news and show her the sparkling addition to her finger.

Her mom reacted quite uniquely. As she let out with a high-pitched nervous giggle of disbelief, she uttered the words, "Oh come on, it's fake, isn't it?" I'd been known to be a practical joker now and then but at this time it was certainly a blow to my self-esteem not to be taken seriously! After a closer inspection of the shiny stone, Marie conceded it was indeed a diamond and we were officially congratulated. The news was spread throughout the land, Julianne and John were engaged.

Being engaged never gave me the feeling I was trapped. Life went on as usual and I wasn't having any second thoughts, until one afternoon while walking along the college campus minding my own business, I heard my name being called. I stopped in my tracks, turned around, only to come face to face with my old girlfriend Regina. She greeted me with the most flirtatious smile and looked absolutely stunning. She was wearing a faded unbuttoned denim shirt that was tied just above the waist, revealing more of her than I'd ever seen, and tight low-cut, faded jeans she was just born to be in. Having not seen her in a couple of years, we talked for a while and tried to catch up on each other's lives. After a lot of chitchat about our old schoolmates and whom we have or haven't heard from, she hit me with the question that planted my feet firmly back on the ground.

"What's new with you?" she inquired.

I replied stuttering, "Oh yeah, I uh, I uh just got uh engaged."

"That's great," she responded, and as the conversation suddenly became strained, she left me with, "Well it's been really good seeing you!"

As she walked off into the distance and disappeared into the crowd of students rushing to and from class, I stood there for a few seconds with my eyes fixated on her sway and the way her washed-out Levi's fit her so well. It was at that very moment I realized I was definitely spoken for.

Planning our wedding was a sure fire way of finding out just how many people we knew and how many people we wished we didn't know. Traditionally, the parents of the bride provide the payment for these extravagant overpriced affairs, but Julianne and I knew there was no way her folks were going to shell out one nickel for our wedding. Julianne graduated college before I did and immediately got a full time job with a bank in Manhattan. She'd always been a hard worker and a diligent student and truly desired to attend graduate school to pursue a career in speech pathology. Graduate school, however, was expensive, so she chose to put those plans of continuing her education on hold, and saved her hard earned money to basically pay for our wedding. Way back in those good old days, a young couple just starting out such as we were, could essentially exist on a minimal amount of money and some big dreams. I was still attending college and was only working part-time at Marty and Morty's hardware store. Julianne earned a very modest salary, so how we ever planned to pay for a wedding with over two hundred guests, was a mystery to everyone.

My parents thought they were helping us out by offering their home to host an open house affair with tents, band, caterers and no restrictions on who and not who to invite. Having that non-conformist mindset, this seemed like a great idea to me. Nobody's feelings would be hurt and both sides could invite whoever they thought should be there. Even my future bride thought this might be the way to go. My future mother-in-law, on the other hand, frowned at the very thought of not having her daughter's wedding at one of the many wedding factories in one of the neighboring towns. One had to keep face. Just because cousin Ro, cousin Charlie, cousin Loretta, and cousin this one and cousin that one were all having their affairs at overpriced chandelier and mirror-studded banquet halls, such as the elegant "Crystal Brook Manor," or the breathtaking "Victorian House," or "Savini's on the Bay," she was unwavering in her opinion we should do the same. In fact, she threatened not to attend if we went through with my parents' open house idea. This was nerve from someone who wasn't planning on laying out even a dime to help us pay for it. For my money I would have said, "Fuck you, don't come," but in order to keep the peace, we followed the path every other engaged suburban couple takes: the catering hall, the limited guest lists, the limos, the tuxedos, the bridal party, the rehearsal dinner, the favors, the wedding band, the invitations, the photographers, the stamps, "the bride cuts the cake," and all the other trappings of the biggest money-making racket in the country.

At this time in our lives we still had some ties to the Catholic Church. I wasn't a practicing Catholic, didn't go to church except on Christmas and Easter, and since we never even considered ourselves to be anything else but Catholic, we got married in the church. One of the requirements of receiving the "sacrament of marriage" was a mandatory "pre-Cana conference." This pre-nuptial program was exactly what it sounded like; a session between the future newlyweds and a priest to discuss the "do's and don'ts" of marriage and the couple's obligations to each other and to the church. They tried to stress the point that sex was designed by God for the sole purpose of pro-creation and that the baby human beings brought into this world were to be raised up in the Catholic faith. This in itself was quite a joke because it was usually inexperienced priests who administered this instruction to hot in the pants young couples, such as Jule and I, who would just agree to anything and say, "Where do I sign?"

In many of life's situations, it's always most helpful to know someone or know somebody who knows someone. To avoid waiting in line, to get out of a tight spot, to evade paying retail or to even wiggle out of attending pre-Cana, it's imperative to know somebody. Once again it paid to have a priest as a family friend. My folks invited Rollie over for dinner one evening and he brought along with him all the necessary paperwork. Julianne and I just signed on the dotted lines and our pre-Cana conference requirement was deemed a done deal by "The Holy Mother Church." Father G not only spared us the pain and inconvenience of having to sit through hours of pre-Cana torture, he also agreed to perform the wedding ceremony for us.

It was on the second of June, 1974 when I left mom and dad, took Julianne for my wife and began a new life of our own. On that Sunday morning I woke up and rolled out of my twin bed for the very last time. I looked around my room not believing for a second the moment had actually arrived. Experiencing a few last minute jitters, thoughts like, "What the fuck am I doing?" flashed through my mind. I took a deep breath, marched myself into the shower and prepared myself for the big day!

I gave my folks a hug and a kiss, and then with a few of my bridal party buddies, headed out on the forty-minute drive to the church. Just before the ceremony was about to begin, Father G stood in the back of the church vestibule with the members of the wedding party and me, and asked how many of us were going to receive Holy Communion. None of us had stepped foot inside a church in quite some time so we weren't so sure if we were prepared to take part. It was at that very moment when Rollie, our earthly connection to Our Maker in the Heavens, gave the entire wedding party an express group confession.

"Is everybody sorry for his or her sins?" he asked.

"Certainly!" we replied.

"Your sins are forgiven, go in peace and let's party!"

Rollie made quite an impression on my friends with his radical penance made easy. After a few magic words a big sign of the cross we were all good to go. Amen.

I will admit that in spite of everything, including having to borrow three thousand dollars from our friend Pat to pay for the five-hour party, everybody had a pretty good time. We figured with the money we made in wedding gifts we'd be able to pay back Pat and have a little something left over to start our new life together. They say, "Never count your chickens before they hatch!" As a group of close friends and relatives gathered together at the in-law's house after the affair (Ray and Marie were now officially my in-laws), my dad asked if we wanted him to place our booty in a safety deposit box while we were away on our honeymoon. This sounded like a most rational idea to me. My new mother-in-law, however, was highly insulted by the suggestion, questioning our trust in her to safeguard our money. Once again, in the name of peace, I reneged on my father's sensible offer. Jule and I were very exhausted from all the day's hoopla. As we sat on her parent's bed, we quickly tore open a few envelopes, scouring for some cash to take with us to Bermuda. After deciding we had a sufficient amount of money, we shoved all the cards and remaining envelopes back into the white goody bag, and along with Jo's mom, placed it up and away into the safety of her parent's bedroom closet...or so we thought!

The long day was finally over. Everyone returned to their homes with their favors and hopefully some memories of a good time. The next morning Julianne and I were on a jet plane bound for Bermuda. Although I couldn't say for sure what was going through her mind, I knew exactly what was going through mine. Suddenly the reality of being a married man hit me right between the eyes. At the tender young age of twenty-one, I made the decision to move out from my castle of comfort on Easy Street. Away from the safety and shelter of the house I grew up in, where I had practically no cares and no worries, where mom cooked my meals, made my bed, paid my bills, and even woke me up in the mornings, I was about to enter a new world. In this new unexplored world of compromise,

I was eventually going to have to stare responsibility right in its ugly face. I was no longer responsible for taking care of just myself now that Julianne was permanently in the picture. Along with the tremendous joy of living together as husband and wife came the tremendous pressure of having to make money to pay the bills. There was going to be rent and phone bills and car insurance and food and gas and electric and Christmas presents for her family and my family. How were we ever going to swing it and still afford any kind of social life or vacation? I hadn't even considered the possibility of us having children! I'd always been opposed to the idea of having to waste my life away working for a living and deep down inside I knew being married wasn't going to change that. Unless I became a rock star soon, Julianne was in big trouble!

We had an excellent time for most of our honeymoon. We stayed at a beautiful hotel where our room was situated right on the pink sand of Elbow Beach and where breakfast was served on our balcony every morning. The weather was perfect, the gourmet food was superb and I even managed to sneak in the opportunity to write a song. But a honeymoon just wouldn't be a honeymoon without the bride getting her period smack dab in the middle of the week. Julianne didn't disappoint me. She was right on schedule, precisely in the middle of the week. Way back then in the good old days, they didn't have all the wonderful drugs that helped ease the pain and discomfort of menstrual cramps, so we both had no choice but to suffer through it. The funny thing was because we were so aware of how incapacitated Julianne gets each month from the severity of her menstrual cramps, we checked the calendar just to make sure that during the week we were on our honeymoon, Martha (the pet name she gave her period) would be nowhere in sight…So much for planning ahead!

Our first week of being together as husband and wife flew by and before we knew it we were back at JFK airport where my good old reliable dad was there to greet us. After having a nice dinner at my folk's house, my father announced that he'd like to speak with us privately. We followed him from the kitchen to the living room and I thought to myself, "Oh no! Not another birds and bees talk!"

"Kids," he said like some wise old philosopher, "remember the most important thing the both of you have to realize is that you love each other and nothing should ever come in between the two of you."

I was thinking to myself, "Okay dad, where are you going with this? Does he think Julianne's pregnant or something? Get to the point already!"

"While you guys were in Bermuda," he softly spoke, and at this precise moment for some reason Julianne thought he was going to tell us that her father died. She held onto my hand and squeezed tightly as my dad continued, "Someone broke into your in-law's house and stole all your wedding envelopes!" Julianne was so relieved her father was all right, the thought of being robbed didn't even register. I was feeling confused, betrayed, angry and violated. Our life together was off to a rocking start.

Before we knew it the police were involved and a full-blown investigation was underway with some of my new brothers-in-law as suspects. We still owed Pat three grand and were now without a way to pay him back. Julianne and I argued daily. We were newlyweds and went to bed each night lying at opposite sides of the mattress. Tensions mounted between our families, everything seemed to be turned upside down, and our lives had become one big mess all over money. I was young, immature and unforgiving and I wanted answers. The problem was I didn't get any until many years later when the guilty party came clean. If only we had listened to my dad, the voice of reason!

The thief was a friend of Julianne's brothers, a neighborhood guy named Kenny, who always struck me as the "Eddie Haskell" type. In other words, what you see is not what you get. My in-laws had never been the best judges of character and the fact they took a liking to Kenny proved it. He knew all the right moves and all the right words to finagle his way into their hearts and household. Kenny would always show up with the right gadget to help Jule's dad tackle some of the landscaping work. Occasionally, he would give Jule's mom an expensive present, usually something that fell off the back of a truck. Unless Kenny was seriously lacking a relationship with his own parents, the one he had with my in-laws was indeed a mystery. Whatever the case, he was in!

It turned out that Kenny was up to his neck in financial trouble with some local mobsters. Out of sheer desperation, he lifted our wedding loot hoping to find a few thousand dollars to lighten his debt and ultimately save his ass. The day I finally learned that Kenny was the culprit, it all became clear. It's funny, but in my mind I suddenly remembered seeing him pacing back and forth past my in-law's bedroom door, smiling at Julianne and me as we sifted through envelopes on the day of our wedding. He was undoubtedly sizing up the job that lay ahead. I never even took into account that it might have been him, but wasn't the least bit surprised when I found out ten years later.

The story goes that he wound up in prison for some other crime he had committed and it was during his jail term he did some soul searching and became, what else, but a Born Again Christian. It appears jail time does that to people; "Son of Sam" too became "Born Again." One day, from out of the blue, something possessed him to call one of my sisters-in-law from prison. He confessed to the crime and asked her to please apologize to us for him. Why he never called us himself, I don't know, and even though we never got all the money back, I'd since learned to forgive him. The last I heard, Kenny had passed away.

It was funny how his confession came about at a time when Julianne and I were being lured into the Born Again movement, a period of my life I can only later explain as temporary insanity.

Life eventually returned to being semi-normal (nothing's ever really normal). Time passed, wounds healed, we paid Pat whatever money we owed him, and after getting over our first major setback, we were finally back on our way down the road to wedded bliss, whatever that meant!

Aside from the typical arguments about where we were going to spend Christmas, Easter, or Sunday dinner, Julianne and I were getting along just fine. Every now and then we would explode over something stupid, but I think it's been said an occasional good fight is healthy for a relationship. One afternoon Jule got mad at me over something I did, didn't do, said, or didn't say, and she picked up one of my guitars and threatened to smash it. In retaliation, I quickly reached for one of Julianne's favorite houseplants and told her if she didn't gently put down my guitar I would tear it apart leaf by leaf. Both the plant and the guitar were unharmed. On yet another joyous occasion, for yet another stupid reason, she locked me out of our apartment, and just in case I may have had my keys on me (which I did), she made sure to slide the security chain in place. I rammed our apartment door like an angry bull and busted the chain lock right off the wall. We never laid hands on each other, just broke or threatened to break the stuff around us.

It felt as though every time we turned around I was renting a tuxedo and Julianne was being fitted for a gown to be in yet another wedding party. Within a year or two practically all of our close friends were married. Those first few years were full of fun times and great memories. We all spent many hours together hanging out at each other's apartments, going to concerts, taking little fun excursions and basically carrying on in the same manner we did before we were all tied down. I was always in some kind of rock and roll band, and whenever we had a local gig, my friends were usually there to support my obsession. As far as I was concerned, life was good. I was still working on my B.A. at Queens College and still employed part time at the lumber store. I didn't have any intentions of ever landing a real full time job because, come hell or high water, I was going to be a super rich rock and roll star. The future was ours and for a while Julianne believed it too. Little by little, however, I was sure she began losing faith.

Jack and Gina were high school sweethearts and they became Mr. And Mrs. Jack Kelly the week after we returned from our honeymoon. Unlike me, Jack actually sought a job but had no immediate luck in finding one. Our absence from the real working world allowed us to spend lots of time together while our wives made their way each day to and from the crowded streets of Manhattan trying to support the likes of us. Sometimes Jack would accompany on the few afternoons I worked. I picked him up at his apartment with the lumber store's panel truck and he would ride with me while I made deliveries to some of the worst neighborhoods of the city. One memorable afternoon, while I was making a pick-up at a Brooklyn lumberyard, Jack stood by minding his own business while I signed some paperwork. Suddenly from out of nowhere, a stack of lumber came tumbling down from a forklift and crashed to the ground all around him. It was an absolute miracle Jack wasn't impaled by a two by four.

On other days we would take walks in the park and try to come up with get rich quick schemes, which sorry to say, we never did. But without fail, each and every weekday afternoon at four o'clock, we made sure we were at either his place or mine, sitting in front of a television to watch the educational program "Mr. Rogers." For some reason we found the seriousness of the show very hilarious and entertaining. By the time Fred Rogers took off his sneakers to put his dress shoes back on, it was time for Jack and me to make our way to the bus stop to greet our hard working wives as they returned from their day at the office.

NERVE GAS

For as long as I can remember, my father used to say I would never die from an ulcer. Nothing fazed me and rarely did I allow anything to worry me. I was always easygoing and had a fun loving disposition. It's been said that opposites attract. I had always been a dreamer, Julianne had always been a realist, and somehow we came together. If she had been more like me, the probability was good we may have starved to death. Julianne had sense enough to work a full time job while I had big dreams. I never realized it, but psychologically, not being the breadwinner had started to disturb me. I must have been having atypical guilt feelings about Julianne bringing home the bulk of the bacon and it began taking its toll on my physical and mental well being. Suddenly one day, completely out of the blue, I developed an annoying nervous stomach. It was as if I was stricken with an uncontrollable condition where my mind was affecting my body. I was caught in this vicious cycle where my nerves gave me such awful stomach cramps I was living in bathrooms and public restrooms. Whenever I ventured out of my home, I would begin to worry that I would ultimately need to find a restroom. That very uncomforting thought alone would trigger my nerves, which in turn would trigger my colon. It was hell. I dreaded going anywhere but I pushed myself, trying as best as I could not to let on to anyone what was wrong with me. Shopping malls, supermarkets, Disney World, road trips, the clubs where my band played; I got to know where all the men's rooms were. This chronic and most embarrassing condition wasn't only taking its toll on me; it was getting to Julianne as well.

Wherever we went I was excusing myself and running for dear life to find a toilet. Early one morning I was driving Julianne to her place of work in the city. While I was in bumper-to-bumper traffic on the expressway, this catch-22 affliction kicked in and I got the worst stomach cramps anyone could ever imagine. Out of desperation I begged Julianne to empty her pocketbook so I could have a place in which to relieve myself. She looked at me in disbelief and cried out, "Are you nuts?? Get a hold of yourself, relax!"

Sweat was oozing from my brow. I squeezed my butt cheeks together as tightly as I could and just as we approached the tolls for the Mid-town Tunnel, I ignored the policeman's signals to keep moving forward and cut clear across the lanes of on-coming traffic, blasting my horn and speeding right into a grimy Gulf gas station where I made a mad dash for the dirty, dingy, disease-infested restroom. I couldn't let this go on much longer. I knew I had to see a doctor.

I never minded seeing a doctor because of ailments such as chest colds, fever, rashes and the like, but as soon as he stretched the rubber glove onto his hand and his middle finger found its way up my "orifice" to probe for the clues needed to diagnose my malady, that's when my dignity put its tail between its legs and ran off. The doctor's examination resulted with a diagnosis of a spastic colon due to nerves. Maybe it was my lack of success in the music business that was getting to me. I wasn't making any money, and the thought of working nine to five did not bode well with me. The doctor gave me some pills that were supposed to relax my quivering innards and he told me that the best medicine would be for me to get a full time job. He advised me to face up to my responsibilities, stop living in fantasyland and join the rest of the world. He didn't have the best bedside manner but I had a suspicion that he was probably right. After returning home from the doctor's office, I held the bottle of pills in my hand and asked myself, "Take a pill? Or get a job? Take a pill? Or get a job?" I took a long hard look at myself in the bathroom mirror and popped a pill. A short while after ingesting the little yellow pill I began to feel extremely weird. My heart started beating so hard and fast I thought it was going to come busting through my rib cage. On top of that I got the worst case of cottonmouth. My tongue felt as if it were just dragged through a sandbox and when I got the urge to urinate, panic set in as nothing would come out.

Julianne was at work while I was home alone freaking out. I called the doctor and he ordered me to get back to his office immediately. He took me right in, checked me over and saw I was a complete mess. It turned out I had an allergic reaction to the medication and had almost every side effect possible. He handed me a different type of pill and suggested I try them instead. Safely back in my apartment, I sat at the foot of my bed. Once again, I held the jar of pills in my hand and was very apprehensive about taking another, fearful it would result in the same ill effects. I was suddenly overcome by a sense of frustration and helplessness. I didn't want to become dependent on pills yet I couldn't go on with this dysfunction. In the quiet of my room I got down on my knees and did something I hadn't done in a long time, began to seek divine help. My heart cried out to God, wherever He was, and to my surprise a peaceful feeling came over me with the assurance I was going to be all right. I walked over to the bathroom and in what I felt was an act of faith, flushed the pills down the toilet and believed from that very moment, my problem was well on its way to being over. Miraculously it was. Was it mind over matter, or an answer to a prayer? Could it be the two are one and the same?

ROCK'S IN MY HEAD

Julianne and I were married for seven years before we decided to start having children. Those seven years took us on quite a roller coaster ride. I continued to chase after fame and fortune, and due to my burning desire to write, became somewhat of a prolific songwriter. Writing was my outlet, my release. It became as important to me as eating or breathing. Whatever was going on in my life, I had the ability to turn it into a song. The band I had started with my college writing partner, Richie, was playing around and gaining local popularity. One weekend while we were playing a gig at a Long Island bar, Eppy, a well-known short fat balding Jewish hippy turned entrepreneur, made his way in. Eppy owned a club called "My Father's Place" where every folk singer and garage band hoped to someday play. Springsteen, The Police, Talking Heads, The Ramones, Blondie, Lou Reed and an endless parade of major stars passed through the small village of Roslyn and performed on the stage of "My Father's Place."

Eppy approached me that evening and assuming I knew who he was, popped the question, "Hey Johnny," he asked, already knowing what my answer was going to be, "How would you like to play at my club?" I didn't want to appear anxious so I played it cool, even though on the inside I was bursting with excitement. Eppy said he saw talent and star quality in me. He gave me his phone number and suggested I call him as soon as possible. Erica's father, Fred, immediately came to mind when he predicted a short fat man with a wide neck would be instrumental in making me rich. I wondered if Eppy was going to be my pot of gold.

Within a few days I placed the call and two weeks later my group was appearing at "MFP" as an opening act for some of our favorite bands. Before long I was roped into signing a management contract with Eppy. He persuaded me to stick with him and it would only be a matter of time before I would be living in a big house on Long Island's prestigious north shore, selling records and touring the world. I saw fame and fortune in the not too distant future. Julianne didn't trust him as far as she could throw him.

Eppy made it clear; I was the artist who he signed, not the band. He kept feeding my ego by reinforcing the idea that I was the star and the other guys in the band just didn't cut it. I knew I was a good songwriter, but as a musician, I was well aware of my limitations. Eppy, slowly but surely, gave me no alternative but to fire my friends from the group. I was blinded by the thought of success and didn't even see how I was being compromised and manipulated. He and all the crew at "MFP" were treating me as if I were already a celebrity. Eppy knew of all the right buttons to push to create a buzz about me. He had connections with the local radio stations, the music press, and the other area club owners. It wasn't long before I recruited a completely new band of all accomplished players. He put us in the recording studio where we recorded our first single. He created his very own record label, on which we were the premier act, and hired a promo man to distribute the forty-five to record stores and radio stations. I was well on my way to national rock stardom, or at least somewhere in the vicinity.

Being a local pop star was a lot of fun and great for my ego but there wasn't much money in it. Whenever we had a paying gig I gave the cash to the guys in the band taking nothing for myself. We developed a following and I began to notice some familiar faces showing up gig after gig. Having fans was great, but the business itself seemed to attract a certain caliber of folks I didn't feel a strong connection to. Excess, greed and lack of humility were prevalent. At times I couldn't even relate to the musicians in my own band. It seemed like everyone had their hand out. Julianne and my friends were one part of my life, the band was another, and there was no common thread between them. One didn't foster the other, and this inconsistency led to the disturbing thought that maybe I wasn't cut out for the music business. To make matters worse, Richie had moved out to California and while he was there he heard my band's forty-five played on a west coast radio station. The song happened to be one I co-wrote with him and although I did give him credit on the record, he wasn't aware of it. Just because the record was getting airplay he was under the impression I was making tons of money. The next thing I knew, I was receiving threatening letters, phone calls and knocks on my door in the wee hours of the morning by some of Richie's close friends who he had commissioned to "kick the living shit out of me!" I was able to convince them I hadn't made a dime on the record and they backed off. Some time afterwards, I managed to track down Rich to a small town in Colorado. I contacted him by phone, apologized for my disloyalty to him and reassured him I was still very, very broke.

Most of the gigs our band played were one-nighters and local enough so we could all go home after the show. On this one summer weekend, however, we were booked to open up for "Southside Johnny and the Asbury Jukes" at a large club out in the Hamptons for two nights. It was too great a distance to be traveling back and forth, so we checked into a cheap hotel. Another reason we had decided to hang in the Hamptons overnight and not risk driving home was because of the van we owned. When we bought it, we failed to give it a thorough test drive and realized, after it was too late, we were unable to make left-hand turns. The guy who sold it to us left town hours after we handed him the cash! It was a miracle that we were able to travel such a long distance and arrive safely at our destination in our "right turns only" suicide trap. My good friend and ex-bass player, Tall Mike, was gracious enough to hang on with the band as road manager. This simply meant he got to help us carry our equipment and drive the dangerous vehicle. It was the first time since we'd been married that Julianne and I were apart.

After checking out of our rooms on Saturday morning, all the guys went their own way except for Samba and I. Samba was the endearing name we gave to our bass player John. John was a remarkable bassist, who in his wire rimmed glasses, held a striking resemblance to John Lennon. John gave a tremendous amount of thought to every note he played as he was always striving for perfection. His pensive personality and his desire to play flawlessly were correlated to a manic depression that almost cost him his life.

Since most of our equipment was in the van, and because it was terribly unsafe to be driving it around the town's small streets, Samba and I smoked a joint and hung out in the parking lot of the club where we were playing. I was slouched down behind the driver's seat while John was lying among the guitars in the back of the van. It was an absolutely beautiful afternoon. The sky was clear and the hot sun was beating down on me and within minutes I drifted off to sleep.

The next thing I knew, the startling sound of a blaring car horn wrenched me right out of my peaceful slumber. Rubbing my eyes I glanced over to my left only to see two stunning women sitting in a Mercedes convertible with the top down. "John, John!" I called out to my napping bass player, "You've got to check this out!" Samba resurrected from his state of semi-consciousness, climbed out from the rear of the van and greeted our visitors with a great big smile.

"Do you guys know if there are any happy hours going on around here?" the girl behind the wheel asked.

John and I were standing alongside the luxurious sports car and trying our best to impress the girls, we told them we were in the band on the bill with Southside Johnny that evening. I don't think they were very interested in the fact we were musicians as they asked again if we cared to join them in their search for a happy hour. When we tried to explain to these two extremely hot young ladies that we couldn't leave our equipment unguarded, the one in the passenger seat slowly and seductively slipped up her skirt revealing most of her inner thigh. There I was miles from home in a situation that could have easily become a future story in Penthouse Forum.

"Are you guys going to come drinking with us or not?" the sultry temptress pouted.

Samba chimed right in, "Listen!" he said, "we can't leave this equipment but I've got some really good weed. I could roll you a joint if you want!"

The girls jumped at John's offer. Without a solitary soul around for as far as the eye could see, there we were; John, two gorgeous girls who were anxious to party, and me. As we passed around the joint, one of the girls made it plain to see what was on her mind. Slouched down in the driver's seat with her legs spread just enough to tantalize, she slid her hand under her skirt and brushed it along her perfect thighs. The girls were getting rather impatient with our dawdling and made it perfectly clear if we didn't slide ourselves into the backseat of their car immediately, they were going to take off without us. I told John he was certainly free to go and I would stay behind with the van. John turned down my proposal. Feeling as if they wasted enough time, they thanked us for the smoke then quickly peeled out of the parking lot leaving the two of us standing in a cloud of dust.

I was happily married with no intentions of ever being unfaithful, so I had my reasons as to why I was not going to drive off with the party girls. If I was unattached at the time I would have said, "Fuck the guitars! Let's go find a happy hour!" Knowing John the way I did, I couldn't understand why he would balk at what appeared like a very good shot at getting laid.

I looked at him and said, "Opportunities like that don't come along every day, man! Why the hell didn't you go with them?"

He looked back at me and with a sick grin on his face, matter-of-factly answered my question, "If I hadn't just jerked off in the back of the van I probably would have went with them!"

"Oh you've got to fucking be kidding me!" I thought to myself, "While I'm sleeping soundly, this nut job's whacking off behind me! Thank God I didn't wake up to witness that!"

The band was picking up some momentum. I was writing a load of new songs, some of them based on slightly exaggerated accounts of the ups and downs of my relationship with Julianne. We were getting interest from some major record labels and Eppy struck a deal with CBS to get us in the studio to record a demo of some of my new tunes. One morning while waiting for Samba to show up for rehearsal, we got the feeling something might be wrong when he was almost two hours late. We placed a couple of calls trying to locate his whereabouts and one of them resulted in us receiving the most upsetting news. We learned that after an unsuccessful attempt at committing suicide the night before, John had been hospitalized. Although John suffered from a bi-polar disorder, it really seemed the band was a place where he was directing his energies, finding both purpose and enjoyment. In a million years I never would have expected this. Everything was put on hold until we were informed that Samba was going to be put away for a long while. After John's sad episode, the band went through a series of personnel changes until I reached a point where I could no longer deal with all the personalities and temperaments. I wasn't happy, I wasn't having any fun, we sounded like shit, and so I put the band to rest.

I didn't know for sure whether Eppy just liked me for the good natured sap I was or if he still saw me as a marketable product capable of making him some money. Still legally my manager, he had an acquaintance who was a prominent name in the music publishing business, whom I will refer to as Mr. K. Mr. K's company handled many easy-listening artists such as Barbra Streisand, Dolly Parton and Cher. I assumed he must have owed Eppy a huge favor when he agreed to meet with me in his Manhattan office for a one on one audition. Gold records displayed proudly on the walls, the city skyline in the background through the huge window behind him, Mr. K leaned back in his oversized desk chair and politely said, "So let me hear what you've got." I was nervous and intimidated, never even getting as far as the chorus of the first song, when he interrupted me and said, "Okay, let's hear another!"

After an abrupt and unsuccessful attempt at tuning my guitar, I clumsily strummed my way through the first verses of three more songs and got the discouraging feeling he wasn't paying too close attention. He leaned forward, tapped his hands upon his desk, told me he'd heard enough and asked me to take a seat outside his office. I slumped down into a chair directly across from an empathizing receptionist and was convinced I just blew it. Within minutes, however, he summoned me back inside and surprisingly I was offered a songwriting contract. I was given an advance that was paid out in weekly installments and they showed up religiously in my mailbox for the next year. All I had to do was keep my side of the bargain by presenting Mr. K with ten songs. In my heart I knew my little streak of good fortune was payback and had nothing to do with my painfully pathetic performance. My hopes of penning a hit record were still alive.

While I was keeping myself busy trying to get a songwriting career off the ground, Julianne was experiencing unpleasant little bouts with anxiety. Returning from work one evening and after nearly passing out on a crowded bus, she felt it was extremely necessary for her well being to quit her job in the city. We went through a very rough period living on unemployment checks and low paying, dead end temporary part-time jobs. There were days we rolled coins as to gather up enough money to buy food for that evening's dinner. Getting by was quite a challenge and a struggle, but since we were young and childless, somehow we managed to pay our bills and just barely survive. We seldom had any extra cash on hand so we didn't do much more than hang out at home and entertain our friends. Julianne had made some new friends at a part-time job she found through a temp agency. More often than not she was partying with her new work companions and coming home stoned. We never had the funds in our overstretched budget to include the purchase of pot, but Julianne always seemed to have a joint in her possession and temptress she was, managed to entice me into getting high with her. It's not that smoking pot was anything new to either one of us, because through the years most of our friends were all smoking socially, but now it was getting to the point where my wife enjoyed being stoned all the time. I always believed there was a time and a place for everything, and even though I wasn't all too comfortable with Julianne's reckless behavior, there was no better time and place for getting stoned than when we were in bed together. Sex and pot were a wonderful combination!

One Sunday her new work buddies planned a trip to ride the rapids at the Delaware Water Gap. In those days Julianne was very daring and would try almost anything at least twice. Tall Mike and Hannah also joined us on this adventure. Having no experience whatsoever in this potentially dangerous outdoors activity, Julianne and I figured it made perfect sense for us to navigate our very own canoe. For amateurs we did an excellent job for most of the journey. Suddenly, however, the current became stronger and it sent our tiny boat racing along the choppy waters. Our peaceful cruise was turning treacherous. We bounced off the rocks and lost complete control as the angry river flipped over our canoe and left us stranded in its forceful flow struggling to stay afloat. The water was over our heads but I managed to grab onto a large boulder that luckily was in my reach. As Julianne was about to drift by, I yelled for her to grab hold of me, which she did, but her weight pushed me under. Every time I managed to get my head above water, I screamed for Mike and Hannah who were fast approaching, to pull Julianne off of me and into their boat. Julianne was rescued and moments later, so was I. When we were safely back on dry land, thankful we had escaped death, an upsetting look came upon Julianne's face. As she reached into the pockets of her totally soaking wet jeans, she realized that the joints she had rolled earlier were completely useless. Talk about priorities! I think she was more upset about the wasted weed than the actuality we could have drowned! Live and learn. When planning to ride the rapids, always be sure to safely place the stash in a plastic bag.

WORKING IT OUT

The fact we were two college graduates who hadn't pursued careers was extremely frustrating to our parents. Jule's parents weren't too comfortable knowing I wasn't supporting their daughter, and my parents weren't too happy knowing Julianne wasn't working to support me while I followed my dream. Sometimes, out of desperation, we would read the want ads in the local papers hoping to find easy ways to make some fast cash. One afternoon Julianne came across an ad placed by a schoolteacher living in our neighborhood who needed a full time babysitter. Her name was Myra and she was in dire need of someone reliable to watch her little boy while she worked. Myra interviewed Julianne and quite understandably fell in love with her. Julianne took the job that not only brought some money into our household, but it also opened up a door for me. Myra got me an interview for an assistant teaching position in the English department at the high school she taught at. Not only did my charming personality (along with the fact that I was a friend of Myra's) land me the job complete with medical benefits, but I was also informed if I went back to college for a few more credits, I could actually become a teacher and make teacher's salary. This could have well been our ticket out of poverty except for one very minor detail; I hated the job!

I had to work side by side with this stuffy old woman named Pearl. Pearl drove me crazy with her meticulous methods, her rules and her regulations. It was her way or no way. The school wasn't in the greatest of neighborhoods and my assignment was to assist Pearl in remedial reading classes. Most of our students were tough below average street kids and gang members who had no problem in wanting to give me a hard time. My dilemma was I related more to the kids than I did to the old bat I was assisting. As the little terrors sat behind their desks struggling over their worksheets, it was my thankless task to walk around the room and answer their simple questions. I found myself hovering over the desks of a couple of female students a little more than I should have. Minimally, every other minute, one of them had her hand up trying to get my attention and both of them dressed inappropriately to say the least. "Mr. Domenico," Sally Jackson sweetly sighed, "Could you please help me with this, I don't understand?"

I leaned over Sally's desk and somehow my eyes meandered into her open blouse before re-focusing onto her schoolwork. She was well aware of what she was doing and for me it just wasn't a healthy or comfortable situation. During my breaks, if I wasn't correcting test papers or homework, I sat in the teachers' lounge and attempted to use the time to write song lyrics. Sometimes Pearl would intrude on my alone time and try to discuss some of her lame ideas with me. She knew I played guitar and thought it would be so innovative if I could incorporate a little live music into the lessons by bringing my instrument to class. "That's a great idea, Pearl!" I would say to her, having absolutely no intention of ever following through. I figured it was easier to patronize her rather than try to make her understand that black and Spanish street kids were not going to relate to my style of white folk rock.

One afternoon, Carol, another English teacher, politely interrupted a conversation between Pearl and I in order to introduce herself, rescuing me from Pearl's annoying enthusiasm. Pearl excused herself and I became immediately indebted to Carol for liberating me. Carol was a cute short girl with a pixie haircut, infectious giggle and a love for rock and roll. We immediately became friends and daily lunch mates. I told her my history then she told me hers, and the next thing I knew she asked me if I wanted to step outside and smoke a joint with her. It was an offer I couldn't refuse; only now I was going to have to face Pearl while I was stoned. She was hard enough to deal with when I was straight, but while being high, it was sure to be torturous. It was.

Next to going home, having lunch with Carol was the only thing that got me through those dull never-ending days. I guess my unenthusiastic attitude with the job became quite obvious and after squeaking by the year, thank God, I was finally let go. It wasn't easy breaking the news to Julianne, but it was just one more thing I wasn't cut out for.

It was another typical morning in our unoccupied lives. We were lazing about our apartment. Julianne was watching a game show and I was fidgeting with my guitar when I got a call from my dad. He told me he got word regarding an available job in the radiology department of a major New York City hospital. The pay and the benefits were decent and a colleague of his was the department chairman. Julianne and I agreed it sounded like this could be a start to a more secure lifestyle, so I scheduled an interview. For one of the few times in my life I was punctual, neatly dressed, and presented myself in a professional manner. I handed my completed application to the gentleman conducting the interview. I shook his hand firmly, took a seat and began answering his many conventional questions. I thought the dialogue was going rather well and not at all intimidating, until he hit me with the question about my interests and hobbies.

"I see you are interested in music John."

"Yes, very!" I honestly replied.

"Do you consider your love of music basically a hobby or are you actually pursuing a career in music to some capacity?" he inquired.

I explained to him how I loved to write songs and had big dreams of having a hit record someday. He looked at me a little dumbfounded and with an expression of sincere concern asked, "If you were ever to have that hit record you're so obviously striving for John, would you leave your job at the hospital should we hire you?"

I looked back at him with an even more dumbfounded gaze and answered him with another question. "If you were to win the lottery would you quit your job here at the hospital?"

"I see," he said and the discussion came to a screeching halt. Moments later as I waited outside his office I overheard him speaking on the phone. "It seems we have a major conflict of interests here. Mr. Domenico's love for his music clearly suggests to me he would not be an asset to our workplace!"

I never knew when to keep my big mouth shut. In spite of dad's connections I didn't get hired.

Ever since my high school days, when I was reading the underground comic books written by R. Crumb, I started to dabble in drawing cartoons. By the time I had graduated college, my notebooks were full of my efforts at being a cartoonist. Like Mr. Crumb's work, some of my sketches were a little risqué, but because of my lack of refined artistic talent, the characters that appeared most frequently in my doodle books were "Unipeds." "Unipeds" are exactly what they sound like, creatures consisting of a single foot and a head. Because I was able to draw heads with very detailed facial expressions and had no luck at all aligning them with a proportionate body, "Unipeds" were born.

One afternoon, Tall Mike happened to be visiting. Mike was forever trying to come up with get rich quick schemes, and recalling some of my freaky drawings, asked me if I still had any of my old notebooks handy. I never threw out any of my creative works (at least up until that time) and knew exactly where to find them. Paging quickly through my illustrations, Mike started chuckling his inane and extremely annoying chuckle, and then asked me if he could borrow the book for a couple of days. Even though he didn't explain to me why he wanted it, I let him have it. About two days later Mike was back knocking excitedly at my door. "John," he said, "Wait until you see what I'm going to show you. You're not going to believe it. We're gonna be rich!"

He reached into the plastic bag he was carefully carrying and pulled out a small object that was completely covered in bubble wrap. Slowly he unwrapped the mystery item and at last unveiled a three dimensional "Uniped" that had been sculpted in clay. It was remarkable; there was my drawing come to life. Mike's younger sister was somewhat of an artist and she was commissioned by Mike to sculpt several different Uniped characters based on my cartoons. Because this little novelty item looked so cool to Mike and me, we just assumed that everyone in every household across America would want one. Immediately we began to brainstorm and "Uniped, Inc." was established. Smurfs were very popular at the time so we figured we could give them a run for the money. Mike and I contacted lawyers, mold makers, plastic companies, novelty companies, and toy manufacturers and after completing our research, we discovered the one very important ingredient we were lacking in order to start a business was money!!! No one would even take us seriously unless we had the finances to back up our big ideas. All I could think about was if we could get Unipeds to take off, I wouldn't have to worry about ever finding a job. I was determined to go full steam ahead with this project thinking this could very well be the answer to my prayers.

We started seeking investors by asking everyone we knew for money. We didn't care who it was; if they were willing to give it up, we were willing to invest it for them. Acting as if we were high financiers, we drew up contracts promising would-be backers generous returns on their investments. Among family and friends, we pulled together fifty thousand dollars to get us started. I even had the balls to take ten grand from a wealthy cousin of mine who lived in Texas and didn't really know me from a hole in the wall. I was amazed not only at the fact that we were able to raise so much money, but also at how expensive it was to hire an attorney! So with absolutely no business experience and a lot of determination, "Uniped, Inc." went into full production, manufacturing thousands upon thousands of washed out looking plastic figurines, each one neatly packaged in its own clear Lucite container. Experience counts for something. We had no idea the clay statuettes Mike's sister had so brilliantly created would lose all of their distinct features and stone-like color when being mass-produced in plastic. We were into this mess for fifty grand; we had to make it work. We took out ads in trade magazines; we displayed our product at trade shows and waited for the orders to come rushing in. We calculated that with the sale of just one thousand displays we could recoup the initial investment. We sold six. Stored away somewhere in the garage of Mike's family's Vermont home are the very expensive molds, thousands of Lucite containers, and endless cartons of dull gray statuettes. The conversation pieces we hoped would take the country by storm never even stirred up a breeze. "Uniped, Inc" went kaput and soon after, as not to be reminded of our failure, I surrendered my "Uniped 1" vanity license plates. Our investors were all risk takers and had forgiven us for not being more prudent with their money. I couldn't understand why another one of my attempts at becoming an overnight success didn't work out.

The strangest job I think I ever had was when I went to work for Sonny at The Roma, a local Italian restaurant. My sister Virginia was Sonny's daughters' basketball coach, and they had mentioned to her that their dad was looking for a lunchtime waiter. Knowing "Uniped, Inc." had failed and I was unemployed again, Virginia recommended me. It was only due to her recommendation I was hired because I had absolutely no restaurant experience. Sonny was the largest human being I had ever encountered and the cast of characters who frequented his establishment were some of the oddest people I'd ever met. Without exaggerating, Sonny had to weigh close to half a ton. Sonny loved to mingle with his customers, so he would usually pull up a chair and plop himself right in the middle of the dining room and the sight of him was dizzying to say the least! Dressed in his white chef's apparel, complete with apron, when looking at him it was as if I were looking at a giant ball of white, not being able to tell where he ended and the walls began. The fat on his ankles drooped over the sides of his shoes. I'd witnessed Sonny consume a dozen bagels within the course of one day. His appetite was insatiable.

The lunch shift staff consisted of two people, Sonny and me. Sonny cooked while I waited and bussed the tables, worked the register and tended bar. Little by little, Sonny taught me how to run the kitchen. I got to know how to work the ovens, the deep fryers, make pizzas, and prepare most of the lunch specials. After a few weeks Sonny got to know me and by gaining his confidence, he entrusted me with the keys to the place. Because of his enormous size and his inability to maneuver about quickly, I almost always ended up in the kitchen to help Sonny cook. More often than not, he was either on the phone with his bookie, entertaining his friends who dropped in from time to time, or flirting with the female clientele.

One of Sonny's good buddies who dropped in on a regular basis was Dominic. Dom was a short, stocky, friendly fellow who was not too fat but you could tell he loved his cannolis and espresso. He reminded me a little bit of "Pauly," Sylvester Stallone's sidekick in the movie "Rocky." One afternoon, Dominic sat across the table from me while I was trying to enjoy my lunch. It appeared as though he was really troubled about something and initiated a discussion about a parking lot attendant who directed some sexual advances at him while jockeying his Cadillac. He continued to tell me that the guy offered to give him gratuitous oral sex. My jaw dropped into my minestrone, as I couldn't believe this man who was practically a stranger, was telling me something so personal.

"What would you have done in that situation," he asked, "Would you ever let another guy suck your dick? I mean if your eyes were closed how could you even tell?"

"There's no way, Dom!" I stated emphatically, "I would have never let it come to that and if the dude persisted I would have thrown him out of my car!"

"Yeah well, I was just curious how you would have handled it," he muttered, "I kind of didn't know how to deal with the situation!"

I had no desire to learn of any further details and from that moment on, kept a safe distance from Dominic, never mentioning a word to Sonny.

Although Sonny was quickly expanding to the size of an elephant, I must admit he had a rather handsome face. On a summer afternoon two attractive women entered the restaurant and sat themselves in a booth. Sonny loved women, so instantaneously he waddled over to their table and planted himself in a chair right beside them, completely inattentive to anything else that was going on around him. As I watched Sonny turn on the charm, I wondered if he thought he was Clark Gable. It was so painfully obvious he was trying to get into the pants of either of these ladies. Surprisingly enough, he succeeded!

Sonny started showing up for work later and later. It seemed that I unwillingly inherited the responsibility to open up, take in the bags of fresh bread, get the ovens running, the water boiling, the sauces and soups hot, and the tables set. There were some days when the customers started flocking in and Sonny was nowhere in sight. I was racing back and forth from the dining room to the kitchen and back again taking orders, preparing them, and serving them. On this one particular day the place was packed and the patrons were driving me crazy. "Oh waiter, check please…where's my coffee…could we have more bread…could I see the wine list…," it seemed like it would never stop. I was just about ready to tear off my vest and apron and go AWOL when suddenly, who came squeezing through the back door, none other than Sonny himself. "Where the fuck have you been?" I shrieked. Without flinching, Sonny took his place behind the stove and as he drained a colander of piping hot ziti, started to explain how the two women who came in for lunch a couple of weeks ago became his business partners. Sonny then went on to tell me he opened up a brothel in a rear apartment of a store three doors down. The reason he was so late for work that day was because he was sampling the goods! Once again my jaw dropped, only this time into the eggplant parmagiana I was about to serve, when Sonny described in detail the double-team blowjob he got just moments ago. "Don't tell a soul," Sonny warned as beads of perspiration dripped off the sides of his chubby face.

Until the day I finally quit the restaurant I kept Sonny's side business a secret. As long as I live, I will always wonder how under all those layers of rolling blubber, those two women ever found Sonny's penis.

Carrying around the hopes that one day I was going to be a big star, I always looked for a mindless temporary job like driving a truck. I didn't want to get myself too deeply involved into anything, this way when the day arrived I'd have to quit, it wouldn't be such a big deal. While I was waiting for success to find me, making a little better money wouldn't have been such a bad thing either! I found my next job at the Valentine Yeast Company through the classified ads in the newspaper. When I applied in person for an interview, Don and Sal, the two brothers who owned this bakery supply wholesaler, were delighted to see my familiar face as much as I was to see them. We all kind of knew each other from the neighborhood we grew up in so I was hired on the spot. Finally I had a real full time job that offered a decent salary and company benefits. The job wasn't exactly an easy one. I reported to work daily at six A.M. where I joined a rather motley crew in picking orders and loading trucks. Then in pairs, we went out on the road delivering hundred pound bags of flour, donut mixes and assorted bakery supplies throughout the tri-state area, including some very funky unsafe neighborhoods. I quickly learned this business was very territorial with mob watchdogs insuring everyone got their piece of the pie and only their piece of the pie. It wasn't uncommon to hear the news of a competitor who crossed the line and ended up with a bullet in his head. I was like a chameleon; always able to blend into whatever situation I may have been in at the time. Most of my fellow workers were lucky if they even completed high school so my college education pulled no weight around the warehouse where not much more than seniority ruled. It didn't take me very long to become one of the gang. I was gaining respect and admiration from my co-workers and my employers, even though I had no intentions of hanging around very long. I kept holding on to the hope that somehow, someday, some way, somewhere, something was going to break for me musically. As much as I liked the great bunch of people I worked with at Valentine, I knew I couldn't make a career out of it.

Although we were very far from being on "easy street," my semi-respectable job enabled us to crawl out of penny rolling poverty. We owned one jalopy after another since we were never financially capable of making new car payments. Julianne became quite an amazing bargain hunter and a coupon genius. It was nearing Christmas during the same year I had began my new job, when Julianne thought it might be a good idea to visit a local flea market to pick up some inexpensive holiday gifts. I had just cashed my paycheck and intended to use some of it to shop. As we perused the aisles occupied by vendors who excelled in presenting the illusion they were giving things away, we stumbled upon a game of chance. I mistakenly felt lucky so I went with my instincts and played a dollar. Amazingly my dollar won me two. The shrewd little conniver who ran the game informed me if I wished to continue to play I had to double my bet. Being the inexperienced gambler I was, I followed the instructions of that two-bit hustler, placed two dollars down and won four. I bet four dollars and won eight. Eight won me sixteen. I just couldn't lose but I also couldn't walk away. I was hooked. When the bets started getting steeper, my losing streak began. Anxiety set in and I shuddered at the thought of losing my entire salary as the heartless con artist behind the booth coaxed me into dropping down yet another bet by saying in a completely mistrusting Snidely Whiplash tone of voice, "You could win it all back with this roll!" Julianne knew we had no choice but to continue to play in order to win back some of my hard earned money. I knew it was over. I knew we'd been had. We lost it all, every cent. That Christmas everyone got Julianne's hand-made macramé plant holders and wall decorations as gifts and I was permanently cured of gambling.

Upon returning home from work one evening I heard the unmistakable sound of a Patti Smith album blasting from our front window. My first thought was, "My God she's going to blow the speakers!" The music was so loud that Julianne wasn't able to hear the ringing of the doorbell. I slipped my house key into the lock of our apartment door, as I usually would do, and as I stepped foot inside our living room I was welcomed this time with the overpowering scent of burning incense. Soft candlelight dimly lit the room as my wife, dressed so I would not mistake her intentions, just completed rolling a long fat joint. She smiled and danced seductively around me to the pounding of the beat roaring from our stereo. Any red-blooded American male would have welcomed her advances and jumped at the opportunity to get it on, so I'm sure my bizarre reaction not only puzzled her, but frustrated her as well. I stretched my arm around her to reach for the stereo and turn down the music. Then I insensitively broke the mood by putting on the living room light and blowing out the candles. "What's the matter with you?" I hollered in confused disapproval, "You can't go on like this!" Jule had every right in the world to despise me that evening. I don't know what I was thinking, but if it were possible to turn back time in order to live a certain moment over again, that would be one of them.

"You're going to kill yourself!" I shouted frustratingly.

With what seemed like pure contempt for me at the moment she defiantly replied, "You're such an asshole! Don't you know the only things worth living for are sex, drugs, and rock and roll?"

Man! How things have changed through the years. My apologies didn't cut it that night and I'm pretty certain that was the last time I was welcomed home in the way most men yearn for. I'm not quite sure whether or not I was worried about Julianne getting high too often or bothered by the thought that I was being manipulated. She was right; I was an asshole!

PART II

THE END OF LIFE AS WE KNEW IT

Julianne's brother Arthur left home when he was 17, not to do what most runaways were doing; that is, go to San Francisco or Greenwich Village to grow hair, join a commune, smoke dope and have sex. Arthur split from his overcrowded house on Shepherd Ave. in North Merrick, Long Island to join the United States Air Force. Before I ever got the chance to meet him, whenever I saw pictures of Arthur posing so proudly in his uniform and military hair cut, I used to think to myself, "How un-cool this guy must be!" He met Mary Helen when he was stationed in Arizona. Mary and Artie fell in love and instead of living together, which was what most runaways were doing at the time, they got married. After they bounced around the country from air force base to air force base, they finally wound up settling on Long Island when Arthur fulfilled his commitment to the U.S. government.

The first time I met Art and Mary was when he was stationed up north in Plattsburgh, New York. Julianne and I were not yet engaged when we decided to take a mini-vacation together and drive eight hours to visit her brother and his new wife. We stayed for a week and the four of us had a blast. It was then I realized for a military man, Artie was a pretty cool guy after all. We saw eye to eye on so many issues, had the same sense of humor, liked the same music and he was almost as opinionated as I was. Whether it was because we had so much in common, because I was a musician, had long hair, or was dating his sister, Art took a liking to me. We had a mutual admiration for each other which soon developed into a relationship that made us closer than brothers.

Art and Mary had their first and only child, who they named Robert, shortly after Julianne and I were married. His military days were behind him so Arthur had to join the working world. He became a hairdresser, got a job in a busy salon and reluctantly joined the hum–drum daily grind of living in the suburbs.

Aside from holidays and occasional family gatherings, it was unfortunate that the four of us seldom made the time to socialize. Having a child to care for didn't lend them the freedom to get out very often. One Saturday, however, Artie and Mary had us over to their apartment for a typical evening of eating, listening to music, drinking wine and smoking pot. We were having a good old time laughing, joking and gossiping about different family members. What started out as a most enjoyable evening, suddenly and mysteriously turned into a nightmare. Julianne excused herself and disappeared into the bathroom for a considerable length of time. We were quite wasted so no one seemed to be too concerned about how long she was missing. None of us had a clue to what was really going on. Jule slowly made her way back to the living room with a pale and petrified look on her face. At first I had just assumed the combination of everything we ate, drank and smoked made her sick to her stomach but she complained she wasn't able to catch her breath. We tried to get her to relax and because it was getting late, I told her it might be a good idea if I took her home. Julianne panicked over the very thought of getting into the car and pleaded to stay the night. Not being able to empathize, I was getting extremely annoyed over the fact that her odd behavior was interfering with my plans to go home. Julianne was having severe anxiety attacks and Artie, Mary and I had no idea as to what was occurring, how frightened she was or how to deal with it. Little did I know, but that night was a major turning point in all of our lives.

The following Sunday morning I got Jule back to the sanctuary of our apartment. She crawled right into bed, and from under the safety and warm comfort of our blankets, she tried her very best to explain the horrifying and disturbing experience she had undergone the night before. Giving it my best attempt to understand, I listened while she described the feeling of not being able to breathe, and how at any minute she felt as if she was going to die. I couldn't really relate and tried to reassure her it was just a bad reaction from the weed we smoked the previous night. I was sure she wanted with all her heart to believe my theory; the only problem was her fear, and therefore her anxiety, wouldn't go away. Right before my very eyes, I witnessed the girl who loved to party, transform into a fragile and fearful soul, afraid to leave the false security of our home.

When Monday morning rolled around I had to head out to work and was somewhat concerned about leaving Julianne alone, especially since she still claimed to have difficulty catching her breath. I made sure to routinely phone home during the day to check up on her. She kept calling in sick at her job until finally she had to quit. Just walking around the corner to the grocery store became a wearisome and sometimes terrifying task for her. The tranquilizers prescribed by her doctor didn't make her well; they only succeeded in making her quite lethargic. She started losing weight, we began to grow distant, and I was finally coming to terms with the fact that what was wrong with my wife was very real and needed to be addressed somehow. I found myself in a most distressing situation. Some mornings Julianne would plead with me not to leave her alone but I wasn't in the position to not show up for work. She didn't seem suicidal, so I felt like the situation wasn't critical and my presence was not necessary. I also knew with my lack of patience and understanding, I wouldn't be of any help to her anyway.

I often thought Julianne's Aunt Helen to be a little eccentric but I truly liked her. For a mother of five, Helen was a very laid-back woman. Whenever we spoke, I almost always got the notion she wasn't giving me her full attention, like part of her was off in the clouds somewhere. Unintentionally, I'm sure, she had a way of making me feel there was something of greater importance on her mind than what I had to say! Helen had a caring heart and a genuine love for her niece. She heard from my mother-in-law about the condition Julianne was in and asked me if it was at all possible if Jule could stay with her to be looked after and nurtured for a few weeks. Since it wasn't feasible for me to be with her during the day, and since I had no clue on how to cope with mental illness, I approved. Most of Julianne's aunts and uncles on her father's side were very devout Catholics. One of her uncles was an ex-priest and one of her aunts was an ex-nun. I was never exactly too sure why either one of them, after getting the divine calling, decided to leave the order, but would have to say it was probably because they no longer wanted to remain celibate. Aunt Helen took a giant step out from the rigid boundaries of Catholicism and joined the Catholic Charismatic movement. Charismatic Catholics were a group not willing to completely cut free from the Catholic Church, but who were seeking a closer relationship with their Lord. They felt there had to be more to their faith than the empty repetitive prayers and monotonous rituals they had been conditioned to accept as proper and true. The Charismatic group was different because, against the advice of their monsignors and priests, these believers actually read their Bibles. Historically, Catholics haven't been encouraged to read the Bible because the hierarchies made them believe the privilege was reserved only for them. With a desire to emulate Bible toting Christians, such as Baptists and Pentecostals, they longed for that personal relationship with their Savior along with the so-called spiritual gifts such as speaking in tongues. They conducted weekly prayer meetings where they read scripture, gave personal testimonies of how Jesus changed their failing lives and healed their diseases. It was at one of those mid-week Bible studies, where Julianne for the very first time since she was stricken with anxiety, felt comfort and peace, and claimed to have discovered a personal relationship with Jesus.

After work I would drive all the way out to Long Island to visit with my ailing wife. Aunt Helen, with her Bible in hand, was always at Julianne's side. In her distant yet intense manner, Helen would preach to me about the love of Jesus in her ongoing mission to win another soul for Christ. She was never embarrassed to boldly approach someone, lay hands on him or her, and in the name of Jesus, rebuke Satan. I'd experienced her antics and listened to her sermons, but in my head, I thought she and Julianne were both fucking nuts! Visiting Julianne was reminiscent of the time I used to visit Samba at the mental hospital after his suicide attempt. When visiting hours were over, I would give Julianne a kiss good night and head home to my lonely apartment. During those long rides I'd get lost in thought wondering where our future was headed. Would Julianne ever get back to being her old self, was she crazy or was I crazy? I prayed for answers and started to think twice about who the heck I was even praying to.

Julianne was finally released from her aunt's care and returned home to me. She wasn't the same girl I vowed to remain with in sickness and health until "death do us part." She had become meek and mellow, characteristics that were never Julianne. No matter how I raised my voice in frustration to argue with her, she wouldn't fight back. Just like in the film, "Invasion of the Body Snatchers," it was as if someone or something snatched her personality and left me holding a human shell with a total stranger dwelling inside. Her smile seemed contrived and she had that faraway look in her eyes. Each night I positioned myself on the edge of the bed as far away from her as I could. Her night table lamp would be on so I would curiously turn, only to find her buried in her Bible, reading intently. This was a far cry from the two of us making love after smoking a joint! I would usually say something that could have easily started an argument like, "Don't you ever put that stupid book down?" Instead, she would calmly look at me and say things like, "Don't you want me to be well?" or "If you loved me you would try to understand!"

I was at my wits' end. How was I going to conform from the lifestyle I was used to? How was I going to share my life with someone who I was convinced had been brainwashed into becoming a religious fanatic. I wasn't so sure if I even loved her anymore because I had no fucking idea who she even was. Day after day I left for work wondering if when I got home I would see a little evidence she may be snapping out of it. Night after night, while Julianne slept soundly, I'd lie awake contemplating whether or not our divorce was inevitable. What I wouldn't have given to have my pot-smoking party girl back!

A warm breeze was gently blowing through our bedroom window. My head sinking into the softness of my pillow, I watched from our bed as our navy blue curtains seemed to float out into the open room and brush against the dresser. I turned to the right and took notice of all the items neatly lined up on Julianne's vanity; perfume bottles, lipstick, make-up mirror and hair brush. I couldn't sleep. As I tossed from side to side my thoughts were running wild. I was so disturbed over the disintegrating condition of our marriage and didn't know where to turn. No one understood my dilemma, not my friends, not my parents. All I knew was I wanted Julianne back, I wanted a normal life and I wanted it soon. As much as divorce seemed like my only alternative, deep in my heart I knew it wasn't. We had too much time invested and I had no desire to have our names added to the growing list of failed marriages. I felt so burdened by a barrage of agonizing thoughts and questions I had all to do to keep from sinking into a state of depression. Knowing that sooner or later I would be faced with having to make some kind of decision, I was overcome with this sudden and urgent need to pray. As I lay there broken and humbled, in desperation

I silently cried out for God's help. I was lying on my side facing away from Julianne who was fast asleep. Hoping my SOS was getting through to my Maker, a rather strange feeling suddenly came over me. Without any warning signs whatsoever, my body seemed to be stricken with some kind of paralysis. I wasn't able to move my arms, my legs, or even turn my head. Then right there at my bedside, a glowing figure with outstretched arms appeared to me. There were no distinguishable facial features, only light within the outline of a human's frame. Desperately I tried to move my arms to alert Julianne but it was to no avail. I tightly shut my eyes and when I reopened them the figure was still present. Surprisingly, I remained very calm. I could still clearly see the flowing curtains, the jewelry box on the dresser, the perfume bottles on the vanity, and in the midst of them, the body of light. I truly thought I must have died in my sleep, and the light was what all those crazy people on talk shows claimed to see when having outer body experiences before entering the other side of this life. My mind seemed to be working, but my body seemed to be lifeless. I lied there motionless only capable of opening and closing my eyelids. Every time they opened, the figure was there. "This is totally nuts," I thought to myself," "this can't possibly be happening," and when I opened my eyes the very next time, the vision vanished. At that very instant my arms broke free and I reached over with puzzled exhilaration to tell Julianne what I just saw. I gently shook her and when she awoke to the sight of my mesmerized face I said, "You're never gonna guess what just happened to me!"

In her semi-consciousness she smiled and said, "Can't you tell me in the morning, honey?" Morning couldn't come fast enough.

The following morning I recounted in detail the strange occurrences of the night before. Julianne didn't find anything about my experience peculiar and didn't even suggest it all may have been a dream. I knew beyond the shadow of a doubt it was no dream and could only reason "Somebody up there" was trying to convey a message to me. I took it as a sign and decided that maybe I should start looking into the Bible a little. Julianne asked me if I would like to attend her weekly prayer group and I even agreed to go.

At the time, another mysterious occurrence got me thinking that maybe God did have a hand in this and He was unquestionably trying to tell us something. It just could be He really did hear our prayers. Someone had given Julianne some flowers back when she was feeling her worst. She kept hoping for a miracle, that her mental health would be completely restored, and although she claimed to have faith, she admitted to me later she had prayed for a sign. The flowers had long since died but Julianne refused to throw them into the trash. She just let them sit there on the windowsill as the brown and dried up petals eventually all fell off. One morning Julianne cried out with excitement, "John, come look at this quick, you're not going to believe it!" Having had no idea what she could have possibly wanted to show me, I came hurriedly into the living room. She stood before me in amazement, holding up what were once the dried up, wilted and positively dead flowers, and pointed to where bright yellow new petals were growing from the lifeless stems. A botanist I'm not, and whether or not it was common for flowers to do this, I couldn't say. But Julianne believed her prayer was answered and that she got her sign. She was secure in knowing everything was going to be all right. I thought, "Why fight it?"

When I walked through the doorway of the meeting hall, I expected to encounter a faction of brainwashed zombies. Instead I was welcomed by the warm greetings of friendly smiles and hearty handshakes from people who appeared to be quite regular. "Praise God, so glad you could join us," a soft-spoken woman said as she directed Julianne and me to the circle of folding chairs in the center of the room.

Julianne already knew most of the crowd and introduced me to everyone as we took our seats. The meeting had order. Someone opened with a prayer. It wasn't a prayer like the ones I was familiar with when I attended church. It wasn't a Hail Mary or an Our Father or some prayer said from memory. This person was talking to God in the same way I would talk to a good friend. When the opening prayer was over, the entire group began to worship together. Eyes shut, hands waving in the air, they were shouting out phrases like "Alleluia" and "Praise the Lord". In turn, each member of the group called out a prayer request, and then they all prayed for each other's needs. So far the evening seemed pretty harmless and my pre-conceived notion that this group was part of a psycho cult was dismissed.

When all the singing, the praising and the holy howling faded to a silence, the inevitable big question arrived. A tall gentleman who wore a rather large cross around his neck and who appeared to have been unanimously appointed master of ceremonies, asked, "Does anyone here tonight want to give his or her heart to the Lord?" I could have sworn that every eye in the place was on me. I sat there stubborn-like with my arms folded as I slouched down in my seat. I glanced around and from the corner of my eye I could see two or three hands that went up. I thought to myself, "What the heck, God must have brought me here for a reason," so I took a baby-step in what I assumed was faith, and reluctantly raised my hand. The next thing I knew I was standing in a line that led to where the same tall man with the perfectly coiffed salt and pepper hair stood waiting. I heard him ask the lady at the front of the line if she wanted to accept Jesus Christ as her Lord and Savior. He placed his hands on her head then started to chant several unintelligible syllables. Almost immediately the woman started to shake uncontrollably. It looked as though she lost her balance and was about to hit the floor when two men rushed up behind her. They broke her fall and laid her out on the ground where she remained still for at least twenty minutes. While witnessing this I thought, "Holy shit! This is fucking crazy!" I found the whole scenario extremely bizarre, but I kept thinking about that vision I had, the dead flowers, and Julianne's noticeable improvement. Maybe there was actually something to this business of being "Born Again." It was my turn to step up to the plate.

In an authoritative tone of voice, the ringleader wearing the cross asked me the same question, "Do you accept Jesus Christ as your Lord and Savior?"

"Why soytainly," I answered as Curly Howard came to mind.

He placed his large hands on my head and began to pray for me. While applying more and more pressure to my brow, as if he was actually trying to knock me down, he sporadically blurted out some of that strange mystery babble.

Again he questioned me, "Would you like to receive the baptism of the Holy Spirit with the evidence of speaking in tongues?"

I was thinking this dude was off his rocker, but I answered him anyway, "Anything the good Lord wants to give me I'd be glad to accept!"

In spite of the fact there was no physical evidence anything was happening to me, that is, no shakes, no gibberish, no fainting, everyone shouted out simultaneously, "Praise the Lord!" It was like I just inadvertently rolled off the assembly line to salvation.

As wacky and as far out all of that Holy Roller behavior seemed to me, it did get me thinking and left me with a much different approach on how to reach God. Certain scripture verses seemed to come alive, genuinely touching me. The members of the group sincerely demonstrated their joy of the Lord and although I didn't fully understand what was happening, I too, soon got swept away with a desire to know Jesus, or at least understand the mystique. It had been years since I disconnected from the Catholic Church, but because I did believe in a Supreme Being and was indoctrinated with the thought that Jesus died for me, the very idea I could have a personal relationship with my Savior felt right. The concept of having the faith of a tiny mustard seed, asking anything in His name and having it, was mind-boggling. Aunt Helen would always say God's word does not return void and it certainly appeared as though she might have been right. Her burning desire to serve the Lord kept her focused and driven, and little by little she spread the Word to most of Julianne's family. She was ecstatic over my sudden budding interest in spiritual matters. I grew to enjoy Helen's company and looked forward to having regular Bible discussions with her and whoever cared to join us. The seeds were planted and now they needed to grow, because one thing about me was that whenever I got into something, I had to go all the way and everyone had to hear about it. I have to wonder though, based upon what I know and believe now, were those feelings I had genuine, or were they the necessary first baby steps leading to my radical behavior in years to come?

Call it miraculous, but Julianne and I bounced back. She was back to being her old self, and spiritually, for the most part, we were on the same page. Well she wasn't quite her old self; the drugs were gone, but thank God the sex and the rock and roll weren't. Our social life resurrected and after a while Julianne stopped attending the prayer group. It was around that time when Bob Dylan released his first Christian album "Slow Train Coming." Dylan had always been an inspiration to me, so I too began writing songs of faith. I attended one last charismatic meeting and by request played the group a song I had written called, "If Only They Believed in You." I wrote it while double-parked in the bakery supply truck on the upper west side of Manhattan. I was people watching and had a moment to reflect about what I perceived as the vast amount of lost souls that seemed to be wandering about with no direction in their lives.

Everyone at the prayer meeting loved it. One guy told me he had a friend who knew Billy Joel and recommended I record the song because between his connections and the Lord, you never know blah, blah, blah...I must have heard that routine a thousand times already. I'm sure he was just trying to help, but the song was just not Top Ten material!

Julianne and I talked to everyone about our exciting new twist on religion. A couple of Julianne's brothers and sisters were very interested, but the only friend of ours who we thought was at all "enlightened" was Toni-Ann. So at least there was someone from within our circle who we could talk to about God. My family was about ready to disown us. They didn't get it at all. They thought we were getting involved in a cult!

We were not attending any church on a regular basis but now and then Jule would bug me about making an effort to go. We weren't very familiar with any other kind of Christian church except Catholic, so to make her happy I would join her in a visit to the neighboring St. Robert's on an occasional Sunday morning. On one such Sunday morning while sitting in my pew, I put aside any negativity I had towards Catholicism and earnestly tried to connect with God. My eyes were fixed upon the huge crucifix hanging high above the altar. I stared at the tortured face of the Christ figure with the red droplets of blood oozing from the crown of thorns and His eyes directed towards the painted clouds on the church ceiling. I prayed what I thought was from my heart. "Dear Lord," I pleaded, "Please help me to land the hit record I've waited so long for. After all, didn't You say 'Ask and it shall be given'?" I wanted so much to feel confident that somewhere in heaven arrangements were being made to make certain my humble request would materialize.

I READ THE NEWS TODAY OH BOY

While watching the news before going to bed on the evening of December 8th, 1980, I was sickened by the report of John Lennon's assassination. Julianne and I couldn't pull ourselves away from the television as over and over again we listened to the newscasters on every station repeat the horrible and unbelievable news. We eventually drifted off to sleep with hopes that tomorrow we would wake up to find it was all just a bad dream.

The sun rose the following morning just like it did on any other workday, only this dark day would be certain to stand out in my memory for the rest of my life. It was difficult finding the motivation to get started. When I arrived at work I stepped inside my vehicle and immediately turned on the radio to listen to the rebroadcast of the news. "How in the world could this have happened?" I thought, "It doesn't make sense!"

I was so terribly distressed I could hardly function. I was traveling solo that day with my ears glued to the radio. The newscaster's words seemed to rip through my heart. It was like a nightmare, as I couldn't believe what I was hearing for what had to be the hundredth time; "John Lennon was shot down in cold blood in front of his home at the Dakota…"

Again I got a sick, empty feeling in my gut as the reality of the situation made my head spin and my thoughts race. *"I heard the news today, oh boy!"* went through my mind as I slowly drove through the saddened New York City streets and in my stupor I could see the shock and dismay on the faces of the many people I passed along the way. In between the continuous news bulletins, the disc jockeys played all John Lennon songs.

When Lennon's all too familiar, passionate voice broke into *"And so this is Christmas..."* I completely lost it and cried uncontrollably as if it were my best friend who was murdered. It was rather difficult trying to compose myself. Part of me wanted to shut off the radio thinking the anguish would just go away, yet part of me needed to keep listening.

I'll never forget returning back to the office that evening, after an emotionally exhausting eight hours on the road, and having to deal with the comments of a visiting salesman when he saw how distraught I was. He was an older gentleman and as he stood before me in his long tweed overcoat, totally unmoved by the events of the day, he said to me, "I can't believe the way you're reacting; it's not as if the pope was shot or something!" While biting my tongue I gave him one of those "If looks could kill" stares. I wanted in the worst way to tell him off but instead I explained to him what Lennon once said in an interview that in my eyes made him even more of an exceptional human being. John gave credit to a much Higher Power by rationalizing how he himself wasn't responsible for creating the musical notes of his songs. "I didn't actually create the notes; for me to make that claim would be ridiculous!" he said humbly. "The notes already existed. They'd always been there. I just collected them, arranged their order and added some words!" Sounding somewhat like a religious fanatic, I continued to try and enlighten this old-timer, by sermonizing him on the charisma of my favorite Beatle. "His perspective was unlike anything we'd been used to hearing," I lectured, "John's vision of peace and oneness was a major influence in my life and the lives of millions. He was a revolutionary, a radical thinker, and an activist, and he was snuffed out way too soon!" I shut the door behind me as I left the office. If life were like cartoons, he would have seen the thought balloon above my head with the words, "You insensitive bastard!" I wonder if my parents had similar thoughts about my unsympathetic reaction when JFK was assassinated.

A little bit later in my life I heard certain Christian acquaintances of mine condemn the song "Imagine" and make judgments like, "If he didn't accept Christ, you'll never see John Lennon in heaven." I'd always felt uncomfortable with that way of thinking and could never really buy into it. In my mind, a man who'd tried his best to wake people up by bringing a message of peace and love to a hurting world didn't deserve eternal damnation. Questions like this one would haunt me for a long time to come. Lennon once made a profound statement saying that the Beatles were more popular than Christ and that Christianity would not last. At first I didn't quite understand what he was getting at, especially since I considered myself to be a Christian. *"Imagine there's no heaven, it's easy if you try. No hell below us, above us only sky. Imagine all the people living life in peace."* If only I would have taken his profound lyrics a little closer to heart, it may have saved me many steps in a long journey ahead. Imagine that!

GO FORTH AND MULTIPLY

Remember John Costopolis, the neighbor who filled me in on the facts of life? Well his dad, George, owned a flower shop not too far from our apartment. Somehow through the grapevine, Julianne learned he was looking for someone he could train as a floral designer and assist him in his store. Julianne had a green thumb, loved plants and flowers, so she let George know she was interested. Julianne's desire to excel in anything she tried her hand at would make her a tremendous asset to anyone's business. George not only hired her, he loved working with her.

In 1981, we were finally sailing upon a long stretch of calm sea. Both of us had jobs, we were healthy, and we were spiritually in agreement. So after almost seven years of the ups and downs of marriage, we decided the time was right to have a child. It was a bitter cold Saturday in January and we spent half the day lounging about in bed. I'm positively certain that was the very day Christiann was conceived.

Jule made an appointment with her gynecologist and I had every intention of being with her on this visit to hear firsthand the definitive answer as to whether or not we were having a baby. About a week prior to our anticipated trip to her doctor I was at work like I was on any other weekday. I was on the truck heading into Manhattan when my partner decided to pull into a greasy spoon diner for a cup of coffee. I indulged in a cup and a buttered roll. It couldn't have been more than an hour or two later when I started to get abdominal warning signs that major intestinal trouble was on the way. For the next fourteen days anything I ate exited my body within minutes. I was diagnosed with salmonella food poisoning and needless to say couldn't wander too far from a friendly bathroom. I made a gallant effort to accompany Julianne on her meeting with the doctor, but two minutes away from home, a sickly mother nature began calling. We had to turn back and I had no choice but to stay behind while Julianne traveled off alone in search of an answer. She did, however, call me as soon as she left the doctor's office to give me the news she was indeed pregnant.

If there's an ill side effect to anything, I could be sure Julianne was going to get it. For the first few months of her pregnancy she not only got morning sickness, she got morning, noon and night sickness. The saltine crackers were at her side always and the romantic sound of the dry heaves was forever present. Four months later, when the nausea finally subsided, Julianne transformed into one of the most beautiful pregnant women I'd ever seen. Her face was radiant, her disposition was joyful and she had boundless energy. Sex was extremely good for a few months because we no longer had the birth control issue hanging over our heads. We could make love with reckless abandon.

For the most part, Julianne would say that being pregnant was a pleasant experience, which was a good thing because the labor wasn't quite so pleasing. No matter how much training someone gets at a Lamaze class, no matter how many manuals someone reads, when a couple is having their first baby there's just no way of knowing what to expect. I was up the entire night looking blurrily into a watch trying to determine how much time elapsed between labor pains. Who knew if the pains she was experiencing were even labor pains at all? As far as I could tell her water had not yet broken. I was hoping that when it finally did, it wouldn't be anywhere where I'd have to mop it up! We were clueless, so we decided the best thing to do was to get her right over to the hospital. After filling out all the countless forms in the admitting office, they took Julianne into the examining room to see just how far she had dilated. Only a few moments had passed and along came a nurse pushing Julianne in a wheelchair. I could tell by the frustrated look on Jule's face exactly what the nurse was about to say, "Take her home, she's not ready yet!"

After four trips back and forth to and from the hospital in the blackness of the same night, I think they felt sorry for us and finally admitted her. My poor wife was in labor for over forty hours while her poor sleep-deprived exhausted husband stood beside her for most of that time, coaching her through breathing exercises and holding her hand for moral support. Other than that, I was pretty useless. After all the preparation I went through to be there beside her when she gave birth, the obstetrician advised me it would be best if I left the room and waited in the lobby. Julianne wasn't having an easy time of it. Because her pains were so excruciating and because she still wasn't dilating, I think they were preparing us for the possibility of a c-section. To be honest, in some respects I was a little old fashioned and sort of favored the idea of playing the expectant father role by pacing the floor of the lobby waiting for the inevitable call from the doctor. I really didn't have the need to witness the miracle of a bloody, slimy head come squeezing out of my wife's vagina. It seemed like an eternity, but I eventually got the call announcing that Julianne gave birth naturally to a beautiful healthy baby girl. "Oh my God," I thought, "I'm a father!"

For weeks before our daughter was born, we read through hundreds of names in those handy little mini-books that alphabetically listed every name under the sun along with its meaning. We settled on the name Christiann. I guess it's because we were waving our Christian banner and that name represented what we believed in. I can still picture as if it were yesterday, when one of my work buddies stopped by because he wanted to see, as he so eloquently put it, "the kid." I'll never forget the sight of Christiann lying on her back in the middle of our queen-sized bed while my rugged co-worker with unshaven face, work boots, rough calloused hands and hooded sweatshirt, stood at the footboard staring down at our newborn for a few seconds then turned to us and uttered one word, "Cute!"

I couldn't tell just how sincere of a "cute" that was but at least he said "cute." As proud parents I guess we expected more of an enthusiastic response like, "Wow, she is the most beautiful baby I'd ever laid eyes on, do you mind if I hold her?" In certain life situations there are those standard remarks we'd all been conditioned to say. At funerals the appropriate comment is, "So sorry for your loss." At weddings, it's "Congratulations," even when knowing divorce is in the very near future. When viewing someone's new born child for the first time, "Cute!" is the customary appropriate response. What else could one say, "What an ugly baby?" Of course not, just smile and say, "Cute," even if it's not a sincere "cute."

After I took that anxious yet hesitant stroll over to the hospital nursery and attempted to pick out my child from behind the glass window where all the newborns were displayed, I was relieved when I was successful in selecting my own child without even reading the nametag. There was that shallow fear hanging over my head saying, "What if my kid's ugly?" But of course it was mine! How could I think it was anything but the cutest baby ever born?

So now that we'd become parents, we were not only facing a future full of important decisions to make, we were also faced with making some immediate ones. *Do we baptize our daughter? If we do, who do we select as godparents? Where do we go to get her baptized and who will perform the Baptism?*

Jule and I were still on the fence somewhere between Pentecostal fanaticism and Catholicism. We hadn't yet reached the point in our spiritual walk where we totally understood being baptized was an act of obedience, symbolizing one's decision to follow Christ, to be made by an individual who has reached the age of accountability. Infant baptism, we later learned, is completely unscriptural, but at that time we were not at all worried about our child's eternal fate, if we had decided not get her baptized. We were still somewhat confined, however, by the trappings of tradition, so we forged ahead with plans to christen Christiann anyway. Once again from out of the religious reserves we called upon the services of Rollie to perform the ceremony. We contacted a local church, the date was set and naturally, as with most of the sacraments, a party was to follow. Because the presence of godparents was an integral part of the baptism ceremony, we had no alternative but to choose some. My best friend Joe immediately came to mind, but because he wasn't a church attending practicing Catholic, some family members disapproved of my choice. So in our continuing efforts to keep peace in the family, we dispensed with our own wishes and chose the youngest sibling from each side, my brother Jim and Jule's sister Elena. (Years later when my brother Jim got to choose his Jewish friend to be the Godfather of his kid, I was confused. Understandably, he didn't dare ask me because of my growing negativity towards Catholicism, but where was the voice of disapproval when he chose a real non-believer, a Jew? After all, the whole point of selecting a Godfather was to insure that the child is brought up Catholic should the parents die!)

In the true spirit of most religious occasions, people usually skip the ceremony at the church and go directly to the party. But an impressive number of our friends and relatives surprisingly showed up at the church, including Aunt Helen and several of Jule's aunts and uncles. Helen's diligence in spreading the gospel was very influential in many of them joining the Charismatic movement. Out of everyone who was present at the service, the Charismatic bunch seemed to be enjoying it the most. They had their very own little cheering section shouting out "Amen" and "Praise Jesus," something that wasn't very common among Catholics. They took it upon themselves to sing a few verses of "This Is the Day the Lord Has Made" and enthusiastically clapped along. Some of my immediate family members had a way of rolling back their eyes, enabling them to indiscreetly inform me they thought these people were kooks. Rollie's familiarity with our family, however, gave the service a personal touch, thus making it relatively short and painless. The party that followed was back at my parents' house where all the guests ate and drank in joyful celebration of a religious rite I was almost certain would have no relevance in the lives of Christiann, Julianne and me. We never really had any intentions of raising our daughter in the Catholic faith but at least we made everybody happy by conforming to the tradition we'd all been accustomed to.

THIS JOB'S GONNA KILL ME

I continued along at my backbreaking job, hauling one hundred pound bags of flour and donut mix on my shoulders, to the pest infested basements of bakeries, donut and coffee shops throughout the city. Some of the sights I saw were enough to make me think twice before putting another donut or pastry into my mouth again. Startled rats the size of cats darted past the stacks of bakery supplies and into the cracks and crevasses of the dank underground when they heard us approaching. We'd find bags of donut mix gnawed open by the hungry rodents who'd burrow their way through the powdery food supply leaving their droppings behind them. Caravans of roaches crawled along the sticky floors feasting on the spill from the broken sacks. Each and every time I escaped from one of those vermin hideaways, I felt as if I needed to fumigate my clothes and take a sterilizing shower.

I had just finished delivering to an uptown route in Spanish Harlem. That afternoon my partner just happened to be a guy who lived in the city. To save him the trouble of having to return to the warehouse and commuting home again, I dropped him off at his Harlem residence, and then headed cross-town on 125th Street toward the Triboro Bridge. I was delayed in traffic and while sitting at a red light all I could think about was getting home to my family. The streets were crawling with inner city stereotypes and it never even occurred to me that my vehicle doors were unlocked. Suddenly without warning, this sinister-looking black dude opened the passenger door of my truck, climbed in and introduced himself in the most unfriendly manner. My heart raced, my palms started to sweat because somehow I knew this uninvited guest was going to be trouble. He held a small gun in his left hand that he concealed in the pocket of his worn out, olive green army jacket. "Listen to what I tell you," he said heartlessly, "or you're going to end up in a hospital or better yet a graveyard, because I have no problem fuckin' killing you!"

Somehow he must have been tipped off and knew there was a safe in the cab of the truck that was stuffed with cash. He ruthlessly ordered me to follow his directions and reminded me if there was a choice between his going to jail and my life, I was a dead man. He wanted my wallet. While trying to reason with him that I had a wife and new baby, I took the wallet from the rear pocket of my jeans and opened it for him to see all I had was five dollars. The creep wearing the navy blue woolen cap on his head took my only five dollars, but fortunately let me keep the wallet. As I slowly and apprehensively made my way along the street full of heavy city traffic, I assured my would-be assailant I would co-operate. Thoughts were rushing through my head and as I quietly prayed for my safety, I unintentionally went through a red light. By doing so, the thug thought I was purposely trying to attract attention and commanded me to make a right turn onto Second Avenue then pull over. His finger still on the trigger, he motioned for me to exit the vehicle. As to why I slipped the keys from the ignition and into my pocket when stepping out of the truck, I initially had no theory, but I thank God that I did. Later I determined that it was divine intervention and until this day I stick to my story! The gunman clutched my arm with his free hand and walked me around to the back of the truck. There he ordered me to open up the rear cargo door, climb inside and remain quiet for thirty minutes.

As I stepped up, the nervous naïve Caucasian I was, I turned to him and made this idiotic request, "Please slide open the lock when you're done so I can get out!"

"Yeah man, sure thing," he snipped, "just get your white ass inside and shut up!" The next sound I heard was the clink of the lock sealing shut the roll-up door.

I frantically walked in circles while imprisoned inside those four tin walls. Every few minutes I put my ear up against the front wall to try and detect whether or not my abductor was still there. I noticed there were some small cracks in the body of the truck where light filtered in and I began hoping I would be rescued before dark. I wasn't wearing a watch so I couldn't really tell how much time had passed. I knew it was getting late and sooner or later I had to make a move. I grabbed hold of the hand truck we used for deliveries and began banging it against the door. Crash! Bang! Crash! "Help," I screamed, "open the door!"

I figured if the thug should open the door, I'd smash him in the head with the hand truck before he even realized what hit him. After ramming my steel friend into the door once again, I heard the faint sound of gentle voice calling out, "Hello, hello, is anybody in there?" Fearing my rescuer might be walking away, I yelled with every ounce of strength I had, "Open the door!"

I then heard the distinct sound of the metal lock slipping open and saw a wonderful liberating glimpse of daylight come streaming in as the door slowly rolled up. Outside the truck stood my hero, a short, stocky white man whose thick-framed glasses made him look a bit more confused than he probably was. While smiling at me he asked curiously, "What did you do, lock yourself in the back of the truck?" Still in the state of panic I snapped back, "No! I was robbed, I was robbed!!" not even thanking the stranger for answering my cry for help.

It must have been quite a sight watching a terrified white man in the middle of Harlem screaming his lungs out, "I've been robbed!" while running towards the cab of his truck. I leaped into the driver's seat, slammed the door, locked it shut and swiftly drove away. After making a couple of illegal u-turns then speeding across the bridge back to the safe familiar territory of Queens, I stopped to call my boss and gave him the bad news.

By the time I returned to the warehouse everyone knew what had happened. My boss opened the truck's safe only to find what he expected; nothing! Three thousand dollars had been fished out. The inner-city bandit must have known exactly what he was doing. He didn't randomly select my truck; he was definitely tipped off. That evening the entire workforce, including the office staff and warehouse crew, took me out to a local bar to try and help me forget my frightening experience. After several shots of Jack Daniels I was feeling no pain and was behaving like my regular class clown self again. Some of the guys were getting hungry so they ordered a few plates of raw clams on the half shell. Raw clams were not one of my favorite things. It was hard enough for me to even look at them, never mind eat them. The first guy to ever pry open one of those creatures and decide to suck down the slime from within must have been either totally wasted or starving to death! I watched everyone in their clam glory as they smothered the slimy things with hot sauce and lemon juice before gulping them down. I suppose it was a combination of my being hungry and the Jack Daniels kicking in that made the clams start to look appetizing to me. "Lemme have one of those things," I said as I reached for the hot sauce. I performed the lemon and hot sauce ritual then sucked the critter from the shell and into my clam-virgin mouth. As soon as my tongue felt its phlegm-like texture I sobered up. I stood at the bar rolling the clam about with my tongue and finally just gave in and swallowed. It was the first and last time I ever did raw clam. When I eventually got home that night, I hugged Julianne and Christiann tightly, immensely grateful I could.

A few days later I was called down to police headquarters where I looked through endless mug shots of black faces, all convicted criminals. After what I thought was going to be an impossible task, I finally picked out the photo of the man who I believed held me up. The officer in charge took the information and assured me they were going to be able to "nab this guy." Months passed, and after receiving several phone calls from detectives who questioned me over and over again as to whether or not I was certain about the identity of the wanted man, the case was dropped and soon forgotten about.

A short time after the robbery incident, Don and Sal asked me how I felt about getting off the trucks, out of the warehouse, and taking a stab at a sales position. It meant sleeping a little later in the mornings, driving a company car, and having an expense account. "John, you're a college graduate, you're smart and you're personable," Don stated, "I think you'd be great at it!" The more he flattered me, the more my hat size increased and I accepted the job. The first couple of weeks were fun as Don and I traveled together. He introduced me as the new sales rep to the owners of his existing accounts and gave me a crash course in how to schmooze. Every day we had lunch in fine restaurants, drank wine and had lots of laughs. That sure beat breaking my ass on the trucks.

After being out on my own for a while, trying to boost sales, I started to realize that not too many of our customers were very fond of Don. "Your fuckin' boss is a crook," they would confide in me, "why should I give you the business when I know he's screwing me, I can buy it cheaper elsewhere!" Everywhere I went it was the same story and it became quite frustrating because how could I argue that logic. If they could get the same product cheaper from the competitor, why not go for it? Each night I would return back to the office with almost no new business and report to my boss that we were just too expensive to compete. I was amazed we had as many accounts as we did. Some were just loyal old-timers; some just kept us around in case of emergencies. It got to the point where I didn't even want to show my face at most of my scheduled stops. The customers never ordered anything over and above their weekly minimum so visiting them was senseless. I started to slack off. I called my friends and met them for lunch. I visited my mom, went shopping, hung out at home and did anything other than what they paid me for. Eventually they came to the realization I was worth more to them by making deliveries rather than driving around all day in the company car, wasting money on gas and tolls. My job was understandably eliminated. It was a little humiliating having to join the ranks of the warehouse crew again but I had no alternative.

I returned to the mindless backbreaking job of lifting, hauling and schlepping, until one morning I piled one too many hundred pound bags on my shoulder and felt a sharp pain in my groin. My partner was concerned I might do further damage to myself, so he was kind enough to deliver the remainder of the load himself. After reporting the injury to my office, I went to see my doctor. Just as I suspected, the doctor informed me I had a hernia and until it was repaired, heavy lifting was definitely out of the question. Surgery was scheduled, I went on workman's compensation and before long my days of schlepping at Valentine were over.

Prior to going into the hospital for my operation, Jule, Christiann and I took a trip to Colorado to visit Arthur. Christiann wasn't even two but she was a terrific traveler. It was the first time we'd ever been out west and we had a wonderful time. Art and Mary lived in Colorado Springs and from their backyard we got the most spectacular view of Pike's Peak. The mountains and the colors made me quickly forget about the city streets of New York, our tiny apartment, and the fact I had to return home to face hernia surgery. At the time, Artie and Mary were also drifting from the Catholic Church, so we were able to have good fellowship with them concerning our new adventures in faith. Every day of our stay was full of fun, laughter and meaningful conversation. As the week progressed, I was dreading going home. Our first family vacation seemed to fly by and before we knew it, we were saying our goodbyes at the airport. Both Art and I could barely keep from crying. Aside from the fact we were leaving one of the most beautiful places we'd ever been to, I knew I was really going to miss Artie and he was going to miss me.

My surgery went well and for the eight weeks that followed I enjoyed spending the time bonding with my daughter. We took walks in the park, made videos, and listened to a whole lot of music. She wasn't quite two years old and was able to identify "The Beatles," "The Stones," "The Police" and Elvis Costello. I thought maybe I could influence her taste in music at an early age. If I had had any indication that the future would bring about the likes of Brittany Spears, New Kids on the Block, or Boys II Men, I would have worked a little harder in molding her musical tastes. I have to say, I loved being able to stay at home and not have to go to work.

Unfortunately, Workman's Comp ran out, and it meant I had to return to the daily grind. My boss more or less told me I had been replaced and he no longer had a position for me. Truthfully, I was not upset in the least bit and I think Don knew he was actually doing me a favor by letting me go. Once again I was knocking on the doors of my old friends at the unemployment office.

NOT IN KANSAS ANYMORE

Christiann was only going to get older so we knew that very soon we were going to need a larger place to live. We were living in a three and a half room apartment, so our bedroom was part nursery cramped with a crib and changing table. It was around this time when we got the news that our building was going co-op and we were presented with an offer to buy our apartment at the insider's price of sixteen thousand dollars. Like an idiot I signed a "no-buy pledge," a legal document drawn up by the tenants' association, a group of furious "forever renters." The know-it-all I was, asked without having any insight of what a great investment buying the apartment would be, "Who in their right mind would pay sixteen grand for this?" Less than two years later, that tiny little piece of real estate was valued at ninety thousand! Who knew? It wasn't the first mistake I'd ever made and it wasn't going to be the last. I'm just grateful my friend Jack's mom was able to buy the place at the right time. As far as I know, she still lives there, so when the day comes when they finally sell, somebody is going to make a hefty profit.

It's funny how things always seem to work out (maybe not the way we want, but nevertheless, they work out). As we were looking around the area for houses we knew we could never afford, we got a call from Julianne's uncle. He owned a house located near the water in Freeport, Long Island, a small fishing and boating village, and wanted to know if we had any interest in renting it. I was born and raised a city boy so I was opposed to living in the land of shopping malls, cookie cutter houses and Saturday morning lawnmowers. The rent, however, was more than reasonable and we really had no affordable options. As much as we loved what was our home for about eight years, it was time to move on.

With many of the things that appear too good to be true, there usually comes a catch. As fortunate as we were to have found a new place to live, the one drawback was we had to share the house with Julianne's Aunt Tess. She was to live on the lower level, which was really an above ground basement turned studio apartment. We were to occupy the main level that included a kitchen, dining room, living room, three bedrooms and a bath. We all were to share the laundry room and the yard. Under the impression Aunt Tess was a "sister in the Lord," we figured what better person to share living space with? Sometimes even the simplest of arrangements can get complicated. Whenever Tess was home we had to learn to keep the television volume down and play our music very low. The walls were paper-thin so we had to be sure to watch what we said and we also had to be sure our company didn't get too noisy. In the meantime, we had to contend with the smell of her strange cooking and the annoying sound of her "Christian talk-radio," which were leaking through from downstairs. We all had to adjust and learn to tolerate each other. At times it wasn't easy for any of us.

While living life many of us just block out the fact that although time never stops, it eventually runs out for all of us. It wasn't going to be long until my unemployment benefits ran out as well as the minutes on Julianne's biological clock. She wanted more children, which put me in the predicament of quickly finding a decent job. It's true I couldn't change what was already behind me, but nevertheless, I was getting mad at myself for still being so unsettled at this stage of my life. Aunt Helen (who was Aunt Tess's sister by the way) didn't live too far away from us now, so every once in a while she would stop in to see how we were doing. She was especially concerned with our spiritual walk and invited us to attend a small "Full Gospel" church she claimed the Lord led her to, which was conveniently just a couple of towns away from us. Jule was more excited about going than I was, but as usual, I went along without a fight.

One Sunday morning we got into our car and followed Helen to a little brick building that was tucked away at the back of a parcel of land where there stood a large cross, the only identifying object suggesting this was a church. Upon entering the doors of this small meeting hall we were greeted by what appeared to be the happiest people I'd ever met. "Welcome, praise the Lord!" they said, smiling from ear to ear. We were handed some literature then shown to our metal folding chair seats. "No one can be this happy," I thought, "These people have got to be on medication!"

On the wall up in the front of the room there was a large cross, less the attached crucified Christ figure we'd all been accustomed to seeing. There was a platform with a portable pulpit, a set of drums, piano, guitars and some amplifiers. It looked more like the stage was set up for a lounge act rather than a church service. The musicians stepped up to the platform and took their places when a guy in a three-piece suit, who appeared to be in his mid to late 50's, leaped up to the microphone and shouted, "Praise to the Lord!" Next thing I knew, the little man strapped on an accordion and the entire band broke into "I'll Fly Away" and everybody was up on their feet clapping and singing. Always the skeptic, I stood like a statue, my arms folded in front of me carefully observing the faces of all those ecstatic people. The music went on and on, song after song, and I thought it would never end. Now and then there would be a long pause between songs. It was during those pauses when most of the congregation would shout out phrases like "Alleluia," "Glory to God" and "Thank you Jesus!" Many of them would start babbling the way they used to do at the Charismatic prayer meetings. At one point the inane babbling, the chatter, the screaming, the clapping and the overall noise level got so out of control I felt as if I were in a sanitarium. I noticed a couple of men who were so into it, they looked as if they were psyching themselves up the way weightlifters do before attempting to press ten thousand pounds. Their heads were shaking and their veins were surfacing through the skin of their temples.

The song service went on for a good hour or so, followed by announcements, a collection or "love offering," as they called it, and a message (what we were used to calling a sermon or homily). The pastor requested everyone stand and read along in their Bibles as he read a passage from scripture prior to preaching a related message. I wasn't totally turned off but I listened attentively and had no problem with most of what he had to say. In my first visit I learned a lot of Bible stuff, most of which made me comprehend, even more clearly, many of the major flaws of Catholicism. The Pastor's name was Ralph and as he stood behind the pulpit delivering the word of God, he testified about his own past life as an entertainer lost in the nightclubs and bars of the sinful city. "In today's vernacular," he preached, "and in the words of Mick Jaggers," a name he mispronounced quite often, "I can't get no satisfaction," implying how the things of this world just can't satisfy.

Applause came from the excited worshippers, and when Pastor Ralph claimed he had "a Holy Ghost check," he brought his sermon to a close. (A Holy Ghost check simply meant the spirit of God was telling him to wrap it up. He could have been confusing Holy Ghost check with hunger pangs, but who was I to say!) The message was then followed by his asking of that same recurring question, "Does anyone wants to give his heart to Christ? If so would they please make their way up to the altar?"

The music started up again, some people went up to the altar, some people stayed in their seats, and some people, including me, made a mad dash for the exit. Aunt Helen met us in the parking lot, "So what did you think?" she asked.

"Oh it was really nice!" Julianne answered.

"How about you John, didn't you find the pastor to be so anointed?"

I nodded and with the best put-on enthusiasm I could muster up, I said, "Yeah, I really enjoyed it!" Whether I wanted to or not, it looked like this was going to be the place we were going to be spending our Sunday mornings for a while.

TWENTY-FIVE YEAR TEMPORARY JOB

Every morning, without fail, I made it part of my daily routine to ride over to the stationary store where I would pick up the newspaper and search the classified ads for a job. One June morning in 1983, I came across an ad that read, *"Drivers wanted. Thirty days only. Summer help. UPS apply in person…"* The ad listed the salary and after some quick mathematics I figured out just how much money I could earn in thirty days.

"This would be perfect," I said to Julianne, "we could pay up some bills and then I could move on to something more suitable for me." I drove over to the UPS building and became immediately disillusioned when I got on the end of a line where hundreds of applicants stood ahead of me. My defeatist attitude told me this was going to be a complete waste of time so I considered just turning around, going home and telling Julianne a lie like I didn't qualify. The girl on line in front of me was pretty friendly, very talkative and she convinced me to stick it out to see what happens. I spent a good part of the day there, as UPS personnel showed us the ropes and told us what would be expected of us. I felt like I was in boot camp. The place was run just like the military and I was beginning to feel if I got the job it would be payback for beating the draft when I was younger.

The last part of my day was a one on one interview with a guy in a suit who told me point blank, "You know, if you work here you're going to have to cut your hair!"

Even though I felt like he was sticking a knife in my heart, I answered confidently, "No problem!"

Well, a few days later I got the call, I got the haircut, and I got the job.

I was told where and when to report, I would be given my brown uniform and my thirty-day assignment. The strangest part about my getting a job at UPS was recalling how years ago, when I was writing songs with Rich Soriano, he handed me the lyrics for a song we collaborated on called, "The Boy from UPS." It was a pathetic tale about a girl who loved a UPS man and how she *"kept his uniform pressed!"* There I was, all those years later, wearing a stiff polyester brown uniform, while Rich was probably out west somewhere with a full beard, long unkempt hair, strumming his guitar and writing some more prophetic stories. Another ironic situation from my past that came to mind that day was the time I attended Julianne's cousin's wedding. Jule's uncle was a UPS driver and a shop steward. At the reception seated at a table were all of his UPS buddies. I remember them to be a loud obnoxious bunch of guys who did nothing but talk about their job. I also remember thinking to myself, "What a bunch of losers!" never imagining that in the future I'd be sitting at a similar table with a similar gang of union men. It's strange how I never even looked back and thought to take those occurrences as warning signs!

I hated UPS. It was nothing like I'd imagined it would be and opposite everything I considered myself to be about. Once again, I found myself surrounded by guys (and a few girls) with nothing more than high school educations, not to say I felt like I was any better than anybody else, but I did have a college diploma. The place had an "us versus them" atmosphere about it, that is, management against unionized labor. The management paraded about clad in suits and ties and thinking they were superior to the hourly. The hourly went about their business in the familiar brown polyester, resenting the fact it was their muscle and sweat that provided the supervisors with their hefty salaries and bonuses. No one had long hair, beards, goatees or demonstrated any form of self-expression. It was a workforce of drones laboring in obscurity.

On my very first day I reported to my assigned center, a rookie among dozens of veterans, and waited for instructions. My manager introduced himself to me then quickly excused himself to enter a screaming match with a seasoned driver.

"Fuck you!" the driver screamed, "I ain't taking this load out with all these stops" and continued to toss boxes from his truck and onto a conveyor belt.

"Either you put those packages back on your car or you're on a fucking seventy-two hour notice!" They referred to their trucks as "package cars."

As I quietly observed the verbal battle going on between my boss and the sweat-drenched driver, my head was literally spinning. I thought to myself, "So this is what it's like to work at UPS! I'm certainly not cut out for this shit!" I was told by some of the other drivers that the majority of those in management and supervision were former drivers and loaders who just couldn't handle the job, turned in their union cards, and joined forces with the opposition. I just kept telling myself, "This is only for thirty days!"

BORN AGAIN AND AGAIN

We continued to attend "The Full Gospel Church" and eventually became official members. There was nothing anyone had to do to become an official member except show up. When the latest copy of the Church directory was printed, our names were listed among its members, thus making us "official." It was at these weekly Sunday services when I started to gain a deeper knowledge of the Bible and became uncharacteristically consumed with a desire to truly understand what it meant to be a follower of Jesus. I had yet to encounter any of the personal maniacal manifestations I saw others experience. Up to this point I still haven't had the experience of "speaking in tongues," which in these circles was evidence that one was filled with the Holy Spirit. I still wasn't sure if I believed whether or not that sort of stuff was for real, even though people all around me were babbling something other than English, Italian, Latin, Greek or any other recognizable language. One thing I did know, however, was that if any of the "gifts of the Spirit" did exist, I wanted them. These gifts included prophecy, healing and interpretation. Interpretation was the ability to decipher what someone who was speaking in tongues was actually saying. Like I said, I wasn't exactly cool with the entire "Full Gospel" program, but because we fled from what I believed were the deceptions of Catholicism, there was a peculiar attraction to this being "Born Again" mystique. We broke away from the non-scriptural homage to Mary and the patron Saints. We became aware of how confession, purgatory, the Pope, guilt, and holy days of obligation were all unbiblical. I comprehended that I could go directly to my Father in heaven and ask anything in the name of Jesus and have it! I wanted all this new information, which was in the form of head knowledge, to take root in my heart. I wanted all those Pentecostal catch phrases I had learned to rattle off, such as, "Being in the world but not of this world," to really have meaning in my life. The one thing I couldn't deny that made being "Born Again" so appealing, was the shared hope there was a safe and easy way out in case doomsday should occur during my lifetime. As a member of God's army, I was assured to be swept away and caught up in the air with Jesus when He returns for us at the end of time, which I'd been told week after week, "Is coming soon!" This "meeting in the air" Born Again Christians talk and sing about is known as "the Rapture." I think I liked the idea of "The Rapture" because it made possible the opportunity to get off the planet and into heaven without having to die and be buried. Over and over I would hear Christians mention how they weren't afraid to die because they knew they were going to be with Jesus. These people would cause me to question the intensity of my own faith because as much as I heard Heaven was a cool place, I was in no hurry to get there! I used to say to people, "Hey! I believe in God and all, but if I saw death stalking me, I'd be running the other way as fast as I could!" I knew I still had a lot to learn and loads of issues to work out, but I sincerely felt I was at least on the right path. I had no idea there would be many paths ahead.

Little by little we became more familiar with some of the other church members. I guess we seemed like a nice enough family and others wanted to get to know us. It's a funny thing, but I noticed how the "Born Again Christians" I knew, liked to make other "B.AC.'s" think they only associated with "B.A.C.'s." They would often refer to the "Don't be unequally yoked" verse from the Bible and tried to make us feel like we shouldn't be associating with our worldly lifelong friends anymore. Before we knew it, our church acquaintances were becoming part of our social life. When we started getting invitations to attend small "get togethers" at the homes of our new Christian brothers and sisters, Julianne would panic and beg me to be on my very best behavior. Although I was trying to "live for Christ," I still had an offbeat sense of humor and couldn't resist going for the laugh. I'd always believed I had to be true to myself and that there was nothing worse than being a hypocrite. I wasn't about to act any differently in front of "Christians" than the way I did with anyone else. By being myself, I eventually found out who of my "brothers and sisters in Christ" I actually had a little something in common with. Maybe there was some way I was going to be able to fit in with the church crowd after all?

One thing I picked up on when visiting Christian homes was that they didn't serve alcohol, nobody smoked (in front of each other at least), the jokes were usually very unfunny and "Christian" music was always playing in the background. I started to wonder just how suited I was to belong to this new social club. I hated Christian music. In my mind most Christian bands were just a bunch of wannabe rock stars who didn't get a break in the secular world, and then decided to take a stab at the Christian market. Their styles were influenced by many of the well-known rock and pop stars, and most of their songs were blatant rip-offs, except of course, for the pseudo-holy lyrics. I hated how Christians got so impressed when popular musicians announced their conversion to Born Again Christianity. Now that he or she became a believer, it was suddenly okay for us to listen to them? I also liked to indulge in an alcoholic beverage or two in social situations. Our Christian acquaintances always seemed to offer sweet drinks, diet drinks and coffee. I'd always hated soda and how much coffee could one drink? I often questioned how the same people who refrained from drugs and alcohol could drink so much coffee. After all, isn't caffeine an addictive drug?

One other thing I noticed about church people gatherings was how early they always broke up. "Well, we've all got to get up early for church tomorrow morning," they would say as they stretched and yawned, the not so subtle hint to grab your coat and exit. Jule and I were being exposed to a whole new way of hanging out, social behavior we just weren't used to.

UPS was not known for being such an easy place to land a job. Before becoming a route driver, there were certain criteria one had to measure up to. These requirements included having a clean driver's license, a neat wholesome appearance, and being drug-free. Once a person began working for UPS, he or she would be put on a thirty-day trial period. At the end of thirty days, odds were that person would get laid off before having the opportunity to join the union. Don't ask me how they arrived at this system, but if someone worked a certain number of days in a given period, he or she would automatically get his or her union book. UPS did, however, figure out a way of building up a workforce during their busy season. They would hire an overabundance of seasonal help, and by dangling the false hope carrot of a permanent position before them, they'd manage to acquire the man power needed to get the packages delivered without having to offer benefits and full scale pay. Before working a thirtieth day, the temporary worker was usually laid off. Very rarely was someone kept on. I've known guys who'd been jerked around for as long as five years before becoming a permanent hire. I was lucky (or should I say not so lucky). After a very brief lay-off period, I was called back and moved quickly along to making my union book. I had become an official full-scale UPS man.

When some of the old-timers would approach me to welcome me on board, I'd always say to them, "This is just a stop-off, I've got other plans."

"Yeah sure kid!" they'd respond as if they really knew, "You're a lifer! Talk to me in twenty years!"

I got the knack of the job very quickly and in just three years had my own route. Coincidentally, the route was in the town of Port Washington, home of the "Salem Inn" and our very first bachelor party.

Julianne and I found our social circle changing. Before I knew it, that little gang of ours was spread out all over the place. My friend Joe settled in New Jersey to be close to his wife's parents. My friend Mike moved to Texas when his office relocated and he couldn't find another local job. I still kept in contact with most of my old friends, but not nearly as much as I would have liked to. New neighbors, co-workers and in our case, church members were all becoming part of our changing lives.

We became regular churchgoers, not only for ourselves, but because we felt we had to establish some religious roots for our daughter and future children. We now considered ourselves to be "Born Again Christians," and with this new spiritual identity came along other big changes. Both Jule's parents and my parents were not too happy about us officially denouncing Roman Catholicism. Attending a church where we actually read and studied the Bible brought along with it a new and clearer understanding of the God we were serving and it also illuminated us to all the non-scriptural doctrine of Catholicism. Just like the infatuation period one experiences with a new boyfriend or girlfriend, the same held true with the new relationship we were having with our God. We were so excited about our new slant on religion and wanted to share it with our family and friends, most of whom thought we were nuts. Many family get-togethers turned into arguments because of our overzealousness about the importance of being born again. One afternoon my dad walked out on us when I looked down on him from my soapbox and said, "Dad, when are you going to acknowledge there's more to talk about in life than movies and restaurants?"

At the time, I didn't realize how badly I must have hurt his feelings. We decided our home was to be a Christian home and we wanted all who entered it to know it. Julianne started watching Christian programming like Pat Robertson's 700 Club and the Jimmy Swaggart ministries. She was reading Christian encouragement books and placing little inspirational knick-knacks all about the house like calendars with scripture verses. We had Bibles all over the place, the King James Version, the NIV, The Book; study Bibles for men, for women, and for children. For Julianne this all seemed second nature, easy and genuine, but as excited as I thought I was about my new found knowledge and deepening relationship with God, there was a lot I couldn't stomach. I loathed Pat Robertson and his faithful sidekick Ben, the Johnny Carson and Ed McMahon of Christian programming. They impressed me as arrogant and self-righteous, a far cry from Christ-like. Although Jimmy Swaggart, adorned in his gold Rolex and diamond-studded matching cufflinks, delivered a strong, powerful, soul-saving message, I couldn't shake the feeling it was all a well-rehearsed act he had down to a science. I wanted to believe I was part of a movement knowing the indisputable truth, yet common sense, logic, and skepticism continually hinted that something was amiss. If all the hopes and promises about being born again were true, then I needed to see them for myself!

Someone from the church told us about a seminar taking place at another neighborhood assembly on a Saturday night. It promised to be an eye-opening revelation of how Satan took full control of the entertainment business, especially rock and roll music. Well aware of how much rock and roll has always been an important part of my life was probably the reason some church colleagues invited us to attend. We asked Aunt Tess to baby-sit (one of the advantages of living in the same house with her) and we went. The meeting hall was packed. Jule and I took seats to the back and watched as two extremely rigid and well groomed young fellows proceeded to rip apart one of the true loves of my life. These guys managed to find satanic influences in practically all my favorite records. The bands they targeted included the Eagles, Led Zeppelin, Pink Floyd, the Stones, and even the Beatles. They were playing records in reverse, revealing evil subliminal messages such as "Worship Satan," or "God is pooh-pooh". To tell the truth, I sat there in childlike amazement. I couldn't tell if I was astounded by the fact so many subliminal messages really existed or that someone actually sat around for years playing records in reverse trying to find them. I couldn't argue; I heard most of them as clear as a bell with my very own ears. Whether or not the tapes were edited to fit the "Rock n' Roll is Evil" agenda was something I only wondered about afterwards! They handed out literature that gave detailed accounts of rock stars dealing with the occult. They explained why they believed Jimmy Page was a Satan worshipper and a member of the black church (black not referring to Baptists or Afro-Americans). They took apart the lyrics to "Hotel California" line-by-line, defending their position the song was about the church of Satan. Of course the main objective of the evening was for all of us good Christian soldiers to run right home, pull out all the evil records from our treasured collections that have been crammed onto the shelves of our wall units, and toss them right into the trash.

The night ended in prayer, as most church related functions do, and the foes of rock left us with this thought, "How can we claim to be living our lives for Christ if our homes are full of this filth and the work of the devil?" Somehow they even got me wondering enough to examine my conscience. Maybe it was time for me to clean up my act.

As we were exiting from the building we ran into Jeff and Sherry, a couple we recognized from our church. Jeff gave me one of those raised eyebrow looks, which perfectly described his feelings of amazement and in his Midwestern accent said, "Well what did ya think of that?" Not really knowing how to describe what I had just seen and heard, I answered by simply saying, "Holy shit!" loud enough so everyone around could hear. Julianne gave me an elbow to the ribs and reminded me where I was and to whom I was talking when she said, "Some impression you must have just made! I can't take you anywhere!" That very same night when I got home, I browsed through my collection of almost seven hundred albums. I began pulling out the records the speaker had specifically mentioned that evening. Out came "Hotel California" and "Houses of the Holy" and "Goat's Head Soup," but when I reached for the Stones' "Satanic Majesty's Request" with its 3-D album jacket, I said to myself, "I can't get rid of this, it's a collector's item!" For some reason I gave up the Eagles album but I slipped the others right back onto the shelves I took them from, where they still remain, safely tucked away in alphabetical order.

...AND THEN THERE WERE FOUR

Samantha was born in June of 1984, three years after Christiann. Julianne had a much easier time with this delivery. The entire ordeal lasted only four hours, almost two days less than the battle she had with our first born. I didn't get to witness the miracle of childbirth with this baby either. I just assumed there would be complications so I opted to pace the lobby floors. Julianne fooled me this time and everything went smooth as glass. This being our second child, we were far more prepared and a lot more relaxed than we were the first go round. With Christiann, Julianne read all the manuals, taking extra-special care to make sure that mothering and parenting would be the most pleasant experience for all of us. No amount of reading material, know-how, or skill could have prepared us for what we were about to face with Samantha, our new bundle of joy!

We got more than a handful with Sam. Although we were familiar with the term "colicky baby," nobody ever warned us how torturous having one could be! A colicky baby is enough to make a parent lose his or her mind, and in a moment of temporary insanity, either kill themselves or the kid! It seemed like she cried every minute she was awake, which was all the time because she never slept. In the middle of the night we would wake up to the habitual sounds of Samantha's relentless whining and crying, and since we knew nothing could stop it, we'd leave her there in her crib hoping she would eventually get exhausted and fall back to sleep. Sometimes she didn't and Aunt Tess would tip-toe her way upstairs to hold and rock our cranky baby. "Oh you poor kids!" she would say to us, "Try to get some rest while I rock her!"

Knowing my wife's aunt was walking around my home trying desperately to rock my daughter to sleep wasn't very conducive to my falling back to sleep. I discovered a secret weapon that usually succeeded in stopping the squealing for at least a little while. I would hold Samantha in my arms face down in a "Superman" position and run through the house as fast as I could. It had the same effect the wind has on a dog when it hangs its head out a car window. Sam would start gasping and the crying would momentarily cease. I think I must have scared her half to death. Until the day she finally began sleeping through the night, Julianne and I were totally drained. It was bloody torture.

Now that we understood infant baptism to be non-Biblical and no longer part of our doctrine, we had to gently explain to our families that Samantha was not going to get christened. They just assumed after our baby was born a christening was to follow. Many of the people who found their way into the various forms of protestant denominations, at one time or another were Catholic, and because tradition plays such an important role in any church, they needed something to replace the baptism ritual. In the church we belonged to, a little ceremony called a "dedication" was performed. It could best be described as a waterless baptism, where the parents were asked to publicly announce they were going to bring up their child in the saving grace and knowledge of their savior Jesus Christ. Some people didn't make a big deal of a dedication, while others felt the need to have a big celebration. Some couples just couldn't break completely free of tradition and even selected godparents for their child. I had no problem at all not turning Samantha's dedication into a major event. I was happy to get away from all the pomp and circumstance of religious tradition. In fact, we tried to undo Christiann's christening by dedicating her along with Sam on the very same day. We got a two for one special! Pastor Ralph dedicated our two girls during a regular Sunday morning service. I wasn't too thrilled about being on display in front of the entire congregation and I hated all the ceremonial formalities, but sometimes we just had to go with the flow. The girls were given their very own children's Bibles and after the service many of the members of the assembly congratulated us, making a much bigger deal out of it than I thought necessary. But in my very best John Domenico fashion, I smiled, I nodded, and I shook hands. So after completing another milestone in our church life, without a celebration or party, we went home and had dinner as a family. It seemed like the right thing to do at the time.

TONGUE TIED

There was a period when somehow I became obsessed with the "speaking in tongues" phenomena. Every Sunday I would look around and see worshippers blabbing away in this unknown language. The pastor would continually preach on the importance of being baptized in the Holy Spirit with the evidence of speaking in tongues. I for one never spoke in tongues, but at the same time, I believed I was filled with the Spirit of God. My unceasing desire to want to know God and live in accordance with His word, made me certain of it. In any case, I started to question the legitimacy of the tongues issue. I deemed if those around me were worthy of this "Gift of the Spirit," then so was I. What was the reason I was not speaking this "Language of God?" Was it because I wasn't living right, and therefore not worthy of such a sacred privilege, or was it a matter of God just not wanting to give it to me yet, after all, we were told God's timing is not our timing! Another thought also occurred to me. Was it possible all those gibberish-speaking believers were simply brainwashed and emotionally charged up or perhaps even faking it?

During my busy workdays, while driving the UPS truck, I was alone with my thoughts and communed continually with my Maker. "Father," I would pray, "if the gift of tongues is for real, please let me have it. Let me know Your ways." Over and over again I would mimic the sounds of the so-called anointed ones hoping I could get it started, "Sha mah nah nah sha mah nah nah alla bah nah nah nah nah..." I had no idea what the hell I was even saying, but I was determined that if there was such a thing as "tongues," I was going to speak it. I talked about this with Julianne and even though I'd never heard her mutter one word, she insisted she was able to pray in "tongues." I was very annoyed by the fact I became so preoccupied with this crazy matter. What in the world was I doing wrong that I could not experience what seemed to come so easily to others?

Late one night as I lay in bed mentally conversing with God, I was once again dwelling on my current obsession with speaking in tongues. Julianne had drifted off to sleep while I lied awake tossing, turning and trying to convince myself that speaking words I wouldn't be able to understand was simply ridiculous and it had no bearing whatsoever on my salvation. I'm not certain if I had eventually fallen asleep, but if I did, the rumbling that suddenly stirred in my gut was surely enough to wake me. I was feeling something very abnormal but at the same time peaceful. The strange stirring started to intensify and slowly creep its way up from my stomach and into my chest. I had absolutely no control as to what was happening to me. I lied still as I felt the rumbling reach my throat and finally erupt uncontrollably through my mouth, accompanied by the most abnormal sounds. The best way to describe what I experienced that night would be calling it a "spiritual orgasm." The unusual occurrence was confounding. I sat up in bed feeling a bit dazed from what I concluded was an encounter with the supernatural and asked myself, "Did I just speak in tongues?" I couldn't understand how Julianne didn't wake up from my loud outbursts. I wondered if it was all a dream or if it actually happened. I knew I had a vivid and wild imagination, but I didn't think I would have been able to fake something that felt so forceful yet so incredibly restful and serene. Perhaps because I was obsessing over something that was proving to be unattainable, I subconsciously created what I'd imagined the experience would be like. Whatever the case, the pleasurable convulsion I described really happened, so I stuck to the story I spoke in tongues. I refused, however, to accept the notion that speaking in an unknown language was real if deliberately psyching oneself into it was the cause that brought it on. For me to have accepted the idea that speaking in tongues was genuine, it had to be an action as involuntary as breathing, as I believed mine was. But who knows, maybe subconsciously I did psyche myself into it. It never happened again. Not even in a dream!

WALKING THE WALK?

So often I heard it preached, Christians were supposed to be "in this world but not of this world." Our pastor repeatedly advised us, that as "new creatures in Christ," the occasional drinking and partying that were once such an integral part of our lives should cease and worldly people should no longer be part of our social circle. Preachers have always had such a way of taking scripture out of context and using it to support whatever agenda they planned on advocating that particular day. Not being too well versed in scripture at the time, a minister could have told me anything and I probably would have swallowed it. This particular teaching about not associating with my "worldly" friends was a little disturbing and quite confusing to me, because if Jesus himself was hanging out with the riff-raff, why was my pastor instructing me not to? If I was supposed to be spreading the gospel, to whom was I supposed to be spreading it if I was only mixing with fellow believers? Most of my old friends were non-practicing Catholics who, except for special occasions, never stepped foot into a church. Every one of them could have given me a thousand reasons why they didn't, yet at the same time they continued to put their children through all of the traditional rituals of a religion they themselves no longer took seriously. In spite of our spiritual differences, no one could have asked for finer friends than ours and there was no way I would have even considered abandoning any one of them. In contrast to me, religious matters were far from being a priority for them. Maybe they had the right idea all along...don't take religion too seriously.

There were, however, some very convincing Sunday messages that persuaded me to rethink some of the strong opinions I had about my behavior. If I was going to label myself as "Born Again," there had better be a recognizable difference between non-Christians and me. If I was going to talk the talk, I had better walk the walk as they say. Whether or not it was a conscious effort on my part, I don't know, but I really cleaned up my language. I would choke on expletives before verbalizing them and suddenly found listening to the very same four-letter words I once used so freely was most offensive. Hearing someone use God's name in vain began to really rub me the wrong way.

One day a fellow UPS worker approached me and asked, "Are you a Born Again Christian?"

I hesitated before answering and told him, "Yes, why do you ask?"

He said, "I never once heard you curse or swear. You're not like the other guys around here!"

At that point I should have asked him, "Then who am I like?" But instead I got inflated with the idea I was so "different." What he said to me that afternoon really mattered. It did my heart good to know someone saw a difference.

Management had arranged for an informal business meeting that took place after work one evening at a nearby tavern. The purpose of this casual get-together was so the drivers could participate in a program by which we were able to openly express our opinions regarding work related subjects. In order to assure a good turnout, free beer was a necessary requirement. While everyone in the room seemed to be having a good time sucking down beer after beer, I refrained from drinking alcohol and sipped a Perrier with lemon. The only thing I could have done to further alienate myself that evening was to have worn a tee shirt that read, "I'm a Born Again Christian, and I don't drink!" Several times that night, however, I questioned my own authenticity. I wanted a beer so bad I could taste it. There was nothing more thirst quenching and besides, maybe a beer or two may have loosened me up. What in the world was I trying to prove by not indulging? Did my bullshit self-righteousness do anything to make anyone in that room think about his spirituality or his walk with the Lord? What kind of an asshole had I become? Was I cutting off my nose to spite my face? If I wasn't being true to myself then how was I being true to my God? I knew I had to look long and hard into the spiritual mirror and do some serious soul searching.

DIAL A PRAYER

In the Bible there are numerous accounts where Jesus healed the sick. Unlike what transpired during the Catholic Mass, the Full Gospel Church made the healing of the sick a major part of the service. Those who were ill and desired healing were asked to make their way up to the altar, where the pastor and the elders of the church were waiting to anoint them with oil and pray in the name of Jesus they be restored to health. Week after week I observed the same formal procedure take place and week after week I witnessed the same people jumping on the prayer line. Always the cynic, I continually asked myself why a sick person had to get anointed and prayed for so many times before God took action, if and when He took action. Believe me, nobody wanted to see miracles more than I did. Every now and then someone would come up to the pulpit, grab the microphone, and boldly give their testimony of how Jesus healed them. The congregation would go wild with applause to a great and merciful God and shout praises of "Thank You Jesus!" The thing that would throw me was witnessing how three weeks later, the same person would be back on line with a relapse or a new ailment. If Christ is the "Great Physician" and He answers prayers by healing diseases, I imagined He would have done the job right, completely and perfectly. I hated myself for always being the "Doubting Thomas," but I couldn't help but wonder if many of those "little miracles" were just "little coincidences".

One day Julianne came home complaining about an irritation in her eye. Day by day the condition worsened. It reached a point where it got too painful for her to even open and shut her eyes. I took her to an ophthalmologist who diagnosed her with a rare and contagious virus we later deduced she contracted from her cousin's baby daughter. The doctor prescribed a medication that temporarily relieved her symptoms but was not very effective in fighting the virus. Although Julianne tried her very best to remain quarantined, it was only a matter of time before we all were contaminated. Christiann had it the worst. My heart broke as I placed the drops of medicine into her fiery red eyes and saw them actually begin to shed tears of blood. My words would just fail to describe the torture this disease brought along with it. It felt as if pieces of glass and sand were lodged behind our eyelids. Without having any control over the natural function of blinking there was almost no relief. Like many new Christians who get suckered into sending monthly donations to Christian programming, we fell victim to Pat Robertson's "700 Club." "Give and you shall receive tenfold!" was one of the best sales pitches I'd ever heard. One particular day I happened to see the "700 Club" flash their Prayer Hotline Number across the television screen as a soft-spoken voiceover proclaimed, "God answers prayer. If you need prayer call the number on your screen and one of our prayer warriors will pray with you in asking Our Master for your needs!" I was so desperate. The discomfort from my eye infection was driving me to madness. In a state of despair I reached for the phone and dialed the number. A "700 Club" prayer partner answered the phone and asked me for my prayer request. I answered with hopeful sincerity and told her about the virus that wreaked havoc on my eyes. In a stern, hard voice she asked me if I had been to a doctor, to whom I answered, indeed I had. She then started to scold me and ordered me to grow up, be a man and give the medicine a chance to work. "Just thank God that you have your vision," she reprimanded, "count your blessings and stop your whining!"

I stood there holding the phone, startled by the way this woman just spoke to me. I was expecting her to rebuke Satan and shout something like, "In Jesus' name I command this virus to depart from this young man..." but instead, I got reproached. I politely said, "Thank you," when what I really wanted to say was, "What the hell kind of a Christian are you?"

During one of Pat Robertson's broadcasts, I watched in disbelief as he stood before the television cameras with his hands raised and his eyes tightly shut, praying that God would redirect an approaching hurricane away from the "700 Club" studios. I thought silently, "What a schmuck!

He's praying God will send the hurricane to flatten another part of Virginia so his broadcast empire could be spared!" His smugness and his arrogance really irritated me.

Pastor Ralph heard the news about how the eye-dwelling virus got hold of our family. One Sunday afternoon, undaunted by the fact that this disease was so contagious, he showed up at our front door in his gray three-piece suit and his little emergency kit of "holy oil." "I want to pray for you," the humble little man said confidently, and opened the tiny bottle of oil. He anointed each member of our family by applying the oil to our foreheads, and then with his eyes closed and his brow wrinkled from the intensity of his prayer, he demanded, "In the powerful name of Jesus, heal my brothers and sisters in Christ!" He then packed up his healing equipment and we thanked him for coming. As he was just about to exit our front door, he turned to us, smiled and said, "See, Jesus still makes house calls."

Even though I was hoping we would have been healed immediately, I guess I had to be grateful we were all eventually well again. Just like any other virus, it had to take its natural course. We were created with a built-in defense system. Our bodies were designed to fight certain sicknesses and diseases and I believe that's a miracle in itself. Maybe we all just have to learn how to be patient and let things work the way God intended.

THE "F" WORD (FLORIDA)

It's a universal expression shared by almost every married person, "In-laws are a pain in the ass." Parents of married children seem to forget their sons and daughters have to split themselves between two families. Every year it was the same old nonsense pertaining to where we were going to spend the holidays. We had to keep a scorecard of our whereabouts for Thanksgiving and Christmas from year to year. I used to think my mother-in-law had a time clock that kept track of the extent of our visits. God forbid we spend a minute more with the opposition! As much of an annoyance the in-laws were, it was a blessing, at times, having them close by. When we lived in Queens, my parents were there at a moment's notice. When we moved out to Freeport, it was nice knowing that Jule's mom and dad, neurosis included, were just minutes away in the neighboring town. Whenever I needed a hand with anything around the house or if ever I had car troubles, I could always count on my father-in-law to be there and tackle the problem for me. An unexpected visit from them, every once in a while, was something Julianne and the kids considered a pleasant surprise. Occasionally mooching a meal from her mom gave Julianne a break from having to cook.

As much as things seem to stay the same, things do change. It's not until the things we take for granted are gone do we miss them. After my father-in-law retired, he determined he could no longer survive comfortably living in New York on his fixed pension. With taxes continually rising and with real estate at an all time high, he decided to sell his house, cash in and go south. So before we knew it, my sister-in-law Elena (who was still living at home) was looking for a place to live because there was no way she was moving to the promised land of American retirees, often referred to as "Heaven's Waiting Room!" It all happened rather quickly. They found a residence in Florida, sold the house, packed up and didn't look back. In a sense I couldn't argue with my father-in law's logic, "Why struggle after working hard all your life?" On the other hand, I had to question how they were able to abandon Elena and the family, including the grandchildren, they left behind. Their moving away may have alleviated some of our holiday scheduling, but the truth be told, there were moments I missed having them around. We knew it was going to be years before seeing them again.

All the while we were living above Aunt Tess she was dating Bob, a cab driver who lived directly across the street in a weather-beaten, waterfront cottage that looked like something out of an episode of Popeye. Bob was a nice enough guy but quite a character. When talking to him, he always pretended to acknowledge me by nodding and saying, "Ah huh!" even though he really wasn't paying the slightest bit of attention. He was easily distracted by the things around him and far more interested in what he had to say. When he was talking, every sentence ended in a question even though he didn't expect an answer. He also had the annoying habit of swallowing between phrases. So long as he could be experienced in small doses, it was difficult not to love him. A true eccentric, Bob must have had a hundred telephones wired up all over his property. He loved collecting junk. He also loved Aunt Tess. Bob decided it was time for him to retire, so he sold his house and his taxi medallion, moved to Florida and bought a place in the same development as my in-laws. In a rather hasty decision, Tess packed her things and went south to live with him. In a way, it was a piece of good fortune for us because now we were able to take possession of the entire house and God knows we needed the room.

During this time frame there seemed to be an exodus to Florida. Aunt Helen's husband had long since passed away. She also decided to cash in on the real estate boom and migrate to the Sunshine State. I wish we could have afforded to buy Helen's house, but at that time we were just about making ends meet and there was no way we could have taken on a mortgage. I was disappointed to know Aunt Helen was relocating. She was someone who I enjoyed seeing from time to time. I admired her eccentricity and spiritual excitement.

NO JOKE, WOMEN RULE

I don't care what anyone tells me, women rule the world. Eve wrapped Adam around her finger, Delilah wrapped Samson around her finger, and Julianne wrapped me around hers. On a wall in our first apartment we mounted a large bulletin board on which we displayed photographs of our friends, favorite places, favorite bands, my bizarre drawings and all the things I felt represented who we were. My guitars were always strewn about somewhere, my fake gold record hung on the wall along with my Woodstock reunion poster. As time went by I noticed the things that characterized me were slowly disappearing from view and replaced with items Julianne decided better suited the décor of our home. When we moved from our first love nest, the bulletin board was destroyed and eliminated from my life. My guitars were restricted to the bedroom and my gold record placed in a cardboard box along with my framed Beatle photo and all the pictures I once proudly exhibited on my walls. The walls were now adorned with what I considered, uninteresting, unoriginal generic "Vogue" prints that could be bought at any local J.C.Penney department store. The worst part about situating those lackluster prints up on the walls was the agonizing ordeal Julianne put me through. Trying to get them level, centered and straight enough to meet her strict standards was exasperating. It started to seriously disturb me just how much of a perfectionist Julianne had become.

"Do they look even to you?" she would ask me over and over because no matter how many times I said, "Yes dear," she insisted on re-measuring. Striving desperately to get my input, she'd question, "Do you like the colors? Do you like the way they contrast with the couch? Do you think they're too small, too large? Are they centered?" I'd nod my head up and down in the affirmative motion and she'd respond, "Well what does that mean, too big or too small, you like it or you don't?"

The truth is, it really didn't matter to me, and did she really want to hear what I thought? I would have been perfectly happy with my Beatles poster, my pictures, my photos and my guitars, but whatever was going to make my wife happy was all right with me. Women don't seem to understand, as long as men are getting fed and having sex, we pretty much don't care about anything else. Sometimes Julianne didn't know when to leave well enough alone.

We were a nice little family, Julianne and I and our two girls, until one day Julianne looked at me affectionately and asked, "John, what do you think about having another baby?"

I looked at her like she was completely out of her mind and said, "Are you nuts?"

"Wouldn't you like to have a son?" she posed.

"Listen Julianne," I apprehensively responded, "We're lucky we can afford the two kids we have now. Why do you want to add another major expense to our lives, and what makes you so sure if we do have another baby it's going to be a boy?"

"Where's your faith?" she questioned, "don't you think God's going to take care of us?"

I had no immediate reply but I was pretty sure I was content having things just the way they were. I wasn't one of those macho guys who aspired to having a son just so the family name could live on.

"What if our country's at war and our son is called for military duty, well there's no way I could allow him to go," I told Julianne in true hippie fashion, "did you ever consider that?"

"If that's the best reason you can come up with, well it's just not good enough," was her comeback.

For months we discussed the subject of a third child and I can't even count how often I would do anything to avoid having sex. It's incredible how sexy and seductive a woman can be when she wants something, especially a baby! Julianne was very much aware of her body clock and knew exactly when she was ovulating so I had to be very cautious and always one step ahead of her. Then one afternoon she hit me with a line that for some reason weakened my resistance and caused me to give in.

"John," she sighed, "I just won't ever feel complete as a woman if I don't have a third child!"

What could I have said? Well, this is what I said: "Okay, if I agree to give you a third child there has to be some stipulations. You have to agree in writing that you're going be the one getting up in the middle of the night. Even if this baby is a boy, you're going to be the one taking him to the rest room if we ever happen to be out with him."

"Whatever you say John, I agree," she happily responded, knowing that as usual she was about to get her way.

If I'm not mistaken, I believe it was on Julianne's birthday when Matthew was conceived, because I recall saying to her during that evening of romance, "Happy birthday honey, I hope this one takes!"

WORK BUDDIES

Although I wasn't very happy about having to spend a good part of my life as a UPS man, the company did provide excellent medical benefits and the opportunity to establish friendships with two very unique guys. Shawn Regan and I both started our careers at UPS at the very same time. Shawn is a full-blooded Irishman, has a striking resemblance to David Letterman and is one of the most brutally honest people on the planet. Shawn doesn't patronize anyone; he calls it just as he sees it. He would always lovingly say to me, "You're the only Italian guy I know with whom I can carry on a conversation without wanting to smack him in the head."

When I told Shawn the news about Julianne being pregnant with number three, he didn't reach out to shake my hand and say congratulations. Instead, he put his hands on my shoulders, looked me right in the eye and hollered at me, "What are you fucking crazy? What were you thinking? You make UPS wages, how are you going to support three kids?" Then he laughed, gave me a hug and his sincerest best wishes. I had to love him.

I'll always remember the day Shawn felt the need to confess to me his admission of defeat, the forfeiting of his bachelorhood, the announcement of his engagement.

"John," he stammered, "I'm getting mm...mmmm...mmmmar... married!"

I thought he was going to choke on those words. With Shawn, there was only one way I could have possibly reacted to his unexpected submission... so I did! I roared, "What are you fucking crazy? What are you thinking? You were my idol; I'm quickly losing respect for you man!"

Shawn laughed his ass off because he knew exactly what my reaction was going to be. He also knew there was a little truth in every word I said. I shook his hand and congratulated him.

I always assumed that Shawn, with his love of independence, his stubbornness, his unbending opinions, his yearly trips to Vegas, his obnoxious obsession with Shecky Greene, Buddy Hackett, and Jerry Lewis and his annual extravagant backyard parties, would always remain single. The first time I went to one of Shawn's parties I was blown away by the experience. The garage was set up like a gambling casino; blackjack, wheels of fortune, just name it. There were life size posters of Elvis, party lights, continuous music and a grass hut where he served fresh strawberry daiquiris exclusively. The food was extraordinary and plentiful, and if my memory serves me well, there was even a roasted pig. After attending one of his elaborate parties, one could easily recognize Shawn was a top-shelf guy who loved a good time.

Shawn and I once made a pact in the company locker room while changing into what we considered our dishonorable uniforms. "John!" he said holding back a belly laugh, "If you see me here five years from now, promise you'll shoot me and I promise I'll do the same for you!" We shook hands on it and laughed a sorry laugh. Whenever we discussed women and the problems that come along with relationships, Shawn always related a story that seemed to sum things up. When his wife gave birth to their son, he told me how he stood looking down upon his naked newborn child thinking, "Son, if I cut it off now, you wouldn't understand, but you'll surely thank me in the years to come!" Knowing Shawn is in the world has given me a crazy sense of security and camaraderie. I love him and will always treasure his friendship.

Another UPS character who joined the ranks a few years after I did, and managed to entangle his way into my heart and my life, is Johnny Fiore, or as we affectionately called him, Figgy. Fig is a really rough around the edges sort of guy. We could always count on him to grab the largest slice of pizza or drink the last drop of a bottle of soda, never considering that maybe someone else may have wanted it. Not a day would pass by, while at lunch, he would knock over his soft drink, spill yogurt on his shirt, or drop a spoonful of macaroni salad into his pocket. Figgy lives by following his base instincts, and although he'd often come across as someone who thinks only of himself, he's got a genuine heart of gold. With John, what people see is what they get. There's not a pretentious bone in his body, yet there is a naivety about him that makes me just love him. The day I broke the news to Figgy that a co-worker of ours, who we all believed had the perfect family, had just gotten a divorce, he looked at me with the same stunned expression a child has after being told there is no such thing as Santa Claus. "No way!!" he said, not knowing if I was putting him on or not, "You're kidding me!!" His eyes opened as wide as the heavens and with a smile that resulted from only astonishment, he whispered, "Holy shit!"

One afternoon as a group of us were having lunch, the word 'cunnilingus' entered the conversation and it was obvious Fig had no idea what the word meant. The look on his face was priceless when I explained to him the word's meaning, and ever since then, just for laughs, he saw to it that it became a regular part of his daily vocabulary.

John has a remarkable talent for doing impressions of unknown people, especially his fellow UPS workers. We knew exactly who it was he was imitating because he had an amazing ability to make his face transform into that person. Figgy would often entertain us with tales from his wild and misspent youth, most of which involved his overindulgence of booze, drugs or sex. Needless to say, he got his girlfriend pregnant, decided to do the right thing by marrying her, and that is precisely why he ended up in the UPS hellhole. I love Figgy like a brother and hope to remain in his company until the day one of us gets called to leave this planet. Both Shawn and John lessened the pain of having to show up for work every day. They hated the job as much as I did and I think the mutual hate helped to get us through the work week. They were both there to listen, console and advise me whenever I had to unload my troubles. They were the only guys who could tell me if and when I was acting like an asshole without me taking offense. Believe me, there have been times I needed to be told!

...AND THEN THERE WERE FIVE

Julianne went into labor on a hot August morning in 1987. This time I made my mind up that I was going to stay with her throughout the delivery and witness the birth of our third child. I stood right alongside her, holding her hand, feeding her ice chips, and coaching her breathing (which I remembered how to do from Lamaze class six years ago). Every twenty minutes or so the doctor would enter the room and examine her to see just how far along she was. There were some iridescent colored liquids coming out of my wife's body I swear Crayola would have been jealous of. It's no wonder why I waited in the lobby during her previous births. A few hours went by and I could tell by the apprehensive look on the doctor's face that things weren't going as smoothly as they should have. Jule had several wires hooked up to her so the doctor could monitor the baby's heartbeat. Lights were flickering, medical devices were beeping and I had no idea what was going on.

Julianne gazed at me helplessly and as she lied there shivering, she shuddered, "John, I can't keep from shaking!" When she spoke those words my eyes lit up as if the secrets of the universe had just been revealed. "Does anybody have a pen?" I asked frantically, as if the very fate of mankind depended upon it. A kind nurse handed me a pen and then on a piece of paper towel I wrote down the words, "I can't keep from shaking." "What a great title for a song!" I cried out and tucked the paper towel safely into my pants pocket. Jule shook her head and looking over at the nurse said, "He's out of his mind!"

Just like the labor she endured with Christiann, Jule was having a real tough time with the birth of child number three. She looked as if she was fighting a losing battle and appeared extremely fatigued. Tension showed in the doctor's face as he swiftly gave orders to have Julianne prepared for surgery, announcing he had no alternative than to perform a C-section. I felt like I was totally in everybody's way.

"This is my cue to leave," I whimpered, "I don't have the stomach enough for this!"

The doctor tossed me a surgical mask and declared, "No way, scrub up! You're going to stay by her side and get her through this!"

This was much more than I had bargained for. I was in quite an ironic situation. Having missed the natural births of our first two children, I was now a participant in the surgical procedure of removing our baby from the belly of its mother. Over and over I kept whispering in Jule's ear that everything was going to be all right. Then in a temporary moment of insanity (or what I thought was practicality at the time), I mentioned to the assisting nurse if it were at all possible for the doctor to tie Julianne's tubes, being he was already in there. Taken aback with my comment, the sweet gentle nurse slugged me in the arm and said, "How can you be so insensitive? This is neither the time nor the place to even suggest that!" Needless to say, I felt like quite the heartless jerk.

Time was moving right along and it was getting down to the nitty gritty. The drugs kicked in, Jule's mid-section was made to feel comfortably numb and the procedure was about to begin. I stood behind Julianne's head trying my best to keep her calm. The nurse was standing beside me trying to keep me calm. We kept telling each other how much we loved each other as I repeatedly kissed her cheek. (Not the nurses, Julianne's!) I was told not to look above the small curtain that had been placed just above Jule's belly as to block the view from the area where the doctor was cutting. It was like driving past the scene of a car wreck, trying hard not to look, yet not being able to resist. Well my friend the nurse saw to it that every time I attempted to take a peek she'd give me a whack.

"Okay everybody," the doctor happily announced, "It's a boy and here he is!" In what to me was an amazing fraction of time, he held up our son, fresh from his mother's womb, completely encased in a coating of blood, ooze and who knows what! They speedily ran our boy through the baby wash then placed him in Julianne's waiting arms. It was quite a fascinating moment to say the least!

So Julianne got the desire of her heart, and at the same time, the thorn in her side. Matthew was quite a handful right from his difficult entrance into the world. We started to wonder about him ever since the morning we found him in his crib with his face covered in paint chips. Most kids will chew on teething rings and the like; Matthew preferred enamel coated wood products. Most kids like to eat candy and sweets, Matthew made a habit of finding hair, rolling it about in his mouth and swallowing it. Without getting too graphic, I must mention there have been several occasions when either Julianne or I had to physically yank strands of hair out of Matt's bottom. I'm sure that must have helped Julianne in making her feel "complete as a woman!"

DOES HE MEAN SMEGMA?

It just so happened, at the time Matthew was born, the in-laws were up from Florida. They came to the hospital to see Julianne and their new grandson. After Julianne and the new baby were settled in at home, her mom and dad graced us with their company for the remainder of their visit. With Aunt Tess out of the picture, we now had the room for houseguests. As nice a guy as my father-in-law can be, he can also be very stubborn and opinionated. If he had something in his head, there was no way anyone was going to change his mind. Late one night, Julianne was sitting in the living room trying to unwind from yet another hectic day of being a mother of three, housewife and host to her parents. My mother-in-law had gone to bed but Jule's dad decided to stay up and chat with us for a while. I was getting tired and since I had to rise early for work in the morning, I said good night and went to bed. As my weary head sunk into the comfort of my soft fluffy pillow, I couldn't help but hear the conversation between Jule and her dad drift from the living room through the paper-thin sheetrock walls and into my bedroom.

"God! I can't believe what I'm hearing," I thought to myself. They were having a debate over the pros and cons of circumcision. As soon as Matt was born we had him circumcised. I don't know exactly why we made that decision, but since my brothers and I were circumcised, I just assumed my son should be. The fact that the doctor strongly recommended it was also a deciding factor. Obviously, my father-in-law was never circumcised because he was trying his hardest to present an argument against circumcision. I sat up in bed trying to catch every word. He accused us of depriving our son from a future of intense sexual pleasure by having him circumcised. He claimed that when the foreskin is removed, it causes the tip of the penis to callous and desensitize. I was thinking to myself, "No wonder he's got nine kids!" as I was trying to understand his pleasure principle. I was circumcised and if my penis were any more sensitive than it is, my heart would have exploded by now. If a man was circumcised prior to having any sexual activity, how could he possibly know the difference between what it was supposed to feel like with or without foreskin? Without getting into any of her newly learned Biblical history concerning circumcision and the covenant God made with Abraham, Julianne told her dad the reason we circumcise today is for health and hygienic reasons. The answer her dad gave her will live with me forever. "It's true Julianne," he said dead seriously, "it's very common that a cheesy substance can form around the tip of the penis if a man doesn't follow proper hygiene methods." I was rolling, "A cheesy substance! A cheesy substance, now I heard everything!"

Julianne finally came to bed, and seeing I was still awake, she shook her head laughing. I gave her look of amazement and without cracking a smile, asked seriously, "Honey, before you come to bed could you do me a favor?"

"What?" she said, "Haven't I just been through enough?"

"Get me some crackers. I have a cheesy substance on my penis!"

She broke up and whispered, "I don't know who's sicker, you or him!" pointing to where she just left her dad.

ALL IN A DAY'S WORK

Most Long Islanders, from what I'd seen, have very unusual relationships with their UPS men. I, for one, didn't and still don't understand it, but there seems to be a fascination with UPS guys. Maybe it's because the packages they deliver usually contain either something pleasurable or something of importance. Maybe it's the way they come and go so quickly that makes them seem so alluring and mysterious. Whatever the case may be, I'd met some very peculiar, some very fascinating, and some very wonderful people while working my route. I'd become such a familiar face to so many of my daily customer, they permitted me to walk right into their homes as if I were a member of the family. I've sat and eaten meals with some folks, watched television with others. Many customers have graciously invited me to swim in their pools whenever I desired. I was even extended an invitation to use a household's shower! Many evenings after coming home from work, I would try my best to convey, in detail, some of the experiences I'd had during the course of my day to amuse Julianne. People just never ceased to amaze us.

Mike the security guard was probably one of the most interesting characters I had ever come across. He was retired from the construction business and took a security position just to occupy his time. When I first encountered Mike he came stepping out of his guard booth with his clipboard in hand. He motioned for me to stop, and in true security guard fashion, jotted down my plate number. I could tell he was new on the job because nobody has ever written down the license number of my

UPS truck. Mike was a short man with a pale wrinkled complexion and although he once mentioned to me he was soon to be seventy, he looked more like ninety. At this particular stop, I would normally drive about a quarter of a mile to a delivery entrance where I would leave the packages in a mailroom. Mike was kind enough (or maybe I should say bored and inquisitive enough) to ask me if I preferred for him to sign for everything and then later he would distribute all the packages to their rightful places while making his rounds. I would do anything to save time, so I pulled over, and Mike helped me to carry the packages into the guard booth. I was able to tell that under his official security officer cap he had lost all but a few strands of silver hair. Around his neck he sported a thick silver chain and an unusually large crucifix that would pop out from under his shirt whenever he leaned over.

"So are you Italian?" he asked in a voice that sounded like he'd been smoking five packs of cigarettes a day for the last sixty years.

"Yeah," I answered, "how did you know?"

"You look like a fucking Italian. I'm Italian. Don't I look Italian?"

How could I have answered, but to say, "Yeah, you look like an Italian? In fact you kind of remind me of…"

"Fuck you! I don't look like anybody!" he snapped back. "Hey, my name's Mike, what's your name?"

I told him my name and I also told him I knew his name was Mike from the nametag on his pocket.

"Fuck you wise guy! I guess you're Catholic too then, huh?"

"No! I'm not Catholic…"

"What are you, Protestant?"

When I told him I was a Born Again Christian he went wild.

"If you're a fucking Italian then you're a fucking Catholic I don't give a shit what you say! Not another one of these fucking Born Agains! Jesus Christ!!"

Mike signed for the packages and as I went on my way he cried out, "Good fucking meeting you John, see you tomorrow!"

After a few days I got it. Mike was lonely as hell. He needed someone to talk to, tell his troubles to, and I was that someone everyday at eleven A.M. Mike looked forward to my daily deliveries and I looked forward to the stories that ached to jump out from his memory banks. Mike was a widower but loved to tell me stories of sexual prowess from his past.

"John, I used to be the greatest pussy eater of all time!" he bragged while smacking his lips.

Mike was most descriptive in all of his tales and too often he told me more than I cared to know. I listened not only because I felt sorry for him, but also because he was so damned funny. Within a few months I think I got to know just about everything there was to know about old Mike.

He enlightened me about his lactose intolerance, "I love drinking a nice tall glass of ice cold milk, but every time I do, without fail, I get the fucking shits!" It must have been my lucky day. I was there to witness it. He did get the shits! As comical as it was, it was also pretty pathetic having to listen to this worn-out old timer telling bizarre tales of his legendary youth. Mike was the only person I'd ever known to boast about being able to ejaculate further than any of his friends in a masturbating competition! He had a daughter in her forties who still lived at home with him. Mike confided in me that sometimes at night she would crawl into bed with him just like a little girl who needed her daddy.

"You know what John?" he asked one day in a pensive moment of deep concentration, "Tomorrow I think I'm gonna bring in my horn and blow. Yeah, I used to blow quite a saxophone!"

"No shit," I said, "I got to hear this!"

The very next day when I drove by the guard booth, there was Mike reclining the best he possibly could in a straight back chair. His head was down, his weary-looking saxophone was resting on his chest and his eyes were tightly shut. The only music I heard that morning were the grunts and groans of his snoring. I didn't have the heart to wake him.

Maria Jones was one of the sweetest human beings God had graced this planet with. The day I learned Maria was almost ten years my elder I nearly flipped. She looked incredible with not a single blemish or wrinkle on her soft velvety skin. One summer morning as I was walking up the stairs that led to her office, she happened to greet me at the landing. I was wearing the famous UPS brown shorts, which I thought made me look retarded, but Maria pointed at my legs, did a little wiggle and with the cutest smile said, "Ooh, would you look at those sexy legs!!"

That was the moment that broke the ice leading to a wonderful friendship. Morning after morning I would sit by her desk and we would tell each other countless stories about our lives. Personal problems, religion, politics, jokes, movies, music, we conversed about everything.

"John I have to tell you something," she said one day smiling, "I had a sex dream about you last night!"

"I don't know if I'm ready for this Maria," I said flattered, "it might make me look at you differently!"

She proceeded to tell me her dream.

"You walked over to my bedside and placed your hands under my covers and began to touch me. Slowly you reached down to kiss my body and I pushed your head away and said, 'No just your hands; just touch me with your hands!'"

"Whoa!" I thought out loud, "What in the world was the meaning of that dream and why are you telling me?"

We were both aware of the harmless flirtation going on between us, but I swear, we did it just for laughs. She once told me she could never have an affair with me because she couldn't see herself getting through it without laughing hysterically. That was okay, because I didn't see her in that way anyhow.

Maria had the most beautiful head of full, silky jet-black hair and though I'd never made mention of it, I truly admired it. Always up for a laugh, one morning Maria summoned me to meet her in the mailroom. She had this huge grin on her face and asked me to close my eyes and not open them until she said so. I had no idea what she was up to but went along with her little game.

"Okay you can open them now!" she said, and I nearly flipped when I opened my eyes to see Maria standing before me with her long gorgeous locks gone from her head.

"You've been wearing a wig?" I cried out in surprise, "I don't believe it!"

She and her sister Angie got the biggest kick out of seeing me with such an expression of shock on my face. Maria then explained to me how her military haircut was a result of the chemotherapy treatments she had undergone for breast cancer. I felt so bad but she assured me the cancer was in remission and she was going to be fine. She felt comfortable enough with me to share her secret and at the same time thought I'd find it hysterical to see her with a crew cut!

Occasionally our conversations centered on God and the great mysteries of religion. Maria was a semi-practicing Catholic and she would take me only half-seriously whenever I lectured her with my testimonies and whatever "Bible wisdom" that managed to stick with me after a Sunday service. Some of those discussions went on forever and never got even close to being settled. (It's amazing at how much I thought I knew until years later I realized I didn't know squat.) Now and then she'd get the evil eye from her boss, reminding her she wasn't on the payroll to be bullshitting with the UPS man. I told her the story about "the cheesy substance" and she laughed to the point of tears. The following day I brought her in a gift. I just knew how she was going to crack up after unwrapping a container of "Planter's Cheesy Balls." The continuing episodes of my in-laws would keep her in stitches and time after time she would try to encourage me to write all these stories down in a book.

Part of my normal everyday routine was making my way up the stairs that led to Maria's office. On this particular day she just happened to be standing at the top step, the very same place she stood on the day when she admired my sexy legs. Only on this day she wasn't smiling her usual smile. I knew her well enough to know something was terribly wrong.

"What's the matter Maria?" I asked apprehensively. She turned her head to hide her tears and walked with me into the privacy of the mailroom.

"Maria, you can tell me! For crying out loud, I'm the one you dream about!" I said, trying to lighten things up a little.

She took a deep breath, then trying to compose herself, clutched my hand and whispered sadly, "John, the cancer's back and the doctors say it's inoperable."

I didn't know what to say or how to react. I stood silent and helpless as I squeezed her hand. She asked me to hold her and as she fell into my powerless arms, I tried to reassure her everything was going to be all right. "I'll pray for you Maria," I said confidently.

She worked up a smile, said thanks and returned to her desk full of paperwork. Maria managed to keep her spirits up while undergoing chemotherapy treatments but after a while she became too weak and too frail to come to work. Eventually I learned she had been hospitalized. I made a few attempts to visit her but each time she was so drugged out, she wasn't even aware I was there. While I was at home relaxing one cold winter afternoon the ringing of the telephone disturbed me.

"Hello," I answered, "Oh no I'm so sorry…"

It was Angie who called to inform me her sister had lost the battle with cancer. While she was still fighting the disease in its early stages I wrote her a song. She asked me if she could hear it so I put on cassette and gave to her. A line from that song went, *"If anyone deserves a place in Heaven, Maria I swear it's you. If only I could be that strong…"*

IN HOT WATER

Summertime is brutal for UPS guys. The interiors of our trucks are always about fifty degrees hotter than the outside temperature. Our one hundred percent polyester uniforms hold in the heat, we sweat like pigs and by the end of the day we usually smell as rotten as low tide. I first met Mina and her three very lovely daughters, Janine, Laura and Doreen on such a summer day. Mina was divorced, lived in a huge house in a very wealthy neighborhood and ran her dress designing business from her home. From what I could tell, either she sold a hell of a lot of dresses or her ex-husband left her quite a bundle to afford living where she did. She was scheduled to be my last pick-up stop of the day. I dragged myself from my truck to the front door. I rang the bell, a big old dog barked wearily, and a frenzied Mina invited me to step inside.

"Hi, I'm Mina. Welcome to my crazy house." Stepping curiously down a long winding staircase behind her were two attractive young ladies.

"Let me introduce you to my girls. This is Laura," she said pointing to the older of the two, "and this is my Janine." For some reason I could tell she favored Janine, a beautiful slender girl with a warm smile, long straight black hair, and terrific figure. Janine looked to me as if she was in her late twenties.

"Hi, I'm John. It's a pleasure meeting you," I said awkwardly.

Mina cut in, "You'll be dealing with my girls because they take care of all of my shipping and receiving."

"Can you give us about twenty minutes?" Janine pleaded, "We still have to finish invoicing a few packages before we send them out."

Well since it was my job to keep the customer satisfied and since there was no way to resist the captivating look in Janine's eyes, I agreed to wait and the girls dashed back up the stairs to their office.

"Listen!" Mina suggested, "You look hot, why don't you cool off and take a swim in the pool while you wait. You look about the same size as my son Denny; I'll let you wear one of his bathing suits!" It sure sounded inviting but there was no way I was going to wear Denny's bathing suit or go swimming in someone's pool who I just met five minutes ago.

"No thanks," I replied shyly, "I'll just wait here until they're done packing."

"Then make yourself comfortable while you wait," she said while leading me into the den.

She persuaded me to sit on this remarkably cozy sofa, handed me a remote control and told me to feel free to watch whatever I pleased on her fifty-two inch wide screen TV. As she made her way out from the den, she pointed to their full-sized bar and said, "Make yourself at home. There's cold beer in the fridge and the bar is open...and it's going to be hot tomorrow, don't forget to bring your bathing suit!"

Thirty minutes later, the girls helped me carry the boxes to the truck, gave me a cheerful thank you and a big wave as I backed out of their long driveway. "Can you imagine?" I pondered, "I'm just their UPS guy. They don't know me from a hole in the wall. This is going to be one crazy stop!"

The very next day I took Mina up on her very friendly offer by bringing my swimming trunks. The heat was excruciating and the only thing I could think about was taking a dive into the cool revitalizing water of that pool. Once again the girls weren't quite prepared with the packing of the day's shipments and Mina inquired, "Well did you bring your suit?" When I told her I did, she seemed so delighted I graciously accepted her offer to go swimming.

"You can change in here," she said showing me the bathroom, "and when you're ready, you know the way. Have fun!" I found my way out to the backyard where stretched out before me was the shimmering clear blue water of their gorgeous in-ground pool. I stepped out onto the diving board and without hesitation splashed down into a refreshing moment of utter delight.

"Who's got it better than me?" I asked myself as I peacefully drifted about on an oversized float, tranquilized by the penetrating rays of the late afternoon sun. Feeling as if at any moment I was going to fall right to sleep, the sound of a barking dog startled me. I quickly looked up only to find Mina, Janine, Laura, Doreen and the dog, frolicking about in the pool beside me. Eight fairly large boobs all supported by skimpy bikini tops surrounded me. "My God," I thought while trying hard not to stare, "if my boss saw me now I'd surely get fired. Never mind that, if Julianne saw me now I'd have some explaining to do!"

I didn't want any of the ladies to think I was feeling uneasy about being in a pool with four beautiful women, so I stayed in the water for just a few more minutes before making a tactful exit. I don't have anything against dogs, but the floating pet hair also prompted me to get out when I did.

"Oh don't go," sighed Janine, "we just got in!"

"My boss is going to wonder where the hell I am," I answered, "and I had better hit the road. Thanks for the swim! I'll see you all tomorrow."

I dried off with one of Mina's oversized fluffy beach towels, changed back into my uniform then loaded their freight into my truck. While on my way back to the UPS building I had all to do to keep my mind on my driving. I was imagining all the wild possibilities. Penthouse Forum readers would have loved them.

Throughout the years as Mina's UPS man, a genuine friendship was established between the girls and me. She considered me part of their family, always extending an open invitation for Julianne and me to attend all of her parties and family functions. We accepted the one to Laura's wedding on the "World Yacht" out of New York harbor and had a really good time, even though it was a little strange being among all of her relatives and high society friends and introduced as "our UPS guy!" Working side by side with Janine on a daily basis launched an intimacy between us that was awkward yet strangely addicting. It eventually became quite a struggle trying to keep my head on straight!

THE BEST LAID PLANS

Upon walking into the front door of our residence, there was a small flight of steps one would have to climb before reaching the living room. At the top of these stairs we kept a safety gate in place for the obvious reason of having an active toddler living on the premises. One morning, before I had to leave for work, Julianne and I were just hanging out in our bedroom talking. I don't know why I didn't heed the warning when it first occurred to me that maybe I should check to see if the safety gate was closed. Suddenly we heard the patter of Matthew's quick little feet go racing through the hallway, followed by the chilling sound of loud tumbling, a thud and unnerving crying. Fully aware of what just happened, the two of us made a mad dash to the living room and found Matthew, just as I suspected, lying on his back at the bottom of the stairs. Julianne let out with a bloodcurdling scream and fell helplessly to the kitchen floor sobbing, "Oh Jesus no! Please God no!"

I'd always been curious as to why fear and dread seemed to override faith in times of trouble. I flew down the stairs and swept Matthew up into my arms. There was no blood or signs of disorientation so I knew there was no need for panic. My immediate problem was getting Julianne to snap out of it. When she saw our son was coherent she was finally able to compose herself. Our hearts got some workout that morning. It was either by the grace of God or the simple fact that toddlers are so limber, Matthew was amazingly unharmed.

They say "all good things must come to an end" and "nothing lasts forever?" Well, Jule and I knew exactly what those expressions meant when we got an unexpected call from Aunt Tess in Florida, announcing her decision to return to the Freeport living quarters which we had so nicely converted into a playroom for our kids. She told us a future phone call would alert us as to her date of arrival. We were quite upset over this sudden news and knew there was nothing we could do to prevent it because her brother owned the house. He would evict us before leaving his sister without a place to live.

It was in the middle of a Saturday afternoon, when without warning, Tess arrived with an entourage of her siblings to help move her back in. We were freaking out. They had caught us completely off guard and were adamant about us getting our belongings out of her apartment immediately. Under my breath, just soft enough so they could hear me, I cursed and swore like an enraged lunatic to let them know how pissed off I was. I knew I wasn't doing a very good job of displaying my Christianity but I didn't really give a shit. She not only ruined our weekend, but also took over an area of the house we furnished and decorated with our hard earned money. I'm probably one of the nicest guys in the world, but that afternoon I was very much out of character, behaving like the biggest prick on the planet. It took us a few hours to move all of our belongings from what was once Tess's apartment. We piled them up in any available space we could find and as we stared at the heap of stuff sitting in the center of our living room, I said, "Babe, we've got to buy our own house. It's time!"

About a week or so later we received a bitter note in the mail from Jule's uncle Sal, our landlord. In his spiteful letter he made it known to us there would be a considerable rent increase and in so many words he advised us to start looking for a new place to reside. So the search began and for the next few months Julianne, the kids and I spent weekend after weekend in the company of hungry ambitious realtors, driving all over Long Island looking for an affordable house.

The adventure of purchasing a first home is a book in itself. It was exceedingly frustrating not being able to afford anything that appealed to us. It was even more frustrating to know we could barely afford the homes that didn't appeal to us. The experience was so trying, Julianne was ready to give up and stay put, but there was no way I could live in that cold, unfriendly environment any longer. Aunt Tess would go out of her way just to avoid seeing us and we would do the same. If she saw the kids outside playing, she would acknowledge them with a quick hello, but she wouldn't even make eye contact with us. It really was a terrible way to live for all involved.

Totally frustrated with house hunting and the high cost of living on Long Island, at the suggestion of my brother-in-law Artie, I left Jule and the kids briefly and flew out to Arizona to seek employment, a home and to see if the grass was truly greener out west. Sitting by myself on the airplane, gazing out at the clouds, gave me several hours to meditate. "What in the world was I doing?" I wondered. Since the day we were married I'd never been anywhere without Julianne and it felt very unnatural. I wasn't even in the sky for an hour and I missed my family tremendously. I started to visualize what it might be like should things work out and we decide to settle down out west. "I have to be out of my mind. I can't leave my family and friends!" I thought to myself, "This trip is a waste of time!" Not that I didn't love Artie and Mary, but there would be just too many people removed from our daily lives should we relocate. I had to try and convince my brother-in-law and sister-in-law to move back to New York instead.

It was towards the end of July and to say it was hot would be an understatement. The temperature reached as high as 118 degrees. The streets were pretty much deserted because no one could stand to be outdoors. The next time some smart ass tells me, "Yeah, it's hot but it's a dry heat!" I'm going to smack him in the head! In fact it was so dry, I felt as if every drop of my body's natural moisturizers had vaporized.

Having spent a couple of days looking at real estate, I learned that even though the cost of housing was a little more affordable in Arizona, from the constant running of the air conditioning, the electric bills were so enormous, the expense of owning a home was comparable to that of New York. I also visited some employment agencies and learned the job market was terrible. A very honest agent at one agency told me bluntly, "Listen John, you've got a good job with great benefits and a pension back home. Don't believe for a minute you're going to find paradise in the suburbs of Phoenix. The grass isn't always greener, you know what I mean?" I thanked her for her honesty and made up my mind to spend the remainder of the week bumming around with Arthur. Bum around is exactly what we did. We ate, we drank, we swam, we soaked up the sun, and we swam and drank some more. At night we conked out on the couch while watching movies, then get up in the morning to repeat the process. I don't recall showering or shaving until the day I left for home! Hanging around with Art made me realize just how much I was going to enjoy retirement one day!

A HOUSE IS NOT A HOME

We finally made a monumental decision by agreeing to stay in Freeport. We'd already been living in the town for almost eight years. By this time we had established some new roots, some new friendships and the kids were settled in the schools. Besides, out of all the towns we researched, the unassuming racially mixed little village of Freeport was the most affordable for us. Although the price of real estate was ridiculously high at the time we purchased our home (thanks only to an advance in inheritance money from my parents), it wasn't nearly as astronomical as it had become. We figured if we really tightened our belts (not that they weren't tightened to begin with) we could actually swing a mortgage. The house we settled on was by no means our dream house, but it was fairly new, was on a really nice block, and all the neighbors seemed very friendly. In fact, we were invited to their block party a few weeks before we moved in and had a pretty good time. Christiann, Samantha and Matthew were thrilled to learn that living all around us were potential playmates. I met Jerry who lived three doors down. Jerry was a recording engineer/producer who gave me a full tour of the full-blown recording studio that was built right into his house. He told me he was looking forward to hearing my music and possibly working together.

While sitting on my future neighbor's stoop, I gazed across the street at the dozens of kids trampling across what was soon-to-be my lawn, thinking with a slight touch of pride, "This could very well turn out to be a good thing!" Little did I know the misery waiting in the wings.

I'd heard stories from fellow first time homebuyers how on closing day, with their few remaining dollars, they would either go out to lunch, dinner, or even drinks to celebrate the occasion. I had every intention that after our tedious ordeal of signing paper after paper and writing out check after check, Julianne and I would partake in such a celebratory meal together. Julianne thought otherwise. She wanted to go straight home. She didn't seem to think closing on our first house was any reason to celebrate.

"This was all your idea," she told me, "I hate that house!"

"Hey, nobody was holding a gun to your head to sign those papers," I retorted, "If you hate the house so much, you had the power to get out of it!"

I couldn't believe it. Most couples looked upon their closing as an exciting and joyful experience. Julianne and I argued the entire way home.

Before actually moving in, we spent endless hours scrubbing, scraping, pulling up soiled carpet, taking down tacky wallpaper, sweeping, vacuuming and basically doing a general but thorough clean up. I never realized just how filthy the house was. There were things growing in the refrigerator that defied description. The toilets required blasting to remove some of the nasty fragments that adhered to the porcelain. If I was extremely grossed out then I could only imagine how sickened Julianne must have been. When it comes to cleanliness and order, I challenge anyone to find a person as fanatical as my wife. After days of inhaling the potentially dangerous fumes from a vast array of household cleaners and working to the point of drop-dead exhaustion, we called on a professional painter to put a fresh coat of paint on every wall in the place. The house was now ready to be inhabited.

Moving day was yet another nightmare. Weeks in advance I went to the local truck rental, left a deposit and reserved a large enough truck to accommodate our move. When the big day arrived, I went to pick up my vehicle bright and early that morning only to find they did not have one available. Somebody screwed up. It was Labor Day weekend and there wasn't a truck to be had anywhere. I had absolutely no choice but to rent the only small van they had left on the premises. All of our family members must have had previous engagements because none of them showed up to help us. While Jule and I started loading the van with the first of many loads of our possessions, we got an unexpected visit from Paul, Carl, Jim and Randy along with their cars, van and station wagon.

These lifesavers were friends from our church who helped tremendously in lightening the burden and the torture of moving. I was deeply grateful for their help, but in all honesty, I cannot go without mentioning the endless interjections of "Praise the Lord" and "Thank You Jesus" were getting a bit nerve racking. I genuinely liked these people but I could clearly detect we were running on entirely different wavelengths. Jesus may be wonderful, but if I heard his name once that day, I heard it at least ten thousand times! Nevertheless, I thank God they were there because without their help it would have taken us an eternity. It took the entire day to get our mission accomplished. If moving shed a light on anything, it was just how much crap we accumulated in such a short time. Boy, did we have junk!

We still had a long haul ahead of us. Boxes upon boxes were impatiently waiting to be unpacked. Furniture needed to be situated. The property needed a major landscaping makeover. It certainly seemed like the next few months were going to bring with them no rest and relaxation whatsoever. Julianne felt the brunt of the move much more than I did because she was the one at home all day dealing with the organizing, the decorating, the shopping and the children. I would come home from work only to find a tired and irritable wife who saw no light at the end of the tunnel.

Way back in the days when I was a kid, I never lacked for friends. There was always somebody ringing our doorbell or calling on the telephone asking if and when I'd be coming out to play. As soon as I would get home from school, I would race through my homework then be out the door involved in a game of touch football, stickball, freeze tag or something to keep me busy until it was time to come in for dinner. During the time we were living at Uncle Sal's place, there were really no other kids in the vicinity who would come knocking at our door looking for our children to come out and play. Occasionally, a "play date" would be arranged with other classmates, where the parents would be involved in the dropping off and the picking up of the kids at each other's houses. Most of the time, Christiann, Samantha and Matthew kept occupied with indoor activities such as playing with dolls, watching videos or waiting for visits from their grandparents. Whenever they were outside, we never had to worry about them roaming too far from the front steps. The only kids on the block lived next door and mostly kept to themselves. To say we were overprotective is debatable. Julianne liked having things in control. Our world was simple and uncomplicated. There was order. I went to work, Julianne tended to the house and to the kids. When I came home from work, we had dinner as a family. After the dinner dishes were done, we watched some television, and then the kids then took their baths, had a little dessert and went to bed. Things weren't running as smoothly in our new home.

Our doorbell was constantly ringing and nine out of ten times it was the neighborhood kids looking for our kids to come out to play. This was all new and very exciting for Christiann, Samantha and Matt. Whenever they heard the sound of the doorbell ringing, they would dart to the front door knowing it may very well be an opportunity to get out of the house. The opposite was true for Julianne. She found it new and very unexciting. Little by little she felt as if she was losing control of the children. She wasn't used to having the kids wander out of her sight and she wasn't used to having the neighbors' kids congregate at our house. Julianne and I were raised in very different households. I was accustomed to having my friends hang out at my house all the time; to me this was a normal way of life and had always expected it would be the same for my children. This was the beginning of the two of us not being able to see eye to eye in our methods of parenting. Daddy was soon looked upon as the easy-going parent and mommy became known as the heavy. I started to see a side of Julianne I didn't understand. Knowing she didn't really have the greatest childhood, I wondered why she wasn't just a bit more lenient with her own children. Our arguments became more frequent and they almost always had to do with the kids, or should I say how I dealt with them.

AUNT TRAILS

My conscience began to trouble me continually about the way we left off with Aunt Tess. So often in church I heard it preached that Jesus said, "If you can't love your brother who you can see, then how can you love your Father in heaven who you cannot see?" I didn't have an enemy in the world and I wanted to keep it that way, so I wrote Tess a letter of apology. At the time I wasn't being the least bit understanding of her situation. I acted selfishly, un-Christian like and said some things that were uncalled for. I needed to make things right between us.

About a month or so after mailing her the letter, we met at a family function. Words were almost unnecessary. We exchanged hugs, said we loved each other and have been comrades ever since. The awkwardness among me and Julianne with her aunts and uncles was finally resolved. At the time, no one could have convinced me otherwise, the problem was remedied by the healing hands of God in response to a simple act of obedience...forgive!

Whenever we spoke with my mother-in-law from Florida, she would always be sure to update us on all the latest adventures and misadventures of the family, whether we asked to hear about them or not. Aunt Helen, who I will admit can leave one with the impression of being a bit eccentric, was often a topic of conversation. As I mentioned several times already, Bible-toting Helen was the one responsible for single-handedly leading a major part of her family to Christ. Aunt Helen had taken on the reputation of becoming a "church hopper," because according to all the latest reports, she wasn't being fulfilled in any one of the churches she was attending. She bounced from denomination to denomination trying desperately to find a place where she felt spiritually comfortable. We had heard she even stumbled back into the Catholic Church for a short time. Many times it was insinuated Helen was just crazy and when she finally found a home among the Messianic Jews, it only reinforced the thought. "Your Aunt Helen thinks she's Jewish," Jule's mom would snicker, "and she goes around saying things like 'Shalom.'"

Truthfully, Julianne and I initially agreed Helen was losing it. It was on one of our trips to Florida we had the opportunity to reunite with her. I couldn't help but take notice of how peaceful she seemed and how calm and soft-spoken she was. She had a whole new approach to the business of God. She now referred to Him as Yahweh and Jesus as Yehshua. She greeted us with "Shalom" instead of her usual "Praise the Lord". Although knowing that we thought she was nuts seemed to amuse her, I felt she was also confident one day we would understand.

One thing I couldn't understand about Helen, however, was how a woman who was so into the Word of God was able to smoke cigarettes the way she did. I guess we all have our vices, but it was those damned cigarettes that cut her life short. We learned Aunt Helen had been diagnosed with lung cancer. What I found to be extraordinary was the attitude she had after learning about her life threatening condition. She blamed nobody but herself, fully understanding she had to accept the consequences of poisoning herself by smoking for so many years. She often told me that only through obedience do blessings come. She looked at her smoking habit as an act of disobedience, defiling her body, the temple of the Holy Spirit. She was all too aware of the penalty.

Helen's body was flown up to New York where the family held the funeral service. As sad as it was, it was also one of the most joyful funerals I'd ever attended. Helen's request was honored as a Messianic Rabbi presided over the services. He spoke highly and lovingly of Aunt Helen, her love of God and her dedication to seeking truth. All but a few of the people in attendance were Roman Catholic so they obviously had no clue as to what was going on. No "Hail Mary's?" No Rosary Bead of roses? I had a sneaking suspicion Helen may have been onto something. It's too bad she didn't stick around a little longer to clue us in. Shalom!

GOING THROUGH THE CHANGES

Julianne was never very good at dealing with change. Once she situated a piece of furniture in what she felt was its proper place, that's where it stayed...forever! "A place for everything and everything in its place" led the list of her household rules. Heaven forbid something was moved ever so slightly, there was no chance it would escape Julianne's watchful eye. With this neurotic mindset, one could only imagine how she handled moving. I believe our relationship took a turn for the worse as soon as we were given the keys to our new home, or should I say house. In all fairness to Julianne, I admit moving can be overwhelming, but Rome wasn't built in a day. From this point on, nothing seemed to make her happy and as the saying goes, "When mommy's miserable, everybody's miserable!"

Life moves on and whether we like it or not, along with it comes change. Right around the same time we moved, another event occurred that Julianne had a very difficult time coping with, her fortieth birthday. For some reason, turning forty had caused her great distress. She refused to celebrate or even acknowledge it was her birthday. I couldn't help but recall her twentieth, when after a night of "Bummer Bowling," the whole gang met back at my parents' house where we threw her an impromptu surprise party. My mom baked a cake and everyone who was there showed Julianne just how much she was genuinely cared for. She even welcomed her thirtieth birthday by proudly displaying her age on a tee shirt my sister had made for her. On the morning of her fortieth, however, Julianne got into her car then disappeared for the entire day. She opened no presents, answered no telephone calls and distanced herself from everyone who loved her.

The months ahead were trying, to say the least. Julianne just didn't seem pleased about anything. I think because she was so besieged by a combination of things, it caused her to lose sight of what was really important. Number one, the house needed tons of work and she wasn't crazy enough about the house to do the work. She had her heart set on buying a big old Victorian. The trouble was, the available number of charming old homes needed major renovation, including electrical and plumbing, and at the time there was no possible way we could afford it. Number two, our house needed cosmetic work and we didn't have the money to afford even that. Number three, being we were now entering our forties, she thought we should have already been settled and all this work should have been well behind us. Number four; our kids weren't toddlers any more. Number five, something hormonal was stirring and no woman wants to confront or even admit that. Number six was my lackadaisical attitude towards everything.

I never knew who I was coming home to. Some nights I'd walk in the front door and get welcomed with, "Hi honey how was your day?" and more times than I could emotionally handle, I'd be welcomed by ice-cold silence. Not fully understanding Julianne's frame of mind and feeling sorry for myself, I took on the role as a victim. I resented the fact I broke my ass at work every day and had to come home to deal with a despondent and discontented housewife.

HERE COMES TROUBLE

One of the major differences between Julianne and me has always been that I'll talk about our problems with almost anyone, while she tends to keep things very private. If someone lends a sympathetic ear, I will pour my heart out. Janine was very attentive and very sympathetic. Each evening while I sat in her office doing my paperwork, we'd tell each other our woes. She was having her share of problems with her fiancé and I was her shoulder to cry on. I was still getting out most of my frustrations and expressing my many feelings by writing songs. Jule's been hearing my songs for years now, and at this stage of our lives, she just wasn't impressed anymore. Janine, on the other hand, was my captive audience. She told me time and time again how much she loved my songs and admired my talent. I was starving for the attention, the appreciation and the admiration, and found myself slowly wandering into what could have easily become a dangerous situation. Arriving at Mina's every evening was becoming the highlight of my working day. Janine knew I liked wine so almost every day during the winter months there was an open bottle of red wine waiting for me. During the summer months, it was usually a six-pack of ice-cold beer that awaited me. I would pull away from the house, smack myself in the face and say, "Why the hell do you even entertain these ideas when you know nothing's going to happen? Anyway, you're supposed to be a Christian!"

Janine was sweet, kind, encouraging and she filled my head with all the things I needed to hear. From time to time she would tell me what a good guy I was and that should Julianne ever leave me she'd gladly take her place. The flattery was overwhelming at times, and what guy doesn't enjoy being flattered? I could only imagine what the neighbors thought when they saw my truck stationed in her driveway for hours at a time every evening. The truth is, vulnerability may have done a number on my imagination, but when I wasn't chitchatting with the family, I was just watching Mina's big screen TV. What seems incongruous to me now was the way I would get up on my soapbox and preach to Janine and her family about Jesus and the need to be "Born Again" whenever I heard them discuss anything that had to do with their defending Catholicism. Mina would get aggravated with me, point her finger in my face and say, "Don't you go talking to me about God, because God has no favorites!"

How could any one of them have taken me seriously? I was drinking on the job and not at all responsibly, and it was clearly obvious what mind games Janine and I were playing with each other. Life at home was far from paradise, but I always regarded myself as someone who could rise above the problems. No matter what fantasies wandered about in my head, I knew in my heart I could never be unfaithful to Julianne. It was a very confusing time and I was most definitely battling it out with my conscience. When I confided in my good buddy Shawn, by telling him about "this girl on my route," he was good enough to remind me, "Why complicate things. One woman in your life is trouble enough. Don't be an asshole."

YOU DON'T KNOW JACK!

My Uncle Jack was my father's brother and for most of his life he lived in either Chicago or somewhere in Pennsylvania. Every once in a while he'd pass through New York to visit my grandparents, so at least it gave me the opportunity to know what he looked like. Jack was divorced twice and several years after my grandfather had passed away, he moved to New York and shared an apartment with my grandmother. She lived on the top floor of a six-story building in Flushing, Queens. It was adjacent to the apartment my Aunt Jean and Uncle Hank lived in. The years passed and so did Grandma and Uncle Hank. Aunt Jean remained alone in her apartment and Uncle Jack in Grandma's. Jack loved his booze, his cigarettes, his women and his dog Pepper. He had a bum leg and walked with a very noticeable limp. The booze and the smokes did their job on making Jack appear older than he was. His bulging eyes were usually bloodshot and his drinker's nose was red from the many broken capillaries. In spite of his eroded worn-out appearance, he still considered himself quite the ladies' man. Couldn't help but to love him!

When our daughters were young, Aunt Jean used to take them on shopping sprees and buy them fancy dresses in Lord & Taylor. Because Jean didn't drive, Julianne would pick her up, and then drop her off at her apartment always making it a point to stop in next-door to visit Uncle Jack, in spite of the dog hair and the stale smell of pets and tobacco. Jack loved getting visits from Jule and the girls and they held a special place in his heart. Especially Julianne, he was crazy about Julianne! Just the simple act of her dropping by to say hello meant so much to Jack. As the years quickly paraded by, Jack's health started failing. He was in the hospital and it didn't appear he was going to be around much longer. All the times I had conversed with my uncle it was always small talk; family, womanizing, work, womanizing…We never spoke about anything spiritual and now that he was getting close to the edge of eternity, I felt driven to speak with him. One afternoon I took the forty-minute drive into Queens to visit Jack in the hospital. I stood beside his bed, looked down upon the frail frame of the man and wondered what in the world must have been going through his mind. For most of the visit I held onto his hand while we made eye contact. We didn't talk much, we said a lot without words. I gave him a kiss goodbye and told him I'd see him again later in the week. "Give my best to Julianne and the kids," he murmured. I made my way out of the hospital and back to my car, mad at myself for not saying what I had planned on saying to him. While heading for home I thought to myself, "What if he dies today without hearing what I should have told him?" I was about five miles away from the hospital when something compelled me to turn around and go back to tell Jack what was so heavy on my heart. When I entered the room he appeared to be a little confused by seeing me again so soon.

"What did you do, forget something?" he faintly asked.

"Yeah Uncle Jack, I did. I forgot to ask you something pretty important and I'm not going to be able to rest until I do."

"What's up?" he asked most curiously.

I was feeling a bit awkward about saying what I knew I had to say, nevertheless, I pushed out the words. "Uncle Jack," I softly spoke, "the funny thing about life is we all know the inevitable yet we try our best to ignore it. What I'm trying to say is, uh, everybody wants to get to heaven but nobody wants to die…"

"What exactly are you trying to tell me John?" he interrupted.

"Uncle Jack," I continued, "do you believe in Jesus Christ and that He died for our sins so we could enter heaven and have eternal life?"

Jack smiled and said reassuringly, "Johnny, I've had a lot of time to meditate. Don't worry; God and me are okay. I believe. Now go on home to your family, I'm going to be okay!"

I held his hand, kissed him on the forehead and told him for the last time, "Love you Uncle Jack!" I returned home with a sense of relief. Even if what he told me wasn't true, at least I knew he'd be giving it some thought.

Within the week Jack stepped into eternity. Wherever that may be…

   One by one all the appliances in our new home started breaking down. First it was the dishwasher, followed by the stove, then the refrigerator and the clothes dryer. It almost seemed as if the house was cursed. This only added to the frustration Julianne had of owning a home she didn't love. As for me, I can deal with almost anything. Just like every other suburban family, whose houses became money-pits by charging the things necessary to keep their homes functioning, we could do the same. It's the American way. You don't need money to get things done, just good credit.

   Just as we were about to dive even deeper into credit card debt, we got a very pleasant surprise. Uncle Jack didn't have much to his name when he died, but a lot of what he did have he left to Julianne and I. Thanks to Jack we were not only able to replace all of our broken appliances, but we did a complete kitchen renovation and were still able to purchase some new furniture. Because nothing was left to any of my siblings, the situation was very delicate. My Aunt Jean was with Jack when he made out his will and he left it up to her to handle his estate. We were asked to keep my uncle's generosity and favoritism a secret, but how were we going to explain our major renovation to those who knew of our financial position? Needless to say, word got out and we took a fair share of needling from my family. Their jealousy pissed me off a little because I would never deny my brothers or sister any good fortune. The fact is we needed it at the time, they didn't.

JIMMY THE GREEK

Another blessing came our way when Jimmy, our friend from church, agreed to take on the job of doing our home improvements. Jimmy's a Greek fellow, very stubborn and set in his ways, yet from what I could tell, a real man of God. "Bless you brother, let's pray!" was something I could always expect Jimmy to say. He would stop what he was doing to pray with anyone, anywhere for any reason. Jimmy was a contractor and did meticulous work. Julianne loved having him around, not only because of how fastidious he was, but because as he worked they would discuss "churchy" things. I guess if I had to leave me wife at home all day long with a contractor, I should consider myself blessed it was Jimmy. As a homeowner, one of the many things I learned was, when dealing with any repairman, serviceman, carpenter, or contractor, prepare to get screwed! Jimmy worked just the opposite; he screwed himself. He did the job for less than half the amount of any estimate we were given and he did the job twice as good as any other general contractor would have done. No matter how much more money I tried to pay him, he refused to accept it.

Jim and I became more than just church acquaintances. After he completed my kitchen, we started going out for coffee every other week or so, just to talk. Julianne thought it would be beneficial for me to be in the company of a Christian man. As rugged a man as Jimmy seemed to be, he would never take the first sip of coffee or nibble of pastry without first saying a prayer. I thought he was a bit much, but I can adjust to almost any situation; if he wanted to pray, I just went along.

Jimmy and his wife Peggy appeared to live their lives based upon very rigid Bible principles. They were both so well versed in scripture, quoting Bible verses from memory so frequently during conversations, I felt spiritually inadequate being in their presence. Unlike Julianne and me, Jim and Peggy never listened to rock and roll, never watched "R" rated movies and never used foul language, living quite the exemplary lifestyle. Peggy came across like a sweet, soft-spoken, modest, almost angelic woman, who in compliance to scripture was totally submissive to her husband. I was under the impression their household was in perfect order and in accordance with God's word, something I knew we could never achieve. A submissive wife was something I just wasn't accustomed to! I was the head of my house as long as I did things Julianne's way!

The talks Jimmy and I had usually centered on our marriages. I complained and he listened. He complained and I listened. After spending so much time with Julianne, he couldn't help but notice how particular she was about things. "God bless you brother," he said sympathetically, "That wife of yours can pick out imperfections the good Lord himself couldn't detect!" Then he would preach to me, sympathetically, about how her focus should not be on minute details and the material things of this temporary life. "What's he telling me for?" I'd be thinking, "Try telling my Julianne! Maybe she'll listen to you!"

Jimmy opened up to me a little bit more than I thought he would and I was actually shocked to learn even a Godly man like him had marital problems. I thought only we worldly guys, with one foot in the world and one foot in the church, had troubles of those sorts. He hated that his wife didn't keep a tidy household, something I surely couldn't relate to! I hated that Julianne was so clean!

I found it extremely odd how my nights of fellowship with Jim usually turned into wife-bashing sessions. "You can't live with them brother, and you can't kill 'em!" Hearing Jimmy vent, reason, and quote scripture to support his views, was starting to make me believe maybe God was a chauvinist, or that He created women just to torture us! Jimmy had carnal thoughts and temptations just like me and every other red-blooded male. If Jim and Peggy, who were so rooted in "The Word," were having trouble in the marriage department, then what chance did a lukewarm Bible dabbler like I have? All of our talking and we came to one conclusion: men will never understand women and vice-versa, Christian or not! We never arrived at a single solution for any one of our problems.

As much as marriage seemed to present one frustration on top of another, Jimmy's recommendation was, "Just keep your eyes upon Jesus, my brother." He closed each evening with the same familiar prayer, "Father thank You for my brother John and this time of fellowship…" Each time I bowed my head, and as Jimmy grabbed my hand while continuing to pray, I thought, "Oh brother, no more prayers, people are starting to look at us funny!"

DELIVER ME...

It's supposed to be the work of every obedient, evangelical Christian to spread the Good News about salvation and the promise of eternal life through Christ. If and when the day comes when I may have to stand before the judgment seat, I would surely want to hear the words, "Well done my good and faithful servant!"

Mrs. Deyo was a dainty sweet gentle woman. I learned soon after meeting her that she was a widow. She resided and worked on my route so I saw her often, if not at one place then at the other. She lived alone, so I guessed she was lonely and seized every opportunity to strike up a conversation with me. UPS guys don't have the liberty to stay in one place for too long, so I always politely tried to cut our discussions short, so I could be on my busy little way.

One day I suddenly realized I hadn't seen Mrs. D at her workplace in a while. Being inquisitive, I asked about her, only to find out she had taken ill. It wasn't long after hearing the unpleasant news when I started making deliveries of mail order prescription drugs to her home on a regular basis. Within weeks I saw her condition worsen and the tell-all kerchief on her head said it all...cancer and chemotherapy. Not even two months prior, she was lifting boxes and stocking shelves at the gift shop where she was employed, and now Mrs. D was so weak it was an effort for her just to come to the door. Many times I would let myself in only to find her slouched helplessly on her sun-faded sofa among boxes of saltine crackers and pill bottles. In a barely audible voice she thanked me for my kindness, and behind an expression of defeat, agony and anger, she painfully conceded her time was short.

Each time I made my way from her front doorsteps back to my truck, I felt as if I were moving in slow motion, growing increasingly powerless and more depressed. I witnessed firsthand what appeared to be a perfectly healthy woman reduced to skin and bones. In my mind I could envision myself taking that bold step in faith, laying my strong hands upon her frail body and crying out with every ounce of my strength, "In the precious name of Jesus, be healed!" Sadly enough, my doubt and fear of ridicule won over and I never even attempted to test the waters by taking a stab at intercessory healing. I never once doubted God could heal, I just didn't think He was going to do it through me. The parable about the mustard seed says volumes... "Faith the size of a tiny mustard seed could move mountains..." How little faith did I have, or where was it I wanted to move those mountains?

One afternoon, however, as I was about to pull away from my dying friend's house, something overpowering stopped me dead in my tracks. Although I was reluctant at first to obey my inner voice, I knew what I had to do. As if I were being forcibly led, I returned to Mrs. Deyo's front door and rang the bell. Knowing how weak she was, I felt bad disturbing her, but at that moment I truly believed a higher force was compelling me to do so. When she finally made her way to the door, I was greeted by a look of puzzlement.

"I don't recall ordering anything else," she said with great effort.

"Listen!" I gently spoke, "This is probably going to sound nuts but I have to ask you something important."

Balancing herself between her cane and the arm of a couch, I motioned for her to please sit down because I was afraid her bones would snap in two, even from the pressure of what little body weight she had. As she slowly and carefully took a seat amongst the pile of blankets, old magazines and outdated newspapers, she did her best to give me her attention.

"Mrs. D," I said as sympathetically as I could, "Death is a part of life we're all going to have to face, but nobody should die without having a relationship with Jesus Christ!"

For the first time in a long while I saw Mrs. D smile. "You're sweet," she murmured, "but don't worry about me. My dad was a minister...I've heard the gospels...and I'm ready!"

I sighed a sigh of relief and told her how glad I was to hear that. She thanked me for caring enough to stop back and saw me out. That was the very last time I saw Mrs. Deyo.

Why I felt I was led to speak with her on that day, I can't say. Since my friend claimed to be certain she was right with God, why did I feel this pressing need to talk with her? Was the spirit of God really talking to me and dealing with me, or was it all something I conjured up myself. Had I been saying my lines as they were written or had I been improvising? Who the hell knows?

I have to say being a UPS man has allowed me to meet many wonderful people. Florence Feldman and I hit it off from the first time I asked her to sign for a package. She lived in a relatively modest house situated among the many prestigious mansions in the well-to-do neighborhood of Sands Point. A nicer, kinder woman, I could not find. Florence loved to talk to me. Some days I would spend up to forty-five minutes just chatting away with her while standing at her back door. She would ask me numerous questions about my wife and kids, not because she was nosy, but just because she loved family and it gave her the opportunity to tell me all about hers. Our conversations covered every topic from music and entertainment to politics and the environment to cooking. Sometimes I tried to quietly drop off the packages on her porch and quickly sneak away from her house, as to not get involved in another lengthy discussion, causing me to fall way behind in schedule.

Florence loved to cook and around holiday time I would always follow the mouth-watering aromas drifting from her kitchen window. I would peak in to see her surrounded by pots and pans, her sleeves rolled up and her hands and apron coated in flour. Whenever I allowed her to spot me, she smiled the warmest smile, quickly wiped her hands on a dishtowel and dashed over to her door to let me in. She always insisted I sample what she was baking and must say her desserts were heavenly. If and when I made it a point to tell her just how much I enjoyed one of her baked goods, she never failed to present me with the recipe to give Julianne. On one such occasion, she even went out of her way to purchase the special baking trays needed to prepare a particular pastry and gave them to me as a gift. I loved Florence.

Mrs. Feldman always told me I reminded her of her son. I met him briefly just once. From everything she told me about him, he seemed like a great guy. He was politically involved as an environmentalist, worked with the underprivileged and was tremendously health conscious. He wasn't interested in achieving the wealth from where he obviously came, but would rather dedicate his life in helping the underdog. Florence bragged about him all the time and I could truly understand why she did.

Florence and I became pretty close through the years and I would even say we considered each other friends. Whenever she spotted me on the road, she'd always stop to say hello and share a few words. I knew she genuinely cared about me and I cared for her as well. One autumn afternoon, when the slight chill in the air made it clear winter was just around the corner, Florence stood alone in her driveway. As I walked up to greet her with the package she ordered from Bloomingdale's for her granddaughter, I could tell from her expression something was terribly wrong.

"Hey, Mrs. Feldman," I called out, "How are you?"

"Not good John, not good!" was her stone cold reply.

She told me she didn't care to talk about it but I was able to gently coax it out of her. The doctors found a tumor in her son's head. Florence was devastated, but I tried to convince her to think positive, to believe in the miracles of modern medicine and to pray.

"Why him?" she sobbed, "Why him?"

The cancer spread quickly, and before she knew it, Florence's favorite son was taken from her. From the day illness befell him, Florence was never the same. She became so despondent, never smiled that big wide smile of hers, and was very pissed off at God. How does one begin telling someone who just lost her son about the saving grace of Jesus Christ, especially when she is Jewish? I was telling a friend of mine, who happened to be a Born Again Jew, about Florence. He gave me a book entitled "The Promises of God" and suggested I give it to her to read. The book sat on my desk for months.

Florence seemed to disappear. Her depression must have caused her to cut down on her mail order shopping. Day after day I would drive my truck along Florence's tree-lined street never once stopping at the Feldman residence. I would think about stopping by to see her, but the idea of knocking on her door without having a package to deliver, seemed a little strange to me. One day, however, as I was doing my route, I finally came across a package addressed to Florence. I stopped the truck at the foot of her driveway and walked towards the rear door of the house where I always left her parcels. The house was dark. There was no sign of Florence. She wasn't standing at her usual place in the center of her large kitchen stirring a sauce or rolling out dough. What disturbed me more was the makeshift wooden ramp extending from the back door to the edge of the driveway.

It was a bitter cold winter morning. As my truck turned down one of the hilly back roads of Sands Point, I saw three figures all bundled up in their scarves, hats, gloves and parkas, taking a stroll along a wooded path. I recognized one of the figures to be Florence's husband Alan. I pulled over and motioned for him to wait up. Alan reached out to shake my hand and introduced me to his other son and daughter-in-law. I told him how sorry I was to hear about his son's passing and asked about Florence. Alan cleared his throat and with great difficulty, managed to share with me the terrible news that his wonderful wife had suffered a pretty bad stroke. My heart broke as I let him know how fond of Florence I was.

The next time I saw Florence she was sitting in a wheel chair. Propped up by a pillow and looking as lifeless as a mannequin, Florence sat expressionless as her homecare worker, who took her out for a stroll, pushed her along past the mansions on Forest Drive. When I drove by, my eyes and Florence's locked glances. I knew I had to get out of my truck and say something. I introduced myself to Lucy, the aide, and explained my relationship to Florence. Florence sat motionless staring blankly into space, and the same angry look she had on her face the day she told me she was mad at God was still there.

"Florence!" Lucy called out smiling, "Someone wants to say hello to you!"

I stood in front of her, but Florence seemed to be looking right through me as she gazed out into the unknown. Then suddenly Florence's lips moved and in a soft gravelly voice replied, "Lots of people used to love Florence, but Florence is not here anymore. Florence is gone!"

I was spooked. It was so weird. "Why her," I thought, "Why her?" I thanked Lucy and drove off into the distance fantasizing once again about laying hands on someone and demanding, "In Jesus' name, be healed!" What a testimony to the glory of God it would have been if Florence became well again. Once again, however, doubt reigned.

On the corner of our block, in a big old Victorian house, the kind Julianne dreamed of owning, there lived the Henderson's. The house needed some major tender loving care, but Dan Henderson loved fishing and the outdoors way too much to be spending his free time replacing windows and power washing cedar shingles. Dan was a Nassau County cop and he was assigned to patrolling the waterways. What better gig could a die-hard fisherman ask for? Dan's wife Cindy was a teacher in the Freeport school system. The first time we officially met Cindy was when she rang our doorbell one evening, a week or so after we moved in, and interrupted our dinner. Upon hearing the bell, my daughters made a mad dash for the door and let her in.

"Sorry to disturb you during your dinner," she said in a not too apologetic nasal whine, as she tried to inconspicuously give the inside of our bare home the once over.

"Oh that's quite alright Cindy," I said trying my best to make her feel as if she wasn't intruding, "would you care for something to drink?"

"Oh no thanks!" she answered, "I can only stay a minute! I just wanted to let you guys know there's been a little outbreak of lice in the schools and since you all have MAJOR hair, I thought you ought to be aware of it!"

"Gee thanks Cindy!" Julianne chimed in almost sarcastically, "I'm glad you told us!"

Dan and Cindy didn't seem like they belonged together, but I'm sure most people thought the same about Julianne and me. Cindy was Jewish and Dan was an Irish Catholic so religious differences obviously weren't a major issue with them. Dan was a soft-spoken guy who pretty much kept to himself. When he wasn't working he was spending most of his time fishing with his son Thomas, who is the same age as our son Matthew. Dan and Cindy also had a daughter Michelle who was our daughter Samantha's age. Michelle used to tell everyone her name was really Dawn, but that's a whole other story. The Henderson's were good neighbors.

One of the dangers of being constantly out in the sun is that the odds are pretty good of getting skin cancer, especially for someone as fair-skinned as Dan. Dan didn't beat the odds, and at the tender young age of forty-four, he developed an aggressive strain of melanoma that spread like wildfire. Cindy was beside herself grabbing at any hope she could that would bring Dan back to health. She tried herbal remedies, witch doctors, acupuncture, homeopathic treatments, ancient Chinese diets and gurus. Julianne told Cindy we were going to lift Dan up in prayer at our church. Cindy was so desperate she began to ask Julianne questions about the church. Julianne mentioned to her how we believed Jesus is the Messiah and even today He heals the sick. Cindy was Jewish. Jesus meant nothing to her, but in her time of great trouble she would have tried anything, even Jesus. After all Dan did come from a Christian background. It was worth a shot.

Cindy urgently pleaded with us to ask our Pastor if he would come right over to pray for Dan because his hourglass was running out. Cindy wasn't thinking at all about Dan's eternal life. She wanted a miracle. She wanted Dan alive and healthy. Heaven and hell weren't a reality to her at this point. Dan not being around anymore was the only reality she was facing. We assured Cindy we would do whatever we could do and placed a call to our pastor's office. The pastor was out of town and time was of the essence. We pondered over and over about whom we could get to come over at a moment's notice and immediately thought of Jimmy. Jimmy was a man of faith, he was bold, and if anything, I could certainly vouch he was indeed a man of prayer. Jimmy agreed to come, provided I would be there with him, because as it says in scripture, "Whenever two or more of you are gathered in my name…" I had no choice but to agree.

When Jim and I arrived at Dan's, it was Dan's sister who let us in. Cindy had stepped out momentarily so she didn't get to witness what was about to happen. Dan was stretched out on a single bed located in the dining room turned intensive care unit. The house was dark and reeked of death. The only sound we could hear was the heavy breathing coming from Dan's emaciated body. His bony, sunken-in face was unshaven and his bulging eyes stared at the ceiling as if he were paying the utmost attention to something up there. I couldn't recall ever seeing something so eerie, somebody I knew about to step through death's door.

Jimmy stepped up to Dan's bedside with me standing just behind him, my hand upon his shoulder for moral support. "Dan!" Jim cried out in a firm authoritative voice, "I don't know if you can hear me Dan, but brother you are moments away from eternity!" Jimmy's words sounded so harsh but that was indeed the bottom line. Wherever and whatever eternity was, Dan was only moments away.

"Jesus died for you Dan," Jim continued, "No man gets to the Father except through Him! Accept Him Dan! You don't want to spend eternity in hell...He loves you Dan...Accept Jesus as your Lord and Savior Dan..." To tell the truth, I was very uncomfortable. The entire scene was completely bizarre to me. Here was a guy completely zoned out on super strength pain killers about to breathe his last breath, as a complete stranger was warning him he had mere seconds to accept Jesus in order to avoid the eternal fires of hell. Could this really be the way God worked or were we all fucking crazy? Dan's sister who was watching from the adjacent room let us know in no uncertain terms, we were fucking crazy!

CAN'T GO BACK, OR CAN YOU?

There's an expression that goes, "Shit happens!" The older I get the more I see just how true it is. Time changes things. Marriage, children, and jobs are all factors affecting why friends don't keep in touch as much as they should or would like to. Pat had been closer to me than a brother. With his divorce from Erica way behind him, Julianne and I played matchmaker by setting him up with Julianne's cousin Rosanna. Pat fell for Ro almost immediately, and after a struggle and a chase they got married. For a few years the four of us were inseparable. Pat and Rosanna lived just down the block from us and every Sunday morning we would all have breakfast together. It was a perfect arrangement of friends and family. Indirectly, my friend Pat was now my cousin through marriage!

We always knew Pat was destined for success and through his hard work, ingenuity, and the support of Rosanna, he quickly achieved it. It wasn't very long before Pat and Ro moved from their apartment and bought their first house. They bought at the right time, making a very nice profit when they sold it, enabling them to move to a more prestigious neighborhood and into a beautiful big home. With an unstoppable drive to forge ahead and with a knack for making money, Pat and Ro moved up again. This time to the land of millionaires on a three-acre plot complete with swimming pool, pool house and rolling hills. Pat started socializing more and more with business associates and an entirely different class of people. For some reason, money attracts money. Julianne and I were beginning to feel like we couldn't relate with them anymore, having nothing in common but our past. Julianne and Rosanna had a falling out over something petty and unfortunately, it affected my relationship with Pat. We hardly kept in touch with each other. See, shit does happen.

Pat was about to turn forty and in the mail we received an invitation to his surprise fortieth birthday party to be given to him by Rosanna. It was to be a classy affair held on a party boat as it circled Manhattan Island. I started to think about what I could give Pat as a present for this milestone birthday. "Your friend is loaded," Julianne reminded me over and over again, "What could you possibly give him that he doesn't already have?" It was then when I got the brainstorm of making him a tribute film on video. Julianne thought it was a great idea and since time was of the essence I knew I had better get cracking. Night after night and weekend after weekend I sat among stacks of photographs, eight millimeter movies, and videotape, trying to create something I felt certain would move him deeply. I called all of "The Bummers" and asked them to send me homemade video clips of them wishing Pat well. In my splicing lab, which was a dining room table covered with movie projectors, video recorders, tape players, cameras, and transferring equipment, I put together a ninety-minute nostalgic film including a soundtrack of our favorite music and an original song, which even made me cry when I viewed it.

When Pat stepped onto the boat everyone yelled surprise and plunged toward him to wish him happy birthday. I maneuvered my way through the well-wishing crowd and when I finally made my way up to Pat, I extended my hand and wished him happy birthday.

"Why the hell don't you call me, you stiff?" he asked.

"Hey, are your fingers broken? You know my number!" I answered sarcastically.

"You're right!" he admitted, "I'm just as much a screw-up!"

I handed him my masterpiece and told him, "I hope you like it."

Having no idea what I just gave him, he simply said, "Thanks, I'm sure I will!"

The following morning when I got home from Sunday service, I saw the light on my phone machine flashing. I hit the button to listen to my one message. It was Pat. The heartfelt emotion in his voice expressed to me just how much he was moved by the video, making all my painstaking work worthwhile. My creating this video and his viewing it made us both realize what a special friendship we shared and that nothing should ever come between us. But as they say, shit happens.

FALLEN ANGEL

Mothers Day was upon us once again. This particular Sunday was sunny and bright and in the lobby of the church everyone was smiling and wishing all the moms, grandmas, and mothers-to-be a very happy Mothers' Day! As eleven o'clock drew near, everyone made their way into the church sanctuary and waited for the service to get underway. The whispering among the congregants gradually developed into a thunderous drone. It was already eleven-fifteen and the worship team had not yet begun to play. Something was obviously irregular on that Sunday morning as the worshippers were all getting fidgety in their pews, turning to one another making assumptions as to what the problem might be. I always try to find humor in any situation, so I was cracking joke upon joke as to what the holdup was all about. "Pastor Ralph woke up with a hangover! No, I know, he ran off to Hawaii with all of the church's money!" For every crack I made I got an elbow in the ribs from Jule, even though everyone around us was getting a good laugh. Finally one of the elders stepped up to the pulpit and said, "What do you say we come together and praise the Lord!" Without missing a beat the music began and with Pastor Ralph and his swinging accordion missing in action, the service began and we were all left to guess as to his whereabouts.

As it is with any conglomeration of people, there is always the privileged someone "in the know" who passes on top-secret information to someone he knows he can trust as to not spread the news around. It's usually not very long before the trust is violated and the gossip spreads like wildfire. When the news reached my ears, I was utterly stunned. I looked around and by the astonished looks and the tears on some of the church members' faces, I could tell who knew and who didn't. Some folks were rendered speechless as they exited the church doors and some loitered in the lobby trying to investigate as to what transpired. This was one of those circumstances when although I desired to know what was going on, once I found out, I wished I hadn't. I had enough garbage in my head I didn't need to know this.

For as long as Ralph was our pastor I'd always perceived him as a meek and humble servant of God. He always had a faraway look in his eyes and I just assumed his thoughts were on God and not on the breasts of the teenage girls of the church. I should have seen it coming. Jimmy Swaggart used to constantly campaign against pornography. He started movements to get smut removed from all the convenience stores across America. In the eyes of the Christian movement, he was a hero, leading one of the largest and wealthiest ministries in the world. I can only imagine what his followers and supporters felt when it was revealed he was caught performing lewd acts with prostitutes in a sleazy hotel room. He was exposed and his empire crumbled. Pastor Ralph would continually comment about the way the girls of the church would dress. He preached about what he considered a proper and appropriate dress code. One Sunday he stressed how he would not permit the little girls of the church to wear shorts to vacation Bible school. It was summertime. It was hot. These were children. It was ludicrous. To me it seemed as though he was very obsessed with the clothing issue and the thought occurred to me, maybe he had a problem. He did. Several teenage girls from the assembly reported, when they went to see their pastor for counseling, he fondled them. When the elders of the church asked him to step down, he put up a fight in a futile attempt to justify his immoral behavior. His self-gratifying actions, including an alleged secret affair with the church secretary, caused a major upheaval in the church. How could men who presumably start out doing the work of God, stray so far? Is there really a devil so powerful working behind the scenes or has all that talk about being baptized with the Holy Spirit and covered with the "Armor of God" been just a bunch of meaningless feel good lip service? How ineffective all of their efforts become. I can only wonder how I would have reacted if my daughters were among the violated.

ONE GOOD TURN DESERVES ANOTHER

Time marches on. My fortieth birthday was right around the corner. Julianne and I discussed it now and then and we decided, instead of a party, she'd take me away for the weekend when my big day arrived. I knew a party was out of the question because first of all, she couldn't afford to throw one that could accommodate the amount of guests we'd have to invite. The other reason I knew a party was not in my future was because our relationship was going through quite a strain. In my mind, Julianne was still going through some emotional turmoil, which I sensed was causing her to act irrationally. We had our good days but we were also having far too many bad ones. Every time tensions exploded into an argument, Jule had a way of blaming me for her misery. It was my fault we moved into a house she didn't love and it was my fault we had no money and it was my fault she lost control of her growing children. I insisted her radical mood swings were hormonal and that the way she perceived things was inaccurate. Since the day we started dating I had to cope with her monthly premenstrual syndrome, which I preferred to call "the Jekyll and Hyde Syndrome." Whatever the reasons were, hormonal, menopausal, psychological, or even possibly genetic, they were affecting our marriage. Without Julianne knowing it, I contacted her gynecologist and explained to him how peculiar she was behaving and begged him to see her. He obliged me and under false pretenses called her to schedule an appointment. He examined her thoroughly, blood work and all, and found her perfectly normal. Although I should have considered this good news, I didn't. Somehow I thought a magic pill would be the answer in turning our world right again. Could it be I was the problem?

Julianne decided maybe it would be a good idea for her to get a part-time job. It would break the monotony of her being stuck in the house day after day without seeing other human beings. It also would lighten our financial burden a little. The children were in school for most of the day so it wasn't like she was abandoning them. She applied for a couple of local jobs, but the CVS pharmacy, located walking distance from our door, offered her employment immediately. She wondered if it was a good idea to accept the job or wait to find something a little more dignified with a little better pay. I understood just how she felt. Julianne was a college grad with a degree in speech pathology and she was considering taking a clerk's position in a neighborhood drug and convenience store. "Listen honey," I said sympathetically, "you're not looking to make a career out of this. It's just for a little spending money and to get you out of the house a few days a week. Besides, they will accommodate you to whatever hours you need!"

Julianne accepted the job, which I thought was good for her socially and at the same time helped paying a few bills. The one drawback about her taking this job was, no different than anything else my wife engaged in, she involved herself one hundred and ten percent. Julianne doesn't like anybody to assume she is ignorant about anything, which she is not, and prefers to give much more than what is required of her. It is just her nature to give her all with anything she tries. It is unfortunate, however, in the unjust world of big business, hard workers, like Julianne, are often taken advantage of and not compensated for their earnest efforts. I hated seeing her wear that stupid red CVS vest and work so hard.

It was the month of August, 1992 and Julianne was in a particularly good mood. I had no idea as to why, but she pestered me to make her an audiotape of all of our favorite songs. One Saturday she went so far as to tell me to put off everything else (including the usual weekend chores) and concentrate on completing this tape. "I want something to listen to in the car," she said, "couldn't you just please do this for me?" So without question I did. When she requested I include two of my favorite songs, Dylan's "Forever Young" and Zappa's "Peaches and Regalia," I should have had a clue something was up.

A few days later, Julianne informed me about her cousin Rosanna calling to invite us to their estate for a barbeque on a Sunday afternoon. What I found really surprising was that she agreed to go without even asking me. Being we're always late for everything, I also found it extremely out of character for Julianne to be hurrying me along when that Sunday afternoon arrived. With a sense of urgency in her voice Julianne called out, "Come on John! Let's get going and get into the car, they're expecting us for three o'clock and don't forget the tapes!" As long as I've known her she's never rushed me to go anywhere, especially to one of my friends' places. I got into the car and we sped away to spend an afternoon in the company of Pat and Rosanna.

I pulled into the huge circular driveway at the end of the cul-de-sac. We exited the car and my family followed close behind me as I unsuspectingly made my way through the gates leading into Pat's magnificent backyard. I was completely oblivious to the fact I was walking into my surprise fortieth birthday party until I heard the loud cries of "Happy Birthday" coming from the sea of smiling faces standing before me. My real birthday was still a month away so at first I was very much disoriented. One by one I focused on each familiar face. There was Gino and his wife Katie, my brothers Bill, Jim and their families, my brother-in-laws and sister-in-laws, my parents, my sister Virginia, all of the Bummers and their wives and children. It was unbelievable. I didn't know which way to look. My eyes turned to Pat who stood in the distance wearing the most gratifying smile and I made my way right over to him.

"This is incredible!" I said ecstatically, "How did you ever pull this off?"

"John," he happily replied, "I can't make videos or write songs and poetry but I can throw one hell of a party! Happy birthday buddy!"

I threw my arms around him gave him a big hug and a kiss and said, "Nothing's ever going to beat this!"

It was amazing just to see everyone having such a tremendous time. The food and drink were superlative and plentiful. The weather was fabulous. The sparkling blue pool water just beckoned the guests to jump in. I felt as if I were living an episode of "Lifestyles of the Rich and Famous!" By the time the evening came to a bittersweet close, I was so tanked up on Tequila I could hardly stand. I lied down in Pat's driveway, closed my eyes and blissfully proclaimed, "Now I can die!" On Monday morning there was no way I was able to get up for work, so I called in sick. I spent the entire day in my backyard lying on a hammock trying to recuperate from the wonderful day before and gearing up for the rough days ahead.

GOOD TIMES BAD TIMES

I guess it would be correct to say I'd always been somewhat of a dreamer and a romantic. I'd always felt life was much too short to be miserable. I didn't have an enemy in the world and there was really no one I knew of who I can honestly say I despised. The only person on this planet who had the ability to cause me mental anguish or depression was my wife. I wanted nothing but for her to always be happy and stay in a relatively good mood. I honestly believed I'd always been a good, faithful and loving husband and a pretty good provider. As I'd said before, the one thing I'd learned through marriage was when the wife/mother is happy, the entire house is happy. When the wife/mother is in a vile mood, there is turmoil in the home. If my life depended on answering the question, "How do you keep a woman happy?" I'd be a dead man. Men on the other hand are the easiest creatures to please and every woman knows it. All it takes is affection, good food and good sex, not necessarily in that order. It doesn't quite seem fair now, does it?

One would think after all the years of being with the same woman and having three children with her, I'd be used to riding the emotional roller coaster. Unfortunately, that's not the way it went. As much as I cherished the good days, I just didn't seem to deal well with the bad ones. Whenever the tension rose between Julianne and me, I became quite prolific by pouring my troubled heart into my songs. My imagination also began to take over and I would fantasize about divorce, infidelity, adultery and all the other un-Christian like thoughts dangerous to my well-being. To make matters worse, each day at work I had to face

Janine who only added to my torment.

I was very much aware life couldn't always be a bed of roses, but as the years progressed, it became apparent we'd been feeling too many thorns. We used to have a lot more fun. We were more spontaneous. I never dreamed we could ever turn into my in-laws, trapped in an inescapable stagnant marriage. We weren't there yet, but it was starting to look more and more like that could be our future.

Julianne and I made it a point to get away together at least once a year for a two or three day romp in a romantic Pocono resort. It gave us the opportunity to get reacquainted with one another. What could be more amorous than a bottle of wine, fireplace and a heart-shaped tub for two? One time, not following instructions, we poured a little too much soap bubbles into the Jacuzzi and before we knew it the entire room was full of suds. It was like an episode of "I Love Lucy" to see the two of us in our birthday suits, scooping up armfuls of bubbles and trying unsuccessfully to toss them into the shower. For some reason after our last visit, for the occasion of my fortieth birthday, we just stopped going. I often suggested we go back, but Jule never seemed to get too excited over the idea, so I abandoned it.

MEET THE NEW BOSS

Meanwhile, back at the "Full Gospel Church," the search was on for a new pastor. For several months a number of visiting ministers (sort of like substitute teachers) would come to the church to preach. It was as if the church were holding auditions. One particular reverend, by the name of Ted, made quite a few repeat performances and his charismatic personality was winning over the hearts of the membership. At first, I even took a liking to Ted. He was vibrant, energetic and his messages seemed to hit home. Ted was a well-spoken, half-Italian/half-Irish evangelist from North Carolina, who knew accepting the job as new pastor would put him in quite a challenging position. A good number of the church members, in one way or another, were related to the ex-pastor. The remaining unrelated, still felt a certain amount of loyalty towards him. Whatever the church decided to do, whether it was hiring Ted or reinstating Ralph, I didn't care. Throughout history, many great men of God have fallen and were forgiven. Who was I to judge? Ted's charismatic preaching, however, made it a unanimous "hands down" decision he was to become the new leader of the flock. I went along with the majority's decision to take on Ted.

After Ted settled in, I was beginning to see he was a pretty slick salesman. He had a tremendous command of the English language. He was a master of alliteration, "...Give gratuitously and a good, gentle, grand, glorious, giving God of glory is guaranteed to guide and bless you greatly." Whenever he preached, the immortal words of "The Wizard of Oz" always came to mind, "You billowing bag of bovine fodder!" The entire congregation fell for Ted and his bag of evangelical tricks and welcomed him with unsuspecting open arms.

Pastor Ted and his wife Greta, a matronly type who resembled Mrs. Claus, were as friendly as can be and knew just what to do and say to find acceptance in their new home. They were also shrewd in voicing their demands, which included housing, transportation, pension, competitive salary and getting everything they asked for. Ah! The business of church!

The new shepherd started forming committees and ministries and doing whatever was in his power to get the members involved. Julianne was appointed church librarian and was given carte blanche to purchase anything she needed to get started. He also got personally involved in selecting musicians and singers for a praise and worship team. It was probably out of his frustration of watching me fall asleep in my pew week after week that made him approach me to play drums. What better way to keep me coming to church knowing how much I loved to play music. He also encouraged the formation of a men's fellowship so that the male membership of the church could get together and bond. Before long we were once again one big happy family praising and worshipping the Lord! Alleluia!!

The guys who organized the men's fellowship knew I played guitar and wrote songs, so they asked me if I would sing a couple of tunes at the next meeting. I don't know if it was because of my agreeable nature or because my ego needed the recognition, but nevertheless, I arranged to do so. I had written a couple of spiritual songs I thought would be very appropriate for a men's meeting and I played them that evening to a very receptive and appreciative group of gentlemen. When I was through playing, Pastor Ted asked me if he could use my guitar to play and sing a favorite old hymn of his. I carried my instrument back up to the podium and handed it to him. When I returned to the pews, just by coincidence, I sat in the front row on the right side of the church. Everyone else was sitting on the left... everyone!

As Ted wrapped his fingers around the neck of my guitar trying to form a "C" chord, he said, "Pray I remember how to do this folks, because it's been years!" He then proceeded to play the tune perfectly, as if he just rehearsed it moments ago! Right then and there I knew this guy was quite the character! When Ted the troubadour was finished entertaining us, he put my guitar down and suggested we pray. He asked if any of us had any special prayer requests. One of the guys called out and suggested we pray for a certain church brother who was taken ill. Mostly everyone, from what I could tell, bowed their heads and began to pray.

Suddenly the pastor cried out boldly, "Let's not summon God like a bunch of whiny old wimps, let's pray like the Pentecostal men we claim to be!!" The first problem I had with his pompous remark was I never claimed to be, or ever desired to be, classified as any denomination or religious affiliation. Don't label me Pentecostal. Don't label me anything! The second problem I had was how as soon as he completed his statement, it was a cue for every man in the room to begin shouting out at ear-splitting decibels what they considered prayer. Now picture this. One side of the church was full of guys jabbering away in "tongues." On the opposite side of the church there was little old me, my head in my hands and thinking to myself, "Please get me out of this asylum! This can't be right!"

While the indecipherable roar of babbling went on and on, with my face still hidden in the palms of my hands, I prayed silently yet fervently, "Lord," I pleaded, "If this is real, let it be by Your doing I join them. If it's not, please let me know. Show me truth Lord, please let me know truth!" Nothing happened. I tried on my own to add to the rumble of masculine cries, but all that would come out was "Yabba, dabba, doo! Yabba, dabba, doo!" Suddenly, I found the situation so hysterically funny, it was difficult holding in my laughter. When we were dismissed, a lot of the guys came up to me and expressed how much my song had ministered to them.

"Thanks brother, your song really touched my heart! It was truly anointed of God!"

How could I have responded to a compliment like that but to say, "Thanks man, no problem?"

I drove home that evening more confused than ever, and thinking out loud in a state of total exasperation I cried out, "Something's fucking wrong with this picture!"

NO HOPE FOR THE FUTURE

We can never tell when someone is going to suddenly spring into our lives, make a connection and become a dear friend. One Sunday morning the pastor allowed this woman, who I'd spotted from time to time sitting in a pew towards the rear of the church, to step up to the pulpit to say a few words. I had no idea as to what her name was until she was introduced as Sister Sue. Sue, sporting a short choppy haircut and a bright "Century 21 Real Estate" style blazer, took the microphone from Pastor Ted's hand and without showing any signs of stage fright, began to solicit the congregation to support "Hope for the Future," a non-profit organization dedicated to feeding the homeless and less fortunate on Manhattan's lower east side. Every Friday evening, Sue exhibited her take-charge personality as she doled out work assignments for the many volunteers who showed up to lend a hand in the preparation of hundreds of care packages for the needy. Julianne always believed part of being a good Christian was helping others, so "Hope for the Future" was right up her alley. Friday nights soon found Julianne behind a cutting board in the large commercial kitchen slicing, dicing and slapping together sandwiches from whatever food products were donated to the cause by local restaurants and grocery suppliers. Sometimes she dragged along the kids and once in a while she dragged along me. Julianne's "take the bull by the horns" personality was very similar to Sue's, in that when there was a job to be done, you could count on them to get it done. This common character trait was the foundation for what became a solid friendship between Sue and Jule.

Whenever I conceded into giving up a Friday night to join the forces fighting hunger, I couldn't help but act up. Always the class clown, I pushed it to the limit by doing and saying whatever I could to get a rise out of Sue. Being surrounded by a crowd of good little Christian soldiers doing the "Lord's work" made it easy to get a reaction. Julianne would cringe, worrying about what I was going to say next to embarrass her, but Sue, on the other hand, curiously enjoyed my warped sense of humor. Like many people who end up finding refuge in church organizations, Sue had a crazy past…sex, drugs, rock and roll…somehow we clicked! I appealed to Sue's fun-loving side. In spite of my sarcasm, cynicism and odd way of looking at things, Sue and I also became good friends, growing closer as we really got to know one another. A true friend is someone who shines through in any situation, someone you can depend upon in good times and bad. Sue has always come through for Julianne and me, but what I love most about her is how she can hold her vodka. When Sue's out of the soup kitchen and free from organizing a lady's potluck dinner, she's helping me concoct a cocktail or polish off a bottle of cabernet sauvignon.

My dad had a slight problem adjusting to some of the friendships that blossomed from our church. Anyone from out of the circle of familiar Bummer faces brought about suspicion. After breaking off an engagement in her pre-Jesus days, Sue has remained available. "Be careful!" my dad would warn me, "I've been around long enough to tell you friendships like this lead to trouble!" My untrusting pop was so convinced Sue had the hots for me and was deviously planning to work her way between Julianne and me. "Dad," I said, "You really have no clue!"

Sue had to eventually leave the organization she put so much of her heart and soul into. Having irreconcilable differences with the founder of "Hope for the Future," Sue resigned and put her energies towards fighting hunger elsewhere.

TAKING THE PLUNGE

It wasn't too long after Ted officially became our pastor when he announced he was going to hold his first Baptism service. Unlike Infant Baptism as practiced by the Catholic Church, where the ceremony is performed by a priest who holds a baby over a fountain while pouring droplets of holy water upon the infant's forehead, Pentecostals believe in the full body immersion of a believer who has reached the age of accountability (usually teenagers). In the Catholic version of this symbolic ritual, the annoyed, head-soaked baby cries, as the proud Godparents promise to raise the child in the Catholic faith, in the tragic event of the parents' demise. Everybody smiles for the camera except for the cranky baby donned in an uncomfortable miniature-wedding gown. After Church, the family and invited guests go to a catered affair where everyone overindulges themselves with food and alcohol. The first obligation of being a Catholic is fulfilled.

Ever since we started attending Full Gospel services, we'd been hearing about the Scriptural approach to Baptism. The Bible instructs that believers are to be baptized in water in the same manner John the Baptist immersed Jesus in the river. Although Julianne, Christiann and I were all baptized as infants Catholic style, something kept nagging at us that maybe we should do what the Bible says and get re-baptized Pentecostal style. When Pastor Ted asked for interested parties to sign up, we came forward. Many of our church pals were shocked to learn we'd never taken the plunge. It was as though we belonged to a club for thirteen years without getting initiated.

Because it's largely inconvenient to hold Baptism services in a river, most Bible based churches come equipped with built in tanks. Pastor Ted was very excited over the large turnout for his premier immersion service. As I sat alongside Julianne, Christiann and the other candidates in the first pew of the church, I felt quite silly dressed in the long brown robe that covered my swim trunks. Many Born Again believers make a big hoopla over a Baptism service, and being this was the new pastor's first, there was a very large number of spectators. When I heard my name being called, I knew there was no turning back. I timidly made my way up to the altar and stepped down into the naval-deep lukewarm water of the Baptismal tank. Pastor Ted greeted me with open arms and a great big Pentecostal smile. He asked me to lean over, speak into the extended microphone, and tell the congregation what compelled me to take this leap of faith. Carefully making sure to avoid getting the electric shock of my life, before a full house, I expressed gratitude for my salvation.

"Do you accept Jesus Christ as your personal Lord and Savior?" the Pastor inquired with a thunderous tone. I answered affirmatively; he placed his hand behind my back and while lowering me into the mysterious water of sanctification, cried out, "I baptize you in the name of the Father, the Son and the Holy Spirit!" The congregation went wild with applause, the Praise Team went into an up tempo foot stomping traditional number, and I went running off to the changing room to put on some dry clothes.

When the service concluded, most of those who turned out for the event came up to us to shake our hands and offer congratulatory hugs and kisses. "Thanks!" I answered, even though I wasn't feeling the excitement I knew they were feeling for us. I guess I conceded to go through the motions because I wanted to have all the bases covered. If getting baptized was really one of God's requirements, maybe it was in my best interest to comply. I kept asking myself however, "How has this changed me? How was this going to affect my life? What did I just prove?" I still felt and thought exactly the same as I did before my submersion, and I doubted very strongly it had any real significance, except maybe now I was considered an official authorized member of the club. I think it meant a lot more to Julianne than it did to me.

THERE GOES TROUBLE

Mina's business was hurting and the expense of living in a ritzy neighborhood like Sands Point was much more than she could handle, so in a decision to downsize, she put the house up for sale. She found a place in a town far from my territory. As much as I was going to miss them and the haven they provided for me at the end of each day, it was a good thing they were moving off my route. The way I was behaving when I entered that house, the drinking and the flirting, was ridiculous. If I were close to someone who was acting the way I was, I wouldn't have approved. I had become too attached to Janine's flattery. A million stories have been told about UPS men and the women on their routes who have complicated their lives. I knew myself better and wasn't about to add another story to the list. The last few days before Mina's move, Janine became more flirtatious than usual and I felt guilty just knowing where my thoughts were going.

The day before the moving vans pulled up to their door to take them away, Janine drove about the town and tracked me down. She caught up with me while I was having lunch with the guys in a local pizzeria. She walked into the pizza shop, called out my name, and asked me if I would step outside with her for a minute. She was striking and the jaws of my fellow workers dropped as they saw me, dressed in my dirty brown UPS uniform, walking off with this beautiful girl.

"Get in the car," she said.

Before I knew it, I was sitting in the passenger seat of her fancy red sports car and we were speeding along Main Street until pulling into the parking lot of the town dock. It was a beautiful afternoon and we sat facing the bay, watching as the sunlight glistened on the water.

She turned to face me and reaching for my hand, told me sadly, "I'm really going to miss you!"

"Are you kidding?" I answered as the two sides of my conscience wrestled, "I'm going to miss you too. My job's never going to be the same!"

She leaned over and threw her arms around me. She looked stunning; her hair smelled amazingly sweet and the softness of her face against mine sent my imagination into a tailspin. I knew I'd better go. "My God," I thought, "Please get me out of this one before it's too late!" (Maybe not in those exact words, but God knew my thoughts!)

For a brief moment we held each other tight, then trying to make sense of the situation, let go. Maybe she sensed my hesitation, I don't know, but the last thing I needed was to let that moment lead us to the next. Sometimes people have been known to find themselves in an awkward situation, and they somehow seem to step out of it and see themselves from a third party perspective, like an outer body experience. That happened to me that afternoon; almost as if I were watching myself caught up in a pointless predicament, in a place where I had no business being, acting out a part so contrary to who I thought I was and what I thought I stood for. Flesh and spirit were most definitely battling it out. In all honesty, I admired Janine tremendously and found her curiously exciting. I was truly going to miss her and at that moment I wanted nothing more than to hold her tighter. I also knew I had a life with Julianne and didn't want to destroy a marriage over confused emotions and some lunch hour sex. I told Janine I'd better be getting back, so she drove me to the pizzeria where I rejoined my friends for lunch. Naturally, guys will be guys, so they were all making assumptions and accusations. "You idiots," I said, reassuring them what was going on in their heads was far more exciting than what was going on in that car!

WHEN YOU LEAST EXPECT IT

One of the crazy things about life is waking up in the morning without any clue as to whom you may meet in the course of each new day. For me it was just another typical workday without much to look forward to except going home. Sometimes, however, I wondered why I was in such a hurry to get home because there was always a pretty good chance Jule would be in a cranky mood, and when she was, I'd start wishing I had put in some overtime. I drove my truck up to the entrance of my next stop, the Sands Point Nursing Home. I gathered together the packages to be delivered, entered the lobby and approached the front desk. Standing before me was a face I'd never seen before, a face that intrigued me from my very first glance. The regular receptionist smiled as she introduced me to the new girl.

"John," she announced happily, "this is Maddie; she'll be joining our staff!"

"Nice to meet you!" she said in a pleasant enough voice.

"Nice meeting you too Maddie," I answered, while thinking to myself, "What a perk to be able to see her every day!"

It took about a week before Maddie and I were having some good conversations. I learned she too was a "Born Again" Christian. She attended a church where her husband (yes, she was married) was a drummer in the worship team. We were both tall, Libras, and not always thrilled with our partners. We spent hours discussing our churches, our marriages, and our frustrations, and tried to encourage each other. In the same way I used to look forward to seeing Janine, I looked forward to seeing Maddie, but even more so. We seemed to have a lot in common and I extremely enjoyed hearing her strong opinions and her points of view. The fact I found her beautiful didn't hurt either. We connected.

Maddie was very motivated and quickly moved up in the organization. In a relatively short time she got an administrative position and moved from the reception desk to her very own office. I spent hours sitting beside her desk talking about everything and anything. I assumed she didn't mind my company, otherwise, she would have found a way to get me to leave. I told Julianne all about the Christian girl on my route, and one day I invited Maddie to visit our church, which she did. I couldn't believe the way our Pastor's eyes were fixed on her and immediately after the service how he made it a point to introduce himself. I think I may have embarrassed him when I said, "Hey Pastor, you really know how to pick out the pretty ones, don't you?"

When things were good at home, I looked at Maddie as a great friend. When things were not so good between Jule and me, Maddie became my virtual escape via my fantasies. When I thought about Maddie I envisioned fun, recklessness and no responsibilities. Julianne represented the ball and chains of a tedious marriage.

Maddie's marriage was rocky and she often spoke to me about eventually leaving her husband, a very bold and unordinary comment from a Church girl. One day she told me she was ready to throw it all in and run away to the Caribbean. I knew she was joking, but when I lightheartedly raised the question if I could come with her, she said, "I'm ready, let's go!" When I asked her if she needed to pack, she laughed and said, "All we need are our bathing suits!"

The very next day when I showed up at her office the first words she spoke to me were, "Did you bring your bathing suit?" Oh brother! How tempting it all sounded, the idea of just running away from all our problems. For months to follow, that was our running joke, "Ready to go?" she'd ask, "Did you bring your suit?" Reality always had a way of slamming me across the head with an iron club.

Julianne and I were going through another rough period and Maddie and her husband were pulling further apart. One afternoon I was sitting opposite from Maddie while she was at her desk. I looked at her. She looked at me. We didn't need to speak. We knew there was nothing we could do but encourage one another in spite of the very strong connection we sensed between us.

"Don't you wish it was that easy and we could just run away together," she asked rather innocently.

Feeling somewhat helpless and a bit exasperated, I reluctantly admitted, "Yeah, but we can't!"

Both of us simultaneously shrugged our shoulders, she laughed, I smiled and we went on with our lives. I guess it's just human nature to wonder, "What if?"

Maddie meant what she said. She divorced her husband, got an apartment of her own and because she was so strongly motivated, accepted a job at another facility for more money. I was going to lose the pleasure of spending a few minutes a day with a woman whose company I truly appreciated. She asked me to be sure to it make it a point to stop by and say so long on her very last day. I stepped into the lobby a few minutes before five that evening. Maddie was standing by the front desk and she looked extraordinary. She was wearing a long black dress, her hair shined and her eyes sparkled. She handed me a business card with her phone number on it and told me to be certain to keep in touch. She extended her arms, we hugged tightly, then she kissed me on the lips and we wished each other well. I saw my reflection in the glass of the building's front door, stopped for a second, and asked myself, "Who is that guy and what's wrong with this picture?"

There's an old joke comparing dogs to men by using this analogy: "Men chase women in the same fashion dogs chase cars. They know once they catch up to them they can't drive them!" I knew this could very well be the last time I was going to see Maddie.

I HATE INTERSTATE 95

Unlike a lot of our friends, Julianne and I were never very big on traveling. It's not that we didn't like going away on vacations; it's just that we never really had the extra money and on the few times we flew, Jule experienced major earaches. The few times we were on our friends' boats, she got seasick and nauseous. On two road trips to Florida we had mechanical problems with the car, so I became quite resistant about driving anywhere. Taking all these things into consideration, it's no wonder we were never really known as vacationers.

Because my in-laws live in Florida, I was forced to take the family down south a few times. The first time we flew, Julianne and Samantha suffered tremendously with earaches from the cabin pressure. Two other times we drove. On the first road trip, all five of us, together with our luggage, were stuffed into a Ford Taurus. Julianne was at the wheel, when at six o'clock in the morning somewhere in the Carolinas, we got a blow out! I was in the passenger seat trying my best to get some sleep when the explosion and the rumble of the car woke me right up. There we were, just after dawn, pulled off to the side of Interstate 95, emptying all of our belongings from the trunk of the car so we could dig out the donut spare tire. I was on my knees putting the micro-jack into place, while Julianne did her best to make sure the oncoming eighteen-wheelers were aware of our susceptible position. The last thing I needed was to get splattered all over the roadside of a Carolina highway. We found our way to a service station, where we patiently waited for the mechanics to arrive for work and open up the shop. The tire needed to be replaced and thank goodness they had our size in stock.

Like everyone who has ever taken the tedious drive along I-95, from anywhere in New England to the Florida Keys, we made a stop at the most famous tourist trap in the country, "South of the Border." We were wandering about the gift shop where Matthew had his eye on this fancy plastic dagger. Since he was on his best behavior, we bought it for him. After what felt like an eternity on the road, we finally arrived safely at my in-laws house in sunny Homosassa Springs, Florida. While the kids were in their assigned sleeping quarters sorting out their luggage, Julianne and I sat around the kitchen table talking with her parents. My father-in-law happened to get a glimpse of Matt's new toy weapon, picked it up and began to tinker with it. Within seconds, he accidentally snapped it in two.

"Oh my God," Julianne remarked, "Matt's going to be so heartbroken."

Her dad's disposition suddenly turned to one of annoyance and he snapped back, "I'm not going to take no shit from any kid! These things happen so I don't want to hear anybody's crap, you hear me?"

"Dad," Julianne cut in, "You broke his new toy so of course he's going to be upset!"

"Oh great," I thought, "This trip's off to a rocking start!" All throughout the week my mother-in-law and father-in-law argued about everything from whether or not cold cuts can be frozen, to their preferences on how to serve broccoli rabe! Jule's mom, knowing what fussy eaters we were, always felt under pressure when she knew we were visiting. Queen of the bargain hunters and never able to free herself of the mindset of having to feed nine children, she bought several pounds of sliced turkey breast when she saw it on sale and then froze it! On the planet I come from, we buy cold cuts fresh on the day we plan to eat them! Somehow thawed out, slimy pressed-turkey slices just weren't very appetizing!

Homosassa is about a two to three hour car ride to Disney World. One day during our first visit, Jule's folks joined us for a romp through the Magic Kingdom, Epcot Center, and MGM Studios. Time and time again I asked myself why we put ourselves through these agonizing adventures. Who's tired of walking, standing, waiting…Who's hungry, who's legs hurt, who's thirsty, hot, cold…it was enough to make me want to strangle Mickey Mouse. It was getting late, the park was going to close, and everyone was getting irritable because of hunger and exhaustion. I suggested we make it over to Epcot and have a nice meal at one of the many international restaurants. My in-laws had become true Floridians and refused to dine out unless it was a "Family Style" or an early-bird special, or better yet, an early-bird special at the "Family Style" (a large cafeteria style eatery popular in Florida). It got way too late and my hopes of eating in Japan or Italy had vanished.

The seven of us all crowded back into the Taurus and drove off into the distance leaving Disney World behind us. The problem was, we had close to a three-hour drive ahead of us and everyone was hungry. The huge red "Denny's" sign towered high above all the other road signs and captured our attention. At my mother-in-law's suggestion, I pulled into the parking lot, and in true "Family Vacation Griswold" fashion we made our entrance into the diner. Matthew was so knocked out from the long day he couldn't keep his eyes open or his head up. I tried to ignore the fact we weren't sitting in one of the cleanest establishments. I was so hungry I foolishly ordered a large salad in a taco shell with grilled chicken, and to assist me in staying awake for the journey ahead, a large cup of stale coffee. We all filled our bellies then hit the highway.

We were traveling the dark back roads of the Orlando suburbs for maybe forty-five minutes, when I could suddenly feel gas skate though my intestines in the same fashion hot water travels through baseboard radiators. At some points the pain was so excruciating, I knew the only way I would feel better would be to expel it. I was trying to keep my mind on my driving and off my extreme discomfort.

"You're kind of quiet, honey," Julianne queried from the back seat, "Is everything all right!"

While pinching my inner thighs in a desperate and futile attempt to divert the pain, I grumbled, "I'm fine."

Using the excuse I needed some fresh air, I opened the driver's side window and inconspicuously began sneaking out farts. I don't know how anyone in the vehicle didn't pick up the scent because I sure did. The road ahead was pitch black for as far as the eye could see. I was beginning to sweat profusely and as my agony worsened, I drove faster and faster. With one eye on the odometer I was trying to calculate just how much further we had to go, because come hell or high water, I knew I had to go! With the other eye I was trying to determine whether the flashing red light in my rear view mirror was heading for me. It certainly was. I pulled over and trying unsuccessfully to ignore my vicious cramps, I greeted the officer with a painful grimace.

"Good evening sir," the lawman spoke, "and how are you all doing tonight?"

I groaned back at the cop as he shone his flashlight into the tired eyes of my wife, my three kids and my in-laws, "I'm not doing too good officer and if I don't find a restroom soon I think I'm going to have a rather unpleasant accident!"

He kindly let me go and pointed me in the direction of a nearby convenience store.

"Thank you so much officer," I whimpered, as I slowly drove away towards my relief station.

"Better not let me find out you were speeding again," he called out, "or I'll have you locked up!"

I pulled into the parking lot of the quiet little twenty-four hour convenience store and bolted for the front door. As I walked in, a sweet little lady with a southern accent welcomed me with a friendly, "Good evening sir!"

"Good evening," I replied, "I just want to use your men's room for a minute!"

"Sure thing!" she called out, "Just be sure to use the one on your left, the other one is out of order!"

It wasn't the most sanitary restroom I'd ever been in, but desperate times called for desperate measures. I whipped down my shorts, dropped down onto the bowl and sighed the longest sigh of relief one could imagine. I was a new man ready to face the road once again. I zipped up my pants then reached over to flush the evidence. I watched in horror as I saw the toilet water along with everything in it slowly rise to the rim with no indication it was ever going to stop. It didn't. Resembling an erupting volcano, the toilet lava spilled out from the porcelain bowl and onto the tile floor. "Oh my God," I shrieked, trying not to step in my own mess. I looked around for a plunger and fortunately for me there was none. "Okay, you'll never be back here again," I thought, "just get the hell out of here!"

I nonchalantly went walking through the grocery aisle and after the nice lady bid me a good evening, I matter-of-factly called out, "Oh by the way, the toilet's not working properly! You might want to call a plumber!"

"No honey, it's all right," she said determinedly, "I'll take care of it!"

"Believe me mam," I said cautioningly, "You really don't want to go in there!"

Her smile dropped right off her face, and all too aware of the ghastly sight she was about to face, she sighed, "Oh dear Jesus!"

When I told my misadventure to everyone in the car they were hysterical with laughter.

"Why didn't you tell us you didn't feel good?" Julianne asked.

"Because some things I just prefer to keep to myself!"

One would think we'd learn from experience and never drive south again, but I was a glutton for punishment, so we did. On one excursion, I threw my back out while lifting a suitcase in our hotel room just outside of Disney World. My lower back hurt so badly I couldn't even stand up straight. I managed to get behind the wheel of our car and drove the three hours to Homosassa where I spent most of my time popping Advil and lying on my in-law's living room floor. The worst part about my suffering was that I knew I still had a twenty-two hour drive ahead of me. When it was time to embark on the return trip home, I positioned myself into the driver's seat, activated the lumbar switch to try and alleviate some of my discomfort, and drove straight through to New York.

I used to be a lot more adventurous in my 30's and 40's, so after having a new transmission installed into our trusty blue '89 Taurus, we attempted another family drive to Florida. Once again, just as if we were programmed to do so, we stopped at "South of the Border." Perusing through the gift shop, this time Matt's eyes focused on the fake dog poop. "Dad can I please get it, please!" he begged. We always had to bribe him to behave, so we promised, if he were on his best behavior at grandmas, we would make a stop on the way home for his dog poop. He was on his best behavior and we kept our promise. When we pulled into the parking lot of "South of the Border," I noticed we were getting some strange looks from other tourists. I parked the car and got out. I couldn't help but notice choking smoke coming from under the chassis and black oily liquid dripping all over the pavement.

"Oh shit!" I cried in exasperation, "What the hell could be wrong now?"

"It looks as though you blew your tranny!" a caring stranger said as he observed the situation.

He gave me the name of a service station situated just a few miles down the road and offered to drive me. What choice did I have? The worst that could've happened was this Good Samaritan would have stabbed me to death and stole my credit cards. He didn't, and the mechanic was very accommodating. While towing our car away, he informed us it would take at least twenty-four hours before he could get the part and repair the vehicle. We booked a room and remained stranded at "South of the Border" for the next twenty-four hours. Twenty-four of the longest hours I can remember! All five of us were cramped into two double beds and I lied awake for most of the night staring at the ceiling while listening to the rumble of the tractor-trailers cruising along I-95.

The transmission was fixed (again) for less than half of what it cost us in New York. We made it back home without any further incident and I swore, never again would I drive to Florida (or any other place more than one hundred miles away). It wasn't a complete loss because my mechanic reimbursed me for all of the charges I had incurred including the repairs, food and lodging.

IT'S A BIG HOLE IN THE GROUND

The stress level I reached when planning a vacation for a family of five was enough to either bring on a stroke or make me want to stay home. There were just too many personalities to contend with, and the fact three of them were female, made it even worse. Julianne and the girls packed enough clothing, shoes, cosmetics, hair products (that includes dryers and straightening irons) to last them a lifetime. I tried my best to travel light, but Julianne always made it a point to "strongly recommended" I pack more; so to avoid further confrontation, I complied.

We took one more vacation as a family, only this time we flew. This adventure was to Arizona to see the Grand Canyon and to visit my brother-in-law Artie. Of course the flight was nothing short of torture for Julianne. She got so annoyed with me because I wasn't sympathetic to her fear of flying, but truthfully speaking, there was absolutely nothing I could have done to stop her ears from hurting or make her any less scared. The flight was a little turbulent I'll admit, but I had the utmost confidence in our pilot. No matter how many reassuring remarks I made or how tightly I held her hand, if the plane was going to crash it was going to crash. No amount of handholding or words of reassurance were going to make her feel comfortable on this flight. Where does the faith go when we need it most?

Needless to say we landed safely and the Grand Canyon was the most awesome thing I'd ever seen. With every step the breathtaking view kept changing. The sight was so overwhelming, it reinforced the beliefs I held that only a powerful and loving Creator could design something so beautiful. The experience was truly humbling. I couldn't take my eyes off of it for a moment, and at the time, I truly believed I could have stayed there forever. My kids, on the other hand, especially Christiann and Samantha, were bored silly and preferred to wait for us in the gift shop (another Griswold moment). "Dad!" they said impatiently, "You're making such a big deal about a giant hole in the ground!"

Julianne and I were leaning over the rail staring at the spectacular view from along the Canyon's rim. I looked over to her and whispered, "You know Jule, I have the most incredible desire to make love to you right here!" (Not necessarily in those exact words).

"You're a sick man!" she said, not once turning away from the natural wonder's magnificence.

I had rented a mini-van so Art and Mary could travel with us and be our very own personal tour guides. They took us to some beautiful spots including Sedona, a New Age paradise full of pyramids and washed up entertainers like Shields from the mime duo "Shields and Yarnell." Even though he appeared regularly on one of my favorite programs, "The Smothers Brothers Show," I found him to be obnoxious and full of himself! He did a little shtick for us and probably wondered why we didn't ask for his autograph. I didn't have the heart to tell him that in all probability, nobody back home even remembers who the hell he is! One thing I did know for certain, Sedona was a city of great natural beauty, an indication, once again, of God's great handiwork!

One of the things I found most amazing about Arizona was how the weather changed as we traveled from the Canyon down through Flagstaff and then into the valley. Within a few hours we went from the snow and sleet at the canyon to sunbathing poolside at our hotel in Tempe. While my kids were splashing around in the pool, Artie and I were lounging in the sun just taking in the surrounding sights. One of them just happened to be a voluptuous nineteen-year old blonde who was vacationing with her mom. It was most difficult trying to keep our eyes off of her, but Artie's gawking was much more noticeable than mine, and Mary caught him in the act of lechery even through his tinted sunglasses. This so happened to put a little damper on things as jealousy seemed to set in and tension mounted between Art and his wife. "Do you guys have to make it so damn obvious?" Mary hurtfully questioned.

Artie clearly explained himself to me that afternoon. "One evening

Mary Helen and I were watching Shania Twain on television. I just happened to mention what an incredible body the singer had and how I'd do her in a minute. Mary freaked out and asked me how in the world she was supposed to compete with someone as gorgeous as Shania Twain. I looked Mary in the eye and told her she was being ridiculous because nowhere in this world was Shania Twain sitting around wishing she could fuck Arthur from Tempe Arizona." Artie's justification of staring at beautiful women couldn't have been summed up any better than that.

MY OBSERVANT MECHANIC

I'd never had much luck at having a good honest car mechanic. After being ripped off and disappointed countless times, my brother Jim introduced me to Lenny. Lenny is one of the most colorful characters to have ever entered my life. He stands maybe five foot five, his teeth are in a state of neglected decay, his voice is hoarse and gravelly, he smokes continuously and he uses the word "fuck" in more ways than I could ever imagine. He's overly opinionated, knows a lot about a little and a little about everything and given the opportunity, will chew someone's ear right off. In spite of his appearance and crude language, he is undoubtedly a quality trustworthy mechanic and good guy. Because he came to know me as Jim's older brother, we seemed to bond immediately. Lenny loves to talk and through some of our conversations I learned a lot more about my brother's personal life than I even cared to know! "When's your fuckin' brother gonna realize you don't fuckin' eat where you shit?" he asked. I played dumb acting as if I knew what he was talking about and Lenny inadvertently revealed some very deep dark incriminating secrets about my youngest sibling.

One Saturday morning while I was waiting to get an oil change, Lenny and I got into a crazy conversation about how marriage is unnatural.

"A man wasn't meant to be with one fuckin' woman for his whole fuckin' life!" Lenny rambled, "It ain't fuckin' natural!"

I stood there grinning, because no matter how I would have responded,

Lenny never reneges on anything he says. I just listened as he segued into another story.

"The other night, Maria went out with her fuckin' girlfriend, so I called my cousin and said why don't we go out and get a fuckin' bite to eat?"

As the smoke from the remaining half-inch of his cigarette drifted up behind his wire-rimmed glasses making him squint, he unloosened my oil filter and continued.

"So we're sitting there in the restaurant and we're trying to decide what the fuck to order, when I see this fuckin' waitress, with a pair of the nicest fuckin' jugs I'd ever seen, serving somebody a sizzling fuckin' juicy steak. My cousin tries to fuckin' convince me the lobster in this joint is to fuckin' die for but I made my mind up that I'm gonna sink my fuckin' teeth into a steak. So after we had a few drinks and I'm feeling a little fucked up, the waitress finally drags her cute little ass over to our table to get our dinner order. My cousin orders his fuckin' lobster and just as I'm about to order my steak as bloody fuckin' rare as the chef could possibly prepare it, the thought occurs to me, 'Oh Christ!' I said to myself, 'I can't eat steak! It's fuckin' Lent!'"

After seeing and hearing Lenny give me that very animated account of his Friday night dining experience, I was about ready to bust with laughter.

"Lenny!" I asked, "Do you really think God cares whether or not you had a piece of fuckin' meat on Friday. He may prefer you give up the profanity for Lent!"

Lenny responded, "Fuck you!"

I JUST BLINKED...

The years between forty and fifty seem to be a blur. Although some monumental moments occurred during that time, for the most part I still have to ask, "Where the hell did the time go?" One would expect that when certain incidents strike an individual, a family, or a country, lessons would be learned. Life would take on a new perspective and the stressing over small stuff would be alleviated. It was during this decade that Julianne and I both unsuccessfully celebrated our fiftieth birthdays, once in a lifetime occasions turned unnecessarily unpleasant. Within the same time frame, Christiann's first love tragically died while she was away at school. On top of that awful news, I got the scare of my life when I was diagnosed with cancer, something that's supposed to happen to the other guy, not me! The entire country felt the jolt upon hearing the sickening news about The World Trade Center coming down in flames on an unforgettable September 11th. Just when I began to wonder what else could go wrong in my little world, I was injured in a serious automobile accident. It was also during this unsteady period when Julianne and I finally agreed to seek marriage counseling. Strangely enough, I became somewhat of a religious fanatic only to ultimately disassociate myself from organized religion altogether. *Life is full of surprises...life is full of surprises!*

A HOUSE IS NOT ALWAYS A HOME

Married life was a continual series of ups and downs. Most of our disagreements were over our children and the way our opinions differed on how to raise them. I have to reiterate, Julianne and I came from very different backgrounds. Almost no one can live their life uninfluenced by how they were reared. Hopefully we make the effort not to relive the mistakes. When I was on my journey through adolescence, my parents always kept an open door policy with all of my friends. My folks were loved and respected by all of my buddies and were somewhat involved in their lives. I always thought it was going to be that way with my kids, their friends, and us. Julianne, on the other hand, spent most of her childhood being a mother to her siblings. She will openly admit she didn't have the greatest time growing up. Jule once told me how she stood over her baby sister Caroline's crib and cried, telling the infant how sorry she felt for her having been born into their family. Although we were familiar with my kids' friends and were fond of most of them, our house was not usually the place they congregated. Julianne, along with all of her brothers and sisters, did whatever they could to get out of the house, so their household was never the central meeting place like mine was. As she got older, I saw Julianne becoming more and more obsessive over neatness and order in the house and it drove the kids and me crazy. It really became very disturbing and upsetting to me to see how my daughters were never able to really bond with their mom. I had always been more concerned about the things that are unseen. Although I didn't always succeed, I wanted to know what my kids thought about, what was in their hearts. Not to say

Julianne didn't. It just seemed to me her priority was having a spic and span home over a friendship with her children. I didn't really care if their beds were unmade or their rooms were a mess. I would only insist upon it to keep mom from getting pissed off. I thought if Jule spent more time trying to be a friend to her kids, trying to understand what made them tick, rather than nagging them about the way they stuffed their sweaters into their drawers, life would have been a whole lot sweeter in our home. Maybe then (and I say maybe) the kids would have tried harder to please her. Julianne has never once taken the responsibility for anything that has negatively affected the relationship between her and the girls. If I'd heard it once, I'd heard it a thousand times, "You haven't been a good father! It's you who turned them against me! You haven't grown up yet yourself!" I will never place all the blame on Jule; we just didn't know how to meet in the middle.

Kids will be kids and are experts at manipulating their parents, pitting one against the other. I admit, at times I hadn't made the wisest decisions, but God bless my wife, she's never admitted to having been wrong! (A trait undoubtedly inherited from her father.) Because they didn't consider our home to boast a relaxed atmosphere, our kids always preferred hanging out at their friends' houses. Most of my brothers-in-law and sisters-in-law split from their nest as soon as they could. Some ran away from home, some got pregnant then got married. Arthur joined the military. That's not exactly how I envisioned our future. I wanted my children to always regard their home as a safe refuge, a place they knew they could run to, not run away from. I'm certain those were Julianne's sentiments as well, she just didn't know how to make them a reality.

Julianne repeatedly accused me of being much too lenient with our children. I'd always felt she'd been too strict with them and we never could seem to compromise. (I believe the definition of the word compromise just means somebody loses.) I can remember all too well what it was like to be a kid and I have wonderful memories of those times. I'd always wanted my children to experience wonderful memories of their own, and my desire was that those memories included good thoughts about their mom and dad. Julianne was great with the kids when they were infants and toddlers but as soon as they started having minds of their own, she seemed to be enjoying them less. I recall a time when she went absolutely ballistic over the way Matthew stuffed his clothing into his drawers. "Fold it right!" she screamed, yanking his shirts one by one and flinging them all over his room.

My kids were looking at her liked she had lost her mind. I was looking at her like she had lost her mind. I was standing in the doorway of Matt's bedroom watching the insanity of my son crying in total frustration and Julianne ranting and raving over his wrinkled tee shirts. "This is because YOU let him get away with this," she shouted, pointing her finger at me. I wanted so badly to speak my mind and tell her what I really thought, but knew doing so would only worsen matters between us. How was I going to tell an irrational woman she was being ridiculous and unreasonable?

When the girls were pre-teens, in an attempt to teach them responsibility, Julianne appointed them the task of pulling the weeds from between the bricks in the yard. I thought it was ludicrous because one shot of weed killer or bleach would have done the trick. Why she made the kids sit in the hot sun performing a mindless chore for the sake of a lesson in responsibility, was something I could only assume she inherited from her mother. I always found it strangely odd how Julianne couldn't recall her own childhood frustrations before using her mom's methods on her own children. I can't even begin to count how many times I called upon God for patience and wisdom. He must have been busy weeding at those needy times.

HI HO SILVER ANNIVERSARY?

I'd often heard that men marry women hoping they'll never change and they do, while women marry men hoping one day they will change and they don't. I just never believed this sentiment would apply to us. Somehow I'd always been able to take a step back, look at Julianne and recognize her as the same girl who stole my heart away in college. I'm the kind of person for whom a good moment will make me forget all the bad ones. It must be some mechanism God installed in me.

I couldn't believe it, but our twenty-fifth anniversary was upon us. It just didn't seem possible I could be old enough to have twenty-five years of marriage behind me! I remembered back when my parents reached that plateau in their married life and Julianne and I hosted a small party for them in our apartment. We, along with my brothers and sister, chipped in and sent them away for a weekend in the romantic Pocono's, heart-shaped tub and all. I had to laugh, because at that time, in my mind, I wondered what my parents were going to do with three days in a place strictly intended for sex and romance. My mom and dad were just approaching fifty, and as far as I was concerned, fifty was too old to be splashing around in a tub for two or looking at love handles in a mirrored ceiling!

Julianne had mentioned to me numerous times how she wanted to renew our wedding vows when we're married twenty-five years. "No way, please don't make me have to go through that!" I would beg her. To celebrate our special day I had booked a trip to Niagara Falls. We weren't planning to actually go until two months after our anniversary to assure we'd have warmer weather and I was totally under the impression the trip was going to be our gift to each other. (As the years went on we weren't too big on giving each other presents on anniversaries because each of us would just run out and charge something, and then I'd only have to pay the credit card bill.) On the afternoon of our twenty-fifth, Julianne handed me this rather large box all wrapped up with a bow and pretty paper. I couldn't imagine what it could be. Thank God my kids clued me in that she had gotten me something very special and strongly suggested I reciprocate. I became too practical in my old age and kind of lost my knack at buying her nice things. She had mentioned to me she wanted an ankle bracelet, so I ran out to a jewelry store and bought her the nicest one I could find. When I opened the gift she had given to me, I was flabbergasted. It was the very same expensive guitar I promised myself I was going to save up for someday. Julianne must have been stashing away her extra cash for quite some time. She really showed me up and I knew I had to make it up to her some way, somehow, so I called Pastor Ted.

"Hello Pastor? This is John Domenico!"

Sounding surprised, he responded, "Yes Brother John, how are you and how can I help you?"

"Pastor," I choked, "a man's got to do what a man's got to do..." and I explained to him how I wanted to arrange it so Julianne and I could renew our wedding vows on Sunday.

"It would be my pleasure!" he exclaimed, and on that very next Sunday in front of the entire congregation, and my parents, we exchanged vows again.

Julianne looked beautiful and Ted made the short ceremony very moving. His words were poignant, Julianne cried and my chauvinist friend Jimmy lovingly ridiculed me as he snapped photographs for the church's archives.

"You wimp," he laughed, "Whatever possessed you to go through with this?"

Once again I used the words, "A man's got to do what a man's got to do!"

After the service, as we stood in the church's parking lot talking with my parents, my father looked at me and said, "Your mother wants to renew our vows for our fiftieth, I told her 'no way.' I don't need to be on display. She knows I love her!" My mom looked at us and with a smirk on her face said, "He's so full of it your father. Is it asking too much of him to once do something to make me happy!" My father was wearing this devious grin on his face when he looked at my mom and tried bargaining with her.

"Okay," he said, "You want to renew your vows; I'll make a deal with you!"

Without batting an eyelash my mom snapped back, "I'm not giving you a blow job!"

SHE'S LEAVING HOME

Somewhere in the Bible it says something about a lifetime being but a vapor. How those words rang true the day we were driving Christiann off to college. Right before my very eyes she grew up into a young lady and it seemed as though I never really got the opportunity to absorb much of it. It was almost as if I blinked and eighteen years had gone by.

Christiann made up her mind she wanted to go away to school. She was always a pretty good student and accepted to all the schools she applied to. She settled on Marist College because they had an outstanding fashion department, which was the course of study she decided upon. I saw Christiann studying fashion in the same way as if I had gone to school to study rock and roll, but who was I to stand in the way of my child's dreams? I was comfortable with Marist because it was the closest "away" school. It was only a two-hour drive, so I figured I could deal with that distance. Even though I wouldn't readily admit it, I guess I was a little over protective of my kids, especially my girls and more so Christiann. She was cute as hell, still is, but had absolutely no sense of direction. She used to get lost just walking around the corner. Julianne would get annoyed with me for always doing too much for her, not giving her more responsibilities and not allowing her to grow up. I guess my doing so was a little selfish on my part as to alleviate my own anxiety and worry.

My church friend Jimmy came through for us once again. He graciously volunteered his services and his van in helping us move my first born to what would be her home for the next four years. Jimmy followed us to the college in his van, which was stuffed with Christiann's belongings. After we unloaded them, he took off, leaving us to be alone with our little college student. We met Christiann's roommate and her parents and were relieved to see they were very sweet people. Our daughter would at least be in good company. Christiann's face was bubbling with excitement, anxiously waiting to decorate her side of the room with pictures, posters and all the finishing touches. After helping her to situate all of her cargo in her dorm, it was time for Julianne and me to leave our girl to get started in her new life away from home. I was bursting with all sorts of emotions and had to put on my sunglasses in order to prevent Christiann from seeing me cry. She got lost in my arms as I gave her a big squeeze. I sniffled, told her I loved her and cautioned her over and over again to behave and to be careful. With my shades in place and Julianne beside me, I walked undecidedly through the corridor towards the exit doors, turning around every two steps to wave goodbye. I was choked up for the entire two-hour ride back home and from deep within my heart I prayed to my God that His protection would always be upon her. Julianne was quiet during most of the return trip. I'm sure her thoughts were not far from mine. A scary thought occurred to me as we cruised along the parkway heading home. I was sincerely hoping the one hundred thousand dollars in student loans Chris would eventually have to pay back was going to be worth it!

I looked forward to most of the holidays and school recesses. It was delightful knowing that Christiann would be safe at home even though the stay was temporary. I was beginning to see, however, that since she'd been accustomed to living away from the reign of mom and dad, the return visits home were sometimes stressful, to say the least. The independent co-ed and her mom were often butting heads, which added to the tension of an already uptight household. I understood Julianne's frustration of seeing her orderly house turned upside down when Christiann came home with piles of junk and dirty laundry, but I knew things would always get done, put away and eventually return to normal. It puzzled me to see how Julianne focused more on the untidiness of the house rather than the joy of having Christiann home.

PROMOTION COMMOTION

Meanwhile at CVS, Julianne grabbed the opportunity to make a career change. A position for a pharmacist technician became available. The head pharmacist knew Julianne to be a conscientious worker and offered her the job. Out of the silly red vest and into a white lab coat, she now worked side by side with a pharmacist in what appeared to be a much more respectable occupation than stocking shelves with cosmetics. She was required to learn a lot of pertinent information and take a very challenging exam. By passing the exam she became the lead technician and certified to work as a pharmacist technician anywhere in the country. I was proud of her. I knew she felt better about herself and the money was a slight improvement. The only downside to this career move was the job required her to work full time. With Julianne's obsessive personality, her desire to excel in all she does, and working forty plus hours a week, it was inevitable things were going to get even a bit more frenzied at home. For the past several years, mom's moods were like the many directions of the wind, and we never knew which way the wind was going to blow. We could go from a house of harmony to one of chaos in a matter of moments.

THINGS THAT GO LUMP IN THE NIGHT

My children took up so much of my energy. If I wasn't physically doing something with them, I was worrying about them. Every time they stepped foot outside our home, I prayed they'd return safe and unharmed.

Samantha had always been a tough kid, very street smart, a great sense of humor and a zillion friends. Contrary to the impression she gave most people, she was also a hypochondriac. We never knew just how serious to take her when she complained about an ailments, most of which turned out to be imaginary. One evening, just after turning in for the night, as I was sinking into that peaceful twilight, Samantha came barging into our bedroom screaming bloody murder. "I've got cancer, I've got cancer!" she hollered with an understandable panic in her voice. I nearly jumped out of my skin as she climbed into our bed crying hysterically.

"Mommy, Daddy, feel my breast! I've got a lump! I've got cancer!" She grabbed my hand and placed it near her armpit where she felt the bump.

"Samantha," I said, pretending to be calm, "You're fine! It's nothing, you don't have cancer!"

I don't handle lumps and bumps very well. Having no choice, however, but to feel it for myself, I became quite concerned over what the noticeable lump could possibly be. Julianne and I tried our best to keep her composed and reassured her it was just a harmless cyst.

With the help of Valium, Samantha endured a cat scan. A few weeks later she underwent minor breast surgery. Just as we suspected, thank God, it was a non-cancerous cyst. But if I said I wasn't worried, I'd be lying.

CELL PHONEY

It seems no matter what church someone steps foot into, there's always a Building Program in effect. Full Gospel was no exception. According to Pastor Ted, our building was too small and didn't allow for growth, the ultimate goal of most evangelical congregations. The two things his church had, opposed to other churches, was $400,000 in the bank, which was donated by an ex-member under the ex-pastor's reign, and it was located adjacent to a large shopping mall. The mall's landlord so desired the parcel of land our modest church sat upon, one day he made Pastor Ted an offer he couldn't refuse. Pastor Ted was by no means ignorant to financial matters, so when all was said and done, Full Gospel Church was moving to a brand new huge location in the neighboring town of Island Terrace without having to spend a dime.

Pastor Ted took it upon himself to be the overseer of the tremendous undertaking, and doing this, his priorities seemed to shift from soul saving to construction. He was always on the phone with contractors, electricians, plumbers and the like. One Saturday morning, immediately following a men's fellowship breakfast, he was leading all the men in prayer. His eyes were shut tight, his arms were pointing towards heaven, assuming heaven was up, and he was beseeching God to bless the men of the church and the construction of the new building. Right smack in the middle of this solemn moment, all communications with God got interrupted when Pastor Ted's cell phone started ringing. The Pastor's conversation with the Almighty abruptly came to a pause. He looked at his phone...he looked at the men. "I'm not going to take this call," he assured us, "unless it's George, the general contractor…" He took a quick peek at his caller ID, and then most impolitely turned his attention away from the men. "George!" he inquired curiously, "What's up?" I assumed God didn't mind being put on hold!

Pastor Ted's vision became a reality. He called for an emergency meeting of the membership so we could decide upon a name for the new church. I voted to call it "Full Gospel Church and Clam Bar" because of the many seafood establishments in the area, but we settled on the rather simple and boring "Full Gospel Church of Island Terrace."

TRY TO REMEMBER THAT KIND OF SEPTEMBER...

I'd always loved the month of September. The sweltering heat of July and August was behind us. We could shut off the air conditioning, open up the windows at night to feel the comfortable coolness in the air. Even though these were all signs winter was just around the corner, and even though September had always been the start of another school year, it was still my favorite month. Okay, I have to be honest; I love it because my birthday falls in September. It's the only day of the year when I got a little special attention. Okay, once again I have to be honest; it's because for years it usually meant getting some out of the ordinary "birthday sex." I don't know why I continue to get so excited anticipating my birthday, because as of late, birthdays haven't been what they used to. To put it bluntly, "birthday sex" just ain't what it used to be. I guess it's a guy thing. Just ask any guy what he wants for his birthday and I guarantee nine out of ten will answer the same!

It was a beautiful morning in early September, the sun was bright and the powder blue sky was cloudless. It was one of those days when I was feeling so good, I wasn't even aware of my own body, no aches, no pains, and no distractions. The load in my truck was fairly light for a Tuesday, so I had every intention of whizzing through the day and getting home early. As I was backing into the loading dock of my first stop, I could see Walter the receiving clerk in my side view mirror. Walter, a stocky Polish fellow who was in his early fifties, was not happy unless he was bitching about something. A Viet Nam vet, who proudly proclaimed to hate Jews, spics, niggers, faggots, and liberals equally, loved "The New York Mets," the music of the obscure "The Rossington-Collins Band," and fishing. Walter was waving his arms frantically and I was trying to determine whether he was warning me to stop or to continue backing up. I could see there were no obstructions, so I backed right up to the bay door. Before I could even take one step onto the loading dock, Walter's warm stale breath was right in my face. His voice quivered with what I couldn't discern to be either terror or excitement

"Did you hear?" he shouted, "A plane just crashed into the World Trade Center!"

Knowing how excitable Walter was and not having any clue as to what was going on, I calmly said, "You're kidding!"

Walter waddled away quickly and made his way into the office where a radio was informing its listeners of the latest bits of information on the crash. I was thinking to myself, "What a freak accident!" when within seconds Walter came running back. He didn't know which way to turn first and looked at me with eyes that seemed to be bulging right out of his flustered chubby face. "A second plane just hit the towers!" he announced just like a town crier.

It was then I knew this was no accident and something very fucked up was going on. A few minutes later the report about the third plane was spreading throughout the warehouse. For the first time in all the years I'd been dealing with Walter, I could see his walls come crumbling down.

My thoughts were racing chaotically and the anxiety was causing my stomach to twist almost to the point of nausea. The first thing I did was to place a call to Julianne just to tell her I loved her. Immediately after I hung up I started searching my mental data banks to recall if anyone we knew was working at the Trade Center. I called Roxie and Jack knowing how close to the scene their offices were located. At first I wasn't able to make contact, but after several hours, I learned of their safety.

I had a truckload of packages to deliver and somehow not a single one of them seemed to be the least bit important. Just like everyone else I came into contact with that day, I needed to talk. My plan of zipping through the day and getting home early was shot. As I would pull up to the customers' houses to make my deliveries, they were already out the door and on their way towards the truck to greet me. "Oh my God, what do you make of this terrible situation?" a worried housewife asked me, as if I had an acceptable answer.

All day long I listened to comments that ranged from, "Who could do such a horrible thing?" to "We ought to bomb the shit out of those motherfuckers!" without any clue as to who those "motherfuckers" were. People's emotions were all over the place. Women greeted me with tears in their eyes fearing this could be the end of the world. Men greeted me with vengeance in their hearts wanting nothing more but to annihilate every human being who resembled someone from the Middle East. Absolutely no one had any idea as to what the truth of the matter was; yet nobody held back from letting his or her opinions fly. I have never been too trusting of our government and I never cared too much for the Bush regime. I had my own theories as to how and why this catastrophe occurred, but for the time being, I just listened. There were some families on my route whose loved ones were killed in that sickening inferno. All I could do was express my sorrow. My political point of view wasn't going to ease their pain.

Lighthouse Road in the wealthy community of Sands Point runs right along the Long Island Sound and when looking out across the water there is a magnificent view of the New York City skyline. I drove my UPS truck along that road on the afternoon of September 11th 2001. I pulled over, stepped out of the vehicle and walked along the sandy beach. I stood alone gazing across the sound as the glimmering rays of sunlight pranced upon its tranquil surface. In the distance, huge clouds of gray hovered over Manhattan Island and through the density I could just about make out the empty space where the towers once stood, or at least I thought so. No different than every other person trying to just live their lives in the "home of the brave," I realized life in the free world would never ever be the same.

The following Sunday there was standing room only in the church. Confused faces were looking for answers as believers and doubters crammed into the wooden pews. Pastor Ted really knew how to play it up. Somehow he managed to get his hands on a cross made from sections of iron girders. The structure stood maybe eight to ten feet tall and upon it hung the helmet of a firefighter. The ominous construction was permanently placed on the church grounds right near the entrance, possibly for sentimental reasons, possibly as an attention getter to attract prospective churchgoers who might be driving by. He contacted all the local policemen and firemen, inviting them to the service. He was able to persuade all who attended to take part in a short procession while "God Bless America" blasted from the PA system. I wasn't quite sure what was nauseating me more, the actual events of 9-11 or the spurious display of patriotism coming from the pulpit.

Antonio led the "Praise Team" that morning. Antonio, with his unmistakable Italian face, was a short stocky son of a reverend, and in my opinion, was nothing more than a wannabe rock star. This was his moment to shine. "One, two, three, four..." he counted, I slammed a rim shot on the snare drum and at a volume much louder than the norm, the "Praise and Worship Team" led the congregation into a lengthy version of "Forever." The song is just a rip off of countless other power pop songs disguised in spiritually uplifting lyrics making them appropriate for church. I was in a real quandary that Sunday morning. I really hated the song yet I was playing with every ounce of passion I had. My emotions were stirring, I was angry, I was sad, I was confused and I was scared.

"Let's praise the Lord!" Antonio shouted, and in response, the congregation applauded, cheered and cried out shouts of "Alleluia, Thank You Jesus!" On that fateful Sunday morning Antonio had nothing short of a captive audience. All across America alarm clocks were set so those who hadn't stepped foot inside a church for years, could crawl out from the serenity of their sleep and try to find favor with their Maker. People needed to be certain God had everything in control. People suddenly felt the need to get right with God. I've got to be honest; I didn't know what the hell was going on. I'd seen the world rapidly declining in the last decade and I'd read enough scripture to deduce it was very possible the "end times" really weren't too far away.

Maybe I was being too harsh forming the opinions I had of Antonio. During that same service I pounded the drums with fury. I didn't understand why, but in some small way it made me feel I was doing my part in a situation in which none of us had any control. Within a month the crowds thinned out considerably. By late October the attendance was pretty much back to just the modest number of regulars. From what was no doubt the greatest "wakeup call" this country has ever known, it didn't take very long before most people fell right back to sleep.

FIRST LOVE FIRST TRAGEDY

Whenever I talked on the phone with Christiann while she was away at school, she would constantly yawn. "Am I boring you?" I would ask her, "or don't you ever get any sleep up there?" One evening she surprised me when the tone of her voice was sweet and giggly as she began to tell me about Trevor.

"Dad," she said, "my friends told me he wants to ask me to the football formal!"

"That's, uh, great Christiann; I, uh, really hope he asks you!" I responded a bit unenthusiastically, because what I really thought was, "Oh no, not a jock!"

From the day she was born I'd been dancing around her with my guitar in hand, singing rock and roll songs and now she was gaga over a football player! On one of our many treks up to Marist we finally met Trevor. He seemed like a nice enough kid and it appeared as though he was crazy about Christiann. The fact he lived in Massachusetts could have been a good thing, by keeping them apart during their breaks; or a bad thing, by the two of them living together at my house during those breaks. It was a bad thing. During two summer vacations, two spring and two winter recesses, Trevor spent much of that time living with us. I wasn't too crazy over the idea of having a houseguest, but if they insisted on being together, I preferred for him to be in my home rather than Christiann being in Massachusetts. One Saturday afternoon while wandering about the house minding my own business, I happened to stick my head into Christiann's room. Upon doing so, I found Trevor, dumb smile on his face, lying in bed with his arms around my daughter, as the two of them were watching TV. Being her father, I was totally perplexed over how I should react. I realized nothing was going on, they were just watching television and the door was open. I also realized, when they were away at school, I had no control as to what they were up to. I also remembered what Julianne and I were doing when we were in college, which was all the more reason why I should have made them get up and out of the bedroom. I was also quite aware of the fact that because this was my home, both Christiann and her boyfriend should have had respect for me, Julianne, Sam and Matt. In the true John Domenico fashion that has irked Julianne for years, I ignored the situation.

As nice a guy as Trevor seemed to be, I wanted to discourage Christiann from getting too serious with him. For one, long distance relationships require too much time and energy to keep flourishing. I wasn't comfortable knowing, if anything should develop between them, the possibility existed she might leave the state. More importantly, was the fact Trevor had a drinking problem. Christiann confided in me on several occasions about confronting him with breaking up if he didn't stop binging on alcohol. I wanted better for my kid. Getting involved with an alcoholic would only create unnecessary problems and eventually cause misery.

Christiann broke up with Trevor for a brief period. He soon came crawling back, however, vowing he would quit drinking. In her heart she had strong feelings for him, so she gave their relationship another chance by accepting his invitation to dinner. Chris called to tell me what a wonderful time they had and she sounded confident about his efforts to refrain from alcohol.

I was stacking as many boxes as I possibly could on my hand truck to avoid having to make two trips into my next stop. As I was making my way into the delivery area my beeper sounded. It was Julianne trying to reach me, but what got me worried was the 911 emergency code that followed her number. (This was obviously before we all got suckered into carrying cell phones.) In keeping with my nature to panic, I did. I grabbed the nearest telephone and called Julianne.

"Hi, it's me!" I said a bit nervously, "What's up?"

"John," Julianne said with a trace of helplessness and sadness in her voice, "Trevor is dead!!"

"What?" I screamed so everyone around me heard.

Immediately I called Christiann, wanting nothing more than to be with her. The sound of her sobbing was breaking my heart as she tried her best to explain what had happened. Being so many miles away from my grieving daughter was killing me. Trying to catch her breath between words, she told me how on the night after their romantic dinner, she caught him at a local college club completely wasted. "Daddy, daddy," she wept, "He hurt me so much!"

Her voice trembled as she continued to relate to me what happened. The same night at two o'clock in the morning, Trevor called her, demanding she'd allow him to come over to talk. Christiann tried her hardest to make him realize he was drunk and discussing the matter could wait until the following day. An hour later she received the disturbing phone call notifying her Trevor had slipped off of a third story balcony and was in the emergency room of the local hospital. I couldn't even imagine the shock and nauseating anxiety that must have taken hold of her. By the time she had made it over to the E.R., he was already gone. I don't know what enabled her to deal with such a nightmare and I don't know how she found the inner strength to cope. I could never be absolutely certain as to where my children reside spiritually, or the extent of their relationships with God, but at that moment, all I knew was, not even faith could have seen me through such a catastrophe. Julianne and I felt it would have been in Christiann's best interest for them to break up, but in no way whatsoever, did we even fathom anything like this could or would have happened.

For quite some time Christiann kept a picture of Trevor on her bureau. Whenever I saw the photo I would get torn apart inside just thinking of the torment his parents must constantly go through. I pictured that dumb smile on his face as he was stretched out upon Christiann's bed, and not for a minute could I believe the young man ready to take on the world was dead. Christiann says she dreams about him from time to time. I say we should never let a day go by without telling our kids we love them.

WHAT GOES AROUND...

Samantha is going to make some man miserable one day. As sweet as she can be, that's how bitchy she can be. Sam has had mood swings that have far surpassed some of Julianne's worst. Basically, she has a great personality, a beautiful smile and more friends than I can keep track of. She's a kid who loves to have fun and for the most part, a kid we've always trusted. Probably because of the influence of growing up in the church, Samantha would always be preaching to her schoolmates about how they shouldn't be getting high. She'd always been very open and honest with me. She would keep me informed as to which of her friends were doing drugs or having sex and always demonstrated her disapproval. Substance abuse and sex were the last things I had to worry about with Samantha.

One of the major issues that triggered conflict between Julianne and me was over the curfew we imposed upon our children. I was too easy going and usually permitted them to push the limit by staying out a little later than the hour we agreed upon. Nevertheless, Samantha always managed to make it home at a reasonable time, sometimes even walking though the door earlier than expected. One night it happened to be twenty minutes past her curfew and she still wasn't home. We were a little concerned because it just wasn't like Sam to be late. Suddenly we heard the sound of the front door open and in strolled Sam.

"Hey, Sam," I called out curiously, "How come you're late?"

"Okay, I'm late!" she snapped, and bolted up the stairs to her room.

Julianne gave me the "what are you going to do about this" look, so I hollered for her to get downstairs immediately.

"Yes Daddy," she complied, standing three-quarters of the way down the staircase staring at me.

"Have you been drinking?" I questioned, knowing something was obviously odd about her behavior.

"Yes Daddy!" she answered without batting an eye.

"What did you drink?" I asked.

"I don't know Daddy!" she quickly answered.

"What do you mean you don't know? Was it beer? Was it wine?" I yelled with extreme concern.

"No Daddy!" she replied agreeably, "It was something somebody mixed me!"

"Are you crazy?" I scolded, "How many times have I warned you to never drink something if you don't know what it is you're drinking. Now go to your room!!"

"Okay Daddy!" she said without a fight and went back up the stairs to her room.

Julianne looked at me like I was an idiot and said, "John, did you see how red her eyes are? She wasn't drinking! She was stoned! How stupid can you be?"

I darted up the stairs and busted into Sam's room to find her sitting cross-legged on her bed.

"Sam!" I asked firmly, "Were you smoking pot?"

"Yes Daddy," she confessed humbly and immediately.

I ranted and raved asking her if she was aware of all of the evil effects of smoking pot and told her she was grounded. Without an argument she apologized and promised to never get high again. I was sensitive to the fact she was stoned and could only imagine how bizarre it must have been seeing her dad (who she knew indulged in the past) reprimanding her the way I was. My wife, the ex-cannabis queen, was waiting for me outside Samantha's room grinning from ear to ear. "Isn't she hysterical?" she asked, while mimicking her busted daughter saying, "Yes Daddy, Yes Daddy!!" over and over again.

It actually was pretty funny but as responsible parents we had to do what we had to do. Six months of being grounded seemed like an unfair and unjust sentence, but Samantha didn't give us the slightest bit of resistance! It was as if she almost enjoyed being grounded. In a temporary moment of insanity, I mentioned to Julianne what a trip it would be to get stoned with our own kid. Just as I assumed she would, she called me an asshole! Samantha succumbed to peer pressure, but as far as we know, she has never smoked pot again. ("As far as we know" is the key phrase here!)

IT'S HER PARTY, I'LL CRY IF I WANT TO

When Roger Daltry posed defiantly and sang the words "Hope I die before I get old…" I don't think any of us who belonged to "My Generation" ever thought we were going to get old so damn quickly. So rather than die, many of us just tried our best to stay young. If anyone told me back in 1968, "The Who" would still be touring in the year 2001 I would have told them they were crazy. Keith Moon died before he got old. John Entwisle got old and died. Pete and Roger are still rocking trying their best not to get old.

I couldn't fathom the idea of my wife, the girl I fell in love with when she was just nineteen years old, turning fifty years old. Yeah, I did the math. She was born in 1951. It was 2001, so that would make her fifty! Even though neither one of us wanted to own up to the fact we were nearing the half-century mark, we did discuss it occasionally. When Julianne turned fifty, we had planned to take a trip to Italy, but when the assholes who masterminded the destruction of the World Trade Center on September 11th succeeded into making the whole world nervous about flying, we thought it best to put our traveling plans on hold. I was faced with making a major decision. I couldn't let an event such as Jule's fiftieth go by unnoticed. One afternoon while I was talking about my dilemma with Jule's younger sister Sara, we tossed around the idea of throwing Julianne a really special party. Sara volunteered her house and my friends Wesley and Pat, who were in the food business, would graciously cater it. Every night after work I would call home and tell Jule I was working late, then speed over to Sara's where we would organize and plan. We designed the coolest invitations. The front had Julianne's baby picture on it with the words "Time flies when you're having fun…" The inside details were written with a personal, humorous touch, and included explicit directions to Sara's place. I worked on a guest list, mailed out the invites and before we knew it, the whole thing snowballed to proportions Sara's house just couldn't contain. I knew Julianne wasn't the type of person who liked being the center of attention, so now and then I wondered if I was doing the right thing. Time, however, was of the essence. Her birthday was soon approaching, so if this was going to come off, we had to work fast and clandestine.

My brother-in-law Gary just happened to be friends with the owner of a restaurant equipped with catering facilities for large parties. Even though it was such short notice, a nice room was made available, and because I was related to Gary, I received a generous discount for what promised to be a top-shelf affair. Pat and Wesley were relieved to learn their catering duties were no longer needed as things were falling right into place. The only problem was now we had to send out correction letters to all those who we invited, notifying them the location of the party had been changed.

The next thing I had to figure out was music. I hated DJ's and I remembered a band Julianne and I had heard at a party several years earlier. Julianne had mentioned to me if we should ever throw a party, she wanted them to play. I thought to myself, "Wouldn't it be a great surprise if these guys were still playing around and I was able to get them for Jule's party?" While glancing through the entertainment pages of the local newspaper, I couldn't believe my eyes when I saw the very band I had in mind was playing at a neighborhood bar that evening. I called the club and got to speak with one of the band members. I explained to him my situation and as luck would have it, they were available on the night of the party. They were asking for a lot more money than I expected to shell out, but I said, "What the hell, I'm in this deep, I might as well go for broke!" I booked "The Blue Scoobies." Once again, everything was falling nicely into place.

I was able to make Julianne believe a story I fabricated that our close friends, along with her sisters and our children, all wanted to do something special for her fiftieth birthday, so we planned to take her out for a celebratory dinner. We were all going to meet at her sister Sara's house where a limo would pick us up and take us to the restaurant. She knew Gary had more connections than the Godfather, so the limo didn't strike her as unusual. Julianne had her heart set on going to her favorite place "Angelo's," but in a pre-arranged telephone conversation I set up with Freddy, the owner of Angelo's, I managed to make Julianne believe he couldn't accommodate us and a restaurant owned by one of Gary's friends could. The plan was working out just perfectly...

I had tee shirts made as party favors with the words *"Time flies when you're having fun..."*and the date of her birthday printed on them. Sticking to a theme, I even wrote a song for Julianne entitled, *"Time Flies When You're Having Fun."* I wrote out chord charts for the band and they performed it with me. Gino and his wife Katie decorated the room, filling it with bright balloons and ribbons. I tried my best to produce everything necessary to make this party an event she would never forget. I invited everyone who I thought played a part in her life; long time friends, relatives, work mates, and even the church members who we socialized with from time to time. I wanted to make certain everyone had a great time, and everyone did... except for Julianne that is!

All of the dinner guests were meeting at the bar, and after everyone arrived, we followed the maitre d to a so-called "private room," where we could dine away from the regular clientele. As we all walked together through the corridor, I couldn't believe Julianne had no idea what was about to happen. The maitre d opened the swinging doors leading to the large party room and as soon as Julianne entered the room, the crowd of one hundred yelled, "Surprise!" as the "Blue Scoobies" broke into The Beatles' "Birthday." Having lived with Julianne a long time, I immediately realized the look of shock on her face wasn't one of elation. She was not a happy camper, and in so many ways she let me know it. I knew I'd be drinking a lot of Tequila to help get me through the night.

Everyone had a blast. The food was great, the band was incredible and I was wasted. My dad was so delighted to see all "The Bummers" together again, he made the suggestion we all get together at his place for a reunion party after the holidays. Everyone was up for it and believe it or not it actually happened.

The "Scoobies" played their last number, and then one by one the guests said their goodbyes, until all that remained were Wesley and Toni, Gino and Katie, and Julianne and me. The gifts were plentiful, and with the help of our friends, we gathered them up and loaded them into the car. Since we arrived by limo we were counting on Gino to be our ride home. Both he and I, however, were in no condition to drive. Julianne, on the other hand, party animal she was, did not indulge in even a drop of alcohol. She took on the role of designated driver. Somehow it just didn't seem normal for the birthday girl to be leaving the party sober and having to drive her inebriated friends and husband home. When we arrived back at our place we all hung around for an hour or so laughing and recounting what was a really fun party.

When our friends finally left us to be alone, Julianne looked at me and said tenderly, "You must really love me to do what you did!" I told her that indeed I did. She looked quickly through her gifts before we turned in for the night. "Good night John," she said in a cheerless and unenergetic tone and rolled over to her side of the bed with no intentions to do anything but fall asleep. I lied awake for a while. I was too wound up to sleep. I was thinking about the words one of her cousins said to me while we danced together earlier that evening. "Boy John!" she said, "my cousin is going to do you big time tonight after this extravaganza!" I gave her the party unconditionally; I was not looking for gratitude sex. There are some moments in life, however, when it just feels right and natural for a husband and wife to complete the day by making love. In Jule's mind, I guess this night wasn't one of those moments.

It couldn't have been more than two weeks after the party when I was sitting at the kitchen table finishing up a late dinner, and from right out of left field Julianne hit me with this... "I'd been holding this in for almost two weeks now and I can't hold back any longer. How could you think I could have liked that party? That party wasn't for me, it was for YOU!" I couldn't believe what I was hearing, and I could feel my dinner churning in my stomach as she continued to unload her pent up feelings at me. "After all these years together I see now you don't even know me. You have no clue as to who I am. How dare you do that to me? You know how I hate parties...how could you?"

She then brought to my attention how I forgot to invite a couple of people. It was an honest oversight and she wouldn't let me live it down. She may as well have just stabbed me in the back, that's how badly it hurt. I felt like I was having a nightmare. Her hurtful words kept swirling around in my head and I couldn't tell if I should've been feeling sorry for her or sorry for me. I just couldn't grasp how any normal, warm-blooded human being with a beating heart could not appreciate a party given in his or her honor… and not just any party; I'm talking about a fucking great party! It was ripping my heart to shreds and wrenching my brain to know she was dead serious about hating every minute of her fiftieth birthday. For weeks to come, we received phone calls from the guests just to say what a great time they had. How immensely pathetic was it that I even had to compose her thank you notes? Here I thought I was doing a good thing and it not only bit me in the ass, it just became something else wedging its ugly way between Jule and me. I just didn't get it…Still don't. Probably never will.

After the episode, "Julianne Rips John a New Asshole for the Party He Threw Her," things were strange in the house. I felt uncomfortable being intimate with my own wife and once again our relationship was straining. Knowing history repeats itself, I knew it would only be a matter of time (how much time, I didn't know) before my emotional wounds would heal and our relationship would once again be on the mend. What I couldn't seem to work out in my head was how a "Christian couple," such as Julianne and I, tended to spend so much of our life together on the mend? I had always been under the impression Christian folks were supposed to be happy folks. Something wasn't kosher!

WIN A SOUL LOSE A SOUL

On the evening of the party, as the band was breaking down their equipment, some of our church friends were saying goodnight in typical "Pentecostal fashion." Knowing the condition I was in, they asked, "Are you going to be attending service tomorrow John? Are you going to be able to play those drums?" This comment sparked the drummer's attention and he asked inquisitively, "What church do you guys attend? Sounds like a nice place!"

We told him all about our Full Gospel Assembly and extended him an invitation. The following Sunday morning, as I tried to keep the beat with a slight hangover, who did I see seated among the fellow worshippers, but none other than the drummer from the "Scoobies." After the service he told me how much he enjoyed it and even expressed interest in attending regularly. He inquired if it was somehow possible to get involved in the music ministry. I told him I planned on being away the following week and asked if he would be interested in sitting in for me. He was very excited about the opportunity, so I introduced him to the pastor and to Brett the Praise Team leader. No one seemed to have a problem with this arrangement, so it was agreed upon that next Sunday the "Scooby" was to arrive at church promptly at ten and fill in for me.

Mid-week I got a call from Brett. It seemed as though Pastor Ted had a change of heart. Suddenly he didn't think it was a good idea for someone who wasn't filled with the "Baptism of the Holy Spirit" to be involved in the praise and worship ministry. (How he permitted me to play is another story!) They wanted me to place the call and break the news to him. When

I tried my best to explain the pastor's decision to the drummer, he had a difficult time understanding.

Sounding somewhat like he was disbelieving me, he said, "I met your pastor and he shook my hand and said he was looking forward to having me aboard!"

"Listen man," I said understanding his disappointment, "this ain't coming from me, it's coming from the pastor!"

"Whatever you say," he answered, not disguising his annoyance one bit, "and I don't think I'll be coming around at all. You guys enjoy your church."

When I hung up the phone I said to myself, "Great job Pastor, we lost another one!"

IGNORE IT SO IT GOES AWAY

I've always been somewhat of a health freak. For over twenty-five years our family didn't eat red meat. I've been taking vitamins since I was a kid. I don't smoke. I read the labels on everything avoiding artificial colors and flavors. I'm aware of every pimple, freckle and blemish on my body. I usually check myself from head to toe when I'm in the shower making sure there are no lumps, bumps, rashes or anything that looks vaguely suspicious.

One morning I was lathering up in the shower and as I was gently washing the family jewels, I felt something that seemed a little out of the ordinary. As my right hand passed over my testicles, one of them felt noticeably different. I kept feeling them, comparing one to the other, and finally convinced myself it was nothing to be alarmed about. Besides, I was way too busy to find the time to see a doctor. One evening, while Julianne and I found a rare opportunity to make love, she also noticed there was something obviously different about my right testicle. I told her it was nothing and tried my best to ignore it. Ignoring it, however, was easier said than done.

Three months after Jule's party, the "Bummer" reunion at my parent's house took place. We all had a great time recalling our glory days. Back in those good old days, when I didn't have a full time job, I had loads of free time in which to let my creative energies loose. I used to draw, write stories, make home-made greeting cards, and then mail them off to Jack, knowing my efforts would always make him laugh. Jack brought some of those demented keepsakes to the gathering. His copy of "Slime" magazine with my picture on the cover as "Man of the Year" was still intact. I don't think I've ever laughed quite as hard as I did that night reading through my parody of "Time." I made up my own news stories, movie reviews, and science news all involving the Bummers. Seeing a photo of our meek and mild friend Mike posed as a gynecologist, with his finger strategically placed in the vagina of a girl I had cut out from the pages of "Screw" magazine, left me breathless. The movie review of "I Want to be Black," with the touched up photo of Tommy Cello's face on the body of a well-endowed black man, also got big laughs!

As much fun it was all being together again, it was also a little melancholy. There are not many people who can boast friendships like the ones we've held onto for so many years. It really did seem like it was just days ago when we all piled on top of a four by eight panel and went gliding along the icy hills of Crocheron Park. All those years ago when our friendships began, my parents were younger than we were on the night of this reunion. The one thing every one of us asked ourselves that evening was where did all that time go?

Gino and I found a few minutes to catch up on the latest events of each other's lives when I mentioned my irregular testicle. "Hey buddy," he insisted, "don't take any chances and have a doctor check that out!"

"Yeah, I'll get around to it," I said, "it's probably nothing!" trying to convince myself there was no need to be overly concerned.

It was one of those nights we didn't want to end, but like all good things, it did. We all departed making a promise we would do this sort of thing annually. But to quote John Lennon again, *"Life is what happens while you're busy making plans."*

IT'S HIS PARTY AND I'LL CRY IF I WANT TO

Nobody wants to get old, especially me, but since there's not a damn thing any of us can do about it, rolling with the punches and doing the best I can seems like the way to go. Roxie wanted to make her husband Mikey's fiftieth birthday something special, so she planned a party at a hotel upstate. All of the invited guests were treated to dinner, a comedy show, followed by a birthday celebration, overnight accommodations and breakfast the next morning. It sounded like it was going to be a really good time and Jule and I were looking forward to a weekend getaway. Because at times I can be such a ball breaker, I was able to get Roxie to book Jule and me a room with one of those "Heart-shaped tubs for two." The hotel was just minutes away from Christiann's school, so we would even get the opportunity to visit her for a little while. Wesley and Toni were also going to be there, and even though it would have made perfect sense for the four of us to drive up together, we didn't. Julianne wanted the flexibility to come and go as SHE pleased. I never seemed to learn to not get my hopes up about anything, because nine times out of ten, something always seems to turn a good thing into a fucking disaster.

Saturday morning, the day of the party, arrived. We had every intention of getting a jump on the day, hitting the highway early enough so we could spend a little time with Christiann and be back at the hotel for a little R&R before dinner. If there's one thing I've come to expect in my long marriage to Julianne, it's that things almost never go according to plan. She woke up that morning with an excruciating headache and the closer it got to departure time, the viler her mood became. Julianne was also not capable of spontaneity. She was unable to step foot out of the house without first doing some housework, headache or not. I completely understand how there are certain chores that need to be accomplished, but Jule became someone who just didn't know how to put fun or her well-being first. I thought her behavior might be genetic, and without the help of modern pharmaceuticals, it seemed apparent, things would never change. She had to make a simple decision; we either had to call Roxie and inform her that Jule was feeling sick and we were staying home, or we get dressed and hit the road. She took her sweet time getting ready and then went into her all too familiar routine of complaining about having nothing to wear. After mixing and matching outfit after outfit and shoe upon shoe, I then had to bite down hard and tolerate the hair drying and ironing procedure. With a two and a half hour drive ahead of us, I started to stress. The mood had been set and I knew we were in for a night of tension.

Our visit with Christiann was short and sweet because just as expected, we were running late. After a very quick hello and goodbye with our college girl, we rushed off to the party as to not spoil Mikey's surprise. When we arrived at the hotel we went directly to our room to drop off our luggage and freshen up a bit. From the second we entered the room, Julianne started to spew out complaints one after the other. "It's freezing in here! It smells musty! Don't think I'm getting into that tub…"

It was brutal. I took a deep breath and tried to calmly explain to her the room had been vacant for a while and once I put the heat on it would be fine. "Roxie paid additional money to get this room for us Jule," I said with a slight hint of resentment in my voice, "if we're not going to use it, let's let someone else have it!" Because she didn't want anyone knowing our business, we left the arrangements as they were. I understood she had a headache, but there was absolutely no reason why she had to mentally abuse me the way she did. If something was wrong in her world, it was always my fault.

We made it over to the dining hall where the cocktail party was already in progress. Wesley and Toni were waiting patiently for our arrival, and as soon as we entered the room, Toni knew Jule was not in one of her better moods. Toni had always been perceptive to what was going on in our relationship. I stepped right up to the bar and fixed myself a drink because a good buzz was the only thing that was going to help me get through the night. I could tell Jule just didn't want to be there and it was obvious everything and everyone was getting on her nerves, especially me.

Dorothy was a friend of Roxie's from way back. The first time I met Dorothy was back in the late seventies when my band was playing in the local clubs. Roxie, Dorothy and several of their friends became our biggest fans. For whatever reason, Dorothy and I seemed to connect and though I'd only seen her a few times through the years, we'd keep up on each other's lives via Roxie. When Dorothy and her husband Steve arrived at Mikey's party, I was almost ecstatic to see her. Since Julianne wasn't too keen on talking to me, I knew Dorothy and I would have lots to talk about. When it was time for all of us to be seated for dinner, whether it was intentional or not, we wound up sitting next to each other. Steve kept leaving the room to watch a football game on the big screen TV at the bar. Julianne ignored me as best she could and directed most of her conversation to Toni and Wesley. I was totally blown away by how much Dorothy and I had in common. We liked the same music, the same bands, the same movies, and had the same political views. She saved the night. I actually had a wonderful time just conversing with her. Several times that evening I was wishing Julianne wasn't even there. Julianne and I were slowly but surely losing our ability to communicate with each other and it often resulted in displays of animosity and hostility.

The celebrating was over and everyone was retiring to his or her room. When Jules and I entered our "honeymoon suite," the first words out of her darling lips were, "Now it's too hot in here! Lower that heat!" We both sat upon the bed and although the room temperature was stifling, I could feel the ice coming from Julianne as she tightly held onto the remote, giving all of her attention to whatever was on the television. I looked over at the empty tub and thought to myself, "What a waste!" She finally let go of the remote, got up from the mattress and locked herself in the bathroom where she was getting ready for bed, or should I say sleep! Extremely annoyed with her and the entire situation we were in, I grabbed the remote and started flipping through the stations. Much to my surprise, I stumbled upon the porno channel, which to the best of my knowledge was supposed to be scrambled, but wasn't. Knowing there was definitely not going to be any intimacy going on in our room that night, I probably should have just changed the channel as to not get any ideas in my head. My curiosity was aroused, so of course until I heard Julianne open the bathroom door, I didn't. The image on the screen of an attractive couple going to town on each other was quite erotic, to say the least, and not at all conducive to sleeping. I quickly changed the station just as Julianne came out of the bathroom. She climbed into bed, buried herself under the covers, turned away from me and curtly said, "Good night!" I lied there on my back as the steamy picture of the couple making love kept replaying in my mind. Thank goodness I drank a substantial amount of mind-numbing alcohol throughout the evening, so eventually I had no problem drifting off to sleep.

I set the alarm for Sunday morning so we'd be sure to make breakfast. Jule's headache must have finally subsided, because as if nothing ever happened the day before, she suggested I fill the tub. Now if I thought like a woman I would have said, "You've got to be kidding, after the way you treated me yesterday!" and ignored her. Because I'm a man, I will openly admit I could overlook anything for the opportunity to get some good away-from-home sex. I climbed into the tub beside her and it was probably the most unromantic bath we'd ever taken together. I think the reason she even suggested the bath was because she didn't want Roxie to have wasted her money on our deluxe room. It doesn't take too much to get a man excited, so when my dutiful wife took notice that I definitely was, she asked if I wanted to fool around. After our bath I jumped at the opportunity and climbed back into bed with her. Even though we were just going through the motions, it was on that morning I knew for certain something was positively wrong with my lovemaking equipment. Why I didn't explain to her right then and there that I thought I might have had a problem was even more troubling than the problem. We were most definitely facing a breakdown in communication.

No different than the hundreds of other times we'd had lovers' spats, things eventually turned around. We forgot about our differences and carried on. I especially hated it when we wasted the rare opportunities to be alone together like the way we did on the weekend of Mikey's fiftieth. I've learned not to dwell on life's disappointments. I simply get over them. It's how I've survived.

THE "C" WORD

Every time I showered, every time I went to the bathroom, every time (though not too often) Jule and I fooled around, I was reminded I'd better go see a doctor. My right testicle became as hard as a cue ball. It was as if it had petrified. Sometimes when I sat down I could actually feel it drop to the chair like a falling rock. It was Presidents' Day; I had the week off, so without saying a word to anyone, I went to see my doctor. My mom worked at his office as an x-ray technician so I had no problem getting an immediate appointment. As I was on my way to see the doctor, I kept trying to reassure myself he was going to tell me it was nothing.

Whenever I felt the need to see a physician, which I thank God was not very often, I went to Dr. Ross. He was the same guy who, when I was in my twenties, prescribed a steady job as a remedy for my nervous stomach. Since he employed my mom, he was like part of the family. He was a very good doctor and a pretty nice guy, although sometimes I felt like his bedside manner could have used a little improvement. Dr. Ross greeted me with a warm smile and a handshake and since my mom already clued him in as to what my problem was, he asked me to drop my pants as he unceremoniously slipped on his rubber glove. I don't care how much I considered him part of the family; I wasn't too comfortable having my balls squeezed by anyone other than my lover or me. As he rolled my testicle about his trained and knowledgeable fingers, he looked up at me and his fretful eyes said it all. "Oh boy!" he commented caringly, "We're going to get you right over to the urologist. I commend you for not putting this off for too long!" "Oh shit," I thought, "Julianne was right! I should have been here months ago!"

Without wasting a minute, he got on the phone with the urologist and made it top priority I be seen immediately. I scooted right over to his office where a sonogram of my testicles was the first order of business. I'm pretty good at reading people's faces and while looking at the expression on the face of the technician who was gliding the tell-all equipment about my balls, I got the sick feeling something was seriously wrong. While consulting with Dr. Rosenberg, my newly appointed and very young urologist, who strongly resembled Doogie Howser, I was informed that the results of my sonogram showed unmistakable signs of something very suspicious. My right testicle, which I'd grown so very fond of during my forty-nine years, was going to have to be removed. Suspicious is just a medical term meaning, "I think you have cancer!" Doogie scribbled some stuff down on a pad and told me to see his receptionist to schedule a date for surgery as soon as possible. The first thing I thought I'd better do was to call my wife.

"Hello Jule," I said, sounding as sickly as could be.

"John, what's the matter?" she asked.

"I'm at the urologist office and…" and before I could finish she cut in:

"You went without telling me! What's your problem?"

I felt so sick and so upset over what I had just heard, I couldn't discuss it over the phone. I also felt sad about not allowing Julianne the opportunity to accompany me during this disturbing ordeal.

"I'll talk to you when I get home," I said feeling sorry for myself, and dropped down the receiver.

The doctor tried to console by saying he couldn't be one hundred percent certain what showed on the films was cancer. He went on to say, worst case scenario, if it was cancer, it was one hundred percent treatable and curable. It didn't matter what he said because he was still going to take out one of my balls. He asked me if I had any questions, and at the moment, all I could think about was how much of a freak was I going to look like. I asked him if it was common practice to fill the half empty scrotum with a prosthetic testicle. He must have thought I was nuts (no pun intended) and reassured me if I was walking along the beach in a "Speedo," no one would be able to tell I had been altered. "This can't be my life!" I thought to myself, "These things are not supposed to happen to me! What's up with this Lord? You're not paying attention! John Domenico is not supposed to get cancer!"

The following day, after the depressing news sunk in, I was moping about the house in a state of confusion. I knew I hadn't been in the greatest of places mentally and spiritually. My recurring conflicts with Julianne had caused me to entertain thoughts a Christian man shouldn't have been thinking. My conversations and the things I was viewing on my computer monitor weren't reflecting the man I claimed to be. I started to wonder if God was indeed punishing me or trying to teach me a lesson. It was about ten o'clock on a Tuesday morning when my telephone rang. I picked it up and was taken by surprise when I heard the voice of Randy, a friend of ours for many years from the original church. I couldn't even remember the last time I had seen or spoken to Randy it's been so long. Randy is a soft-spoken woman who sincerely says "God bless you" and "Praise Jesus" with her every breath. She was just as surprised to hear my voice, as I was to hear hers.

"What are you doing home?" she asked, "I figured you and Julianne would be at work as I only intended to leave a message!" I told her I had the week off and I guess she could tell by the tone of my voice, I was upset.

"What's wrong my love?" she asked with purest concern.

"Well Randy," I replied with a deep sigh, "I got some bad news yesterday" as I continued to tell her of my prognosis.

Without skipping a beat and without a word of pity, she said with utmost conviction, "God is calling you back. He's sending you a wakeup call! You've been wandering away from Him and He wants you to come back!"

Randy's words hit me like a ton of bricks. I hadn't talked to her in such a long time, how could she possibly have known I was going astray in my thought life? I took her words to heart and spent a good part of the day just praying and doing some soul searching. "She was right!" I thought, "I have to get myself right with my Maker!" The following Sunday morning I told my disturbing news to the pastor and a few of my church cronies. When it came time during the service for those in the congregation to step up to the altar if they needed prayer, I was right up there in front getting anointed with oil and having the elders of the church lay hands on me. The news spread throughout the church and everyone and their brother was praying for me. If this was indeed a wakeup call, I thought awoke.

March 6th, 2001 was the day I said farewell to my right nut. For forty-nine years it hung in there for me, producing the seed that fertilized the eggs that brought forth my children and enduring the pain of a few wild pitches. I was in and out of the hospital the same day (only because I insisted) and to be honest, the pain level was minimal. I was able to walk almost effortlessly into my house and up the stairs to my bedroom. When I looked down between my legs to see my manhood wrapped up in a gauze sling, it was quite unsettling. I had at least a couple of weeks before meeting with my urologist again and until then, I tried my very best not to think about the information that awaited me. The possibility was very real; cancer may have made itself a home inside my scrotum. If it was cancer, the next thing left to determine was whether or not it spread. There was no sense in worrying or in making postulations. I had no choice but to take it one day at a time. I have to say though; I expected a little bit more of a pity party than the one my wife and kids threw for me. They could've at least let me have had the opportunity to say, "Don't feel sorry for me, I'll be all right!"

The moment of truth had arrived; it was the day of my follow up appointment with my urologist. Julianne accompanied me on this visit because she knew if the news were negative, I would fall apart. Doogie looked like a junior high school student as he leaned back into the large office chair that appeared to swallow him. With the lab report and the results of my latest CAT scan spread about on the desk before him, without flinching, he gave me the distressing news. In almost the same manner a mechanic would tell a customer he needed a new water pump, Dr. Rosenberg told me, just as he suspected, what I had was undeniably cancer. After I heard him say the word "cancer," my hearing shut down and all I could see were his lips moving. My heart tried to escape me by sinking to the soles of my feet and my stomach felt as though it had turned completely inside out. I almost felt as if I were melting, oozing from my chair, slithering down along its legs and finally to a hiding spot under his desk. Everything seemed to be spiraling as I felt my blissful little world come crumbling apart.

"How is it I could have cancer?" I wondered, "This can't be possible, this is me we're talking about!" I remember hearing these keywords, as my mind seemed to be circling through a cyclone of confusion, "radiation, chemotherapy, lymph nodes, and surgery." He must have known I wasn't hearing a word he was saying, so he directed most of the conversation toward Julianne. He explained, even though my CAT scan was negative, with the type of cancer I had, removing my lymph nodes would probably be the best approach. He went on to further explain, since my strain of cancer didn't react well to radiation, chemotherapy would most likely be the prescribed treatment. After he described the path testicular cancers usually take, from the testicle to the lung then to the brain, he once again reassured me the disease was one hundred percent treatable and curable, recommending I read Lance Armstrong's autobiography. By the time our little conference was over, I felt totally helpless, hopeless and nauseous.

I was then instructed that my next move would be to make an appointment with an oncologist. He made some recommendations, but thanks to my dad and all his medical connections, we found Dr. David at New York Presbyterian Hospital in Manhattan. My father assured me, no matter what the cost, he would see to it that we found the best in the business. I called Dr. David's office for an appointment and because I was able to name drop, he saw me almost immediately. I was told to have all my medical records, including films, lab reports, CAT scans etc. forwarded to his office at once and he would see me for a consultation.

Julianne accompanied me on my first visit with Dr. David. He explained the implications and the complications of lymph node removal and enlightened me to the statistics, in over eighty percent of these surgeries, the nodes are clean. He continued by mapping out my alternative. He said if I went for the surgery, I would probably never have to see him again. The surgery, however, was extensive, the recovery time long and there was no guarantee against plumbing dysfunction. He said I also had the option to choose the "aggressive watch program." This program required a five-year commitment from me and involved blood tests and x-rays. During the first year the visits were to be monthly, the second year, every two months, and the third year, every three months and so on. After carefully reviewing all my records, Dr. David ruled out both radiation and chemotherapy, which I must say was a tremendous relief, especially since I was very fond of my hair! There was no way I wanted to go through another operation, so I agreed to the five year aggressive watch.

During those years, while I sat gratefully in the waiting room of the oncology department, I would look around and see all those who were not as fortunate as I was. Folks too weak to stand were sitting in wheel chairs awaiting their next dose of chemo. Women wearing kerchiefs and men wearing caps were trying to cover up the way the treatments had caused them to lose their hair. Looking into the tired and frightened eyes of some of those patients, I was sure not one of them had ever expected they would be in such a depressing situation. Cancer always happens to the other guy. None of us ever expects that one day we could be the other guy.

Most of the guys at work thought I had hernia surgery. I don't know why, I suppose it's a guy thing, but I didn't want to spread the news around that I had a testicle removed. We guys are proud of our nuts! We were born with two and we want to die with two! In my case, however, if one of them could eventually kill me, I'd rather live with one than die with two.

RECOVERY

My recuperation period was eight weeks. During that time I got the opportunity to once again do a little soul searching. I was reading the Bible almost daily and I was spending some quality time in thought with my Maker. I wasn't exactly sure where He was leading me, but something inside me was stirring. I wrote a couple of songs, one entitled "Drifter," which tells a story of someone who drifts away from God until tragedy strikes, then comes crawling back begging for forgiveness. Somehow, for whatever reason, I believed that was precisely what had happened to me. I made a million excuses why I had backslidden and why my thoughts seemed to have steered me away from God. One excuse was the constant tension in my marriage, but the truth of the matter was, nobody was to blame but me. I knew I had to start getting more serious about taking care of my spiritual affairs. Amazing what a little disease can do.

I also got the chance to do something I'd wanted to do for a long time. I was finally able to put all my songs in a file on my computer and printed out my complete songbook. Working long hours at UPS resulted in most of my personal things becoming quite disorganized. In some way, my time away from work was a blessing. It gave me the chance to finally get some things in order. Looking back on all the songs I'd written through the many stages of my life, however, was an eye opener for me. Far too many songs were about my roller coaster relationship with Jule. It was somewhat painful for me to recognize just how different we were and how many times I'd felt we'd become so unsuited for one another.

Almost every day I had the pleasure of getting treated to lunch by one of my visitors. I felt like a human being again, away from the rat race of the working life. I grew my beard and fell into this wonderful groove of pretending to be independently wealthy by spending my days going for walks on the beach or eating at my favorite restaurant. I was sure the waiters were beginning to wonder what my story was. Not having to go to work and being on disability surely agreed with me. Of course the help I received from my parents made my situation a lot less worrisome. Their giving me a little advance of my inheritance money helped to lighten the financial burden somewhat. There's a bright side to every situation, it's only a matter of choosing to see it. I treasured every minute of my eight weeks at home. Okay, maybe not every minute. There were moments when I sunk into a little depression because I expected a little more attention from my kids while my activities were still somewhat restricted.

"Need anything?" Matthew would yell from the bottom of the staircase, and if he didn't hear a response within seconds, he'd vanish. He'd either be out with his friends or down in the basement engrossed in e-mailing his buddies or pounding on his drums. Kids have their own agendas and my disability interfered with them. I wonder if that's just the way they handle things. I still can't get over the way Christiann dealt with Trevor's death. I would have been completely devastated if I had to experience something as tragic as that. Maybe she has a built-in defense mechanism and a natural ability to cope. I guess we all have our own ways of dealing with things. I wonder how I would have reacted if I was a kid living at home and my dad had gone through what I did. Oh well, what the heck, sometimes there's just no choice but to accept things the way they are, like it or not. (By the way, five years had passed with no incidents or reoccurrence.)

OPPOSITES ATTRACT?

From time to time I would get the crazy notion, tragedy brings about good. Because I faced a minor bout with cancer, I had this feeling Julianne and I would grow closer. Then again, I thought as a result of 9/11, Americans would put their differences aside and work harder for the common good, but I was wrong.

For at least eleven years we never seemed to agree on the issues involving our children. Julianne believed I had intentionally taken sides with the kids, turning them against her. I won't say I'd always made the wisest decisions, but that was the furthest thing from the truth. I'd always tried to be fair and honest with my kids, but whether it was the way I gave them some leeway with their curfews, or not grounding them for achieving anything other than high marks in school, an argument always seemed to ensue over my leniency. Julianne demanded much more of her children than I did. I just wanted my kids to enjoy being kids while they were still kids! If there was anything I was sure about, it was how quickly the years pass. No two ways about it, Julianne was more demanding and stricter than I was, so it was only natural for them to come to me with their requests rather than go to mom. It had never been my intention to win favor with my kids or have them not respect their mom. I knew deep down our children had good character, were conscientious and moral, and for the most part, I trusted them with all my heart. In all fairness to everyone involved, I never believed I was doing the wrong thing. Julianne certainly felt she too was doing the right thing, but many times we just didn't see eye to eye. In hindsight, due to stubbornness and not communicating,

I realized how often we didn't put up a united front. Most children are clever and know all too well how to pit mom and dad against each other. The way I perceived things, however, was that if it wasn't Julianne's way, it was the wrong way. Many times she claimed it was her desire for me to be the head of our household. What I thought she really wanted was a puppet, someone to reinforce her laws. Our disagreements would turn into cold wars and for days, sometimes weeks, we would avoid each other at all costs. Discussion was next to impossible and when we went to bed, we would lay as far apart from each other as we could without falling off the sides. Like always, we eventually we made up. This obstinate behavior would drive me crazy, because in my mind, it was such a waste of precious time.

I'd often pondered how two people who chose to share a life together, and who claimed to be Christians, could grow so far apart. Julianne had a remarkable and uncanny ability to lecture me on what an immature, rebellious, irresponsible father I was and any turmoil in the house was entirely my fault. She insisted I was to blame for the poor relationship she had with her children. I would run the scenarios over and over again in my head, trying to determine whether or not Jule was right and that possibly, I was the problem. Each time, however, I realized things about Julianne that revealed to me she may have had some deep issues needing to be dealt with. On the one hand, I felt like I was enabling her by not letting her know my honest feelings, but on the other hand, keeping the peace seemed like the better thing to do at the time. So often I saw her behaving in the same way she would tell me her mother did when Julianne was a kid. If our children helped out by cleaning the kitchen, for instance, it was never good enough. Hell, sometimes I would try to lend a hand around the house and painfully aware of how finicky she was, I would purposely try to do the best job I could. I remember one day how I scrubbed the bathroom for hours. I wanted to make sure everything sparkled. Julianne gave it her usual inspection and instead of saying, "Thanks honey, nice job!" she found the one minuscule spot I had overlooked. Maybe I was over-reacting to her criticism, but no different than our children, I would think, "Why bother? Nothing we do is ever good enough."

Jule just never knew how to relax. The slightest thing would trigger, what I considered, irrational behavior. If a chair, a table or even a cushion was just slightly out of place, it made her uneasy. A crumb on the kitchen counter, a drop of toothpaste in the bathroom sink or hair in the bathtub could easily set off the next argument. She couldn't tolerate how no one else in the household would straighten up after themselves. The problem was, we couldn't see "the filth" she claimed to see. We also didn't see the need to have our home as sterile-clean and orderly as she thought it had to be. It occurred to me, an obsessive-compulsive disorder might not be out of the question. No matter what it was we purchased, she'd be guaranteed to find a defect or an imperfection. Most people who came into our home on the worst day would find it immaculate. In my wife's eyes, however, it was never clean. This unconventional behavior was getting progressively worse as she got older. More times than not, I felt like we were becoming totally incompatible. Everyone who knew us saw the problem, but no one, including myself, had ever suggested to her that maybe she needed some professional help. I kept hoping things would eventually get better. Sometimes they did and I magically forgot how miserable she'd made me. Sometimes we would even fall temporarily back into wedded bliss. Unfortunately, it was not very long until we fell back out.

SABOTAGE

Time marches on and my favorite month was once again approaching, September. This was going to be the September of my fiftieth birthday. All of my friends were either calling or e-mailing, wondering what Julianne was planning. I asked her what we were going to do for my fiftieth and without hesitation she said, "You already had your party!" I wasn't exactly sure what she meant by that comment until she reminded me she was still harboring bad feelings about her fiftieth. "That party you threw for me was really for you! Why don't you just admit it?" she said, without the slightest consideration for my feelings.

I was beginning to notice, whenever a happy occasion was on the horizon, Julianne's mood seemed to mysteriously and coincidentally shift into an argumentative one, oddly bordering on depression. Was it possible she was bi-polar, was there a hormonal problem, or did she just really despise me? Life for the average suburban family man can be rather uneventful. Most people looked forward to diversions. We lived a Monday to Friday workweek, chores on the weekends, not much excitement going on except maybe going out to dinner with friends now and then. When a special day came along such as an anniversary, a birthday, Valentine's Day, I saw it as an opportunity for us to share some special out of the ordinary treatment as a break from the monotony of the daily grind. Nine out of ten times I was disappointed, as my spouse either had a headache or was mad at me for something I was not even aware of. Within a time frame of five years for example, Valentine's Day in our home was completely uneventful and unromantic! On two of those five, she didn't even open my cards. Is it any wonder why I'd come to despise February fourteenth?

I believe it was on our fifteenth wedding anniversary when we planned on staying at a Marriott for a weekend getaway. I worked my ass off that Friday in order to get home early enough so we could make our eight p.m. dinner reservations. Upon entering the house that evening, I found Julianne sitting on the couch in front of the television, nowhere near ready to go. I couldn't believe my eyes. I assumed she'd be anxious to leave and find her showered and dressed. I obviously assumed wrong when she unenergetically said with a stretch and a yawn, "I guess I'd better get ready!" I counted to ten, tried not to show I was upset and did my best to not create any tension. In spite of how annoyed I was at what I perceived as her disinterest, we made it to the hotel just a little late and ultimately enjoyed a candle-lit romantic meal. When dinner was over, however, so was the evening. Julianne got an upset stomach and we ended up spending good money on a luxury hotel room so we could sleep. I was getting quite the inferiority complex.

On our twenty-eighth anniversary she was pissed off at me about something, probably had to do with the kids again, and was talking to me only out of necessity. Nonetheless, we went to dinner that evening with our friends Paul and Maria, who happen to share the same anniversary date as ours. The four of us did nothing but talk about our rocky marriages. The thing that was most unsettling to me was how we all claimed to be Christians. Weren't we supposed to be different? Weren't we supposed to be forgiving? If we couldn't get along and forgive our spouses, how in God's name were we going to be a light in the darkness of a lost world? Once again, there was no anniversary affection and a year later I found the unopened cards I bought her in the glove compartment of my car.

The girl I took for my wife was fun loving, daring, passionate, and open-minded. She maintained, while she grew up and matured, I didn't. If maturing meant eliminating fun from my life, well then maybe she was right and I hadn't matured. Many of the things we liked to do together when we were first married were no longer even considered. Julianne no longer liked to go to the movies, so we rarely went. She hated to fly, so we rarely took those Caribbean vacations most couples long for. She hated sailing, so we almost never went out on boats (and a couple of my best friends owned beautiful boats). We no longer frequented the beaches in the summertime because for some strange and unwarranted reason, she went through a period when she didn't like her body and wouldn't wear a bathing suit in public. The truth is, she had nothing to be self-conscious about, and she had a fine figure. I never liked confrontation, so I would usually let things just roll off my back and move on, but as I got older, my frustration with my wife's idiosyncrasies started to get the best of me. I spent endless hours trying to figure out how she developed such low self-esteem. It was very possible it could be linked to the emotional scars from her childhood. She refused to splurge on herself. Anything she bought had to be on sale and usually came from discount stores. If she had a coupon it made it all the more easier for her to spend her money. Never have I denied her anything. Never have I given her a hard time about spending money, so I never understood how she became such a penny-pincher, other than the theory, she thought herself as undeserving.

One Christmas I gave her a diamond and sapphire ring, something she had mentioned to me at various times she admired. I was bowled over when she complained to me about the shade of the sapphire stones and questioned me as to where and why I bought it without her approval. I just couldn't fucking win! Some of my friends had asked me time and time again how I hadn't divorced her yet!

My brother-in-law Art suggested to me many times, ever since his sister "found Jesus" and became active in the "Full Gospel Church," her behavior changed and not always for the better. "She's bound up by religion," he would say. In the past I'd never given it much thought, but at that point, I was starting to wonder if he was right. Maybe I was being insensitive and impatient with her, I didn't know. What I did know was that we've already wasted too much of life's precious time. Of all the let-downs and disappointments I'd had through the years, what occurred on my fiftieth birthday was absolutely the worst.

IT'S MY PARTY AND I'LL CRY IF I WANT TO

Seeing that Jule had no intentions of initiating any form of a gathering for my "special day," it was left entirely up to me. I told Wesley if we could all get together at our old standby, "Angelo's," it would be cool. Everyone agreed to meet there Saturday evening at eight. I called Freddy in advance just to be sure he could accommodate all of us, which needless to say, he did. From the moment Julianne woke up that morning, I knew this night might very well be one of the worst nights of my life.

Just as I expected, the morning greeted her with one of her pounding headaches, but it didn't stop her from doing housework all day. When the evening finally rolled around, she took her sweet-ass time getting ready, went into her usual routine of complaining about having nothing to wear, and finally asked me if I would go without her.

"Julianne," I pleaded, "please get ready, it's late. They're all going to be there waiting for us. You have to go!"

"Don't you do this to me! Don't you rush me!" she demanded, "I hate this shit!"

What else could I do except to bite my tongue, count to ten and hope she would eventually get into the car? I should have gone by myself. She didn't say two words to me for the entire thirty-five minute ride to the restaurant.

When we finally got there everyone was waiting with smiles, kisses, hugs and presents. Everyone also knew by the look on our faces, there was major trouble in paradise. Julianne was as standoffish as she could possibly be. She didn't crack a smile, spoke only when it was absolutely necessary and totally ignored me. The wine was flowing and all of my buddies tried as best as they could to keep the spirit of the evening lively and happy. Julianne drank a cup of tea, refused to eat a thing and reminded me several times she wanted it to be an early night.

Pat had recently divorced Julianne's cousin Rosanna and that evening was going to be the first time Julianne would meet his new girlfriend Diane. Diane was trying so hard to warm up to Julianne. She was uncomfortably aware that because of Jule's loyalty to her cousin, meeting each other might turn out to be very awkward. If looks could kill, Diane would have been dead ten times over. I was so embarrassed, but before long the wine kicked in and I was able to ignore the evil stares coming from Julianne, to live for the moment and celebrate me.

The gang sang "Happy Birthday," we ate our cake, drank our espresso and it was finally time to call it a night. I prefer to call it a disaster. As I said my "Thank yous" and made my farewells, Jule impatiently rushed me along. She took the keys from me and insisted upon driving due to the amount of wine I consumed. When we got into the car, she quickly started it up, slammed the gearshift into reverse, and while recklessly backing out of our parking spot, almost ran into Pat and Diane. "I should have run them over," she said maliciously, "How does he fucking stand her?"

Julianne sped the whole way home with her angry eyes fixed on the road. My thoughts scurried like startled mice running in a thousand different directions while I sat totally speechless in the passenger seat beside her. My confused emotions were wedged somewhere between depression and fury. The depression eventually took over. It's probably not even necessary to mention, but in case anyone's wondering, there was no "birthday sex" again that year. It was yet another milestone memory in my life.

I received a lot of great gifts from my friends that night, but I would have returned every single one, just to have back the magic of yesteryear with my wife. At the moment, that didn't seem likely, so I figured I might just as well enjoy the presents. I thought Wesley and Toni's gift was great. Jule, on the other hand, deemed it as selfish and thoughtless. They gave me a pair of front row seats for the following Sunday evening's performance of the off Broadway show, "Love Janis".

"You better find somebody else to go with you," she clamored, "because I'm not going on a Sunday night. How dare they buy you tickets without asking if you already had plans? How inconsiderate of them!" I just couldn't understand this irrational thinking and her very distant and bizarre behavior. The woman who was confronting me wasn't Julianne.

"Julianne, we don't have any plans for next Sunday, so why are you getting so crazy," I questioned, "You're making way too much of this!"

Maybe I was dense, but I just couldn't follow her reasoning. When she started to bluster about how she didn't consider Toni or Wesley to be her friends, just mine, I determined there had to be something deeply disturbing her.

"Jule, how could you even think that? Toni's been your friend for over thirty years," I bellowed in bewilderment, "You can't be serious!"

Our heated discussion soon turned into a full-scale screaming match, only this time, I was doing most of the screaming.

"Don't you see you've got a problem?" I yelled. "Everyone who knows you can see it, why can't you? Your sisters, our friends, my family, your friends! You need help! Nobody thinks like you! Nobody!"

I was trembling and with my last ounce of strength, I cried, "I can't take it anymore!" I told her I thought we should seek counseling. Everything I had said seemed to fall upon deaf ears.

"I don't need counseling!" she retorted, "Maybe you should go!" and mistakenly I did.

DEAF EARS

Out of sheer frustration I went ahead and called my pastor, the same guy I had once called to renew our wedding vows. I told him I was having some personal problems and needed to talk with someone about it. He agreed to see me and then one evening in the informal atmosphere of his living room, I confidentially poured my heart out to this "Man of God." I didn't hold back anything and felt I was being as honest as I could possibly be. To say I "let go" would be an understatement. He got quite an earful as I divulged my slant on the history of Julianne and me. It was hurting me to say many of the things I said because it wasn't the way I wanted anyone to perceive my wife. Pastor Ted gave me a look of deep concern then asked me point blank, "Do you love her, John?"

I didn't respond immediately. I took a deep breath, sighed and finally answered him; "I wouldn't be here looking for help if I didn't love her!"

I didn't expect to walk out of his home with the definitive answer on how to restore my marriage, but I did expect a little more than, "I'll pray about this John and then I will prayerfully approach Julianne!"

I had an uneasy feeling that maybe I shouldn't have disclosed so much, but it was already too late. Pastor Ted never spoke with my wife, and betraying the confidence I put in him, revealed my personal business to others. It was only a few weeks after my so-called counseling session, when I heard from some church friends of mine, the news had leaked out, "John and Julianne were having marital problems!"

Julianne wasn't very happy about me talking with the pastor. I was so beside myself, I really believed he could have helped us. Jule and I were in the midst of what was a low point in our marriage and I was scrambling for answers. I knew eventually we would make up and continue on, but in the meantime, the stress was tearing me up and wearing me down. It was really a terrible way to live.

ONE STEP FORWARD TEN STEPS BACK

On the night of the "Love Janis" show I wound up taking Samantha with me. On the way into Manhattan we hit so much traffic, it was inevitable we would miss the entire first act, so we turned around and went home. After explaining what had happened, the theatre management was kind enough to let me exchange the tickets for a future show. By that time, the domestic turbulence had subsided somewhat and Julianne accompanied me to the show. I had purchased a couple of more tickets and took Samantha and Matt along. We actually had a good time doing something together as a family for a change.

For a fiftieth birthday gift, Julianne and my kids chipped in together and bought me tickets to see the Rolling Stones, tickets that were very hard to come by and very expensive. The one thing Julianne and I did together quite often was to attend rock concerts. It still was one of the things we had in common, a love for rock and roll. Somehow the music had a way of bringing us back to who we were before we had to contend with all the complications of raising children and trying to make a living. Unfortunately, the shows were way too few and far between. What disturbed me was how our faith and the promises it held hadn't been enough to keep our relationship from continually falling apart. Something had obviously not been right for a very long time. Was it us? Why weren't we living examples of the faith we claimed to have? Was it all just nonsense?

Mick and Faith are close friends of ours who we met in the church. Every year they would attend a married couples retreat in Blue Mountain, Pennsylvania, and at this time they had asked us to come along. Many years ago Mick had an affair that resulted in him and Faith splitting up. As badly as she may have been hurting, Faith said she remained faithful and prayed about her situation, leaving matters in God's hands. Mick eventually asked Faith to take him back. They reconciled and she totally forgave him. Today their marriage appears to be strong and they get along just wonderfully. I had never been unfaithful to Julianne, yet one would think by the way we rarely seemed to get along I was out whoring and coming home drunk every night. If there was a marriage needing help, it was ours. We agreed to go.

The session was to take place Friday thru Sunday, to be led by a Christian couple with numerous degrees in counseling and years of life experience. At first I was a little reluctant to go because I tended to hate most Christian group activities, but due to the degenerative state our relationship was in, I was willing to try anything. While in the car on the ride to Pennsylvania we got into a heated skirmish over something miniscule, I think it was the traffic. It didn't take much to spark an argument. "If you want to just turn around and go home it's fine with me!" Julianne said indifferently. I drove quite a distance already so I wasn't about to turn around, although a side of me wanted to just scream, "Fuck you Julianne, I've had it I'm out of here!" Of course I said no such thing and kept driving. When we finally arrived, we were taken back by just how beautiful the surroundings were. We were way up in the mountains, smack in the middle of nowhere, for what was supposed to be three days of prayer, teaching and hopefully, healing. I snuck in a couple of bottles of wine just in case.

The weekend essentially went pretty good. The speakers were very enlightening and both Julianne and I were convicted. We actually left the retreat feeling renewed and back in love. We were able to see and talk about our differences and for at least six months, I felt we were closer to the Julianne and John of the good old days than we'd been in quite a long time. As the old saying goes however, "Good things always come to an end!" Before very long, Blue Mountain and the blessings we were able to take away with us had all faded to black. Because I wanted desperately for things to be good, I couldn't keep my big trap shut and told everyone what wonders the retreat had done for our marriage. I spoke way too soon. The same old shit started hitting the same old fan and we were back to being our same old selves. Our marriage motor was stalling again. We desperately needed to refuel; only we didn't.

They say sixty percent of all marriages end up in divorce. Statistics also report the divorce rate among Christians is higher than it is among atheists. If that isn't a distressing bit of information, I don't know what is. Through the years, Julianne and I had saved all the wedding photos that came with the newlywed's thank you cards. It's amazing to me how most of those happy couples ended up divorced.

LOVE REALLY DOES STINK

Pete's a co-worker of mine who was married for sixteen years before his wife pulled the rug out from under him. She was involved in an offshoot fundamental church Pete didn't care to associate with. For as long as I'd known Pete, I could say he was a hard working guy who lived for his family. He was proud of his accomplishments; he built his own home, raised two kids and never settled for second best. He prided himself in being a top-shelf sort of fellow. Most of the guys at work were a little bit jealous of Pete's perfect suburban life.

One day Pete confided in me by revealing that he and his wife Joan had separated. I was in total shock. The story goes that Joan told Pete he no longer fulfilled her emotionally. The bottom line was she met a man at the church who just so happened to fulfill her in more ways than just emotionally. I'm pretty sure in any Christian church "Thou shall not commit adultery" means don't fuck around with another man's wife! Pete gave his woman everything. He even went as far as to get a vasectomy because she didn't want to have any more kids. The biggest kick in the ass was she allowed the "church guy" to knock her up! Needless to say, Pete filed for divorce and was faced with moving out, paying child support and alimony. Where's the justice? She was the one who was unhappy, she was the one who was unfaithful and he's the one who got screwed! Pete had to move back in with his mom, work as much overtime as UPS would allow, and basically, start his life over again.

My friend Pat's story is a little different. Why he and Rosanna decided to get divorced after twenty-five years and three children is debatable. Pat, however, is extremely wealthy. No matter how opinions may differ, money talks and Pat was able to buy his way out. He may have lost millions but he still had millions.

Somewhere in Scripture it implies, God frowns upon divorce. I can certainly understand why. It's not healthy for children as it destroys the structure of the family. It causes bitterness, animosity and stress, all of which take a toll on one's physical, mental and emotional well-being. Somewhere in Scripture it also says that Solomon, whom God favored and gave infinite wisdom, had one thousand wives and three thousand concubines. He had more lovers than Wilt Chamberlain! When one of Solomon's wives gave him an attitude, he simply moved along to the next. If today's average man tried emulating the ways of Solomon, he'd lose everything he'd ever worked for and wind up living in his car, if the judge even allowed him to keep that! Man, how things have changed.

My good friend Tim (he's the one who had set me up with the suicidal blind date) has the most romantic story of how he swooned the love of his life into marrying him. Tim and Brianna both attended St. John's University in Queens, New York. Tim is a songwriter/poet and he was crazy about Brianna. The feeling, however, wasn't mutual. Timmy labored for many hours trying to compose the poem that would eventually sweep Brianna off her feet. He wasn't succeeding.

Brianna left the United States to go study abroad. The only information Timmy was able to gather was the name of the city where she would reside while in England. With that and a pocket full of hope, he boarded a jet plane and flew to England in pursuit of Brianna. He roamed the streets of that cold and lonely British city hunting high and low for the woman who he thought he just couldn't live without. Tim recounted to me the night he walked for hours in the rain, asking anyone and everyone he met, if they had any information on the whereabouts of the girl whose picture he held. A sympathetic couple took him in for the evening, fed him, and provided a place to sleep while his clothes could dry. At daybreak, like trying to find a needle in a haystack, he continued his search. Love triumphed, and at long last he found his fair maiden. His persistence won Brianna's heart and after she returned to the states they were married. Tim and Brianna had two sons and their life together seemed like something right out of a storybook.

Tim and his family moved to Florida. In this world of corporate downsizing and cutthroat practices, many people like Tim have no choice but to relocate where their employer tells them to. While on one of our visits to Florida visiting in-laws, I took a ride down to Clearwater to spend a little time with Tim. We caught up on each other's lives, much of the conversation having to do with the ups and downs of being married. "John," Tim said very wisely, "I take a calendar. For every good day Brianna and I have, I mark the day with an 'O,' and for every bad day we have, I mark the day with an 'X.' If at the end of the month the 'O's' outnumber the 'X's,' I know things aren't so bad."

I thought his idea was terrific and as soon as I got back home, that's exactly how I planned to gauge how my marriage was going. He continued almost secretively, "Well John, my 'X's' have been far outweighing my 'O's' and I want out. Promise not to tell a soul, but I met someone who excites me, someone who I seem to have so much more in common with. Brianna and I have grown so far apart. We have different agendas, different interests, we rarely have sex, and when we do, it's passionless!" I really couldn't believe what I was hearing, although I certainly understood. Here was the same guy who flew to England on a whim to win someone's love, and he was telling me the flame had been totally extinguished. Tim invited me over to his place for dinner that evening. My eyes followed Brianna about the kitchen while she prepared some quick chopped turkey tacos for her unexpected company. Only moments ago Tim had confided in me about another woman in his life. I couldn't help but feel as if I were betraying Brianna.

In this fast moving world of high-speed technology, Tim had found romance on the Internet. Tim was still a writer, a very good one at that, and something about his words sparked the interest of a woman web browser from Maryland. Under the pretense of work related business meetings, Tim would leave town to rendezvous with his cyber-space lover. He was living a secret life, separate from Brianna and the kids, but eventually he got caught. Tim came clean and Brianna filed for divorce. The love story of all love stories came to a bitter end.

It's very strange when close friends of mine go through divorce, because I've always considered their spouses to be friends of mine as well. I had my doubts I was ever going to see Brianna again, in the same way Erica, Hannah (who I think about often) and others seemed to be out of our lives forever.

FULL HOUSE

You just can't hold back those hands of time. Every day life goes on and with it comes good news and bad news. Julianne and I had really been missing Christiann and graduation day was weeks away. "I can't wait until she's back home with us!" Julianne would say in what seemed like a rare sentimental moment, "I can't wait to hug her!"

It seemed like only minutes ago I was wearing sunglasses to hide my tears when I left her at school. Now she was about to graduate, and after being on her own for four years, she would have to readjust to living back home with her family. After not having her as a part of the household for such a long stretch, we were going to have to acclimate to having Christiann, her laundry, her appetite, and her new sense of freedom among us again. It was only a matter of time before mother/daughter conflict began to show its ugliness.

I was so glad to have Christiann home. It's only natural for a father to worry about his daughter and all through her college career there wasn't a day that went by when she wasn't on my mind. Christiann was very fortunate to have landed a job almost immediately after graduating, but with the loans she had hanging over her head, she had to face the cold hard facts and realize she wouldn't be able to live anywhere but the old familiar surroundings of home for a while.

Samantha had decided to go to college locally and live at home, so with Christiann's return, the nest was again full. We all had busy schedules. Julianne, Christiann and I worked full time. Samantha and Matt went to school and had part time jobs. Sometimes there was just no time for getting things done. Meals had to be prepared, there were dishes to clean, laundry to fold, showers happened late, and hairdryers were squealing past midnight causing "mommy" to frequently lose her patience. I resigned myself to the fact that being a parent is a tough job, requires tremendous sacrifice and more often than not, is thankless. Jule, on the other hand, expected our kids to do more to help out around the house and she needed me to be the enforcer. In all fairness to Julianne, having the kids pull their weight wasn't asking too much. In all fairness to the kids, Julianne's obsession with order and cleanliness was more than even I could handle. I always felt like I was stuck in the muddy middle.

I'd always considered myself a laid back kind of guy. Ever since my little bout with cancer, I'd become even more laid back and have tried my best not to stress over the little things. But put five adults (three of them being female) with very different personalities and busy agendas all together under one roof, and there is most probably going to be conflict. My laid back approach to life was surely being put to the test.

THANKS BUT NO THANKS

While checking my e-mail one evening, I opened up a letter from Roxie. "Sorry to have to tell you this," it read, "but Dorothy's husband Steve passed away last evening from a brain aneurysm." I had to read the e-mail over again. How could this be possible? We just saw him not even a couple of months ago. I couldn't help but view Steve's untimely death as another wake-up call.

I thought about Dorothy, wishing there was something I could do or say to ease the pain or give her some hope. Roxie gave me Dorothy's e-mail address and told me it would probably be a good thing to send her a note. I wrote her a heartfelt letter and ever since then we'd become regular e-pals, writing each other regularly. I sent Dorothy a couple of letters telling her all about the hope I believed we had in Christ, and after thinking I'd done my part on giving her a spiritual uplift, she requested I stop any correspondence having to do with God because, quite frankly, she was not a believer. This was very disheartening to hear how a friend of mine, with whom I had so much in common, had no hope of anything beyond what this earthly life had to offer. I certainly understood one's reluctance in swallowing the whole "Born Again" package, but to not believe in a Creator or Supreme Being, with the hope there was another side to this crazy life, in my mind, had to leave one with the haunting feelings of hopelessness and frustration. Maybe it was unrealistic of me to expect someone who had just lost her husband to suddenly find hope in the few standard Christian clichés I had e-mailed her. I also had no idea, I still had lots to rethink and learn.

GONE BUT NOT FORGOTTEN

One thing that really stinks about aging, is the way everyone around me, including my friends and loved ones, are growing old too. Certain scenes from out of my past have clung onto the walls of my memory banks, so from time to time I can view them like a television rerun. One of these scenes involves my dear old Uncle Hank.

I will never forget the family barbeque at my Aunt Mary and Uncle Eddie's home in Connecticut. My Uncle Hank had always been quite a character, always ready to crack a joke and get a laugh. We were all seated around the redwood picnic bench, passing along the many taste treats prepared by Mary and Ed. The "Chicken ala Barbara," an uncooked piece of barbecued chicken with a funky cheese topping, named obviously after my cousin Barbara, was a must to avoid. Uncle Hank wasn't his usual self that day. It looked as if his thoughts were off in the distance, and from across the table I watched him as he slowly sliced his medium-well steak. He took a small bite, chewed for an unusually long time and seemed to almost gag as he swallowed. He didn't make a scene but appeared to be terribly upset. My Aunt Jean and my dad huddled around him and asked if he was all right. Uncle Hank was shaking his head "no" and pushed his plate away. Jule and I were in our twenties at the time. Even though we were both unaware of Uncle Hank having a serious problem, we had an uncomfortable feeling something might be wrong. It was that worrisome look on his face I will never be able to put behind me.

It wasn't very long after, when my Uncle Hank was hospitalized and diagnosed with cancer of the esophagus. It was killing me to see this man who was such a big part of my life, this man who would do anything to get a laugh out of me, wasting away in a hospital bed. I regret that my kids never got to know my Uncle Hank. They would have loved him just the way I did.

At Hank's wake, my brother Bill and I were sitting at the rear of the funeral parlor laughing so hysterically, people were starting to give us dirty looks. We were just recalling all the things Hank did that cracked us up, and thinking about how we were going to miss his antics. I sometimes wondered what the visitors were thinking when they came to pay their last respects and saw him laid out among the flowers and a crucifix, my Jewish uncle Hank Schwartz getting a Christian send-off. People often make such a big deal over religious differences. It's funny how when someone dies, we reason that it really doesn't matter.

From way back when before I began grade school, my family lived with my mom's parents. For an Italian, my grandfather was a very large man. Unlike my grandmother, who had totally lost her accent, my grandfather spoke very broken English. He was a laborer and each day when he got home from his grueling job he would plop down in his recliner and join me while I watched my daily dose of the "Three Stooges." My grandfather had no clue as to what they were saying yet he would shake with laughter. In Italian he would cry out, "Clowns!" then laugh some more.

My grandfather entertained himself by playing the guitar and mandolin. When I took up the instrument, he would sit down with me and try to teach me some new chords. It totally amazed me how his enormous fingers were able to maneuver about the narrow guitar neck, precisely holding down each string and not hearing a buzz when he strummed. I guess in some respects, I take after my grandfather. He was a hard worker who loved his music and loved his wine, two of my favorite things.

Grandpa suddenly got taken ill. At the time, I wasn't quite sure what he had but sometime later, learned it was pancreatic cancer. I was married then and can recall dropping by to visit my folks and check in on gramps. Without knocking, I walked into his room where I saw my mom and my grandmother holding him in a standing position while trying to change him. It was the only time I'd ever seen my grandfather undressed, but the sight of him standing there completely helpless, was something I don't think I'll ever be able to forget. My grandfather, who in my eyes was once a man of steel, was reduced to the mere bones that were hardly able to hold the sagging folds of skin hanging from them. He left Grandma way too soon. I dream about him now and then. In one dream I envisioned him walking about the house confused as to why we all seemed so surprised to see him. I was so elated to have him back that I didn't even attempt to tell him why.

Gino and I met when we were six years old in our first grade class at St. Fidelis. Except for some recent political differences (he's become uncomfortably right wing) we pretty much share the same easygoing outlook on life. All throughout our eight years of grammar school, Gino and I were so close we were like members of each other's families. When we were in fifth grade, he playfully and unexpectedly jumped on my back in the schoolyard. I came crashing down to the ground with my mouth wide open, slamming my front tooth against the cement pavement. The tooth was gone and the pain was excruciating. Fate, coincidence, or convenience, Gino's dad has been my dentist from that day forward. God bless him, he's over eighty years old and still practicing dentistry. God bless me too, I'm still his patient. The office hasn't changed a bit in almost fifty years, with the exception of all the added duct tape holding most of his antiquated equipment together.

When I used to hang out at his house, his mom, Betty, would draw pencil lines on the edge of the kitchen pocket door. The lines represented each of our heights and were labeled with our names and dates. She took these measurements periodically to keep track of how we grew. I towered over Gino in those days and I think it must have bothered him. This was his mom's way of trying to prove to him he would grow. Eventually Gino did have a growth spurt and almost caught up to me.

Just recently Betty passed away. After the funeral, a group of us went back to the house Gino grew up in. For me it was like taking a journey into the past. We went right to the kitchen where, although they were a little bit faded, the pencil lines on the edge of that pocket door were still visible. As I walked about those old yet familiar surroundings where Gino and I used to hang out as kids, I couldn't help but get the eerie feeling it was just moments ago when we were playing stickball in his driveway. I could almost hear Mrs. D. interrupting our game by calling out Gino's name so he could make a run over to the local market for groceries. Her passing took a piece of my past with her.

These wonderful people were all such a special part of my life while I was nonchalantly on my journey towards adulthood. Knowing they and others like them are gone, makes me feel, in a sense, as hard as I try to piece together a life, a part of it is always unraveling.

ARE YOU HUNG UP?

Don't ask me how, but in one way or another, all of us have a hang-up, if not several hang-ups. There has got to be at least one thing in each of our lives we're hung up about. Whether these idiosyncrasies are hereditary and with us from birth, or just quirks we develop from our environment, I really don't know. Most of us have a character flaw or two we are often aware of, but for some reason, just can't seem to overcome. Julianne has a thing with tidiness. She's physically unable to leave the house without straightening out the faucet over the sink or neatly arranging the mail on the kitchen counter. One day my mom suddenly developed a fear of being a passenger in a car. Since then she sits in the back seat and buries her head in a newspaper. My sister Virginia would rather walk six flights of stairs than take an elevator. For the longest time my brother Bill would refuse to use public rest rooms. His bladder control amazed me. Like a camel, he could hold his water for days if he had to. As I got older, I completely realized when it's time to go, it's time to go, doesn't matter where it is! There are probably thousands upon thousands of us out there with bathroom hang-ups, but nothing could beat the story I'm about to relate about my sister-in-law, Elena.

Coming from a family where the mom was hung up about trying on clothes in a department store dressing room, the child was bound to develop a few weird habits. Don't ask how my mother-in-law would ever get her clothes to fit her correctly, because whenever she decided to try on a garment in the store, she would put it on over the clothes she was wearing…in the dressing room no less! Sometimes modesty can spawn into a neurosis, I guess. Well, Elena was one of the many with a bathroom psychosis. If she could possibly help it, she'd absolutely refuse to take a crap in somebody else's house. Maybe it was because she didn't want people to think of her as someone who actually took a crap! There's an unwritten double standard men live by; it's okay for men to fart and shit but never a woman! Men like to think of a woman's bottom as always being pink, fresh and clean!

One day Elena happened to drop by our house while nobody was home except for my daughter Samantha. Elena's stomach must have been acting up, and since none of us were around, she felt safe and secure in using our bathroom. In this world, timing is everything! As luck would have it, just as she flushed, the toilet started to back up and at any minute Julianne would be arriving home from work. When Elena saw her poop circling the bowl and rising to the top, she completely freaked out. There was no way, no how she would allow anyone to see her poop, so she did what any normal American girl would do. She reached into the toilet and physically removed her "deposit" with her hands. She then put it into a plastic bag, ran out our side door and dumped the evidence into our trash just as Julianne pulled into the driveway.

The perspiration was flowing from Elena's nervous brow and seeing the horrified expression on her sister's face, Julianne asked, "My God Elena, are you alright?" Succumbing to the embarrassment and ridicule she knew was going to follow, Elena confessed. When Julianne was finally able to maintain herself, she asked her sister, "Why didn't you just use the plunger?" The great mystery was finally revealed; Elena actually poops!

Weeks later, Elena and her husband David threw a family dinner party at their apartment. Midway through the meal, I excused myself from the table and wandered off to the bathroom. I took my time in the john just to make everyone think I was having a little intestinal problem. Unbeknownst to anyone, I snuck a Baby Ruth bar into the bathroom with me. I held the chocolate under running water for a few seconds to make it appear authentic, then returned to the dining room holding the slimy candy bar in a piece of toilet paper. "Hey, Elena," I announced before everyone, "You're toilet backed up, where can I dump this?" Elena turned beet red as everyone roared with laughter. I realized what I did was cruel, but I just couldn't help myself. That was just one of my hang-ups!

WHO'S HE TALKING TO?

Jerry, an older gentleman from church, was one of the sweetest, most sincere human beings I'd ever had the pleasure of knowing. He'd always seem genuinely happy to see me, greeted me with a "God bless you Brother" and a gentle handshake. Every Sunday he and his wife Gilda sat in the very same pew, Jerry always on the right, Gilda to his left. Jerry always wore one of two suits, with the idea that church was a place of reverence where one should dress appropriately and respectfully. His Bible, wrapped in a leather book cover, was a permanent fixture in his hands and seemed as worn and well- used as his suits. Often times, those who sat in close proximity to him could witness him weeping and tenderly kissing his Bible as if it were one of his grandchildren. If I hadn't known him, I would have thought he was simply nuts.

Jerry's voice had a most interesting tone. The way in which I could best describe it would be to call it something between the "Brooklyn-ese" of "The Honeymooners'" Ed Norton, with the inflections of cartoon classic Yogi Bear, if that's possible to imagine. Although a gentle and soft-spoken man, he had no problem crying out at the very top of his lungs sudden outbursts of, "I love you Jesus" or "Thank you, Lord!" Jerry was obviously an extremely emotional person and I couldn't help but sit back and observe him week after week as he raised his open Bible towards the heavens, shouting praises to God at a volume level just slightly below a scream. What was most interesting, though, was how Jerry always faced the front right corner ceiling of the church. He would carry on conversations with God, as his body shook with what appeared to be joyous convulsions, waving his Bible, never taking his eyes from that corner of the room. People started to wonder if God was really hanging out up there!

A regular occurrence at a Sunday service was when someone in the congregation would suddenly blare out loud enough so an entire neighborhood could hear, those unintelligible phrases, which the church defined as "praying in tongues." I'd always secretly thought, "What good are those prayers if nobody in the church had any clue as to what they meant?" Ah! But that's where the gift of interpretation came in handy. A few seconds after the inane babbling faded to silence, the congregation patiently waited for someone to interpret what they just heard. For whatever reason, often times, Jerry believed he was divinely appointed to be the interpreter. As the silence filled the room, Jerry nervously twitched and waited. Since nobody else seemed to be stepping up to the plate, with his emotions taking hold of him, Jerry obeyed his calling and took the stage. Considering this mystery message was supposed to be coming from God Himself, I started getting suspicious when Jerry's translations sounded more like Jerry than God!

"My children," Jerry would cry out in his unique vocal styling, "I am only a prayer away!"

"Only a prayer away," I thought, "Those were the lyrics from one of the hymns we sang only ten minutes ago!"

"My children," Jerry continued, "Read my Bible daily!"

As much as I liked Jerry, it certainly seemed to me he was fooling himself as well as anybody in the church who took his words seriously. But Jerry just went on and on saying whatever seemed to be on his mind. Any minute I expected him to say something like, "My children! Don't forget to take your vitamins!"

It was preposterous. I could understand letting this slip by once, but it was becoming a weekly event. The Pastor himself knew Jerry had to be stopped, but how was he going to tell someone who really believed he was working hand-in-hand with God, that he wasn't. Pastor Ted took the bull by the horns and came up with his own interpretations, which were only slightly more believable than Jerry's. Before Jerry could part his lips to speak, the pastor was on it. Once Jerry heard the Pastor take on the sanctified task of being the medium between Heaven and Island Terrace, his twitch settled, and he seemed relieved to have had the burden lifted from him. What was wrong with me that I wasted my Sunday mornings sitting through these charades? In a strange way, I guess I might have found it all oddly entertaining.

GETTING RESTLESS

Sunday upon Sunday, for over twenty years, I had been faithfully attending services at the Full Gospel Church. I'd always been a "roll with the punches," "go with the program" sort of guy even when it came to church matters. Suddenly, all that began to change and I was becoming spiritually restless. Church was becoming more and more like a sideshow. The pastor's messages were getting uninspiring and predictable. I would look around at the congregation and try to determine if anything going on was genuine. Were people just conditioned and acting upon their overactive emotions and imaginations? Was the "Spirit of God" really working or was everyone just fooling themselves, going through a bunch of empty repetitive motions? The songs were getting more and more lame; the "speaking in tongues" was contrived and almost everything that happened, including the pastor's bad jokes, were becoming major distractions. I would put my head in my hands and plead with God to help me make sense of Sunday mornings. I needed Him to show me some truth. Week after week the feeling was getting stronger, the ninety minutes we spent "keeping the Sabbath holy," was nothing more than a gathering of the self-righteous, arrogant and judgmental. Sunday sermons were becoming nothing more than high school pep rallies, reassuring us we belonged to the one true team. At least that was the way it struck me.

I couldn't put my finger on it and I couldn't exactly express it in words, but something about "church" and how it influenced our lives started to deeply trouble me. I was having regrets about the way Julianne and I, as impressionable young Christians, kept our children from simple things like celebrating Halloween. We made our children think, as Christians, we should not partake in what we came to believe was "Satan's Holiday." Every year we made them choose to sit in the library while the rest of the school marched in the Halloween parade. While all their friends were trick-or-treating, my kids could not participate in the fun. I wasn't really sure what we were trying to prove. Did my kids really think they were any more special in God's sight than all their schoolmates who were having a good time? How was a kid expected to understand the origins and all the spiritual connotations about a day of dressing up and getting candy? The trouble was I began to rethink things too late. I loved and celebrated Halloween when I was a kid and I turned out just fine.

Christmas was another fiasco in our house. Okay, everybody knows Christmas is supposed to be the Christian celebration of the birth of Jesus. Every year the church would put on a Christmas play that would bring home the message of "the true meaning of the holiday." We would attend at least two Christmas services where the appropriate scriptures were read and the pastor's message would once again emphasize…"the true meaning of the holiday." Christmas hymns were sung and by the time anyone stepped foot out of that church, he or she would have to have been completely retarded to not know the "the true meaning of the holiday".

But let's face it, to children especially, without a present to open, who cares about Christmas? I remember waking up every Christmas morning at the crack of dawn, snooping around the house to see what Santa had left for me. My dad thought he was being clever by hiding the "special gifts" in the basement. After we were done ripping through all the gifts left under the tree, he would ask my siblings or me to go downstairs to get him his cigarettes or his keys. He would stand at the top of the stairs where he would listen to our shrieks of excitement when we found either new bicycles or a full set of drums. Every year he would dream up another silly request to get us to go downstairs. He didn't realize we were already on to him. The first thing we would do every Christmas morning was to check out what mom and dad had hiding for us in another part of the house. Then towards the end of our gift opening ritual, we would wait patiently for dad's signal, a request of some kind, usually resulting in a trek to the basement. We pretended to be oblivious as we made our way down the steps then faked our outbursts of surprise.

Things didn't quite go that way in our house. My kids would all sit together on the couch staring wide-eyed at all the pretty bows and ribbons that filled the living room floor. We all waited patiently for mom to get out of bed and finally make her grand entrance. No one was allowed to open a gift until someone read the Christmas story from the Bible. Then the kids sang "Happy Birthday" to Jesus followed by the traditional playing of the Nat King Cole Christmas album. The children waited so tolerantly to get through the frustrating yearly ordeal so they could start ripping away at the Christmas wrap.

I never let on to anyone, but even back then when I considered myself a Born-Again Christian, the Christmas morning routine used to make me nuts. After sitting through hours of Christmas messages, songs, presentations and scripture verses, I was sure we all got the crux of "the true meaning of Christmas." For Christ's sake, why couldn't we have let the kids just be normal kids?

THE TURNING POINT: BE CAREFUL WHAT YOU PRAY FOR

"Who knows why things happen, the fact is they just do..." are lyrics I used in a song I had written some years back. I don't know what compels people to think the way they do, dream what they dream, or feel what they feel. As my neighbor Lewis would say, "It is what it is!" I believe I've always been the type of person where what you see is what you get. I can't stomach hypocrisy and I especially don't like being fooled or lied to. This held especially true when it came to spiritual issues. For quite some time I'd been crying out to God to help me make sense of things. In my mind there was too much confusion associated with religion. How could everybody possibly be right when it came to God? The main focus of my daily prayer life had become for Him to give me enlightenment so I could get a little bit closer to the absolute Truth, if in fact there was such a thing.

One evening in late November, I was in my car driving along the parkway, and I remember passing the mall and being stunned by the amount of cars scrambling about looking for available parking spots. The place was absolutely filled to capacity. I couldn't help but get that oppressive feeling, the holiday season was once again upon us. Working for UPS, all Christmas meant to me was more and more boxes and longer and longer workdays. My own stress level was starting to escalate to such soaring levels that I had reached a point where I wanted to hibernate through the Christmas season.

Just imagine this guy sitting behind the wheel of his 1999 Honda

Accord, turning off his radio because he couldn't stand the sound of another Christmas song and staring at the bumper sticker on the car in front of him that read, "Jesus is the Reason for the Season." This was yours truly at the moment where I started to unravel. As I continued past the lines of bottlenecking automobiles trying to squeeze their way into the mall entrance, I suddenly felt flushed and feverish, kind of like I was having a mild anxiety attack.

An inner voice seemed to keep repeating over and over, "Well, who do you say I am? Who do you say I am?" I shook my head a few times and feeling a little spooked wondered, "Oh my God! What's wrong with me now?" Was God trying to communicate with me, and if he was, why? In that brief moment I got this crazy notion I had just unveiled this great cover-up, like I had made a monumental breakthrough. I just couldn't stop thinking about it. This "supernatural" experience suddenly made something very "clear" to me: Jesus' name was not Jesus… it was Yehshua. For whatever reason, it made perfect sense. But if that made sense, I then speculated, where else had I been misled? If anyone driving along side of me could have looked into my head and heard my thoughts, they would have surely steered clear of me. I was initially alarmed as to where these thoughts might be coming from and why they were even in my head, because in church we would constantly be warned about the devil lurking about behind the scenes inciting questions and doubt. Was I losing my faith, or worse than that, was I losing my mind?

As strange as it seemed, after some rationalizing, I deduced I'd had an encounter with God on that November evening. I somehow imagined His divine finger singled me out of all those hundreds of cars, and by getting my undivided attention, He put me on (as Cat Stevens called it) the "Road to Find Out." On that evening my spiritual life got turned upside down. Could it have been an answer to my relentless prayers or was it just my over-active imagination at work again?

I just so happened to stop by my sister-in-law's house the very next day after my thought provoking car ride. Sara was one of Julianne's younger sisters who had three kids and a demanding husband so she was always on the run. It wasn't unusual for her to cut me short and be on her busy way. This time however it was different. Sara put aside her errands for the moment. She needed to talk.

Sara had been attending Pentecostal churches just as I had for so many years. She'd always been diligent about reading her Bible and until around this time, her Christian walk had been without incident. I started to tell her what happened to me last night on the parkway and how all of a sudden I was troubled by the name Jesus. She stopped me in my tracks, and with a burst of exhilaration in her voice cried out, "Me too!" Sara then shared with me the issues she was confronting. "John!" her words gushed forth with excitement, "We're all saved! There's no hell! It's bullshit and the scriptures prove it! We've been deceived!"

She related to me how on this one evening while she was reading her Bible she suddenly became besieged by questions concerning matters of faith. She wasn't satisfied with the conventional answers mainstream Christianity had to offer, so she decided right then and there to investigate. Sara was so energized by some of her early discoveries that she was drooling as she spoke.

"Look here!" she shrieked, her voice suddenly rising an octave, "Hell's not a place of eternal torment! It's an incorrect translation used just to instill fear!" Sara was flipping through the pages of her Bible so quickly I was getting dizzy keeping up with her. On her kitchen table sat her laptop computer which was open to a website cross-referencing English, Hebrew and Greek. Like a whirlwind she skipped through scripture while simultaneously clicking her mouse. "John! We have to study! This is amazing! We've been taught lies!" It was as if she unearthed ancient scrolls. We both felt this was too much of a coincidence for the two of us to be concurrently sharing similar experiences and having reservations about our belief system.

"Mom, what's for dinner?" Sara's three kids whined in unison, as our intense conversation left their question unanswered.

"Can't you see I'm talking to Uncle John?" Sara chided her children, "I'll call you when dinner's ready!"

From that day on we were practically in daily communication with each other reading, talking and learning. It was stimulating, yet so out of character for me, a guy who just wanted to play rock'n roll and have fun. In a million years, I would have never believed this could happen to either one of us. We did, however, face some obstacles along our journey for knowledge, and among them were my wife and Sara's husband Gary, who both thought we were nuts.

One day I gently approached Julianne and said with the hope she would grasp what I was about to convey, "Julianne, I got this remarkable revelation I think I need to share with you!"

Already disinterested in what she assumed was going to be an off the wall comment she said, "What now, John?"

I answered cautiously, "We shouldn't be calling on the name of Jesus! His proper name is Yehshua!"

"John," she said somewhat annoyed, "It doesn't matter! Call Him whatever you want, I call Him Jesus and I'll always call Him Jesus! You're not Jewish!"

It was becoming increasingly difficult to sit through Sunday services. Week after week it was the same salvation message I'd been hearing for years. Time and time again it was the same game of tag between Jerry the interpreter, and whoever else was bold enough to challenge him. It got to be such a joke, that from our pews, several of us would make eye contact and start cracking up. We would make bets as to who would be the first one to beat out the other in interpreting the tongues. My money was always on Jerry. It was disturbing to me how the pastor would allow the bizarre, almost blasphemous behavior to continue, especially when we were supposed to be taking such things seriously.

Another regular occurrence at a Sunday service was the altar call for anyone who desired the "baptism of the Holy Spirit" with the evidence of speaking in tongues. In layman's terms, that meant in order to prove the spirit of God has actually taken hold of someone, he or she would outwardly babble the unintelligible language of heaven. People lined up as the church elders would lay hands upon them, psyching them up for this on the spot encounter with the Holy Spirit. Every so often someone, usually a woman, approached the altar with the desire to have this infilling of the Holy Spirit and got what was called "slain in the Spirit," or in other words, she would pass out. The pastor or church elder would place his hand upon the forehead of the candidate, applying enough pressure to cause the worshipper to lean backwards and just about lose her balance, while being forcefully encouraged to inanely jabber. Before long the entire church got caught up in the frenzy. Everyone began to clap, scream, and praise God. The woman would start to shake uncontrollably before passing out into the arms of the ushers who, in these situations, were always on hand to break the fall. She was then left to lie on the floor of the church in a temporary coma, while other congregants simply walked over and around her continuing to rejoice in the Lord. Twenty to thirty minutes later, the woman would regain consciousness and return to her pew, convinced the Holy Spirit had penetrated her very being. It was a freak show, where for almost two decades I had a ringside seat to witness the madness. Many Protestant religions have criticized the strange traditions and rituals of Roman Catholicism, and with good reason, but I felt as if I were involved in one of its offshoots with peculiar rituals of its own.

The messages I was hearing in my church every Sunday were leaving me bone dry spiritually, and couldn't compare to some of the profound teaching tapes I had been listening to by Messianic lecturers. I acquired a real education pertaining to the Hebrew roots of Christianity and became quite a wealth of information, sighting what I viewed as the many inconsistencies of the faith. To me, it was almost as if Christianity hijacked Judaism, then put their own spin on the traditions that had existed for centuries. Many of the teachers I began listening to were ex-pastors, ministers, and preachers who were once affiliated with some form of Christian denomination and claimed to have come out by having similar encounters as Sara and I did. I became fascinated with the Old Testament and through many of their teachings learned how to use the Scriptures to challenge and dispute Christian doctrine. I remembered how exciting it was for me when I fled the stagnant, deceptive conventions of Catholicism and found a new perspective in the Born Again experience. That feeling was erupting in me again. Something was telling me my days in the Full Gospel Church were numbered. What I didn't realize at this very impressionable time in my life was how anyone with profound Bible knowledge could skillfully use the scriptures to support almost any agenda.

I began reading many of the historical accounts relating to the birth of Christianity and the plight of the Jews. I became so dogmatic and stubbornly inconvincible. There was no way I could possibly be wrong. I got myself into so many unsettled arguments with issues ranging from Jesus' name to what day of the week the actual Sabbath was. One evening over coffee and dessert at a friends' house, I turned a pleasant visit into a full-blown debate when I went into one of my rants.

"If the letter 'J' wasn't introduced to the English language until the early sixteen hundreds," I hollered, "How could He possibly have been called Jesus? It doesn't add up!"

"John, you're insane!" my friend answered, "It's no different than John translating to Giovanni! It means the same thing in a different language!"

"You don't know what you're talking about!" I retaliated, "Yehshua does not translate to Jesus by any stretch of the imagination! If there's really power in His name, doesn't it only make sense it should be the real name?"

"Listen to yourself!" my buddy challenged, "How can you prove anything you're saying?"

"Oh my God!" I argued in frustration, "How blind can you people be? In any language, Elvis is Elvis and Popeye is Popeye! How the hell did Yehshua become Jesus?"

At any moment I thought we were going to start throwing crumb cake at each other! We were all too blind to see, it's not a name or a word that brings results, but the magic of belief.

It didn't seem to matter where I was or who I was talking to, I always instigated conversations that eventually led to my assaulting someone with my opinions. One afternoon I was really on a roll as I tried to sell my friend Andy, a new Christian, the gospel according to John, that is, me: "Don't you realize the early Catholic Church compromised by incorporating many pagan rituals into its dogma just for the sake of winning converts? How the heck do you think they came up with Easter, Christmas and the Sunday Sabbath? Do the math, man! If Jesus died on Good Friday, as they claim, then rose on Sunday, how could they state He was buried for three days? Buried Friday, rose Sunday...that's only two days according to my calculator!"

"Whoa! Slow down there, Johnny boy!" Andy pleaded, "You're killing me!"

"Andy!" I continued with my onslaught, "I researched and I'm telling you there are over twenty thousand different sects of Christianity worldwide still feeding from those pagan roots. Why don't Christians stick to the same scriptures Jesus taught from and follow the same traditions Jesus followed?"

Andy responded calmly by saying, "Because all that changed when Jesus came and died for us. His death on the cross set us free from the law!"

"No it didn't" I yelped, "That's what they want you to believe! God is the same yesterday, today and tomorrow, and if the Bible affirms, Jesus came NOT to abolish the law but to fulfill it, then how did Christianity arrive at the conclusion everything changed when Jesus came?"

Andy looked at me like I had two heads, probably didn't have a clue as to what I was driving at, and said, as he desperately tried to get away, "It was nice talking to you John, I'll be praying for you!"

I found myself thinking about Aunt Helen and the journey she was on before she died, wishing somehow I could speak to her. I felt certain I would have understood and appreciated her efforts so much more. I had no idea how crazed I had become. Little did I know, however, this was just another stage and the beginning of a long strange trip.

PLANNED SPONTANEITY

Angelo's Coal Oven Pizza had become our favorite spur of the moment Saturday night restaurant. We knew all it took was giving Freddy a thirty-minute warning, and by the time we arrived, a table would be prepared for us no matter how many people were in our party. One of the great things about going to Freddy's, besides the food, was that nine out of ten times we never knew what surprise the evening was going to bring. Wesley, Toni, Julianne and I had become regulars and the Angelo's crew always treated us and whatever friends we dragged along like family. It never failed, almost every time we went, we ended up closing the joint. The chairs throughout the dining area were placed upside down on top of the tables and the smell of cleaning fluids began to sneak its way into the air as the busboys and waitresses scurried about to complete their last minute closing chores. As his crew left for the night, Freddy locked the door behind them, put up the "closed" sign, and then usually dropped a bottle of homemade anisette onto our table. After a long stressful day, Freddy finally would get a moment to sit down and unwind with us. By that time, all the alcohol we'd consumed throughout the course of the evening had kicked in, and I'd typically start talking silly and the result was a lot of good laughs.

Peter and Renee were friends of ours from the church. Unlike many of the holy-roller types we'd met at the Full Gospel Church, Pete and his lovely wife took a liking to the finer things in life and knew how to have fun. For the longest time I'd been telling them all about "Angelo's" and suggested we should go one Saturday night. Well that long-awaited

Saturday night finally arrived. As we made the thirty-five minute trip from the south shore to the north shore of Long Island, Peter kept repeating, "Where the heck is this place? I'm telling you, this better be good!"

While driving along the winding back roads of Port Washington I reassured him, "Don't worry we're almost there and it's going to be great!"

I politely held open the front door of the restaurant to allow my friends to enter before me. When Julianne and I stepped inside we were very confused about what we were witnessing. Freddy's face seemed to light up when he saw Peter and Renee and instantaneously the three of them were standing before us hugging and kissing as if they'd known each other for a lifetime. "Pete! It's so good to see you!" Freddy cried out, smiling from ear to ear as if he'd just rediscovered a long lost friend.

A waitress led the four of us to our table where Julianne and I sat completely dumbfounded by the little scene we just observed. Pete and Renee really had us going by explaining how somewhere down the line they had family connections to Fred. "What a small world!" I thought, until Freddy walked over to the table. The big grins on each of their faces looked as if they were about to burst, and within a split second, they did. Too much of a coincidence for my money, I knew there had to be a reason for what was going on and indeed there was. Pete was pulling a practical joke on us. After asking me at least a thousand times where we were going, he managed to get the address and phone number of Angelo's and set the whole thing up with Freddy prior to us getting there. This was a candid camera moment if ever there was one!

Wesley, Toni, Julianne and I were having dinner there one evening when Fred introduced us to his best friends Victor and Nancy. Our first impression of Victor was one of a character right out of the late fifties. Wearing a tight black tee shirt, cigarettes tucked into the chest pocket, black jeans and his jet-black greased back hair, he spoke with the heaviest Brooklyn accent. Thirty-three came out like dirty-tree. His wife Nancy appeared to be very plain, quiet and soft-spoken. Victor and Nancy brought along several bottles of their own wine and were very generous in sharing them with us. Victor had that glassy gleam in his eyes showing he'd already had a bit too much to drink. Victor was very animated when he spoke and his use of the word "fuck" in all of its forms was very entertaining. All in all, Vic and

Nancy seemed like a very nice couple, and by the time the night was over, it was as if the six of us had known each other forever.

The women of Full Gospel Church were planning a weekend retreat and though it was very much out of character for Julianne to attend such gatherings, she decided to go. When she returned from her inspirational weekend on a Saturday evening, we met up with Wesley and Toni and once again had dinner at Angelo's. When we arrived, we were surprised to see Victor and Nancy were there, so the six of us sat together. As the conversation progressed, Julianne had mentioned she had just returned from a Christian retreat. When Victor heard that, it seemed as if his face lit up. I was ready for him to say something like, "Don't tell me you're one of those fuckin' born agains!" but instead he stunned us when he said, "Praise God! I love the Lord!"

In the far corner of the restaurant the television was on and a news bulletin regarding something horrific occurring in the Middle East was being broadcast. Without flinching, Victor began to give us a history lesson, referring repeatedly to the Old Testament, to explain why there is such turmoil there. We were nothing short of amazed at his Bible knowledge. Vic and Nancy gave us their testimony about how they came to know Christ, how much they were both on fire for God, how they raised their children to do the same, and strangely enough, how they abhorred organized religion and no longer stepped foot inside a church. We were all flabbergasted, to say the least. A book really can't be judged by its cover. We couldn't believe this character who was smoking, excessively drinking, talking like a truck driver and dressed like a thug, was a Born Again Christian? Well as expected, we closed the joint again that evening listening to Victor converse all about God, Jesus, and being Born Again, while Freddy looked at us like we were all crazy. I didn't say much. I'd heard it all before and wasn't looking to have a confrontation with someone who seemed to know his way around the Bible quite a bit more than I did. I let him assume we were on the same page.

Peter and Renee called us on a Saturday afternoon asking if we had any plans for the evening. We were toying with the idea of going to "Angelo's" again with Wesley and Toni, and knowing the four of them would get along tremendously, we invited Pete and Renee to come along.

They accepted the invitation, but asked if it would be all right if their friends Stan and Gloria could join the party. Jule and I had met Stan and Gloria before so we said, "Of course! The more the merrier!" We called Fred in advance to give him a heads up that eight of us would be arriving soon. Fred told us that Victor and Nancy were also planning to come in, so he set up tables for all ten of us.

Everybody was introduced to one another and we all took our places around the table. The food kept coming, the wine kept flowing, the jokes were flying and everyone was laughing and having a grand old time, until Victor, in a slightly inebriated state, started making some ethnic remarks. Sometimes it's not very difficult determining one's ethnicity and it was easy to detect Stan was Jewish. Victor, however, either wasn't aware or didn't care and was relentless in what was no longer a playful bombardment of Jew jokes. Stan politely excused himself from the table and with the pretext he had to get up early in the morning, he said to Gloria, "Come on babe, I think we'd better go!" The jovial atmosphere changed rather quickly as we all pleaded with Stan to stay. Gloria walked up to Victor stared him right in the face and said, "You know what? You're a fucking asshole!"

She then turned around and joined Stan as they exited the front door. Somehow I was feeling a little responsible, since in a roundabout way, I was the connection between Victor and Stan. Everyone felt terrible, except for maybe Vic, because he may have been too drunk to feel anything. The night ended early and it was probably the last time we went to Angelo's with any expectations of having a good time. I wouldn't have been surprised if that was going to be the last time Julianne and I would see Victor and Nancy. I remember having a few words with Victor about how my views on Christianity were changing and how my interest in its Hebrew roots had been stirred. I also remember how he pointed his finger in my face and lectured me about how Jesus shed His blood for me. Most of all, I remember how this Bible waving disciple was so verbally abusive to our Jewish acquaintance Stan. Sometimes alcohol acts as a truth serum. Being in an intoxicated state may unknowingly bring out what's really in the heart. I got the message Victor didn't care for Jews. It was disturbing. I couldn't understand how someone who was so well versed in Scripture and dedicated to Christ could harbor such animosity in his heart towards Jews. Jesus was born a Jew, lived his life as a Jew and died a Jew. What was Victor's problem? What a goyim!

DON'T TALK WITH YOUR MOUTH FULL

One thing about my friend Sue, if she was determined to accomplish something, come hell or high water, she was going to do it. She made up her mind, that even though she was old enough to be the mother of her classmates, she was going to go back to school and study to be a dental hygienist. Sue wasn't burdened with the responsibilities of a husband, children or a mortgage. She lives with her mom, thus it allowed her the opportunity to do so and achieve her goal with honors. Before graduating, however, she had to prove her skills by testing her abilities on live subjects. Sue asked me if I would kindly volunteer my mouth. Since she would do just about anything for me, how could I refuse? I surrendered a damp dreary Tuesday vacation day by spending the entire afternoon secured to a dentist's chair in a college classroom with my mouth pried open while Sue picked, scraped, brushed, flossed and ripped my gums to shreds. In spite of all the blood I lost she got a good grade! But like with most favors, there's always payback. Whenever my mouth was free from an intruding mirror, pick or scraping device, Sue had to listen to me passionately carry on about how Jesus was not really the name of the Messiah, how the rapture is a myth, how Christmas and Easter had evolved from man-made pagan traditions and how the Bible was poorly translated from the Hebrew to the Greek leaving many Christian doctrines questionable. I thought Sue was by no means a closed minded person and would always be interested in learning something new, but from the way I carried on she must have thought I'd lost my mind. My sense of urgency made me appear like a lunatic who had just learned that Martians were about to attack the earth and it was up to me to inform everybody.

"Okay Johnny!" she said trying to appease me, "Now open wide so we can get finished here!"

"Don't you see?" I yelped in frustration, "We've all been brainwashed with a bunch of lies, Sue!!"

I wanted so desperately for her to see what I saw and feel what I felt but I was beating a dead horse. Sue was hopelessly indoctrinated.

"One day you're going to understand what I'm talking about Sue, you'll see!"

Little did I know, sometime soon I'd be doing some picking and scraping of my own that would eventually reveal God in ways I'd never even considered.

OY VAY! IT'S THE UPS MAN

During this new phase in my life, I was driving everyone, including my family and friends, crazy. I had this notion, just because people liked me, they would naturally listen to whatever it was I had to say. The truth of the matter was, because people liked me, they didn't tell me to shut up and go away! I was thoroughly convinced I was on a mission from God and my objective was to enlighten all who happened to cross my path, or at least make them think like I did! I had the strongest feeling the Almighty and I were on the same team and I absolutely believed He was choreographing my days. The events of this one particular day "proved" it to me. The day's mission: Talk to Jews!

I was a wealth of new ideas and information and now I was unleashing it on the workplace. One of the daily stops on my route was the Community Synagogue in Sands Point. Some time ago, a sweet woman named Marsha worked in the office. She was very tall, had a cartoon-like face, dressed very flamboyantly, and took a liking to me. Every day she had a box of sugar-raised donuts on her desk (never deviated, always a dozen sugar-raised) and never let me leave the office without offering me one. I always accepted. One day while she was working diligently behind her computer, I started messing with her.

"Hey Marsha, what would happen if I touched this?" I said while pointing to the cables coming from her desktop.

"Don't touch that!" she insisted.

I don't know how it happened, but all of a sudden the cable slipped out from the computer, her screen went black and several hours' worth of unsaved data was lost. Her eyes bulged from her rubber-like face. She pointed to the door and instead of killing me, said, "John, get the fuck out of the office!" I tried to apologize but her finger remained pointed towards the door as she ordered me to, "Just leave!"

About ten minutes later I returned. Marsha stared at me and wondered how I had the audacity to be coming back so soon and asked, "Now what do you want?"

"Marsha?" I asked timidly, "Can I have a donut?"

She laughed and reaching for the box said, "Go ahead you brat!"

It was Friday during the week of Passover and Easter. I was just on my way out of the synagogue office after completing a delivery, when Annette, the office manager, gave me a great big smile. While trying to be politically correct she said, "Have a great weekend and a happy Easter or Passover or whatever it is you celebrate!"

That was all the spark I needed to ignite my motor mouth. I was feeling very bold and right there in the midst of the Rabbi, the Cantor and various other temple personnel, I started ranting.

"You know!" I said eagerly, like an energized know-it-all, "Christian and Jew should both be celebrating Passover. It's disgraceful how separate we've become!"

The Cantor turned to me and asked rather smugly, "Do you have any idea about the origins of Easter?" I immediately went into my dissertation.

"Absolutely," I declared while rambling whatever information had been stored in my brain. "Easter Sunday is rooted in Paganism. Esther was impregnated by the sun and became the goddess of fertility, hence the rabbits and the colored eggs and every other screwy tradition that evolved into the Christian celebration of Easter!"

The Rabbi seemed to be very impressed with my knowledge and appeared to enjoy my bashing of the tradition of Easter Sunday. The scene was almost ludicrous, the UPS man lecturing these two learned men as the office staff looked on.

"How you guys have refused to accept Yehshua as the Messiah baffles me!" I declared. I went on without compromise, "Your own holy books prophesied His coming! How do the Messianic Jews get it and you don't?"

The rabbi replied adamantly, "The Messianic Jews are twisted! They have it all wrong! And as far as Christians and Jews celebrating together, it will never happen because we all have too much to lose!"

I looked straight into his eyes and answered defiantly, "The only things we stand to lose are our prideful traditions! You, my friend, have everything to gain!"

Annette shrugged her shoulders, rolled her eyes, looked at me as if to say, "Please deliver your packages and go!"

On that note, the Rabbi raised his eyebrows and left the room in a huff! Apologetically, I said, "I didn't intend to piss him off!" and exited the office imagining I had accomplished something.

That very same day, sometime later in the afternoon, I was about to drop off a package on Lewis Lane, a typical suburban street lined with cookie cutter houses. Robyn was waiting at her door as I pulled up to the house. I'd known Robyn for quite a few years. She was a pretty woman, mother of two girls, probably in her early forties at most. Through the years we'd had many conversations dealing with everything from raising kids to politics, but never engaged in any talk about religion. By the look on her face I sensed something might have been troubling her.

"What's the matter Robyn?" I asked, "You look so sad. Is everything all right?"

Robyn sighed, "I don't know, John, I'm just feeling down. My mom is sick and I'm facing the possibility of losing her. I'd never had to cope with something like this before."

I felt bad, and as I was trying to think of some uplifting words to say to her, she said something that sent my spirit into a whirl.

"John!" she whimpered, "I'm Jewish. I have no hope!"

Assuming I was Catholic, she confided in me by saying, "I'd never admitted this to anyone, John, but I'm jealous of you Catholics and your belief in heaven. You guys have something to look forward to!"

"Robyn! Hold on!" I told her comfortingly and enthusiastically, "First of all don't envy Catholics! As far as I'm concerned they've got it all wrong too! You have more hope than you think you do! Your God, their God, my God, it's all one and the same."

Robyn looked at me as though she wanted to understand but had no clue as to what I was talking about. To confuse her even more, I continued,

"Your Torah and our Old Testament is the same book with the same prophetic message about a Savior! Read it Robyn and see for yourself!"

"I've been feeling so empty, John, I even sought counseling from the Rabbi over at the Synagogue, but between you and me, he's an asshole!"

Making use of whatever knowledge of the scriptures I had, I did my best to illustrate the confusion caused by organized religion and tenderly tried to reassure her God loved her.

"Thanks, John!" she wept, then hugged me as if I'd just rescued her from a sinking ship.

I told her about Sara and how diligently she and I had been studying the Bible. Robyn then made my day when she asked, "Do you think your sister-in-law and you could come over one evening to share what you've been learning? It would be so cool!"

Her request sent my spirit soaring and I answered her eagerly, "You pick the date and we're there!"

Much to my disappointment, weeks later I realized Robyn just had a bad day. She never brought up the topic again. For a brief moment she slipped into the reality of mortality. I guess the new Lincoln SUV I saw parked in her driveway pulled her right back into the contentment of the illusion…

Even later in the afternoon on still the very same day, as I was making my last few deliveries, I was taken by surprise by a third occurrence, and told myself it was a sign. Marlene was the director of the Hebrew school over at the synagogue. She also happened to live on my route. While stepping out of my truck to deliver a package to Marlene's residence, I noticed she was standing in her driveway loading up the rear of her station wagon. She greeted me with her usual big warm smile and told me her family was about to head over to Grandma's for Passover Seder.

"Did you hear about the 'fiasco' at the synagogue this morning between me and the Rabbi?" I asked her.

She laughed, "Oh yes, the story is getting around!"

Contrary to how Robyn felt, Marlene said, "Don't you just love him, he's so brilliant!"

Marlene was such a sweet woman and the last thing I wanted to do was rile her up about her esteemed Rabbi. I'd been delivering packages to Marlene's house for fifteen years and had had many wonderful conversations with her about the simple pleasures and problems of life. That afternoon my spirit got another jolt. From out of the blue, Marlene looked at me and with a childlike curiosity asked, "Do you believe the Messiah already came?" Why she would pose such a question, I didn't know, but at that moment, I could have sworn there were hidden cameras on me! In three separate instances during one day I was given the opportunity to "witness" to Jews about Yehshua, and in each case they listened or at least tolerated me! Like a wind-up toy I repeated all the Biblical jargon I'd been sputtering throughout the day. Marlene seemed to be listening attentively as she placed the last few items into her car, but when she sweetly said, "You are so wise and wonderful," the thought came to mind that perhaps she was patronizing me and I was keeping her from the things she needed to do.

"Before I go Marlene, let me give you the names of some great teaching tapes by a Rabbi who had accepted Yehshua as his Messiah!"

As she politely told me she had to be going, inching her way back to the front door of her house, she said, "I'd be more than happy to listen to them and I'd love to continue this conversation but please give them to me next time you stop by!"

As Marlene made her way into the refuge of her entry, she smiled what was probably a smile of relief, and said the same words that started this whole day off, "Have a happy Easter or Passover or uh, holiday!"

What I didn't realize in my zealousness, one day in the near future, I'd be looking back on that day, disagreeing with everything I claimed to be so sure about.

PICTURE WINDOW

Due to the nature of my job, I spent many hours by myself. I had lots of time to think, meditate and pray, or what I preferred to term "being in communication" with my Maker. Maybe because I was less distracted, it seemed like a lot of things appeared to me while I was driving. One morning I happened to get this visualization of a large picture window. Centrally placed on this window was an intricately designed stencil. When standing back and looking out from it, I could see how the stencil blocked out some of the light, hence creating pretty designs and an interesting view. After gazing out of this window time and time again, one day I happened to notice the view was slightly different. A piece of the stencil had worn away allowing a little more light to pass through. With each passing day, another piece of the stencil dried up, flaked off and fell from the glass allowing more light to enter, thus changing the panorama. One afternoon, while the overworked western sun was shining its very brightest, I decided to take a razor and scrape away the remainder of the stencil. When the stencil was completely removed, the sunlight shone through that window like I'd never seen before, revealing its entire splendor and creating a most spectacular view. It occurred to me, religion was that stencil. It blocked the light and stifled the truth. Until it had been completely removed, I would have never seen the Light in all its fullness, just the pretty designs it created. I knew I had to eventually sever my ties to organized religion. The view I'd been seeing until now had been greatly distorted. I don't know who said it, but I believe, *"The more illumination men have, the less they can be induced to believe what is not true."*

GRANDMA

My grandmother lived to be ninety-six years old and remained as sharp as a tack. She had an incredible memory and for as long as I can remember, she would entertain us with stories of her life reaching all the way back to her childhood. My personal favorite was the one about the fish store my grandparents owned. Friday, of course, was the biggest day of the week for selling seafood, especially in the Catholic Italian neighborhood they lived in. Every Friday just before closing, my grandmother would give away all of the unsold fish. It was bad enough how the news of this "giveaway" spread about by word of mouth, but Grandma also put up a sign announcing the availability of free fish. So after a while, business naturally decreased while the amount of people showing up for free fish at closing time increased. A businesswoman she was not.

My parents heard her stories so many times that it probably drove them crazy whenever they would see my kids captivated by the long and detailed accounts of her younger days. Sometimes it used to really perturb me when I would see my mom or my sister mimic grandma behind her back as she told her tales. I don't know if they were jealous because she was stealing her great-grandchildren's attention, but I would think to myself, "How could they? Let the lady live out her life with dignity for Pete's sake!"

Grandma lived with my parents, so I imagine having her around twenty-four seven could have been the reason they would lose their patience with her periodically. "You don't know what it's like!" my dad would inform me, "Picture having your mother-in-law living with you seven days a week, three hundred sixty five days a year!"

Being the oldest grandson and living with her for most of my childhood, my grandmother had a special place in my heart. I can remember asking her to please wake me up on time for class when I was going to college. She would step softly into my room and whisper, "Psst, Johnny, it's time to get up for school!" as she grabbed my foot and gently shook it. I would turn on her like the wolf man and growl, "Leave me alone Grandma, let me sleep, don't you know my class was cancelled today?"

Of course I was lying to her. Then after not waking up on time and realizing I was going to be late for class, I would scream at her (in a loving way, naturally), "Why do you believe me? I told you to make sure I get up! Thanks a lot Gram!" That abuse, combined with the way I pounded on my drums day after day, had to have driven her nuts!

In my eyes, my grandmother and grandfather appeared to be very close. I can't ever recall hearing them argue or seeing them fight. My grandfather died quite a number of years before my grandmother did, and it was sad to see how grandma had to carry on without her trusted companion. Thank goodness there was my mom, my dad and my sister (who's yet to leave the nest) on hand to take care of her. Sometimes everyone's patience wore thin. Sometimes out of frustration or human frailty, my mom or my sister would inadvertently say things that would hurt Grandma's feelings. It seemed, without Grandpa by her side, Grandma may have lost some of her spunk. Just once I would have liked to hear her say, "Virginia! Go to hell!"

She had a few bouts with her health as she approached her nineties but always managed to bounce back. Her last illness however got the best of her and little by little she grew weaker. Grandma required a lot of attention and a lot of assistance, more than my mom could handle, so they hired a nurse to be with her throughout the day. The nurse was a Jamaican woman named Velma. Velma was a gentle, kind-spirited Christian woman who really seemed to take to my family and they took to her. Velma liked to read her Bible when Grandma slept, and from what I gathered, often spoke to my dad about the need to be "Born Again." My mom, my dad, my sister, my brothers and my grandmother have always been rigid, unbending, traditional Catholics. There was no way anybody, especially the hired help, was going to introduce any new ideas into their unwavering Catholic household.

One day I was visiting with Grandma. She was sitting in her wheelchair at the kitchen table doing her best to get down some lunch. She reached over, touched my hand and looking at me with ninety-six years of life experience etched upon her memory, spoke faintly, "Johnny, life is too short!"

"It sure is Grandma!" I answered, "It sure is!"

Just then Velma entered the kitchen smiling and nodding in agreement after overhearing what was just said. In her lively Jamaican accent Velma asked curiously, "So John, I understand you don't belong to the same church as the rest of your family?"

Someone in my family must had clued Velma in to the fact I didn't attend the Catholic Church any longer, so it made it easy for her to talk to me about her place of worship. When my dad just so happened to have entered the room, Velma looked for my approval as she said, "I've been telling your dad he needs to be Born Again! Does he know about the Rapture?"

I know she must have been disappointed when I gave my long-winded answer. "I changed my thinking on that one, Velma! I'm pretty certain there is no such thing as the Rapture, it's just another hokey false hope put upon men by fanatical Christians! In fact, it was an idea that originated in England in the 1800's by an over-enthusiastic woman of the church. I just can't believe all believers in Christ are going to be swept up in the blink of an eye and meet their Savior in the clouds, escaping the wrath of God on the earth!"

Velma was taken back a little by my response but it didn't stop me from pressing on. "What would make any human being believe he or she was worthy enough to be miraculously beamed up from the planet, while millions of other good souls were left behind to be tormented?" I asked.

Whether or not she grasped what I was saying, I couldn't tell, but I knew for sure my dad and my grandmother were totally confused, having absolutely no idea what Velma and I were discussing. Grandma just stared at her turkey sandwich while dad had a smirk on his face that silently declared, "You're both insane!"

Grandma was content to be surrounded by statues of dead saints, rosary beads and the like. Dad, I believed, would have preferred if I'd just shut up. It was bad enough he had to politely put up with Velma; he certainly didn't need to listen to his fanatical son's sermonizing. In the words of my dad, "I'm a good guy, I love my fellow man, and I try to do the right thing! Isn't that what it's all about?" Hmm…was he on to something?

I was making my last couple of deliveries of the day when my cell phone rang. It was Julianne who gave me the expected, yet heartbreaking news, my grandmother had passed away. For whatever reason, it hit me hard and my eyes just wouldn't stop from tearing.

"Are you alright?" Julianne asked.

"I'll be okay," I said despondently.

There were so many thoughts rushing through my head. Did I show her enough love? Why didn't I give her more time? Would she have understood if I tried to talk spiritual matters with her and why didn't I ever try? Is she at peace in heaven, wherever and whatever heaven may be? Were her last months happy ones? Memories of my grandmother were passing through my mind as if I were flipping through the pages of a photo album. She was absolutely right about one thing; a lifetime certainly goes by quickly.

Having a loved one die can be quite an unsettling time. During her last few months, my grandmother needed round the clock care and attention. It was a draining and stressful time for my mom, so in a sense, her death was a relief. Nevertheless, my mom took it pretty hard. I guess she had a lot of questions of her own. It's just the way life goes. We all thought we were doing our best, and then when the curtain fell, we began to second-guess ourselves.

I dreaded the wake and the funeral. With my anti-Catholic attitude, I was all equipped to criticize every word the priest was going to say. Even though in my heart I was grieving, in my head I was fantasizing about having a battle of wits with the priest, should I hear him say anything not scriptural. I pictured myself jumping to my feet in the middle of the service and shouting out, "Show me where it says that in the Bible!" I had to promise Julianne I wouldn't embarrass her with my idiotic behavior.

Just as expected, and true to form, the parish priest who presided over the funeral service didn't deviate a bit from the standard Catholic procedure. There were vestments, incense, candles and signs of the cross. There were Hail Mary's and Our Father's. There were bells, water, wine and wafers. There was also a homily or sermon or whatever it was they called it, when the priest talked in so many circles, I lost him two minutes after he began. He tried so ineffectively to make sense of death, Heaven, Jesus, Baptism and all the confusing mysteries of the faith, all I remember thinking was, "How and where did he come up with all this nonsense?"

The priest walked around my grandmother's coffin, sprinkled it with holy water and waved incense over it. I looked around the church watching everyone, including my parents, my brothers and my sister, listening and watching so attentively. "How in the world could they buy into this?" I wondered. Somehow I envisioned my grandmother's spirit floating about above us. She had a big grin on her face as she gently spoke to me, "They're all going to have to see for themselves!" As angry as I was about having to sit through what I considered an inane ritual and witnessing my loved ones taking it so seriously, I was at peace about grandma.

YE OF SUCH LITTLE FAITH

It was August 2003. I was in my usual hurry, bouncing about from business to business making my afternoon pick-ups, when I noticed the lights had gone out at one of my stops. Port Washington is a relatively wealthy town but for some reason it wasn't unusual for the community to experience frequent power outages. I live in Freeport, a village that doesn't share the same wealth as Port Washington, but we do have our own generators, we do supply our own electricity and rarely does our power go out. I was joking with one of the employees at the power-less warehouse where I was picking up packages, "In my little town we never lose power the way these rich folks do!"

He looked at me as if I had my head in the sand and with his eyes about to pop out from his head, shouted excitedly, "Haven't you heard man, the entire east coast is without electricity?"

Suddenly I got that too familiar disconcerting feeling, recalling it was on the job when I heard the news about the planes hitting the Twin Towers. No differently than millions of others, I thought this was another terrorist act.

Utterly aware of the fact my daughter, Christiann, was at work in Manhattan, I dialed her office only to get a busy signal. Phones weren't working, cell phones were out of service and computers were down. I became a bit frantic thinking about Christiann. I just prayed she wasn't stuck in an elevator or a subway. Knowing she wasn't very familiar with getting around Manhattan, I was worried. I flew through the remainder of my route and headed back to the depot, but with all the traffic signals being out, the journey seemed like it took forever. Vendors were standing out on the roadways trying to sell their frozen items before they melted or spoiled. Everyday people were helping direct traffic. Nobody had a clue as to what was going on. Everybody just needed to get home.

When I finally made my way back to my hometown of Freeport, I noticed the traffic signals were functioning. Upon entering through the front door of my house I felt the cold blast of air from our working air conditioning. "What's going on?" I asked Julianne. She told me that independent little Freeport still had power. Our streets were overridden with cars because the filling stations in our town were still able to pump gasoline. So while the remainder of the east coast of the United States was without power, there we were with the comfort of central air on a hot summer night, able to watch whatever television was being transmitted.

The thought of Christiann walking about the dark streets of the city was killing me. Cars were forbidden to enter Manhattan so I couldn't go searching for her even if I wanted to. She was finally able to make contact with us by calling from an old-fashioned phone booth located in front of Macy's. When I spoke to her she was as calm as could be while I was carrying on like a nut case. Amidst all the fear and confusion that encased our little section of the world, she finally made it home by two o'clock in the morning. Her co-worker's husband was a New York City cop who was permitted to enter the city by car. I was so grateful to him for getting my girl home safe and sound. The Bible is chock full of lessons about faith and how it conquers fear. All it took was a power outage and my rock-solid faith seemed to go right out the window.

TIME TO SHIT OR GET OFF THE POT

All my talk about leaving the church and I found myself still there. I didn't know if it was because I was trying to keep the peace with Julianne, if it was because I liked playing the drums, or if I was just a masochist? Sunday after Sunday, I sat behind the drums with a very bad attitude. I was just waiting for something or somebody to push me out the door. In the meantime, while doing my utmost to keep the beat, I would look out at the congregation and try to single out any individual who I thought I'd be able to confide in, and intelligently discuss all my newest thoughts and feelings, including why I'd become so turned off to The Assemblies of God and its doctrine. Somewhere among the sea of spellbound worshippers I zeroed in on a few.

One Sunday after the Praise Team had just finished rehearsing for the morning's service, I was standing alongside the pews having a talk with Benny. Benny is a Jew who had accepted Christ as the Messiah. He was also a Sunday school teacher and very well versed in scripture. Benny liked me. We talked a lot about music and our chats reminded him of his former days as a "Deadhead." I figured, "Who better to talk to than him?"

Benny and I talked about how agonizingly ridiculous our services had become. I believed, for a while, I had a comrade in Benny. While we were discussing how anything remotely Jewish had been snuffed out of Western Christianity, Brett the leader of the Praise team passed by and tapped me on the shoulder. Folding his hands and rolling back his eyes was his way of signaling me it was time to join the others in the back room for our pre-service prayer time. For some reason, Brett's intrusion annoyed me so much that I just lost it and under my breath blurted out, "Don't tell me when to fuckin' pray!"

Benny's eyes nearly popped out of his head when he heard my profane outburst, then looked around to make sure the church walls weren't caving in. As if he'd just saw horns sprouting from my forehead, he said, "I think it's time for you to step down brother, you don't belong in the Praise team anymore!"

Driven by a passion to wake other church members out of their Pentecostal stupor, I would confidently approach anybody who I felt would be open to the "Gospel of Me." As interesting as I thought they might have found my twist on the Testaments, the truth was, most were just humoring me. They thought I was off my rocker. If my convictions were as strong as I led everyone to believe they were, I should have just fled. But I seriously thought I could have initiated a stirring and an exodus.

Peggy was a singer in the Praise Team who genuinely seemed to pay attention to some of my viewpoints and opinions. Peggy was married to Jimmy. This was the same Jimmy who preached to my dying neighbor, rebuilt my kitchen, and bonded with me for bi-weekly cappuccino meets. He was an unyielding fire and brimstone kind of guy, who was uncertain about my salvation when I admitted to him I was having many reservations about Christianity. So very unlike her husband, Peggy had an open mind and made it a practice to research everything we spoke about. She was very encouraging and I looked forward to our weekly conversations. What struck me funny was how Peggy, who knew her Bible forwards and backwards, would always be amazed by my unusual spin on familiar Bible passages. I had found an audience for my opposing standpoints on topics such as "The Rapture," "Speaking in Tongues," and "God's Wrath." I found someone who appreciated my views on Easter Sunday, Christmas and the need for Christianity to return to its Hebrew roots. Quite a few people in the church, however, found Peggy to be very odd…Figured! Who was more wacky, her or me?

Every month on a Saturday morning, the men from the church would gather together for an informal breakfast and fellowship. Why I hadn't left the church yet still baffled me and how I got roped into cooking for all these ravenous fellows puzzled me even more. So while the men mingled, I kept busy flipping pancakes. I have to say, in all honesty, I couldn't relate to most of the guys, so I was better off being stuck in the kitchen. There were some men whose company I enjoyed, however, and Hector was one of them.

When speaking with Hector, I had to listen carefully, as his Argentinean accent brought about a little difficulty in understanding every word. Two years prior, Hector's wife had died after a long bout with cancer and it wasn't until then we got close. Hector once attended a Bible college and really knew a lot more about scripture than I did. I started to confide in him about the new path I was treading and my disenchantment with the church. He was pretty much in total agreement with everything I said, so I figured from that day on I had a companion in Hector. What I couldn't get a grip on was why either one of us was even there?

After all the men filled their bellies, I escaped from the kitchen to indulge myself in a few of my made from scratch pancakes. I took a seat at the table already occupied by Pastor Ted, Jimmy, Hector and a couple of other fellows. They were involved in a conversation about what was a recent Rhode Island nightclub tragedy where one hundred people died after the pyrotechnics of the band "Great White" accidentally set the place on fire.

"Could you imagine the looks on the faces of those poor souls when they went from the fires of that nightclub into the eternal flames of hell?" the Pastor asked with a conceited air of self-righteousness.

I got a bit taken back by his cocky remark and asked, "What makes you so sure they went to hell?" Today I would have asked him, "What makes you so sure there even is a hell?" but at the time I didn't know any better.

"Well brother," he confidently responded, "I think it's safe to assume, if one is frequenting those types of establishments, he probably isn't walking with the Lord, so I'm not being too presumptuous by saying that hell is a likely possibility!"

My next question was going to be, "What makes you so sure any body goes to either heaven or hell immediately after dying?" because as far as I knew, at that stage in my journey, the Bible said that everyone must face the final judgment before entering heaven, hell or wherever it is people go after they die.

I wanted so very much to confront his arrogance by telling him that he was not only full of himself but that he was also dead wrong! I surrendered to my good sense, however, backed off and returned to the kitchen to wash pots and pans. I'd patronized many nightclubs to see some of my favorite bands and God was usually right there with me! I'd never go anywhere without Him.

What made this spiritual journey of mine even more interesting was discovering that besides Sara, my brother-in-law Art in Arizona and my sister-in-law Caroline in Florida, were also dissatisfied with mainstream Christianity and were seeking answers to their questions. The three of them discovered Internet Bible chat rooms that dealt with the subject of religious discontent and they communicated with hundreds of people fleeing from organized religion. I wasn't much a fan of creating cyber-space friendships, so although I didn't partake, they continually filled me in on whatever information they'd gathered during our continuous phone conversations. I was becoming increasingly convinced we were called and a divine movement of the Spirit of God was behind it all. When I would attempt to discuss with Julianne the conversations I had with her siblings, she used to say to me, "My sisters and my brother are nuts!"

SUNDAY MORNING SIDESHOW

On a Sunday morning service, the week after Pastor Ted had so "enlightened" me at the men's breakfast, he preached with such vim and vigor about the extreme importance of being baptized with the Holy Spirit and the evidence of speaking in tongues. He was galloping from one side of the altar to the other pointing to various members of the Praise Team. (What the pastor considered an altar, I considered a stage for Sunday Morning Theater)!

"Peter!" he roared, "Have you been baptized with the Holy Spirit with the evidence of speaking in tongues?"

Peter, with his hands raised in the air replied proudly and affirmatively, "Yes Pastor, I have!"

"Brett!" the Pastor cried out, "have you been baptized with the Holy Spirit with the evidence of speaking in tongues?"

"Alleluia! Yes I have! Praise the Lord!" Brett replied like a good little soldier, as if the entire contrived scene had been rehearsed moments before.

This question and answer routine seemed to go on forever. One of the requirements of being a member of the Praise Team, according to the "Assemblies of God" instructional guidelines, was each singer and musician must be filled with the Holy Spirit. There was no blood test, x-ray or MRI that could tell if someone had the Holy Spirit. You could only go by one's word. I knew for a fact Antonio, our guitarist, did not speak in tongues and the church had no problem with him leading song services. He even made it a point to mention to me how he thought the whole concept was ridiculous. Nevertheless, whatever Pastor Ted was up to, it was working perfectly. The place was in a frenzy.

I think he knew better than to call out my name. I sat at the drums and was furious about what was going on. I was annoyed at myself for even having to take part in such an exhibition. People were coming up to the platform as the elders of the church were laying hands on their heads, praying that each needy seeker receive his or her infilling of the Holy Spirit. It was a common practice for the elders to push hard against the foreheads of the people waiting impatiently for the Holy Spirit to mysteriously come spiraling down from heaven and permeating their being. If the inductees to the "Baptized in the Spirit" club should have happened to fall to the ground, it only added to the drama. On one such occasion I heard with my own ears as an elder actually coached a believer into speaking in tongues by saying, "Repeat after me, mosh-anna-manna-nah-nah-nah-nah.".

While the pastor was prancing about, successfully psyching everyone up, the Praise Team broke into a couple of the church's top ten hits. The singers harmonized, "No other name but the name of Jesus, no other name but the name of the Lord!" My spirit cringed. "That's not His name!" I kept thinking, "what a total scam this is!"

That was the straw that broke the camel's back. I absolutely knew I couldn't take part in his circus sideshow much longer. Pastor Ted and his antics were about to push me right out the door!

LIKE FATHER LIKE SON

One balmy Saturday evening, friends of ours from the church had a little backyard graduation party for their daughter. Many of the guests were folks from the congregation including Pastor Ted, his wife, along with their son Ted Jr. the youth pastor and his wife. Who says there's nepotism in the church??? Anyway, Ted Sr. started bidding everyone goodnight, not even hanging around long enough to have a piece of graduation cake.

I was sitting beside Ted Jr. and asked, "Why does your dad have to leave so early? The party just started!"

He looked at me like I should have already known the answer and said, "He has to get home and prepare his message for tomorrow's service!"

At this point I was certain I was done with the church, so I enjoyed nothing more than being an instigator among these holy-rollers and stirring up a little trouble.

"You've got to be kidding me!" I said, "You mean to tell me he waits until the night before to put together his Sunday morning message? What the heck does he do all week long?"

The good son started to justify what his dad did with his time and I cut him short.

"Hey! If his message is all prepared (which it was, I'd seen a few of them all neatly typed and double-spaced) why does he openly pray at the start of each sermon for the Holy Spirit to guide him? I was under the impression the Holy Spirit was running the show!"

Teddy boy replied quickly, as if he'd answered these questions before, "To make sure God approves of what he's about to preach!"

I was up there on the platform Sunday after Sunday and I'd never seen him deviate from his script, but I didn't push the issue because I think he got the message loud and clear.

"Hey Ted!" I continued, "You know as well as I do, if he needed to, he could always resort to his file cabinet full of past messages...I'm sure he's got some good ones we haven't heard yet!"

Ted smirked, and then got up to refill his paper cup with some more fruit punch. Sometimes I just couldn't help but voice what was on my mind. I was talking to a kid whose dad had set him up with a decent paying undemanding job, a place to live, and a state of the art office, all funded by the hard earned money of the church members. What really killed me, though, was how the spiritual advisor of our kids openly admitted to me he prayed to God by typing his prayers out on his computer! He would send God e-mail! I should have asked him if God's e-mail address was GodisGood@yahoo.com.

JUST WHAT I NEEDED TO HEAR

The following Sunday, the Pastor's "Spirit inspired" message was about the doctrine of the "Assemblies of God" organization. From the pulpit he clearly defined what we, as members of this holy ensemble, were required to believe. Once again, the Baptism of the Holy Spirit with the evidence of speaking in tongues was an issue that carried a lot of weight.

"If you don't believe in the Baptism then maybe this isn't the church for you!" he boldly suggested. With the flair of a crafty politician the Pastor continued, "We believe in the Rapture of the church, that we will be swept away in the twinkling of an eye, to meet with the Lord in the air before the days of tribulation! If that doesn't suit you then maybe this church isn't the one for you!"

I sat motionless in my pew, getting more and more irritated as others around me cried out shouts of "Amen" and "Alleluia," with the exception of a few. Benny headed for the exit doors, rolling back his eyes and giving me a look that clearly stated, "I've had enough!" I felt a tap on the shoulder. I looked around to find my friend David, another disillusioned member of the flock, shaking his head and grinning. I knew he could read my mind. Maybe this was no longer the church for either one of us.

After attending Full Gospel Church for over twenty years, rarely missing a Sunday and being a loyal and faithful member of the Praise Team, I finally made a decision to take a few weeks off before officially departing. Even though I still had some friends there and even though I knew I'd never hear the end of it from Julianne, I had no choice but to leave. In a telephone conversation with Billy our keyboardist, I explained my feelings and conveyed to him I desperately needed to take a break. He told me he admired me for following my heart and understood perfectly why I had to do what I had to do. I was so ready for a vacation from church!

CAN'T JUDGE A BOOK...

I've always been up-front with my feelings. I try to be honest with everyone and that's probably why so many people trust me and confide in me. Sometimes they tell me more than I care to know.

Unlike what so many members of the church were akin to believe, to me, it was no secret Peggy and Jimmy's marriage wasn't really made in heaven. Jim gave the impression he was an unbreakable soldier in God's army, standing firmly on Biblical principles; while Peggy often came across as the wholesome, untainted almost virginal submissive wife. Jim was funny. He was a hell fire doomsday lecturer, yet whenever he preached, he was always sure to include a line or two questioning how God could love an undeserving slug like him. Jim came from an Orthodox Greek religion, which wasn't a far stretch from Catholicism. Both faiths really excelled in burdening its members with guilt, superstition and wrath.

Peggy sang with the praise team and had the voice of an angel. One could almost imagine a halo hovering above her saintly face and wings sprouting from her shoulders. Christian or not, guys are guys, and a handful of my "church brothers" had made their fancies about Peggy known to me. I'd never had a problem admitting where my mind has wandered every thirty seconds or so in a church service. There were in fact some fine looking women who have passed through the doors of our humble church. Most men preferred keeping their fantasies to themselves, not letting on they'd spent a good part of the worship service staring at some woman's ass. We're supposed to look. It's perfectly normal. That's the way God made us!

In the eyes of many, Jim and Peggy fit the picture as having the perfect "Christian marriage." Both of them were very involved in church activities. Jim was considered a "prayer warrior," often called upon to lead prayer services, and Peggy, as his subservient wife, was never far from his side, always available to play guitar and sing "White as Snow," a church favorite about God forgiving us our sins. If knowing the truth set one free, then I had to question just how much truth they knew, because to me it seemed as if they were both wearing the shackles of religious bondage. Jim and Peggy put up a great front. Both of them were unhappy and I was one of the few acquaintances of theirs who knew it. They were two very different people who just happened to meet in church and let their naïve hearts fool them into thinking their meeting was not by chance, but by the matchmaking department in Heaven. It was only a matter of time before the front would come crashing down.

Hector wandered about the church like a lost puppy dog. He had never seemed to get over losing his wife, and in the two years since she'd passed away, he hadn't dated. He tried to keep himself occupied by learning the guitar and as fate would have it, if there were such a thing, Peggy was readily available to teach him. The two of them started spending a good deal of time together in what appeared to be innocent companionship between fellow churchgoers. Like I said, a lot of guys had their eyes on Peggy, but nobody would even think of making a play for her, not even lonely Hector. First of all, she was a married woman. Second of all, this was church for crying out loud!

There were quite a few single women in the church who had expressed interest in Hector. He was a slim, well-proportioned, handsome widower with pathetically sad eyes that could make any needy female want to mother him. Peggy, who later confessed to me she regarded her marriage as a prison sentence, fell under Hector's spell and eventually did the unthinkable. Late one hot summer Saturday night, as Hector and I sat out on my deck drinking a few Peroni's, he spilled his guts. To say I was stunned would have been an understatement. My brain nearly exploded with all the mental images.

It's usually only a matter of time before scandalous news items surface. Before long, the Hector and Peggy rumors were flying, and so were the opinions and insinuations of the congregation. This caused quite a ruckus throughout the church. The only way Pastor Ted knew how to handle the situation was to strongly request Hector leave the church. This action raised questions: Why was Hector asked to leave and not Peggy. Why wasn't Jimmy asked to step down from the positions he held as church elder and substitute Sunday school teacher? Without knowing all the details about their crime of passion, people started to point fingers, and even though everyone was well aware of the fact, "it takes two to tango," Hector was standing in the line of fire with a target on his back. I, however, being a friend to Hector, Peggy and Jimmy, was very well informed of all the juicy details, which put me in a very uncomfortable position. I wasn't about to choose sides or turn my back on any of them, even though I knew they all played a part in this truly awkward situation. I completely understood how and why things happened the way they did, yet I couldn't condone that Hector messed around with another man's wife, and not just any man's, Jimmy was his friend! My association with both Hector and Peggy made me an outcast in the eyes of some of the church folk. I was advised not to support Hector by embracing with any comforting words of encouragement. His "brothers in the Lord" turned on him so fast and were so unforgiving, it was pathetic. Wasn't it Jesus who said, "Let he who is without sin cast the first stone?" Well quite a few stones were being cast at Hector, which only reinforced my reasons for wanting to abandon the assembly. The church was acting more like a lynch mob rather than the guiding sympathetic brothers and sisters who Hector, Peggy and Jimmy needed in this time of trouble. In the months ahead, no one was quite sure of Hector and Peggy's whereabouts, and I had to do my best not to divulge to the gossipmongers, any of the information given to me in strictest confidence.

Benny, who had been teaching Sunday school in the church for years, had always been a thorn in the pastor's side. He was never one for restraining himself when it came to voicing his opinions. Benny did not agree with the pastor's unjust decision in asking Hector to leave the church and not Peggy. Furthermore, he was infuriated when Jimmy wasn't asked to step down from teaching a Sunday school class or leading a prayer service. Somewhere in the Bible it states when a man's "house is in turmoil," he should resign from such positions. The pastor must have figured losing Hector was not as big a loss as losing Jimmy, his kids, his parents, and his handyman talent. The feud between Pastor Ted and Benny went on for weeks, until Benny was finally asked to step down from his weekly duty as a Sunday school teacher, supposedly because of his insubordination. Because some of Benny's latest unconventional Sunday school lessons got some influential church members' noses out of joint could also have had something to do with it. Some of the discussions Benny and I have had caused him to rethink a few things. After prayerful study, he brought some new tricks to some old dogs. Some people are just comfortable in their blindness and would rather not hear new ideas, so they made their dissatisfaction with Benny known. After twenty long years, Benny and his wife Shirley sort of followed my footsteps and resigned from Full Gospel Church. They, however, marched right into another local congregation whereas I refused to involve myself in another branch of the same Sunday morning charades.

CRASH AND LEARN

Whatever happened to the life we once dreamed about? Where was the wraparound porch of the old colonial in the wide-open spaces of the Berkshire Hills; why wasn't I strumming my guitar from a rocking chair in front of the crackling fireplace; why wasn't Julianne tending to the garden or baking a fresh apple pie? How was it that the cards dealt us a life in the demented rat race of shallow suburbia? How was it that the peace and solitude of living a simple country life as an artist had been replaced with the stressing shrieks of a discontented life partner? Why was I feeling so sorry for myself? Was it too fucking late to be asking those questions now? The wise old folks from the generations before had warned us time and time again how quickly life passes by. None of us believed them until we saw it for ourselves. Our children were now adults and it seemed like it all happened in the blink of an eye. Before long they would all be permanently out of the house, which was why I couldn't understand Julianne's latest onslaught of complaints.

"These kids don't pull their weight around here!" she would holler, "they're just boarders and I want you to take money from them!"

Granted at times they treated our house as if it was a hotel with Jule and me as the caretakers, but then they were too young for it to bother me. I guess I just couldn't see things the same way my wife did; not to say I was right and she was wrong, we just looked at things differently. I'd always believed with all my heart (as I'm sure Julianne has) we'd been blessed with wonderful kids. Certainly, there's always room for improvement, but that holds true for all of us. I never believed she really meant it when she made her groundless statements about not being able to stand her children or that she wanted them out of the house or even that she wanted to take money from them. I'd always felt those unjustifiable outbursts were brought on by a combination of things. Her frustration with my easygoing nature, the obvious difference in our child-rearing skills, her not-so-wonderful childhood, genetics, her obsessive-compulsive controlling personality and the fact she could no longer control her children, all added to her agitation. Whatever the reasons were, it tore me apart whenever I heard them. I became extremely depressed over the condition of my family and so weary of Julianne's demands. All I would think about was how it usually takes a tragedy to wake people up, and I had this uneasiness that something might happen to one of us. We'd already been through Trevor's death, 9-11, and testicular cancer, how much more did we need? I began to pray unceasingly for the protection of my wife and kids on a daily basis. I don't think I would have been able to handle it should anything tragic had happened to any one of them. Not even to Julianne when I was really pissed off at her. My only mistake was not including myself enough in those prayers.

It was Saturday, just three days before my fifty-first birthday. Since my fiftieth was such a letdown, I was hoping maybe this year I'd be pleasantly surprised. It doesn't take much to make me happy; a little TLC does it every time.

I had my usual list of Saturday morning chores set out before me: the bank, the post office and my monthly adjustment with my chiropractor, Dr. Fazio. Several years ago, I suffered a back injury at work and workman's compensation is covering a lifetime of chiropractic treatment. I picked up the yellow pages, let my fingers do the walking, and since Dr. Robert Fazio was the nearest chiropractor to my home, I called for an appointment. When I first took a gander at the Doc and saw a rather overweight practitioner of natural healing, I wondered, "How serious is this guy about health if he allowed himself to get so rotund?"

Initially, I had some serious doubts about his practice, but when he got me walking again after suffering with crippling back pain, he gained my confidence. Besides, he's got a terrific sense of humor and we've had some great laughs for those twenty minutes he'd fiddle with my spine. I had a nine-thirty appointment with Dr. Bob and as usual I was running a little late. The doc's a cool guy, so punctuality was never an issue. As I was scrambling to find my wallet and keys, I could hear Julianne mumbling with exasperation while searching for something in the kitchen cabinets. She was also about to leave the house that morning for a field trip with the kids from church.

"Have you seen the plastic travel cups?" she asked in frustration, "Your kids never put things back where they belong, now they're lost!"

Whenever there was a problem, she referred to them as "your kids."

"These kids are just boarders. I'm telling you John, I want you to take money from them!"

I was thinking to myself, "Here we go again!" and that eerie premonition about tragedy crept back into my head. In order to put an end to her latest episode of faultfinding, I stopped what I was doing and began to help her search the cabinets. Surer than shit, I found the travel cup where *she* obviously placed it, way back amongst all the plastic crap crammed into the cabinet above the refrigerator.

"Thanks!" she said to me, then kissed me goodbye as I rushed out the front door and into my car.

There's nothing I hated more than to hear Jule loudly lecturing me about what she felt were the shortcomings of our children. It would depress me terribly, but instead of letting the annoyance get the better of me, this time I turned my thoughts heavenward and prayed. "Father," I pleaded, "Wherever You are, please bring this family together, I really can't take it anymore."

As strange as this may sound, that morning as I opened the door of my Honda Accord, I could almost swear I had another one of those quick outer body experiences. From up above looking down, for a brief moment, I could actually see myself climbing into my car! I didn't give it any thought and drove away with joyful anticipation of sharing some funny stories with Dr. Bob.

The traffic on Atlantic Avenue was light. As I headed west in the left hand lane, I could see there were no cars ahead of me for miles. The doctor's office was just blocks away. In my mind I was running through some of the errands I planned on doing that afternoon, when from out of nowhere, without warning, everything came to a screeching halt. All I could hear was the terrifying sound of metal hitting metal. I felt pain shoot all throughout my body; I saw shattered glass and gray smoke. Thousands of thoughts were racing through my head with such intensity, I was unable to focus. Then I suddenly became aware of the premonition I'd been having about a tragedy bringing my family together. I truly believed this was the end of the road for me. I was thinking about all the things I would never get to accomplish. I was terribly upset about being taken away from Julianne and the kids. I wasn't ready to die and if by any chance I was to come out of this mess alive, I didn't want to be physically mangled. Within seconds, my life flashed before my eyes and simultaneously a million thoughts rocketed through my throbbing brain.

Suddenly, the cyclone of confusion I was spinning in became still, and the motion of my hurled vehicle ceased. I compared the scene to the one in "The Wizard of Oz" when Dorothy's house came crashing down from out of the twister into Munchkin land. I came to the realization I was still alive and conscious when I saw smoke rising from the dashboard. I figured I had better try to get myself out of the car before it exploded. With whatever strength I could muster up, I pushed my way out of the driver's side door and hobbled out onto the road as shooting pains pulsated through my chest and leg.

"John, John!" I heard a familiar voice cry out, "are you all right?"

I glanced around and saw Arnie, a friend of mine from the church, come running over to assist me. Just by coincidence, he happened to be passing by the scene of the accident. He laid me down trying his best to comfort me and take charge of the situation. As I lay, completely overwhelmed by what just happened, I cried out as involuntarily as breathing, "Oh fuck! Oh fuck! Oh fuck!"

When I opened my eyes to see Arnie standing over me like an angel who had come to my rescue, I apologized for my language.

"That's okay!" he laughed, "just take it easy!"

I reached for my cell phone and called home. Samantha answered, and after I told her what just happened, I could hear her scream, "Oh my God! Daddy, are you all right?"

Julianne and Sam arrived at the scene immediately, and within minutes the ambulance followed. Strangers were standing all around as they watched me get placed onto a stretcher and carried away to the nearest hospital emergency room. I couldn't believe this was happening. Things like this always happen to the other guy, not me! I was really pissed off knowing my weekend was shot. At that moment, I had no clue I was going to be laid up for the next several months.

I wasn't in the emergency room for more than five minutes when visitors started to arrive. The first one at my bedside to show his concern was none other than Pastor Ted. The man, who'd been annoying the living daylights out of me for months, was at my side thanking God for my survival and praying for my quick recovery.

My dear friend Helen was the next one to arrive at the scene. Helen liked to call herself my Puerto Rican mother, even though she's only ten years older than me. In her youth she was a slender woman with a terrific figure, but after a work related accident, Helen gained a considerable amount of weight and has had more health issues than anyone I know. Yet every Sunday she was right there in her front row pew, shouting out the same unintelligible phrases, praising and worshiping God, and was usually the first one on line waiting to be anointed with oil for a healing. Helen always claimed it was Jesus who had healed her, and then testified about the "miracle" before the entire congregation. Unfortunately, in the weeks that followed, she was back on line again with another ailment. Helen is a woman of tremendous faith and as eccentric as some people find her, I truly love her.

Helen entered the ER crying as if they were lowering my casket into the ground. Not long after I left the house that morning she had called to ask me out for breakfast. She told me I'd been on her mind for days and in obedience to God, had been praying for me. Who knows, maybe her prayers were the reason I'm here to tell about it. Helen squeezed my hand, touched my face and through her sobbing, told me how much she loved me. "Thanks Helen! It's nice to be so loved," I said, reassuring her I would be all right as Julianne and Samantha looked on.

An endless procession of visitors passed through the emergency room that morning to check in on me. The ironic thing was they were all from the church I'd just recently decided to leave. After Julianne had called the church to inform them she wasn't going to be able to make the field trip because I was in an accident, the news spread like wildfire. I love most of the people from the church. They are warm, caring, and praying folks. I guess I was just a lot less willing to accept the things they did. I kept wondering, "Was God trying to tell me something concerning my decision?"

HOSPITAL-ITY

Anyone who's ever spent time in an emergency room will have stories to tell about how absolutely torturous and miserable it is. People linger for hours before finding out what's actually wrong with them. I was getting very impatient. I was confident that I was fine and I wanted to go home, but until I got the approval of a doctor, I had to stay put. After lying there for what seemed like an eternity, it was imperative I get up and use the bathroom. I asked Julianne to reach for my sneakers so I could stroll over to the men's room. After she placed the sneakers on my feet, I carefully slid off the bed to stand. Immediately, streaks of sharp pain surged through my right leg like a succession of exploding missiles. My leg gave out from under me and as I was about to hit the ground, Julianne and my brother Jim, broke my fall. I was dreading the strong possibility bedpans and urinals might become a necessary part of my immediate future. After a series of x-rays and Cat-scans, the prognosis was I had fractured my hip socket. There was no question about it, I was being admitted. I wasn't going home. I was devastated and as depressed as can be.

The next four days found me confined to a bed with my right leg in traction. The bed was too small, the blanket too short and my roommate was a whining spoiled brat who needed to have the daylights kicked out of him, even though he was badly mangled in an auto accident much worse than mine. He abused his parents, he abused the nursing staff and he annoyed the crap out of my guests and me. He continually whined, demanding heavier doses of pain medication. I was hoping his nurse would accidentally assist him in overdosing. I found it rather miraculous, however, once his girlfriend showed up, his constant bellyaching ceased. The curtain separating us was pulled entirely around his bed giving him total privacy. The "ooh" and "ah" sounds escaping from behind it left very little to the imagination. Oh, how I wanted to just smack him!

My stay in the hospital was an exhausting one to say the least. The visitors and the phone calls were relentless. Not to say I didn't appreciate the company and the genuine concern, but I didn't have five minutes alone to even fart in private! My brother-in-law Art called from Arizona at least six times one day just so we could talk for a few minutes without any interruptions. My back was killing me from having to remain in basically one position for twenty-four hours a day. I smelled like sewage and I was on the road to being constipated for the first time in ages, because there was absolutely no way I was about to crap in a bedpan! I was also preoccupied on what the decision of the orthopedic doctors was going to be. I was told I was going to be transferred to another area hospital where hip replacement surgery would be performed. I was a helpless, frustrated wreck!

My favorite September day was upon me once again. The one day of the year I'd looked forward to for over fifty years, and here I was celebrating my fifty-first birthday from a hospital bed. I don't care what anybody says, except for maybe Julianne, we're all babies when it comes to our birthdays!

That evening my room was jammed with family and friends. Julianne and the kids, my parents, Gino and Katie, and to my surprise my good buddy and co-worker Figgy, were all on hand to help me celebrate. I got lots of cards and gifts, but the one thing I'd been looking forward to annually but haven't been getting lately, the birthday sex, wasn't going to happen again this year (unless my roommate's girlfriend accidentally stepped behind my curtain). When visiting hours were finally over, and all my guests had left for the evening, I looked down at my leg and sighed a long sigh of self-pity. The phone rang. I picked up and once again it was Art. I could always depend on Art to come through with the birthday call. I was really feeling depressed so his call couldn't have come at a better time. We talked for hours trying unsuccessfully to figure out this crazy life. After our conversation, I felt a little less sorry for myself and drifted off to sleep.

With every day my situation improved. On day four, the doctors allowed me to get up from bed. I was forbidden to place any pressure on my right leg and used a walker to inch my way from place to place, those being the toilet and the shower. After having my first bowel movement and a nice hot shower since the day of the accident, I was taken to the radiology department for another series of x-rays.

A few hours later, my doctor dropped by to deliver the good news, my fractures were perfectly aligned. He told me if I promised to remain off my leg we could forego surgery, allow the bone to heal naturally, and go home on Saturday. He explained to me, however, upon leaving the hospital, Home Care services would be providing me with a tension bed that was to be set up in my home. I would be instructed to remain in this cumbersome contraption until I healed. At this point, I didn't care what they were sending me home with, as long as I was going home.

If my child was in the hospital, regardless of how young or old, I would be there as often as I could, or until I was told to get lost. My folks were there constantly, and I think it irritated Julianne to see them there every time she arrived. Julianne and I were never given the opportunity to spend any time alone together. I understood her frustration, but at the same time, I didn't have the heart to tell my folks we needed a little breathing room.

On that very same day when the doctor gave me the news about being discharged, Julianne came scooting over to the hospital right after getting out of work. When she entered my room, I could sense her annoyance when she saw the permanent fixtures of my mom and dad standing at my bedside. She greeted me with a quick kiss hello and anticipating an elated reaction, I presented her with the doctor's plan of action for me.

"Julianne," I said grinning from ear to ear, "I have good news and I have bad news!"

"What?" she asked still with that perturbed look on her face due to my parents' presence.

"I'm coming home on Saturday!" I informed her.

"Great!" she replied, "What's the bad news?"

Knowing Julianne the way I did, I had a feeling she wasn't going to be too thrilled when I answered, "...and all this paraphernalia is coming with me!" pointing to the iron crane surrounding my bed.

Julianne's face dropped to the floor and in complete exasperation asked, "And where are we supposed to put all this?"

When I heard her response to what I considered good news, my heart sunk, and by the expression on the faces of my parents, so did theirs. Behind Julianne's back, my mom signaled me in sign language, alerting me I was welcomed to stay at their house. Her invitation didn't help mend my broken heart. Jule felt the tension coming from my folks, I felt the tension coming from Jule and I couldn't even get up from bed to run away from it all. Julianne was flustered, and in her frustration, she came out with a stream of hurtful lines that only worsened the situation.

"Don't be an idiot," she said, "It will be better for your law suit if you stay longer in the hospital!"

She topped that with, "You didn't give this much thought, did you? Who's going to move furniture and rearrange things to accommodate this huge bed?"

Given the choice, I think Julianne would have rather had me stay in the hospital than have had to rearrange furniture. Not for anything, but at this point, I thought it would be a blessing if I had just died. After the two of us had a rather ridiculous argument, Julianne stormed out of my room, and the curtain closed on this day of good news. For an encore, I called home only to have her hang up on me. If ever I felt like a loser, this was it! Before closing my eyes to float off into the peaceful solitude of sleep, I prayed for a solution to my problem.

The next morning greeted me with a surprise visit from my doctor. There had been a slight change in plans. My release date had been moved ahead to Friday, and as long as I promised to put no weight on my leg, the tension equipment would not be necessary. Needless to say, I promised to be on my best behavior, and God knows how relieved I was to learn our household would not be disrupted by the presence of the monstrous medical machinery. When I broke the news to Julianne, so was she! With a vastly improved outlook than the day before, things were looking up!

QUESTIONS AND NO ANSWER

That same afternoon, Pastor Ted unexpectedly dropped by to see me. I told him the news about my returning home, to which he responded with a heartfelt "Praise the Lord!" This was probably the only time during my week's stay in the hospital when I didn't have more than one visitor; it was just Ted and I and the curtains. Even my obnoxious roommate was gone. I figured this had to be the moment. If ever there was going to be a time to discuss with him my disillusionment with the church, it was now. I told him all about my parkway revelation and how I believed it put me on this path of new discoveries. I explained my quandary with the name Jesus not being the Messiah's rightful name. I questioned him about the pagan origins of Easter and Christmas. I asked him how and why Christians abandoned the seventh day Sabbath and conformed to Sunday? I asked him why he thought Catholicism adopted pagan Sun god customs and why Christianity seemed to forsake her Hebrew roots. As quickly as they came to me, I fired off question after question at my supposed spiritual leader. I think I took Pastor Ted by complete surprise and I'm sure he must have thought I was taking myself way too seriously. He answered me by saying, "John, I look at Full Gospel Church as the perfect church for imperfect people. No church has it all."

He tried to appease me by explaining how Bible scholars have debated these issues through the ages, each side successfully using scripture to support their arguments. I knew Pastor Ted was living quite the comfortable lifestyle, with a substantial pension due him not too far off in the future. He needed to defend his position, even if it meant using lines out of scripture that might have been completely out of context, and jumping over puddles by answering questions with questions. Ted was such an expert at slanting words he could easily have been a politician. Maybe he assumed he distracted me enough to land safely. I wasn't at all satisfied with his answers, and I truly felt at one point he knew it. No further explanation was needed as to why I made my decision to resign my position as drummer of the Praise Team. He knew he lost me, and just how lost I was, I had no clue.

THERE'S NO PLACE LIKE HOME?

I arrived home Friday morning, and even though I was maneuvering about with crutches and a walker, it was good to be home! For the next few months I was more or less confined to having my ass permanently attached to the massaging recliner on loan from my sister-in-law Sara. She was also kind enough to hook me up with her wireless laptop computer, on which I was able to write and communicate with the outside world.

For the first few weeks I needed help getting in and out of the shower, putting on and taking off my socks and pants. Julianne still had to go to work every morning so taking care of me was quite burdensome. There were a few times when she totally lost her cool. The daily arrival of visitors and the accumulation of all the junk piling up around me in our den had to be unnerving for her. As the weeks passed, I was able to do more things for myself as I got to be more skilled at hopping around on crutches.

Not having to go to work agreed with me tremendously. To me there was nothing greater than having time for myself. Every morning after Julianne and the kids had left the house, I retreated to the den where I wrote, had on line Bible studies with Sara, Arthur, and Caroline, and listened to Scripture teaching tapes until either visitors arrived guests or my family returned home. My disability also equipped me with the greatest excuse as to why I wasn't going to church. The sad thing was, the further along I deviated from traditional Christian teaching, the further apart I seemed to be growing from Julianne and those around me who loved me. I was beginning to feel as if I were living two separate lives and no one cared to join me in my new one. No matter who came by, the conversations sooner or later turned into religious debates over the touchy topics I almost always instigated, such as church doctrine, Easter and Christmas, Old Testament law, and the name of Jesus. I probably didn't realize it at the time, but I was becoming obsessed with acquiring knowledge, not only to find answers but also to fuel my rebellion. No one was totally disagreeing with me as to the legitimacy of some of my arguments, but how and why after twenty somewhat years I decided to cut myself off from the church was troubling them greatly. I'd always been somewhat opinionated and now I was on a mission to shove all my newly formulated opinions down everyone's throat. I don't think I would have been very far off by stating that Julianne was beginning to hate the very sound of my voice, and rightfully so! She probably didn't know who I was any more. Sometimes I felt as if I was wandering about in the wilderness and everyone was watching me as if I had finally lost my mind.

After spending my entire day fixed to the recliner, my only escape being an occasional visit with my porcelain friend, the toilet, I looked forward to finally hobbling up the thirteen steps that led to my bedroom where I could retire for the evening. My only problem was, I had to lie on my back with my right leg elevated. I kept waking up in the middle of the night due to the discomfort of back pain. The only reprieve I had was to get up and walk to the bathroom. The clunking of my walker would wake Samantha and Julianne, and by morning both of them were feeling a little edgy. Samantha wasn't the most sympathetic daughter, and often made it known to me just how much the sound annoyed her.

One Saturday morning, when all of the kids were out of the house, Jule turned to me and posed the question of all questions, "How long are we supposed to wait before we can make love again?"

My response could only have been, "When there is a will there most certainly is a way!"

I knew my disabled situation had Jule mentally stressed to the point where she probably wanted to strangle me, and I was aware that spiritually, she believed we were divided. Sensitive to those feelings, I could only conclude her suggestion was strictly brought on by a purely physical need. This was a Kodak moment for sure as the two of us contorted every which way as to successfully make love, yet move gently and carefully as to not shift my healing hip socket. As graceless a situation as it was, at least for me, it turned out to be quite memorable.

THE WEDDING FEAST

Long before my untimely accident, we had purchased airline tickets for Julianne, the kids and me to fly to Naples, Florida to attend our niece Melissa's wedding. A week prior to our pending departure, the doctor gave his approval for me to take the trip, so long as I remained on crutches. Everyone in Julianne's huge family attended, not so much because they cared to attend yet another wedding, but because they hadn't seen each other in so many years, it was a great excuse to have a reunion. Most of us stayed at the same Best Western and we all extended our visit for a few days so we could spend some time together. Julianne and I hadn't seen her parents or most of her siblings in such a long while we figured it was bound to be an enjoyable and emotional time. My father-in-law was beginning to show his age; Julianne's many nieces and nephews had all grown into stunning young women and handsome young men. Naturally, Sara and I couldn't wait to see Arthur and Caroline so we could bond and feed each other the latest findings and predisposed interpretations from our excavations into scripture. The four of us were on a mission to prove ourselves right and everyone else wrong. We all awaited the arrival of the rich and nonconforming younger brother Joseph and his wife Corinne, who didn't disappoint us with their eccentricity. The four days proved to be interesting to say the least.

The misadventures began at the church during the wedding ceremony. The bride's parents (my brother-in-law Bobby and his wife Mary) were still Catholic, so the service was held in a Catholic Church, Mass and all the trimmings. I know it was immature on my part, but sometimes it was almost impossible for me to resist cracking a joke or making a sarcastic comment while observing those stuffy Catholic Church rituals. I couldn't help but take notice of how serious and pious a performance many of the churchgoers put on, with their unceasing genuflecting and makings of the Sign of the Cross. Some of us, I shamefully admit, behaved rather disrespectfully. All I needed to do was look at the smirk on Art's face, as he walked about the church pretending to light votive candles or observe the Stations of the Cross, and I cracked up. Sara heard me laugh, which caused her to crack up, which pissed off her husband Gary. Caroline saw Sara laugh, which caused her to crack up, which pissed off her husband Tommy. Meanwhile my mother-in-law was pissed off because an usher didn't walk her down the aisle, not giving her the special attention and respect she thought she rightly deserved. Her attitude pissed off my father-in-law because anything she said or did pissed him off. We were off to a rocking start.

When the proud father of the bride stood up at the pulpit and read verses from Revelations, I turned to Caroline and gave her a look of total exasperation. He read an account from the Bible about "The Wedding Feast of the Bride" as if he were auditioning for a Broadway play. As far as I was concerned, the verses had no significance whatsoever to the situation at hand. The wedding feast as a symbol of Jesus returning for his bride, the church, seemed to be missed by whoever picked out the Scripture readings. It appeared that whoever inappropriately selected the lines having to do with "End Times Prophecy," did so, simply because they included the words "wedding" and "bride".

Later in the service, the priest instructed anyone who did not partake of the Holy Communion yet desired to receive a "special blessing," could fold his or her arms in a crisscross fashion over their chest and receive one. I'm still not quite sure where he came up with such a custom or what that "special blessing" was for that matter. I thought I had heard it all. How the Roman Catholic Church hasn't entirely crumbled by now is indeed a mystery.

The reception that followed was the typical gathering of relatives and friends from two completely different walks of life. The only time people seemed to mingle was when they accidentally bumped into one another on the dance floor, otherwise, everyone retreated to the security of their own table in their own little corner of the room. An invisible wall seemed to separate the bride's side from the groom's. It wasn't until the party was just about over when everyone smiled at each other as they were leaving and said, "So nice meeting you! Hope we run into each other again soon!"

I usually do my best to circulate at this sort of an affair, but since I was on crutches, I remained for the most part an observer. *"This is one of those times I thank God I'm alive"* were the words to the song the D.J. was spinning. Mostly everyone appeared to be dancing and having a good time. I wanted in the worst way to lose my crutches and get out on the dance floor with them, but I was reminded of the possibility that insurance fraud detectives might be spying on me. I stood in the background gazing across the room. I was watching my daughters dancing away with their cousins. They'd all grown into such beautiful young women. Glancing over, I could see Art and Mary sitting quietly at their table tending to the needs of their grandchildren. "Damn!" I thought to myself, "Here we are assigned to the tables their aunts and uncles once sat at. It doesn't seem so long ago when we were the cousins dancing wildly while poking fun at the old-timers!"

Sitting across from Artie and Mary were Joseph and Corinne. It's hard not to love Joe and Corinne. Both are very successful hairdressers, so beauty and youth are of the essence. Joe with his pearly white Hollywood smile, manicured fingernails, tint of the week hair and Botox brow, sat beside his wife who modestly flaunted her fuller lips and newly enhanced cleavage for the entire evening. When using surgery and cosmetics to help maintain a youthful look, I thought the idea was not to make it look so obvious! In spite of their preoccupation with appearance, they were always a lot of fun to be around.

In total contrast from the makeover world of Joe and Corinne, one gentleman who really stood out in the crowd was Bobby's longtime friend from Long Island, Harry. Let me begin by saying Harry was probably one of the nicest human beings anyone could ever have the pleasure of meeting. Observing just how vain we all are when we attend these elaborate parties, worrying about our hair, make-up and clothing, encountering Harry suddenly puts things in perspective. Born with a rare birth defect similar to elephantitis, Harry was shortchanged by nature in his physical appearance. I don't think I could accurately describe the disfigurement this unfortunate man has had to live with throughout his life. I couldn't even imagine the torture he must have endured as a child, from the stares and comments of others. At a time when Harry was contemplating suicide, he met Bobby. Bobby's friendship inspired Harry to go about living his life as if he were no different than anybody else. Unlike the Phantom of the Opera, Harry didn't wear a mask to hide his deformity. He was confident and well adjusted. He held a job, traveled and socialized…things I'm not so sure I would attempt if I were in his shoes. Everyone who knew my brother-in-law Bobby knew all about Harry. Regrettably, no matter how familiar one may be with Harry, sometimes it's quite difficult refraining from staring at his grotesqueness.

The music was pumping and the party seemed to be in full swing. As Harry was walking through the crowd, his sights were set on my mother-in-law who was idly sitting by at her table.

"Come on Marie, let's dance!" Harry suggested, as he reached out his hand out to her. Marie's face flushed with dread as she fumbled for an excuse to escape from dancing with the gentle monster.

"Oh no, Harry, I uh, I can't. I, I uh, I'm not feeling well," she muttered, as the disappointment showed in Harry's one functional eye.

My father-in-law was repulsed by his wife's refusal to indulge Harry and then Sara, who also witnessed the scene, jumped up and joined Harry on the dance floor. I would have guaranteed if any of my brothers-in-laws had asked my mother-in-law to dance, she would have miraculously become Ginger Rogers. What is it they say about beauty being skin deep?

The D.J. really worked the crowd into a dancing frenzy that ultimately culminated with the customary Donna Summer song "Last Dance." We all made our way out into the comfortably warm south Florida air, then headed back to Joe and Corinne's room at the hotel for a post reception party. Because the wedding food had been so unappetizing, everyone was starving. We threw some money together and sent David (Elena's husband) out for whatever fast food he could find. He returned with mounds of french fries, chicken sandwiches, and burgers from the local McDonald's. You'd never believe we'd all just come from a wedding by the way we scoffed down the greasy garbage most of the population of this country considers food. Within moments after the late night snacks arrived, my mother-in-law made her grand entrance into the room and the first words out of her mouth were, "What's there for me to eat?" Just as if she were royalty, a couple of her kids wasted no time tending to her wishes by preparing her a plate with half a chicken sandwich and some fries. "I hope this doesn't give me indigestion!" she moaned, as she quickly downed those fries.

Taking into consideration what I learned about her family history and how she lacked validation from her own mother helped me to understand Marie a little bit better. It also showed me the effect a parent can have on a child, even many decades later. Brothers, sisters, in-laws, nieces, nephews, cousins, parents, and grandparents were all crammed into a hotel room with two double beds. Joseph entertained everyone with tales of his misspent youth and his mother's neurosis. He was hysterically funny and my kids were amazed by the similarities between their grandmother and their mother. "Oh my God, that's mommy!" Christiann blurted out as the room filled with laughter. Julianne wasn't feeling too well so we retired for the night. I was told the partying went on until dawn and everyone had a laugh riot. I was sorry we missed it.

The next morning, the family infiltrated the dining area one by one until before long it was a complete takeover. I was sitting with my father-in-law having my morning coffee when my instigating brother-in-law Arthur walked over and just so happened to mention to his dad that I had my doubts we walked on the moon in 1969! "You mean to tell me you think the moon walk was a hoax?" my father-in-law inquired with disbelief. I explained to him how I thought there was a lot of corruption in our government and I wouldn't put anything past them, even faking the moonwalk. What a mistake that was! For the next hour or so, he called me everything from a leftist, no-good liberal, flag burning hippie to a communist, and gave me a dissertation on why I should get down on my knees and thank God I live in a country where I can openly make unpatriotic remarks such as the one I did. The more I told him I preferred not to talk about it, the more I felt he antagonized me. I was on my best behavior. I didn't argue; I just let him talk. Not once did I even mention my strong disapproval of the Bush-Cheney administration. I swear, not once did I utter one political peep. I'm still waiting to get even with Art for that one!

The weather was fabulous during our four-day visit. Every day the sky was clear, the sun was shining and the temperature was a constant eighty degrees. That same afternoon the whole entourage was hanging around the pool and it was only a matter of time before the subject of food arose.

"Who's hungry?" my sister-in-law Maryanne called out. Instantaneously, suggestions were flying as to where or what we should have for lunch. We figured the most practical thing to do was to have a few pizzas delivered poolside, until those of us from New York quickly realized we were in Florida where good pizza was not easy to come by. I was elected to search the Yellow Pages and select a nearby pizzeria that delivered. As I was trying to make a head count, to determine just how many pizzas I would have to order, my mother-in-law's piercing voice cut through the clatter of everyone calling out as to what toppings they wanted, "I can't eat pizza, do you think they can make me a turkey hero?"

My patience wearing a little thin with mom, I snapped back, "It's a freaking pizza shop; you want a turkey hero you go to a deli!"

Then my extremely attention-starved brother-in-law, Gregory, chimed in with hopes of saving the day, "Mom! I have turkey and cheese in the refrigerator in my room. Why don't you let me make you a sandwich?"

Mom refused Gregory's offer because that's just what she does. She does to Gregory what her mother did to her! Why should she have to eat the day old cold cuts from her affection-deprived son, when everyone else was getting a fresh store bought treat? Gregory then began to walk around for the next half an hour mumbling and complaining about his mother who never stopped complaining! In a sick way I was finding this all very entertaining. Well to make a long story short, the pizzeria was closed so we decided to send Sara on a Burger King run because after all, how much worse could Burger King be than Florida pizza? As we took up a collection and gave Sara our orders, the shrill voice of mom, who never seemed to get up off her ass, penetrated my skull, "Sara! Make sure you get me a chocolate shake!"

Now if anyone saw my mother-in-law, they would see the last thing she needed was chocolate shake. It gets better! Her Royal Highness didn't want to sit in the sun anymore, so she removed herself from our company and went into the dining room located behind the pool area. Upon exiting, however, she expressed her desire that her loyal servant Gregory presented her with her meal as soon as it arrived. "…and don't forget the chocolate shake!" she added. I wanted to tell Gregory if anyone needed exercise it was his mom, to let her get up and get it herself, but I administered some self-control. I said nothing.

Now in spite of what anybody thinks of my brother-in-law Joe, he knows how to have fun. He travels equipped. The trunk of his black Lexus held a week's supply of wine, booze, an ounce of weed, and a bag of apples he cleverly constructed into bongs! For the evening he suggested that Julianne, the kids and I hang out with Corinne and him and get a tour of the highlights of Naples and then all have dinner at a good restaurant for a change. He made an announcement if anyone else cared to join us, they should meet in the hotel lobby by four-thirty so we can get to the gulf before sunset.

Well, four-thirty arrived before we knew it and nobody showed up at the meeting point except for my immediate family, Joseph, Corinne and Joe's daughter Meg. Because time and the sunsets wait for no one, we decided to hit the highway. Just then Art's son Bobby came dashing into the hotel lobby sulking.

With a take charge attitude Joe asked, "Are you guys coming or not? We're leaving in two minutes!"

Bobby started whining about his parents not being ready. Art was in the shower, Mary was taking a nap and he felt guilty leaving them behind.

"Fuck this!" Joe exclaimed, "We've got to go!" and so we did.

The section of Naples we sped through, in order to get to the beach before sunset, was beautiful and obviously expensive. Mercedes', Lexus', Jaguars, and Cadillac's were parked outside every home and condo. The trees and shrubs were perfectly manicured and the streets were clean enough to eat off of. Racing against time, we pulled into the first parking lot led to the beach. As we stepped out onto the sand, the sun hung in the sky before us like a giant ball of orange fire and had just started to make its descent. As it appeared to slowly submerge into the hypnotizing blue waters, we stood in awe at the spectacle. At the very moment the sun kissed the horizon, the dolphins sprung from the water, arcing, and then splashing down again. It was one of the most amazing displays of nature I'd ever beheld. What a joy it must be to live there and witness that every day. That single moment was worth every penny we spent on making the trip to Florida.

After we digested the beauty we just saw, Joseph took us into downtown Naples where we enjoyed a delicious meal at a fabulous restaurant. Spending the evening with Joe and Corinne was definitely the right choice. Just as we were about to head back to the hotel, my cell phone went off and it was my disappointed and very aggravated nephew Bobby.

"Hey, Uncle John, Where are you guys?"

I couldn't help the excitement in my voice when I told him all about our evening.

"Where are you?" I asked.

"Oh I'm sitting in "Carrabba's" with EVERYBODY!" he answered, "It's crazy!"

As I was on the phone listening to Bobby describe the dysfunction going on inside the restaurant, as fate would have it, right up ahead was the neon "Carrabba's" sign lighting up the street. Joseph hit the brakes and swerved into the parking lot. With a big shit-eating grin on his golden bronze face, Joe suggested we go into the restaurant and break balls a little bit. Because of the hassle involved with using crutches, I passed, but my son, Matthew, who was always up for a laugh, joined him. The next thing we knew, Matt and Joe were getting back in the car and Joseph's jovial disposition had turned to one of anger. "They are all a bunch of assholes," he fumed, and "they can all kiss my ass!"

I thought he was joking around until he explained the unwelcome reception he received from the family. Somehow it seemed that Joe's intentions were misread, their jealousy was evident and attitudes started flying. When dealing with a group of over forty people, family or not, there's just no way everyone is going to be pleased. So as Ricky Nelson said, "When you can't please everyone, you've got to please yourself!" We did!

Later that evening, the entire mob gathered around the hot tub. At first the air was thick with tension and needless hurt feelings, but Joe reached into his bag of tricks and pulled out a couple of bottles of wine. It didn't take long before the air was cleared and the bad attitudes dissipated. Once again everybody was hugging and smiling. As much as I'm part of my wife's family, I'm still an in-law and had to often observe from the standpoint of an outsider. Even though they rank high on the dysfunctional chart, (what American family doesn't), in their own way, they all genuinely love and care for each other. I guess we can't ask for more than that. By the way, the marriage soon ended in divorce.

HOME ALONE

Our four-day mini-vacation in the warm Florida sunshine was just about over. The Arizona crew consisting of Arthur, Mary, their son Bobby, his wife Angie and their two children were the first to leave for the airport. I always got all choked up whenever I had to bid farewell to Artie, this time was no different.

Joseph, Corinne and Meg packed up the Lexus and headed back to their home in Boca Raton on the sunshine state's other coast. We made the usual parting promises to stay in touch and visit soon, but in reality we knew, unless somebody died or got married, it would probably be another seven years before we saw each other again.

Julianne, the kids and I were the next group to break away. David had graciously volunteered to drive us to the airport in his rented mini-van. While we were in the middle of the "good-bye hugging and kissing ceremony," Samantha's cell phone started ringing. It was a co-worker calling from New York who had just heard Julianne's name announced on a radio station. She had ten minutes in which to call the station and claim her prize. Jule just so happened to have the station number in her purse. She made the call from the hotel lobby, and in the company of her remaining family, won money in a radio contest. We were headed home with good news!

The weather in New York was cold, damp and depressing, and though it was good to be home, a few more days of soaking up the sun would have been nice. For Julianne and the kids, it was back to business as usual. I, however, still had at least two months of disability time ahead of me. During those months, I resorted to spending several hours a day conversing with Sara, Arthur and Caroline via e-mail and telephone, about our religious philosophies. I was rethinking everything I'd ever been taught. I was totally convinced, or should I say deceived, that God (or Yahweh, as I was calling Him then) allowed me to survive my accident in order to afford me the time to study, learn and as I melodramatically put it, "draw Him closer to me." Julianne, however, saw my enthusiasm as something dark, disturbing and dangerous. I knew the differences in our spiritual viewpoints were creating tremendous tension in the home, so I tried my best not to discuss any of my newest theologies with her and basically kept my spiritual life a secret.

Little by little, I was alienating many of my old church buddies also. No matter who dropped by for a visit, it usually resulted in me clobbering them over the head with my latest insights, views and opinions. A few of them thought I was crazy and wrote me off completely. I didn't seem to care, because it only confirmed what I understood the Bible to mean in the verses about disharmony arising among family and friends for the sake of seeking the Truth. Besides, I figured what kind of Christians were those who had claimed I'd gone off the deep end yet hadn't thrown out a rope to rescue me?

I was sure God had been talking to me. I had reasoned that whatever I was feeling was a direct result of divine guidance and had nothing to do with my own prideful desire to be right. Most of my life I'd never taken anything too seriously and now I'd had an obsession with knowing as much as I could about Old Testament and the history of Christianity. I became passionate about discussing whatever I learned with others. I figured if Jesus himself continually referred to the Old Testament scriptures (the Torah) when He taught, then I'd better have a deeper knowledge and understanding of the Hebrew roots I'd felt Christianity abandoned. At the time I thought in order for me to get through to people, I needed to have the facts, or in my case, the ammunition!

MERRY CHRISTMAS

Christmas was right around the corner and for the first time in my 51 years I did not want to have anything to do with the holiday. All my fact-finding about how the celebration of Christmas evolved, made me not want to observe the holiday any longer. I had figured since I was still recovering from my accident, I had the perfect excuse not to shop, put up a tree, or decorate the house with all those stupid lights imported from of all places, China, a land certainly opposed to Jesus. For once I wouldn't have to untangle miles of twisted wire or try to figure out why every other bulb was out. Julianne wasn't the least bit interested in my disenchantment with Christianity or my desire to eliminate it and its traditions from my life. She wanted the tree, the lights, the presents and the house decorated even if she had to do it all by herself, which she pretty much did! It seemed as if the more I voiced my opinion about how much I despised Christmas, the more Julianne added to our display of decorations and ornaments. I never took into consideration how this bizarre change in my character had to distress her. Suddenly, I was sabotaging the celebration of a tradition we all just took for granted.

One evening about a week before Christmas, she dragged my crutches and me to a place called "National Wholesale Liquidators," a very large discount store run exclusively by Middle East immigrants. Every employee in the store was Muslim, had no fondness for Christmas or Christianity, yet the establishment certainly profited from the holiday. The place was so mobbed it was almost impossible to fall down. We waited on the checkout line for what seemed like a lifetime and made holiday small talk with fellow frustrated shoppers. I was certain it was the billions of contaminating germs floating around in that uncomfortably hot and overcrowded store that caused me to get an end-of-year sore throat and stuffy nose. I was so annoyed about getting sucked into the trappings of Christmas again, because I thought for sure, this would be the year I could slide. It was no different than any other year and the pile of gifts that accumulated in our room waiting to be wrapped grew continually higher and higher. Totally contrary to what we promised ourselves we were not going to do again next year, there we were, up again on Christmas Eve until almost four o'clock in the morning buried in wrapping paper, tape, ribbons and bows. Our nerves were on end and our contempt for one another grew deeper. I was so tired I had to keep sneaking off into the bathroom to splash water on my eyes just to try to stay awake. This year especially, the holiday ritual was extremely torturous for me. Maybe because I wanted to make a statement, maybe because I thought it really mattered, maybe because I had no idea I was still on a journey, whatever the reasons, I was taking it all much too seriously and was ready to eliminate Christmas from our lives. Julianne was ready to eliminate me from her life.

I cringed when Julianne asked, "Aren't you at least going to church for Christmas?" I assumed it was quite obvious how the very thought of this insane holiday made my spirit twist, so why for one minute did she think I would want to go to church or even feel the least bit guilty about not going? I failed to realize she was probably worried about what she regarded as my spiritual welfare. I saw a bumper sticker that read, "Christianity has pagan DNA." In a way I thought there was some truth in the statement.

To try and appease Julianne, I decided to visit my old friend Jeff's church for Christmas service. Jeff and Shirley were the couple we met at the "anti-rock and roll seminar" we attended when we first joined the Full Gospel Church many years ago. Well Jeff was now the pastor of his very own church in a quaint little beach community known as Point Lookout. I made sure to sit all the way in the back in the last pew in case I needed to make a quick and inconspicuous exit. Upon walking through the church's front doors, I was met by the official "Greeters" who attempted to bait me with their great big welcoming smiles, an invitation to return, and the weekly bulletin chock full of important announcements concerning the church's busy agenda. I glanced over the almost capacity crowd and recognized a few familiar faces from the same church I had left. Everyone who was aware of the unrest in my ex-church gave me "the look," assuming they knew what brought me to this new assembly. I felt like setting them straight right then and there by saying, "Hey, you have no idea folks, because if you did, you'd probably be running from this church too!" I promised myself I would keep my thoughts to myself and give Jeff and his flock a fair chance.

Jeff's "Praise Team" was pretty top notch as far as church bands go. The lead singer and rhythm guitarist looked great in a tight tee shirt and jeans, and could have easily been a contender in "American Idol." He had a strong voice backed by some talented and seasoned musicians. The bassist was once a member of The Turtles and Frank Zappa's Mothers of Invention. Unfortunately no amount of great musicianship could help me relate to the same lame songs I'd heard in church for so many years... pseudo-holy pop. The Christmas service was no different than anything I'd heard or seen any place else. I sat for close to two hours as over-anxious Sunday school teachers directed their students through torturous renditions of "Silent Night" and "The First Noel," as they tried to re-enact what happened on that "cold winter's night" over two thousand years ago.

The Christmas service was dreadful but I didn't dare express that to Jeff when he approached me at the end of the service and asked what I thought. I promised him I'd come back again as long as he gave me his word he would have lunch with me one afternoon. I tickled his ear with just enough information of how disenchanted and disillusioned I'd become with mainstream Christianity. He wanted to hear more of what I had to say and seemed eager to meet with me. I returned for another two Sunday services before we met.

I SAID A MOUTHFUL (LUNCH WITH PASTOR JEFF)

On a brisk Wednesday afternoon in January, I met Jeff for what turned out to be a three-hour lunch at the Imperial Diner in Freeport. We reacquainted ourselves by talking about our families. Jeff asked me endless questions about the scares I had with cancer, the auto accident, and if and how it altered my faith in any way. I completely opened up to him holding back nothing. I felt like I could relate to him because of our familiar pasts, growing up with the hopes and aspirations of one day becoming successful rock stars. I confided in him about the struggles Julianne and I were having in our marriage and although he offered some good advice, such as praying about it together, I knew it was not going to work in our situation. He and Shirley were much more on the same page spiritually than Julianne and I had ever been. Gradually the conversation turned to one of church and spiritual matters. I explained to Jeff about all the things that had been stirring up inside me for a while; how it seemed like the masses have been manipulated to believe half-truths and lies propagated by preachers, priests and rabbis alike. I told him how disconcerting I found it that people didn't seem to think for themselves or ask questions. My words came rushing towards him like a speeding train, trying my best to verbalize how the Christian world had abandoned its Hebrew roots and adopted pagan rituals and traditions of man rather than adhering to Scripture. I explained to him how I viewed churches as nothing more than comfort clubs, created by men for men, to make people feel good about themselves and their relationship with "the Man in the sky." Jeff was married to a Jewish woman; if anyone understood what I was talking about, I was certain he would.

"Jeff!" I said lovingly, "You are in a responsible position, where you will be held accountable more than the average street corner Joe!"

I'm not sure if he was just patronizing me, but after a short pause, Jeff sat back and in what I felt was sincere and heartfelt, he replied "John, I'm in total agreement with just about everything you said. Christianity is in a sad and unhealthy state! Whatever we spoke about today will not be taken lightly!"

After two or three annoying cell phone interruptions he went on to explain to me how I never struck him as the typical "Pentecostal Believer," how he always saw a healthy rebellious streak that encouraged posing questions and seeking answers. Then he asked me straightforward, "What did you think of my church?"

"Jeff," I replied, "I'm just a guy searching for the Truth, and in all honesty, I have to say although I've only been to a couple of services, I find that you compromise too much to keep the members happy."

Once again he was in agreement but attempted to justify why he did what he did. His congregation was comprised of some old-time staunch Catholics who still held on to the traditional Holy Communion as being the actual body and blood of Jesus. They were also generous in their tithing, so Jeff offered his members a choice on Communion Sundays, matzos or wafer, that is actual or symbolic Jesus consumption. On some occasions I heard he even sported the traditional reverend's collar. Money makes the world go round!

I felt pretty good after talking with Jeff and told him I would most likely give his church another chance. The following Sunday morning I got into my car and headed over to Point Lookout. The parking lot of the church was full so I parked down the street. As I walked towards the white antiquated building with the steeple on top and heard the polished sounds of the "Praise Team" playing a song from the "Pentecostal Top Ten" coming through the stained glass windows, I stopped in my tracks. "What am I doing?" I asked myself. I continued to walk and slowly climbed the steps leading to the church's front door. I reached out, placed my hand on the doorknob then froze. A voice spoke softly but sternly to my heart and specifically told me not to enter. "Seek the truth and not the ways of man!"

Maybe that was the voice of God; maybe it was my own heart speaking to me. Maybe sometimes they are one and the same. I made a quick about-face, returned to my car then drove down to the beach where I sat in silent meditation.

I sent Jeff an e-mail the following week telling him how good it was to see him and how enjoyable and insightful it was to speak with him. I also explained to him, as gently and honestly as I could, what happened on that Sunday morning when I just couldn't step foot inside his church. I told him how I was looking forward to meeting with him again and perhaps socializing as a foursome with our wives in the very near future. Jeff never responded. I hadn't heard a word from him since we had lunch together on that Wednesday afternoon.

COMMUNICATION BREAKDOWN

In spite of all the hardships, disagreements and troubles I'd had with Julianne through the thirty-three years we'd been together, the truth of it all was I still loved her tremendously and really couldn't see myself being without her. It was just unfortunate how we stopped communicating and created a gap we rarely tried to bridge. In as much as I might have made it appear that she was the culprit in most of our conflicts, I admit at times, I too could be a real pain in the ass to live with.

Recalling the time when Julianne first "found Jesus" and became "Born Again," way back before we had children, I thought she was completely out of her skull. We were so NOT on the same page with each other it was frightening. I hung in there. I didn't give up on us and somehow we eventually began to share the same spiritual vision. I remember how Julianne understood how it had to be very strange and unnerving for me to see her going from somewhat of a party girl to what I considered a religious recluse.

Almost twenty-five years later I was the one who was undergoing a spiritual transformation and it was Julianne who thought I'd gone off my rocker. I couldn't begin to stress enough about how sure I was these changes in my spiritual outlook had come not from me, but from a higher power due to unceasing prayer and a desire to grow spiritually. I was confident it was only a matter of time before my wife and children would understand where I stood. I anxiously anticipated the day when she would come out from the confines of "Full Gospel Church" and the "Assemblies of God," and the two of us would once again be in spiritual agreement. I wasn't claiming to know everything, but at least I felt certain I was on the right road. I would often quote the Bible where God commands, "Come out of her my people!" There was no doubt in my mind those words were intended for all people to get out of "Babylon," which represented organized religion. There was no doubt in Julianne's mind, I was insane!

There was no denying something wasn't right with our marriage. Even though we had a very active social life with friends and such, when we stepped back into the privacy of our own home, the fun stopped. Julianne rarely smiled and the passion and joy we used to know years ago, as lovers, were almost non-existent. It was like we were just putting up with each other. We kept looking for a little light at the end of a deep dark tunnel. Once in a while, however, we got a glimpse. I imagine it was that glimpse that kept us from totally giving up. Besides not being able to afford it financially, we were both under the impression God did not approve of divorce ("Let no man separate what God has brought together").

After so many years of marriage behind us, one would think we would have had our differences worked out. Julianne still blamed me for coming between her and the kids. She still couldn't get over the fact I threw her an unwanted major party for her fiftieth birthday. All of a sudden we even had political differences, which we'd never had before. I had such contempt for George W. and his White House cronies and I don't know if it was just to antagonize me, but Julianne would defend him. Ignoring everything Bush stood for, such as the war in Iraq and gay rights, Julianne voted for him based solely on his claim to be a Christian opposed to abortion. It infuriated me, not because of her stand on abortion, but because she believed voting for him would change things. He was after the Christian vote and his anti-abortion platform would almost guarantee it. It perplexed me how most Pentecostals were pro-war Republicans and how preachers managed to endorse Bush from the pulpit. I always saw Jesus as a man of peace. It was the difference in our belief systems that made it almost impossible for us to have meaningful conversations any more. Jule believed I was no longer walking the pathway to heaven and my fatal decision to leave the church was a bad influence on the kids. Our children were now adults; they had to make their own spiritual decisions. Besides, how could I expect them to go to a church I refused to step foot in. That would be most hypocritical. Witnessing our behavior wouldn't have encouraged anyone to want to go to Julianne's church, especially our kids. With all the animosity that had been building up inside us throughout the decade, the slightest spark could have easily triggered an explosion.

On one unforgettable evening, when the entire family was sitting around the dinner table, all hell broke loose. After she was done eating, Samantha took her napkin, crumpled it up, and placed it in her plate. Julianne reproached her and asked her to remove the napkin from the dish. Samantha wouldn't honor her mother's simple request and with a tone of annoyance snapped back at her. "Why? I'm done eating and I'm going to clean off the table now, what's the big deal?" That was the spark which led to an all out war.

"Sam," I asked, even though I thought her mother's request was ridiculous, "Why don't you do what mom says and take the napkin out of your dish?"

"Why?" Sam hollered back at me, "It's stupid. I'm going to clean off the plates anyway!"

Julianne chimed in by saying, "Well then get up from the table now and start cleaning!"

Samantha sat there defiantly, picked up her glass and said, "I'm not finished with my drink yet!"

Well one thing led to another. Christiann sat there shaking her head in disbelief; Matthew kept calling Samantha an idiot. In retrospect, I probably should have sent Samantha to her room, but to me it seemed as though Julianne kept unnecessarily provoking Sam. Fully aware of how high-strung Samantha could be, Jule knew just what to say to get her riled. Sam on the other hand knew exactly how to continue antagonizing her mom. The entire scene was so out of control I didn't know how to react, so out of sheer frustration I simply shouted, "Can't you people talk without screaming?

Flames shot up in Julianne's angry eyes. If looks could kill, I wouldn't be writing this right now. With malice in her voice, Julianne turned to me and said, "Don't you dare talk to me. We're finished! Just keep sticking up for them!"

"Jule," I whined, "Come on, let's not..."

I didn't even get to complete my sentence. Jule stormed out of the kitchen and for the next three long months we were in a cold war. We slept as far apart from each other as possible. We spoke only when absolutely necessary. As far as I was concerned, we hit a new all time low. I was an emotional mess. Going to work day after day to an unfulfilling job was bad enough, but then having to come home to marital problems made matters even worse. It was all I could think about, all I could talk about. I spent three months complaining and ragging about the woman I married to anyone who would listen to me. It sucked big time. She built a wall around her that nobody could penetrate.

I needed help. I needed to talk to someone who could get through to Julianne and the only person I could think of was, once again, her gynecologist, Dr. Rizzo. She loves Dr. Rizzo. I was grabbing at straws, but knowing Jule's history of PMS and menopause, I was thinking many of our problems could be a result of her hormones being out of whack. Coincidentally, Samantha happened to have an appointment with Dr. Rizzo, so I decided to take a day off from work and accompany her with the hope of talking to him personally. He obliged me.

"Jule driving you crazy?" he asked with a sympathetic smile.

"I don't know what to do Doc," I answered forlornly; "I'm starting to feel like divorce is the only way out."

"Take it from me!" he said, "You don't want to do that. You think you've got problems now, divorce only multiplies them!"

He was talking from experience so I couldn't argue. He asked me to explain to him what had been going on, and since I knew how busy he was, I fired away trying to plead my case quickly and concisely. As soon I was through conveying my woes, he immediately picked up the phone, dialed my house and under the pretense she was due for a check-up, left a message for Julianne to make an appointment "pronto!"

"John," he said confidently, "She needs an anti-depressant. There are a lot of wonderful drugs out there today that can help her. The only problem is getting her to recognize she needs them."

I left his office with a glimmer of hope. I got home only to discover my hope was shattered when Julianne ignored his message. She told me in no uncertain terms she wasn't going to make an appointment.

One of my shortcomings was the need I had to vent and tell everybody my business. I was explaining my dilemma to Figgy and a couple of work buddies and their reactions only confirmed what Dr. Rizzo said.

"Ever since my wife has been on Prozac," Figgy admitted, "My life has been so different. She turned from a mean-spirited bitch into an angel! You got to get Julianne on something! I'm telling you, it works!" At the time, Figgy had no idea what his future held; a wife addicted to prescription pain killers and a divorce!

I couldn't believe how many guys had their wives were on anti-depressants. As much as I wanted my life to turn around, drugs just didn't seem like the right and natural thing to do. As bad as I was feeling for myself, I was feeling worse for Julianne. It didn't seem like anything could make her happy. Maybe drugs were the answer, the church sure wasn't. How come the "Joy of the Lord" she often spoke about never seemed to shine in her home life? Where were the so-called "Fruits of the Spirit?" Whenever I would sing my marital blues to Figgy he would ask me, "I thought Julianne was really religious?" Even he didn't get it!

IT WAS A GOOD FRIDAY

Easter season was upon us again and I received an e-mail from Benny who was now an active member in his new church. He was going to play the part of Judas in his church's production of "The Passion" and asked if Julianne and I would like to attend. I mentioned it to Jule and she agreed to go. I guess Julianne figured anything that would get me inside a church was a good thing. The performance took place on "Good Friday." I attended only to support my friend Benny in his acting debut at his new place of worship, and not to observe "Good Friday." My attitude, at the time, was that the death and resurrection of the Messiah was something that should be observed and honored every day of our lives. "Good Friday" made for a neatly packaged three-day Easter weekend.

The play was actually quite moving. The guy who played Jesus did a fine job and Benny was deserving of a "Tony Award" in his portrayal of Judas. Too bad Mel Gibson didn't know about Benny before he made his film! After all the post show congratulatory hoopla, Benny, his wife Shirley, along with Julianne and I went to a diner. We discussed all the scandals and the gossip of the old church and naturally they tried their best to sell us on becoming part of their new congregation. I didn't know why, but for some reason Benny had this notion my soul was in jeopardy because I fled from organized religion. He just couldn't accept my declaration that my relationship with my Maker was stronger than it had ever been before. Shirley kept asking me if I was all right. She was strangely interested in my job and how I was relating with my co-workers. She inquired about my ties with friends and family. I found her interrogation to be rather odd until

I put two and two together. She must have assumed because I stopped going to church my entire life was falling to pieces.

"Are you happy about everything in your life right now?" she questioned with a look of genuine concern.

"Shirley," I answered confidently, "The only thing that's not right in my life at the moment is my relationship with her!" pointing to Julianne.

My comment opened up a can of worms and the four of us began to openly discuss the problems Jule and I were currently experiencing. Benny, God bless him, by pointing out some lessons from the Bible, helped us to see just how unforgiving and stubborn we'd both become. We realized we had to put all the bad stuff behind us and start anew. That evening was the first step in a long walk which began a healing process for Julianne and me. The next day we spoke and came to an agreement we should seek some counseling. On the evening of the same day, we made love in a way reminiscent of thirty years ago, passionate and beautiful. There was still a spark. I wanted that spark to set off an inextinguishable inferno. I also wanted world peace!

GLORY, GLORY, PSYCHOTHERAPY?

We each confided in our wonderful friend Toni-Ann. Sometimes I'd feel sorry for her having to listen to each of us dump our problems on her. Toni is great. She loves both of us, understands both of us, never takes sides and would never want to see us split up. Toni gave us the name and number of a marriage counselor highly recommended by a friend of hers and strongly suggested we call. There was no doubt about it. Things weren't going to miraculously turn around after one good weekend, so I took the first step in trying to permanently repair our marriage and dialed Bonnie. Years ago if anyone ever told me we would succumb to sitting face to face with a psychotherapist, I wouldn't have believed it for a minute. I completed dialing and waited anxiously for the unknown voice to answer. When I got the answering machine I took a deep breath and left my message... a desperate cry for help. A week had passed and there was no return phone call.

Knowing that my medical plan included counseling, I called my local union hall and asked if they could recommend any in-network marriage counselors who practiced in the areas near my home. Almost immediately they responded with a list of ten local licensed social workers. It was just after ten thirty one evening when Julianne and I perused the list. It was just like grabbing at straws. "We have to start somewhere!" I said apprehensively, "Let's just pick one, give him a call and go from there!"

Just then our telephone rang and I could see by the caller I.D. it was Bonnie. "Sorry it took me so long to get back to you John!" she said in one of the most cheerful voices I'd heard in a long time. We must have talked for at least twenty minutes while Julianne listened, signaling me from the couch as to what questions to ask. Before I could commit to anything, there were things I had to know, especially if she accepted my medical plan. "Don't worry about insurance!" she directed in a take-charge tone, "Let's meet first then we'll take it from there!"

Besides the fact she told me "Psychology Today" selected her as one of the top therapists in the country, I didn't know what it was, something in her voice made me trust her. I booked the appointment for the following evening and agreed to pay her fee. Although I really considered it unaffordable, how could I put a price on saving our marriage? Julianne agreed she'd prefer to go to someone like Bonnie, who was recommended by a friend, rather than randomly selecting a nice sounding name from a list of unknowns.

I didn't know if it was common practice for shrinks to place bogus names on building directories and office doors in order to insure patient confidentiality. As far as the cleaning lady in the corridor knew, I was visiting "Tele-tron Technologies, Inc." As far as everyone sitting in the waiting room knew, I was no different from them, troubled and seeking help in getting his head fixed.

So there I was, sinking down in the waiting room couch pretending to read a magazine, while trying to imagine what the heck could be wrong in the lives of the other three patients in the room. At the same time, I was wondering what the heck I was doing there! On the wall in the waiting room was a list of doctors' names and beside each name was a buzzer, that when rung, would alert the doctor his or her patient had arrived. I walked over to the wall, looked for Bonnie's name, hit the buzzer, and then plopped back down onto the couch. I figured out that behind the door across from me, there were several little offices, with several shrinks, counseling several people with several problems. I waited impatiently to meet the woman who I was about to unload all my troubles upon.

The door swung upon and out stepped a blond woman, who I estimated was around my age and who was a bit heavier than I'd imagined. "John?" she asked, as she smiled, looking directly into my cautious eyes. I nodded and responded, "Bonnie?" With what seemed like a look of approval she apologized for running a little late and guaranteed she'd be with me in five minutes.

I stepped into Bonnie's little office and was greeted by the sweet fragrance of incense or scented air freshener. She motioned for me to take a seat on "the couch." As I sat down and glanced about the room, the odd wall décor and the many burning candles gave me the impression I was about to enter the world of a "new age" disciple. I was partly wrong in my assumption. I later presumed, although she was spiritually liberal in her thinking, she seemed to be bound by some of the old Irish Catholic superstitions. The simple fact she would bless her office with holy water when each new patient entered clued me in.

Bonnie leaned back in her chair and said, "Okay, tell me all about Julianne!" I went on for what seemed like hours but not once did I ever talk about my wife in a demeaning or hostile way. Bonnie asked me if I loved Julianne. I took a deep breath and said, "If I didn't, I wouldn't be here talking to you!"

My forty-five minute session turned into almost two hours. I touched on everything including Julianne's background, my background, my cancer, my accident and my spiritual direction. Bonnie was particularly interested in where I was spiritually and mentioned how somewhere down the road she would like to meet with me solely to discuss the matter. She told me she had strong feelings I possessed special gifts and she could help me to bring them to fruition. Hey, I was always up for a good conversation about the supernatural and Bonnie's comment sort of confirmed what I had been feeling...I was on a mission to try and awaken people to the hypocrisy of organized religion and its traditions. The first order of business, however, was for her to meet Julianne to see if she could help our unhealthy marriage. After hearing my side of our story, Bonnie's first presumption was Jule had OCD (obsessive compulsive disorder), was very depressed, had issues stemming from her childhood and was in need of an anti-depressant medication. Now there were two professionals arriving at the same conclusion. That was my diagnosis all along, but convincing Julianne was going to be like trying to change water into wine. Both Bonnie and I were anxious to see how she and Julianne would connect.

When Julianne returned home from her first session with Bonnie, she seemed pleased. For the first time in a long while it appeared as though Jule and I were on the same page with a desire to make this work. The only problem was Bonnie did not accept my insurance plan. Psychotherapists didn't come cheap and we knew that weekly sessions were way beyond our means and according to her we were in need of at least two years of counseling! I sent Bonnie an e-mail and explained how much we both desired to continue to see her, but also tried to make her aware of our financial situation. She responded by saying she would lessen her fee a bit, to try to work out something so our out of network benefits would cover some of the expense. Months passed. I kept writing out checks without receiving a penny in reimbursement as my claims kept getting denied. There was no doubt Bonnie was helping us, but it was costing us thousands. The big question was how do we let money stand in the way of a possible healing? If she could help us to get our marriage on the right track it would be worth millions. She was great at what she did. After each session I felt this warm closeness with my wife that had been lacking in our marriage for a very long time. Bonnie essentially told us we had to put the fun, the passion, the spontaneity and the playfulness back into our life together. We always left her office aspiring to work at becoming a united front. The only way we were going to bring peace and harmony into our home was to show our kids we were in love and in agreement. In all honesty, sometimes it wasn't easy. Every now and then I could feel us falling back into our old ways and just like a drug addiction we needed another session.

Bonnie must have really liked us because our sessions always ran way over the allotted time. Sometimes I thought we were there so she could share with us the events she was facing in her own life. At one of our later sessions Bonnie asked Julianne to share any dreams or aspirations she may have had. Julianne made mention of how she would have liked to adopt or foster a child. She described to Bonnie how for years she kept the information about adopting folded up in her wallet before recently discarding them. Bonnie couldn't understand why Jule never shared this dream with me and Jule's reply was that she just assumed I never would have supported it. I was not only surprised, but I was saddened to think I had stopped her from realizing a dream. Bonnie then went on to divulge to us her plans to fly to the Ukraine and adopt a baby. Bonnie described to us how the poverty there is beyond definition. Mothers can't afford to keep their unwanted babies so these unfortunate souls are placed in facilities until foreigners adopt them or they are sold into sexual slavery. Bonnie was so confident God had called her to take on this undertaking. She told us about her recurring dreams, where night after night she would actually see from behind bars, the sunlight shining on the face of the baby she was destined to adopt. Going strictly on faith and prayer, Bonnie was going to close up shop for a couple of months and set out on her mission from God to a land where the water wasn't even fit to bathe in. We gave her a lot of credit. I don't care how many dreams I had, I could never do anything that extreme!

Our last two sessions with Bonnie, before she left on her journey, were intense. She showed no mercy as she worked Julianne and me hard in an exercise on communicating our feelings to one another. For some reason, I was feeling a little uncomfortable and Bonnie was suggesting there were issues deep within me she needed to bring out. Bonnie was very intuitive and insightful. I believed she was able to see something in me I'd managed to keep hidden from everyone, possibly even myself.

"We'll save that for when I return John!" she said grinning, "I don't want to open up another can of worms!"

"Come on!!!" I moaned, "Let me have it!"

She refused to even hint at where she was headed and assured me it would be best to wait.

After the session we all exited the building together. We wished Bonnie well on her excursion into the unknown, and assured her she would be in our prayers. As we turned to walk toward our car, Bonnie said, "You go John. I want to have a few words alone with Julianne." This was a little unnerving to me. What in the world was she going to say to her that I couldn't hear? What little secret did she unearth about me and was planning to share with my wife?

When Julianne finally entered the car I turned to her and asked curiously, "What did she say?"

"Nothing," Julianne replied, "And don't hound me because I can't tell you. Honest it was nothing!"

I hounded her. In fact, I became quite a relentless pain in the ass. She never told me!

It was going to be over two months before we'd be seeing Bonnie again. I was hoping Jule and I could hold out during her absence. She had become our crutch, our drug, the inspiration we needed to help us rekindle the passion we once knew. When problems arose it was comforting to know a visit with Bonnie was only a few days away. She gave us the tools necessary to assist us in dealing with our children and each other. It was entirely up to us to use those tools and put whatever we learned into practice. Most times it worked; sometimes it was a struggle. Julianne was trying hard. Many of the methods we needed to utilize, in order to recondition ourselves, went against her nature. Maybe way back in our younger days we were too blind, too stupid and too in love to notice how different from each other we really were. Responsibility, children, health, and the pressures of everyday living bring out the things in people, that in more carefree days, they may have overlooked. We knew of couples who just gave up trying and went for the big divorce. We knew of other couples who just stayed together for the sake of their children and resigned themselves to dying miserable. I didn't want us to be either. Sometimes I wondered if we were just fooling ourselves, but it was those glimpses of light that kept us moving forward.

FANCY MEETING YOU HERE

I often wondered if there was any truth to the concept that nothing is a coincidence, that everyone we meet in our lifetime we were destined to meet, that nothing is by chance. It certainly seemed, at this time in my life, when I'd become completely absorbed in discussing deeper things, such as the personality of God and the purpose of life on planet earth, several people with similar questions and interests have crossed my path. How old friends and family tended to avoid these delicate topics of discussion while my new acquaintances just couldn't seem to get enough, led me to believe these encounters were unquestionably not coincidental. Maria, the office manager at the construction company; Jackie at the science lab; Joe, the mechanic at the automotive shop; Hidalgo, the stockroom clerk and Suzanne, the sales rep at the carpet showroom; Mona and Ross, both sales reps from the stainless steel plant; Cynthia and Annette, the administrative assistants from the Community Synagogue; and Karen from the chiropractor's office are all folks who shared with me the common desire to talk and question. These delightful people all expressed genuine interest in whatever questions I would raise or topics I would just so happen to bring up, and when the opportunity arose, each of them enjoyed bouncing ideas back and forth, with the hopes of getting a little closer to answer the unanswerable. There had been days when we'd gotten so caught up in conversation, I ran hours behind in delivering my route. The one thing I discovered we all had in common was the feeling there was a lot more to life and to the supernatural than what the books, the priests, the rabbis and the ministers have told us.

Some of the most interesting chats I'd had were with Mona, and it wasn't because her blouse just about covered the nipple line of her large breasts. Mo is Egyptian and a non-practicing Muslim. She fell in love then got engaged to a Catholic man who insisted upon getting married in the church. In order to do so, Mo was required to denounce her Muslim faith and convert to Catholicism. Over and over I would implore her, "Don't do it Mo! Don't become Catholic! If anything, drag your fiancé out of that pagan rooted cult of idol worshippers!"

Mona laughed, "What the fuck do I care?" she said, "I don't believe any of their bullshit anyway. I'm just doing it to make his family happy!"

All decked out in my UPS browns I would stand beside Mo's desk like some evangelical psycho, conveniently quoting anything I could pull from Scripture to help me prove whatever points I was trying to make. Afterwards, it always amazed me how I'd be able to command the attention of everyone in the office as I spewed out my opinions laced with what bits and pieces of Bible knowledge I had. I even made an impression on Ross and Larry, both who were Jews and thinking twice (or at least pretending to be) about everything I was preaching. I guess it only proved either I was very entertaining or they knew less and were content in their unawareness. The ironic thing was that as convincing as I may have sounded, the near future was going to find me wanting to eat my words as I began twisting in yet another direction.

ONLY IN FLORIDA

Julianne's dad was diagnosed with prostate cancer. Somehow I felt as if steering clear of cancer was similar to dodging raindrops in a storm. The reports of his health had fluctuated from bad to good to bad again, so Julianne thought we should go down south for a visit and see for ourselves exactly how good or bad the situation really was. I would have liked if he could've come up to New York to see specialists from Sloan Kettering or Cornell University Hospital, but my father-in-law was very stubborn and insisted he was in good care down there on the outskirts of redneck country in Homosassa. We weren't confident about the quality of medical care available to him where the main road was lined with boiled peanut stands, topless carwashes, topless hot dog vendors, adult bookstores and churches.

My brother-in-law Gregory picked us up at the airport in Tampa. It was early July and it was a humid ninety-five degrees. We appreciated Gregory doing us the favor, but the truth of the matter was he had nothing else to do. The situation with Gregory hadn't changed much from over thirty years ago when his mother chased him around the kitchen table with a broomstick. He still mumbled incessantly, he still was hard of hearing, his stomach had inflated to the size of beach ball about to explode, and he was still most annoying in his relentless effort to win attention…from anybody. I promised myself I was going to be kind, sympathetic and understanding but must admit it was most difficult.

During many a conversation with Gregory he would unintentionally bastardize the English language by using the wrong words in common everyday expressions. "I know this town like the back of my head!" he once said to me and I had all to do to keep from laughing as not to hurt his feelings. His brother Art came up with the term "Gregory-bonics" to describe, in a word, Gregory's misuse of idioms and familiar phrases. Some other examples of "Gregory-bonics" would be: "I'm not going to spend another red dime..." or the time he was trying to say, "I'm obsessed," and it came out, "I'm infested!" One afternoon, while Gregory was a passenger in Arthur's car, I heard Arthur had stopped the car in the middle of the road and made his younger brother exit the vehicle. "Get out!" he shouted, "Until you learn to speak right and use those expressions correctly, I'm not talking to you!" Gregory got out of the car and walked home!

For as long as I've known Gregory he'd been a victim of circumstance. Many years ago he injured his back while at work and had been on permanent disability since. He could no longer afford the luxury of a damp Long Island basement apartment so he moved to the promised land of Florida, just minutes away from his mother, the one person from whom he'd forever been seeking affection. Another one to jump on the "Born Again Christian Bandwagon," Gregory learned how to paraphrase Bible passages for the situation at hand. Whether or not he really believed in what he was saying, if it was just his way of gaining acceptance from his siblings or rebelling against his Bible-ignorant parents, I couldn't say. Divorced from an abusive wife, abandoned by his teenage son and financially penniless, I assumed it had to be some form of faith pulling him through. Do the promises of being a good Christian ever manifest themselves in this life or is it all about the next? Gregory has always been a good-hearted soul. One day I hope he gets comfortable in his own skin and stops trying to win the approval of the ones who made him turn out the way he did.

When we arrived at my in-laws home we noticed my brother-in-law Joe's black Lexus in the driveway. He knew we were coming so he drove over from Boca Raton to spend a few days with us. I'm glad he did. Joe always was and still is all about excess. Where there is Joe, there is usually fun. The first thing we did was to crack open a bottle of wine and the second thing we did was to run out and buy a bottle of "Grey Goose" orange vodka. God knows we were going to need it. With Joe around I knew we'd be in for plenty of laughs. Joe holds a special place in my mother-in-law's heart. Years ago, when he was living home, he stumbled in one night completely wasted. In an attempt to straighten out, he dunked his head into a bathtub full of cold water. His mom happened to walk in on him and to this day you can't convince her otherwise, he was trying to commit suicide. Ever since then, she's treated Joseph a little differently from the rest of her children.

Of all the Florida family folk, the person I was looking forward to seeing the most was my sister-in-law Caroline. To look at her you would think she was a groupie for a rock n' roll band rather than someone so intent on studying the Bible. Earlier I had mentioned, when Caroline was a baby, Julianne stood over her crib saying with a sigh, "I feel so bad that you had to be born into this family!" Well in a nutshell, Caroline is a sweetheart but somehow ended up creating a tough life for herself. She dropped out of high school, met the guy who turned out to be her downfall, and like all of her siblings, couldn't wait to get out of their parents' house. She got married and had two kids. Although her husband Tom was a hard worker, he could never hold down a job long enough to give his family any stability because of his vices…drugs, alcohol and women. In addition to that he was physically abusive. But no matter how much we all tried to convince her to get out, she remained. Caroline never had a job and was dependent on the man who was ruining her life. By the way, it was during that time when Caroline also became a Born Again Christian. I remember an incident which occurred when we all first got into the "Jesus Movement." Sara, Caroline, Joseph, Julianne and I were visiting an evangelical church when right in the middle of the service Tommy lit a cigarette. The pastor called him out and ordered him to leave the church. Tom stood up defiantly, got into a staring match with him and said, "Make me!" Today I would have almost applauded him. But back then, my belief systems being what they were, it was extremely uncomfortable.

Tom was a wanted man in three states for drug trafficking and an alleged hit and run, which finally resulted in Caroline filing for a divorce. So my in-laws, with the help of most of their children, pitched in to buy her a place to live in the "manatee capital" of the world, swinging Homosassa! Caroline got herself a little part time job and was trying to get her life in order. Spiritually, however, at that juncture of my journey, I believed she was in an amazing place and that's one of the reasons why I couldn't wait to see her! Just like Sara and I, she had come out from organized religion and diligently studied in an earnest effort to seek the Truth through Bible studies and Internet websites. Caroline fled from mainstream Christianity and immersed herself into the Torah, so much so, she legally changed her name to Rachel. I guess she felt it was better suited to what she believed! At one time I loved talking to Caroline. For some reason, my perspective on things fascinated her and her knowledge of Scripture absolutely amazed me. She mentioned to me how she never forgot when a long time ago, before we became pre-occupied with religious matters, I told her to think about the world of microscopic organism living on our very fingertips. The thought mesmerized her and her wonderment amused me. We enjoyed each other's company immensely.

She appeared to have had tremendous faith and believed wholeheartedly that whatever hardships she was undergoing, her Heavenly Father would see her through. I had mixed emotions. Just like the song says, "To everything there is a season," there had to be a balance. There is some truth in the expression, "God helps those who help themselves." Caroline's enthusiasm for the "Higher things" was wonderful, but wasn't it now up to her to provide for her family? Caroline spent endless hours in front of her computer in Bible chat rooms ignoring the lives of her kids. Even though, at the time, I believed my faith would get me through life's tight spots, I knew the importance of taking responsibility for certain things. Money just doesn't come falling down from heaven; you have to work for it. It's the duty of a single mother to provide her kids with stability. I know it's easier said than done, but if it takes working more than one job, if it takes telling the kids they are loved a thousand times a day, it has to be done! In my mind, I didn't see how things could change without an honest effort on her part.

Through the years it had become increasingly difficult to converse with my mother-in-law and father in-law, especially since he was on a mission to convert us back to Catholicism. Eventually I learned to keep the discussions light and be passive. I would just listen, nod, and view their behavior as a form of entertainment, like watching a sit-com! Since moving to Florida, my in-laws have switched from being Democrats to Republicans. He has become so right wing, I think with enough prodding he is capable of shooting me in the head with the gun he keeps proudly on the premises. He was pro-Bush and pro-war. A man who I can remember spoke out against prejudice, now referred to the southern blacks as the ones with the "shiny skin" who "know their place," unlike the arrogant northern ones. If I hadn't heard it with my own ears, I wouldn't have believed it for a minute.

He prided himself on being a devout Catholic. He would argue about what it says or doesn't say in the Bible yet had never read it. He was very devoted to Mary, "The Blessed Mother," and as often as we all tried to explain to him his devotion to her was unbiblical and not winning him any favor with God, he refused to listen. Even with guests in the house, he would give his wife the eye and pressure her to join him in his daily ritual of reciting the "Rosary." It was crazy! We were all going in different directions trying to find the path to God, yet each of us was trying to force the other to see it in our own respective ways.

When I was a kid going to Catholic grammar school we were forced to march in a procession every May. Across from the school there was a grotto dedicated to "The Blessed Mother." In the middle of the grotto were big stone-like statues of Mary and little children kneeling about her. "Oh Mary we crown thee with blossoms today!" we would sing as we paraded across the street and into the church grotto carrying flowers. It was a special honor to be the student who was chosen to climb the ladder and actually place the halo of blossoms on the head of the statue of Mary. I used to get so disappointed because I was never chosen. In my young, fragile and innocent mind, I thought I was deeply involved in a real supernatural and spiritual observance. Just another one of the many misconceptions instilled upon millions of unsuspecting Catholics like my father-in-law. Because Mary was the birth mother of the physical Jesus, Catholics figure there was more of a chance of getting prayers answered by going through her instead of directly to the Source. Because Jesus obeyed his mother at the wedding feast in Cana by performing his first miracle, many keepers of the faith illogically assume that Mary will come shining through for them simply because Jesus would never deny His mother! Not much crazier than speaking in tongues, I guess!

For the entire week, Julianne and I had to listen to her dad preach about how his greatest desire was for all his children to come back to the Holy Mother Roman Catholic Church. Although he was somewhat happy to see his children becoming more spiritual, he truly believed we were all missing out on the joys of being Catholic. I imagined it was this same kind of thinking that made him assume uncircumcised men had more sensitive penises and heightened sexual pleasure than the circumcised ones. How could he possibly know without experiencing both? In other words he was saying, because I'm this way, you should be this way too!

The development in which my in-laws decided to settle down and live out their "golden years," a retirement village known as "West Maple Woods," is a beautiful countrified community centered around two golf courses. Most of the people who live there are retired professionals. From my perspective, my father-in-law, a blue-collar worker from Brooklyn, and my mother-in-law, a frugal suburban housewife and mother of nine, stuck out like sore thumbs. The best way to describe the situation would be by comparing them to the Clampett's living in Beverly Hills, only Ray and Marie didn't strike oil. The only thing he really had in common with all of his neighbors was his love for golf. Naturally the sole purpose of his relocating to the area was to be able to afford becoming a member of a semi-prestigious golf club and play as much golf as humanly possible. Being a golf club member brought along with it some requirements, however. One of them was spending a certain amount of money annually at the club's restaurant. We had the honor of being their guests on two evenings.

As long as I've known Julianne, her folks were never the type to go out to restaurants. Even though they were living in Florida with no mortgage and a substantial income from my father-in-law's pension, all the years of having to feed nine children on a modest income, the tight budget mindset was something they were never able to surrender. For them, going out to eat was looked upon as an unaffordable luxury. Always looking for a bargain, they found it too extravagant, wasteful, and usually a rip-off.

Witnessing while mom interrogated the waitress for the exact price of every "special," or listening to her try to convince me to go for the "two for one" house wine, was entertaining to say the least. When she told us about her recent visit to "Applebee's" and how she demanded to see the "chef" because she was disappointed with her meal, we had all to do to keep from choking with laughter. All I could picture was a greasy looking teenager, who probably didn't wash his hands after leaving the bathroom, asking my mother-in-law, in broken English, what was it exactly, she didn't like about her microwave prepared entrée? Only in Florida!

I'd never cared for red meat and for at least twenty-five years Julianne and I hadn't indulged. One of the things that Caroline, Sara, Artie, and I had embraced with conviction, concerning our spiritual walks, were the dietary laws found in scripture. There are certain animals, such as pig and shellfish, the Bible deems as unclean and man is instructed not to eat them. I once considered the Bible, among other things, to be an instruction manual or guidebook for living. There had to be very good reasons why it was recommended we abstain from certain foods. So solely for health reasons, I decided to abide.

When Caroline ordered horseradish with her prime rib, I poked her and asked, "You're not going to eat horseradish are you?" She gave me that dizzy blond look of confusion and asked me why.

"It's unclean!" I answered, "Horseradish is made from horse. Horse, like pig, is considered unclean!"

"You're kidding!" she shrieked, "Thanks for telling me! I didn't know! I won't eat it now!"

Julianne rolled her eyes giving her sister the "Why do you believe him look" and Caroline got hysterical over just how naïve she could be.

In my inflexible obsession, I looked at the Bible in much the same way a new car owner followed the manufacturer's suggestions found in the owner's manual. To me, the Bible contained directions for living life. They were not salvation issues, but guidelines for physical, spiritual and mental health. Disobeying the commandments didn't send one to hell; it only brought about consequences he or she would have to face in this life. I deduced, since God is unchanging, wouldn't it only make sense His ways remain unchanged? If the Bible is indeed the Word of God, and if pork and shellfish are among the list of unclean things our very Maker advises us not to eat, why are they staples in almost every household? If the Bible contains instructions for observing the Passover meal from generation to generation, and if Christians supposedly observe the Bible, why have they replaced it with the Easter Sunday dinner at which they eat the traditional big fat Easter ham? Why do Christians stuff their faces full of shellfish, the traditional Christmas Eve fare? Coincidence? I didn't think so! Even though I was blind to my own double standards, it disturbed me to see people use the Bible merely as a tool of convenience, where its words were taken literally or metaphorically for whatever agenda anyone may have had at the moment. I thought people needed to make decisions. Where should they allow traditions to end and their health begin?

LOSING MY RELIGION

The trip to Florida did us a world of good. For obvious reasons, every time Julianne was in the presence of her parents for any length of time, she had an awakening. (It was just unfortunate it was always a temporary fix.) Sometimes we had to witness firsthand what could very well be our future in order to make a conscious effort to try and change it.

For the most part, Julianne and I had been getting along pretty well for a span. We were starting to enjoy each other's company and promised ourselves we should do more traveling and basically try to have more fun. I had to say since we agreed to try some counseling, there had definitely been a change for the better. It had been a while since we'd last seen Bonnie and one evening when she came to mind I decided to e-mail her. I was curious about how her trip to the Ukraine went and in a brief letter asked her to tell me all about it. The very next morning when I sat down at my computer, I noticed Bonnie had already responded. Upon opening her mail, I was saddened to learn her trip was unsuccessful and cut short due to a tragedy that struck her family. She explained how her son-in-law, who was in the U.S. Air Force, was killed when his plane crashed during maneuvers. Bonnie stated how the family was devastated, she asked for our prayers and concluded that Jule and I should seek counseling elsewhere because it would be a long time before she would return to work. We seemed to have come so far with Bonnie we had no desire to start all over again with someone else.

I couldn't help but wonder just how much God had to do with her Ukrainian expedition for it to turn out so horribly. Do our own desires and inspirations deceive us to the point where we are convinced it's God actually speaking to us? Were Bonnie's dreams divine messages from above or workings of her own mind? Why would a loving God, who we believe interacts in our lives, allow so many innocent unwanted babies to suffer while waiting for someone like Bonnie to rescue them and then have the rescue mission fail? I truly didn't know!

Twenty-two years of working for UPS had enabled me to meet and talk with many people. A friendly guy, I would talk to practically anyone and had no problem speaking my mind about anything. The trouble was I became almost obsessed with spirituality, the purpose of life, and the manipulative tricks of organized religion. No matter who talked with me, I had a way of segueing any conversation into my favorite topics. Most people, especially my co-workers, simply dismissed me as being nuts. It amazed me how even my close working buddies had no passion about their spirituality. Life meant nothing more than working to acquire things and holding onto the religious identities they inherited from their parents and the generations that preceded them. It drove me crazy, when during our lunch hour conversations, the only responses I would get from them was, "Oh Johnny, you're going to hell!"

Julianne still wasn't happy about my refusing to attend church on Sundays. She lectured me by saying if I truly had convictions about observing things like Torah, Passover and the seventh day Sabbath, I would get up off my lazy ass and go worship with her sister Sara and the Jews on Saturdays, suggesting I find a Messianic congregation. I knew she was almost right. The truth of the matter was I didn't want to belong to any organization or adhere to any new rules. It just exasperated me how Christianity deviated so far from its humble beginnings. You can't talk the talk unless you walk the walk and my problem was, way down deep in my heart, I started to have my doubts about everything I'd been professing for the past year or so. My search was becoming mentally exhausting. I suddenly surmised that every Saturday or Sunday couldn't possibly be the appointed Sabbath, because according to scripture, Sabbaths were determined by the cycles of the moon. Strict followers must realize the Sabbath changes monthly. With the many adjustments that were undergone to establish the calendar year, it became virtually impossible for anyone to keep a Sabbath as originally intended. I'd concluded... Saturday, Sunday, Monday, or Tuesday...

what difference did it really make? In fact, what difference did any of my ramblings make?

The Catholic Church, in her ongoing struggle for power, chose Sunday instead of Saturday. Any book on Church history will expound on how Sunday became the new Sabbath. Rome hoodwinked her loyal followers into believing missing Church on Sunday was a sin and nobody wanted to die with sin on their souls. Penances were once sold as a means of cleansing one's soul. Later, mandatory weekly offerings ("tithes") from her gullible supporters helped the Church to grow into one of the richest institutions in the world…all in the name of God! Obviously the congregations didn't see the absurdity or the hypocrisy of the traditions that soon carried over into all her rebellious Protestant subdivisions.

My brother-in-law Arthur was spending the summer in New York and staying at Sara's house. I love Art and always considered him more of a best friend than a brother-in-law, but I must admit, I was beginning to understand him less and less. Maybe I was jealous, but Artie found a way to beat the system (or make the system work for him). Somehow he managed to qualify for social security disability, claiming to be diagnosed with chronic fatigue syndrome, Epstein Barr disease, or in his case, too damned lazy to work sickness! Art and I used to spend many long distance hours ragging about our spouses, but I couldn't believe it when just before their thirtieth wedding anniversary, he put his little bit of money where his mouth was and filed for divorce. He moved out of his comfortable home in Arizona to a low rent apartment in a low-income section of northwest Florida. Art's separation from Mary lasted six months. Their communication via e-mail and telephone led them to believe they had made a mistake so they got back together. To date, however, they haven't remarried! As much as I love Mary, I wondered whether Art really missed her or the creature comforts of his spacious Arizona home. Since he was able to spend an entire summer away from his wife, I'd have to bet it was the house he missed more! But who am I to talk, what do I know? I'm certainly not in a position to judge…

Art said how he was looking forward to getting together with Sara and me and having intense Bible studies with the hopes Julianne would join us. Julianne always made it known she was secure enough in her faith and didn't need to delve into the far-out places we'd been going. Every other day Artie would call me from Sara's to tell me about the great all night Bible discussions he and Sara shared. He also expressed his disappointment and disapproval that I wasn't present during any of them. Although I promised him I'd be joining the Bible studies, my long day at work, household errands, and busy social calendar kept me away. Besides all those very legitimate reasons, to be quite honest, I started losing my enthusiasm. Having gained a somewhat deeper understanding of Scripture than I'd ever had before, gave me the self-assurance and the confidence to know that disassociating myself from the Pentecostal church was the right thing to do. Somehow, I had this feeling my journey didn't end there. For me, there were many more forks in the road ahead. As far as Art and Sara were concerned, I felt as though I might soon be heading in a different direction and traveling solo.

Sara had found a small storefront congregation not far from her house that seemed like just the place we'd been looking for. What prompted Sara to investigate was the sign in the window displaying the Star of David and the word Yehshua. Just as she presumed, a Jewish fellow who believed in Jesus as the Messiah led the small assembly. At this point in my unsteady walk, I needed to be in a place where the teaching was deep and able to set me on fire, so both Sara and I decided to attend. The congregation was so small that when we entered on a SUNDAY morning (which I found rather strange), all attention was directed towards us. I guess they were glad to see some fresh blood in the room. Sitting through the first service wasn't too strange or unfamiliar. It was interesting to hear the Pastor read in Hebrew, translate to English and then explain the Scriptures with the customs and traditions of the time. The proceedings, however, were typical of most church services; there was singing, announcements and a message. The songs they sang were the same ones I used to play at the Full Gospel church. The yarmulke-clad pastor used the names Jesus and Yehshua interchangeably, which I found to be a little unsettling because it lacked conviction. He spoke to us about growing up Jewish and the anti-Semitism he had to tolerate as a teenager. The story about his conversion from a young man who hated Christians to what he referred to as a "completed Jew" (one who has accepted Christ) was compelling. At first I wasn't totally sold on what I was hearing from his Judeo/Christian pulpit, but I returned for some future services with hopes of getting a little more meat.

It was on my fifth and final return visit when Artie joined me for a mid-week Bible study. Because of a prior commitment, Sara couldn't make it that evening. In spite of my convictions, I typically tried to avoid confrontation. If I didn't like what I was seeing or hearing, I'd just quietly fade from the scene and not go back. Art, on the other hand, always liked a good discussion or better put, a friendly argument. The Bible study wasn't anything we hadn't heard in the churches we came from. As the pastor started to discuss the rapture, the meeting of believers in the clouds before earth's demise, Art raised his hand to challenge what he had considered to be an incorrect statement. Arthur always had his ammunition handy, ready to back up his own viewpoints with Scripture. The pastor appeared to be perturbed by Artie's interruption and requested he save his questions for the end. Art asked indignantly, "Isn't this supposed to be an interactive study where we could all learn something from each other's standpoints? Forgive my outspokenness but this study seems to be conducted more like a dictatorship, your way or none!"

Turning to me Art said, "Come on John, let's get out of here. I heard enough of this bullshit!"

"Relax man! You can't be rude," I said persuasively, so we stayed.

When he was done teaching, the pastor made a mad dash to the rear of the room where we were sitting, then got into a game of dueling scriptures with Art. Both parties had strong convictions and were able to utilize Scripture to prove their opposing slants on the same subject. Tolerant of each other's opinions, but not the least bit convinced, neither side budged an inch. They both finally shook hands and agreed it was okay to disagree. Everyone can't be right, but is it possible, everybody's wrong? Obviously, what I was seeking wasn't there either. Neither of us ever went back.

My spirit was once again becoming restless. There was no getting away from the fact that all of us involved weren't living exemplary lives. Not that anybody's life is perfect, but with all our so-called scriptural knowledge and this desire to want to get closer to Yahweh, one would think our lives shouldn't be so dysfunctional. Julianne was growing more distant from her sisters and brother not to mention me. Gary wasn't getting along at all with Sara and although he never told us straight out, he thought we were all a bunch of lunatics. Caroline's personal life was a real mess. Her teenage daughter was promiscuous and both of her kids were doing drugs. My in-laws were praying to Mary for all of us to return to Catholicism, my mom still prayed to St. Anthony, my sister Virginia dove head first into studying theology, and Julianne continued to believe speaking in tongues and the rapture were for real. Art was still legally divorced to Mary and collecting social security disability checks for an illness most of us believed was in his hypochondriac imagination. Our kids remained confused, not knowing what to make of any of this insanity, while all of us had our heads in the sand studying God's word! It didn't add up! Life seemed a whole lot better, and Julianne and I were a whole lot happier, when our only concerns were sex, drugs, and rock and roll.

PART III

ANOTHER FORK IN THE ROAD

The older I'd become, the more I'd begun to believe my life had been a journey and the people I'd met along the way were meant to be there. Each and every step of the journey had been part of a learning process where at just the right moment someone had entered my life to help bring me along to the next level.

I pulled my truck into the large circular driveway of the Rubinstein's Shorewood Drive home. It was very rare when their Vietnamese housekeeper didn't greet me as I made my way up the walkway leading to the front door. This was one of those rare days when Elise was on hand to accept her delivery. "Hey!" she happily cried out, "I haven't seen you in quite a while. Where have you been?"

Elise is a very plain, natural-looking, pretty woman who I would've had to guess was in her forties. I gave her all the details about my car accident and how it kept me out of commission for a while. Her reaction was heartfelt and compassionate. I told her how being laid up allowed me the time to think, rethink, study and begin writing a book. She invited me to step inside and before I knew it, I lost all track of time. One topic led into another as the two of us, a wavering Christian and Jew, entered into a beautiful and enlightening conversation about our unconventional views on spirituality. She seemed excited and surprised to hear me discuss unworldly issues the way I did and I was delighted to finally speak to someone who understood my feelings. In our brief conversation, I found Elise to be so soulful, gentle and spiritual, with such a thirst to know her Creator more genuine than anybody I'd ever known, including Julianne,

Sara, Art, and Caroline. She referred to God in a way that appeared so real, unlike anything I'd ever heard. It was almost as if she melded with the very spirit of God. There was no way I could perceive her soul to be in jeopardy of any kind. Elise appeared to love God deeper than any Christian I knew. I suddenly became aware of how much time I was spending at her house. I told her how refreshing I found our discussion and as much as I didn't want to, I'd better be going. Before I stepped back into my truck, she recommended a few books she thought I might enjoy reading. She wanted to write the titles down but I assured her I would remember, knowing in all probability, I'd never get the chance to read them.

On another day, on another street not too far from Elise's, I was making my daily delivery to the home of a very successful well-known novelist. I became pretty friendly with her secretary, Ronnie, after we discovered we shared a passion for red wine. As far as I could tell, Ronnie and I were around the same age because with each time we talked, I discovered we shared many of the same interests. Her boss just released her latest novel, so I mentioned I was taking a stab at writing my first book and how the process seemed to be taking forever. Ronnie asked me what the book was about and my brief synopsis sparked yet another discussion about the great mysteries of God. When Ronnie recommended I read the very same books Elise did just days ago, I got the feeling this had to be more than coincidence. Like me, Ronnie had become quite disenchanted with religion and was seeking something deeper than what church had to offer.

Although I was still fairly confident that Christianity had indeed strayed far from its Hebrew beginnings, and through a series of historic events her followers were steered way off course, I stepped down from off of my soapbox and gave my opinions only when I thought it was absolutely necessary. I mellowed out considerably and my discussions with Sara, Arthur, and Caroline were becoming far less frequent. People around the workplace, who knew me as a fun loving crazy guy, were thinking I'd become a religious fanatic. I also felt bad about my fanaticism becoming just another thing dividing Julianne and me and causing confusion with my kids. I had to make use of those expensive tools Bonnie showed us. Julianne was very set in her beliefs and I knew there was no chance of influencing her to even entertain broader views. I decided to play down the sermonizing and concentrate more on the two of us enjoying each other's company.

Each and every day I was grateful for my friends. Gino and Katie gave us yet another reason to be grateful. Because they chose not to have children, they'd been able to be more adventurous than most of the people we know. They live their lives by following their hearts, and their hearts led them to Prince Edward Island where they purchased a beautiful house on a cliff with a breath taking view of the water. The next best thing to owning a piece of paradise is having friends who do and who want nothing more than for their friends to enjoy it with them.

We spent one summer vacation with Gino and Katie on PEI and had a magnificent time. I felt a tender closeness to Jule I hadn't felt in a while. It was truly one of the most beautiful places we'd ever seen, a landscape adorned with red cliffs, crystalline blue water and bright green grassy hills. As far as I was concerned it was a little bit of heaven on earth.

One evening while the four of us were just lounging around after a long day of perusing the island, I was glancing over at the many books my friend, the child psychologist, had displayed on his bookshelves. It was as if I were drawn to them like a moth is drawn to a floodlight. Positioned directly in front of me at eye level were a few of the books Elise and Ronnie had suggested I read. Of course, Gino graciously let me borrow them, one of which I started reading that very evening. It was on that night I felt as though guiding arms from another dimension physically picked me up and placed me on yet another path, filling my head with questions and needing to find the answers. There was no doubt in my mind I was destined to read those books.

Because I'd always had a passion to write songs and play guitar, I seldom allowed myself the time to read. Suddenly it seemed as though my music took a backseat to an all-consuming desire to read and to write a book. The subject matter of the books I chose to read covered a wide range of topics including the history of Christianity, the scientific approach of creation, Eastern religions, meditation, reaching a higher consciousness, quantum physics, mysticism and mythology. By piecing together the information I was gathering from reading book upon book, a whole new, very real world of spirituality opened up to me, undoubtedly different from anything mainstream religion had to offer. Life, death, creation, science and many of the wonders of the universe started to make more sense to me than anything I'd ever heard from a pulpit or Bible study. Even the Bible was taking on a different perspective. By no stretch of the imagination was I attempting to totally discredit the Bible, but I could no longer accept the idea every word had to be taken literally. I now approached much of it as metaphorical, connecting science and scripture. Maybe what was written in Genesis was just an attempt at explaining the unexplainable. Question after question entered my head as I rethought the Bible verses I once leaned upon. Was the world really created in seven days? Was a day really a thousand years? Did God actually scoop up the soil from the Garden of Eden with His own hands to form Adam? Was it possible the "Big Bang" theory wasn't a too far off explanation of creation and all that resulted from it was by God's design? Were the acts of disobedience by Adam and Eve, eating the fruit from the tree of knowledge, symbolic for another kind of seduction? Were Adam and Eve even actual people? What was a tree of knowledge? Was religion a concept conceived by a group of controlling forces to stop men from thinking? I believed in the same way the spirit of God might have inspired the writings of men of long ago, it was also inspiring men of this age. Reading several accounts about the how, why, when, where and by whom the books of the Bible were written and later compiled had made me aware of how men with agendas had manipulated people by compromising, distorting and stretching truths. For as long as man has been on the planet, he's been searching for the answers as to why we exist. Although religion has been responsible for endless wars, senseless deaths and divisiveness among men, and because it doesn't offer definitive answers, it has given man a sense of comfort in its ongoing effort to anesthetize our minds. Whether it's the promise of Jesus breaking through the clouds in a blaze of glory to sweep all his loyal followers back up to heaven with him, or the roomful of virgins Allah has waiting for those who die in his service, religion provides man with purpose and hope. (Why Nirvana for Muslim men depicts an orgy with seven virgins and not seven prostitutes is rather strange. Except for the fact there'd be no one they could be compared to, I would imagine that sex with the prostitutes has to be a lot better. Virgins are not all they're cracked up to be. Besides what did those poor virgins do to have to be deflowered by some barbarian? Was this their hell?) For centuries there have been feuds between religion and science and their opposing theories that attempt to explain our existence. I trust one day we will discover how science and religion will prove their doctrines can co-exist. It was staggering for me to learn almost eighty percent of all matter is not visible to the human eye because it cannot retain light. Matter is energy, so could it very well be spirits are invisible matter and therefore energy? Is God simply the source of all energy and everything in creation comes from that energy? My questions were endless…but the one undeniable conclusion I arrived at was that God is unconditional love, an ideology I couldn't connect with conventional Christianity.

My Catholic upbringing taught me, God is the big spirit in the sky who looks like a wise old man with a long white beard. He (of course He's a man) holds a staff in his right hand and eternally sits upon a throne while angels who bow before him are constantly at his beck and call. We were also taught that somewhere in the midst of eternity, just 2000 years ago, He chose to come down to earth by becoming one of us because we so desperately needed some direction. Because of His unyielding love for us, He allowed himself to be beaten to a pulp and crucified on a tree, taking the heat for the sins of humanity. He then miraculously rose from the dead. By simply believing in the tale of His death and resurrection and accepting it was done for our sake, we will gain entrance into His kingdom in heaven when we die. For practically my entire life I cruised along assuming this was the undeniable truth. Suddenly it no longer made sense. How our eternal lives could be based solely upon a book of stories that have been inaccurately deciphered throughout history is preposterous. I couldn't perceive how Yahweh, God, or however we chose to address Him, could be so hard to please, that nothing less than the last drop of Yehshua's blood was a satisfactory sacrifice for the redemption of the entire human race. By equating God with pure love and the creation of infinite universes, the Christian message of salvation no longer seemed significant. It all started to become so clear that heaven wasn't a far off place attainable only by a chosen few who followed the rules. I now perceived heaven as a state of consciousness reached only when the mind of God aligns with ours. I now understood it to be God's intention that ALL men be redeemed. God loves the wicked and the righteous. If I wasn't right, I was surely in deep trouble!

RETHINKING THINGS OVER

It's not easy dismissing much of the information absorbed by our spongy little brains from the times we were toddlers. Until we learn to believe in ourselves, if we couldn't believe our parents, teachers and clergymen, whom could we believe? As parents we continue to tell our children the fantastic feel good tales about Santa Claus, the Easter Bunny and the tooth fairy and are deeply saddened when they no longer believe. (Whether it's because we see their innocence vanishing or ourselves growing older, I don't know.) Somehow or other, the day inevitably arrives when kids are able to reason it's mom and dad putting those presents under the tree and not the jolly magical character with the white beard, red suit and flying reindeers! I remember feeling excited and proud when I discovered the simple truth. Until the day the kids become enlightened to the fact there is no actual Santa, parents have a little bit of an edge on keeping them in line: Better be good or Santa's going to leave a bag of black coal for Christmas! Not too different from the warning we still heed from beyond the pearly gates: Better be good and believe what we were taught or God will send us to hell! Long after the kids learn mom and dad buy the gifts and there is no Santa, the presents still continue to appear under the tree each year. Similarly, would anything change once someone rationalizes God is not the wrathful old man in the sky? The sun will still rise and set, people will go on living and dying, and as the earth spins, the quest for truth and the purpose of our existence goes on. God is eternal therefore creation is eternal. There has to be a distinction between what we believe as truth as opposed to what we grow out of.

When parents set down a list of rules for their children to follow, it's not for the intent of punishing them, but for the well-being and protection of the child. God inspired man to make a list of commandments, not to ultimately banish us to hell for disobeying them, but to instruct us on how to safely conduct our lives. Following these living instructions should make one's life run rather smoothly. Choosing to not follow them could result in unnecessary complications. Stick your finger in the fire and you are definitely going to get burned.

The very first thing I learned in Catholic school Catechism class was "God is everywhere." Until recently, I never really understood just how profound a statement that was. If God is indeed everywhere, everywhere must include hell, and if hell is the absence of God, then how can hell exist? If we could only learn to break free from the religious shackles that bind us to accept the many misconceptions we've created concerning who or what God is, then maybe men could co-exist in love and freedom. God is indeed everywhere. The omnipotent spirit who designed the universe is present in each and every living creature. It has become so very clear to me, how with Him as the Source, all things are connected. Most of us are so tangled up in our busy little lives going after bigger homes, faster Internet service, bouncier breasts, bigger biceps and more luxurious cars, that we don't have the slightest clue of how to tap into the eternal energy of our Creator. Instead we recite the repetitive prayers memorized at childhood, make signs of the cross, and say robotic grace. Some people go through the motions week after week sitting in a church pew while pretending to give the minister's sermon their undivided attention. Some people stand before a great wall and place their handwritten prayer requests into the cracks hoping God will honor them. Some light candles, some sing songs, some fast, some kneel, some dance and some talk in strange tongues, when I wonder if all we have to do is to be still and silent. The world is full of many distractions. If for a few minutes each day we could somehow block out the ever-present commotion and learn to look within, it is there we will find Him. There are no bolts of Holy Spirit lightening being hurled through the atmosphere infusing us with supernatural powers. The spirit is already within; we just have to recognize it.

Every now and then I would think about Bonnie. Losing a son-in-law in such a senseless accident had to take a long time to get over. Checking through my e-mail one evening I was pleasantly surprised and immensely curious when I saw I'd received one from her. It was a pleasant note informing us she was returning to work. She thanked us for waiting on her and asked if we'd like to schedule our next session. When I mentioned to Julianne that Bonnie wanted us to make an appointment, she asked almost hesitantly, "Do you think we have to go back?"

The truth of the matter was we were getting along much better than we'd been in years, so I answered her with just a hint of uncertainty in my voice, "Not unless you do!" I could tell Julianne was let down by my answer.

"Why? Don't you think we're all right now?" she asked.

Even though we seemed to be in good shape at that moment, I couldn't abandon the thought that the possibility of a relapse did exist. Another session could have been like preventive medicine but we agreed not to go for any further counseling. I replied to her e-mail by explaining how well Julianne and I were doing and for the time being we would not be in need of her help. Bonnie's follow-up letter expressed her delight in our success and therefore her triumph, but at the same time tried to alert me not to be fooled by this blissful burst of harmony. She warned us that this pleasant stretch would most likely be temporary and reassured us if and when we crash-landed, she'd be there for us. She concluded her correspondence with one last comment that really caught my attention. "I have a spiritual message for you John," she wrote, "God has a mission for you. Listen for His voice and go where he leads you!" "Holy smokes!" I thought, "Just what the hell is that supposed to mean?" Did Bonnie know something I didn't know or was this just a sly way of getting me back into her office?

I couldn't get Bonnie's foretelling comment out of my head. If she truly received a message from God meant for me, well then I had to hear it. After vacillating about whether or not I should continue corresponding with her, I decided to send Bonnie yet another e-mail. I told her I was very interested in hearing what she had to say and suggested we should meet for coffee one evening. Bonnie's immediate reply disappointed me to say the least.

"Thanks for the invite to have coffee," she wrote, "but I don't think it would be very ethical. Perhaps you should schedule an appointment so we can further discuss the gift God has given you. We both work for the same

Boss! Affectionately, Bonnie!"

"Okay, so let me understand this!" I reasoned, "God gave Bonnie a message for me, but in order to find out what it is, it will cost me one hundred and fifty dollars! Nonsense!" I never responded to what I considered an insulting suggestion. It's always about the stinking money! If God had to tell me something He could certainly tell me himself!

Meanwhile my three comrades, Sara, Arthur and Caroline (I mean Rachel), had reached the conclusion I was out of my mind and had slipped into what they thought were the snares of New Age thinking. I'd also been lovingly warned about the possibilities of not making the rapture or even burning in hell. How does a human being deny his own thoughts? Is it possible for someone to simply put up roadblocks to keep the endless succession of questions, doubts and debatable viewpoints from entering his or her mind? If what the Bible says is true, that is, if one has faith the size of a mustard seed he can move mountains, what does that say about the atrocious condition of the planet? There are millions upon millions of people who claim to be Born Again Christians, baptized in the Holy Spirit, with Jesus as their personal Savior, so why aren't there any mountains being moved? If someone were thoroughly convinced the end of the world was at hand, Jesus was coming back any day now, and he or she will escape Armageddon, why would they be concerned about environmental issues? The need to protect and care for the earth wouldn't be so urgent. The need to stand up against an indifferent government wouldn't seem to be of utmost importance. It had finally occurred to me how religion's underlying purpose is to keep people asleep. Christians think the earth will eventually be obliterated and their eternal lives will take place in a far-off place known as Heaven. They haven't deduced that the Heaven they long for is right before their very eyes...but they'll never see it through the veil of religion.

If a person truly believes God has His watchful and judgmental eye on this earth, and by breaking His laws he or she may suffer the penalty of eternal damnation, I can't imagine why they would risk it? Why do so-called God-fearing people continually cheat, steal, commit adultery, and even kill? Could it be, deep down inside they don't take God seriously? I could no longer fathom how the great designer of the universe, the Being who created everything from the sun to a daisy, the very Spirit who breathed life into man, who loves us unconditionally, would conceive a place solely for the purpose of tormenting His disobedient children forever. I, as a mere mortal, wouldn't even consider sending my worst enemy to a place such as hell, no less my own children, so how could a loving God? So in order to understand the disobedience and the evil so prevalent in the world did men create the concept that lurking behind the scenes is Satan, the Devil, Lucifer, or as he is often called the Great Deceiver? Is Satan's greatest trick to make us think he doesn't really exist? To confuse matters even more, why did God graciously give men free will in spite of our weak nature? Wouldn't that make life nothing more than a chess game between two opposing forces and we are the game pieces? The idea of a loving God creating His nemesis and then allowing him to wander the universe instigating chaos and destruction upon His children is baffling to me to say the least. The standard Christian comeback to that method of thinking is, "God gave us the remedy...Jesus the Messiah." If that were the case, then do we all just exist in God's fishbowl for His entertainment? Then again, if our boundless all-seeing Creator already knows the results, how entertaining could that be? I concluded it all comes down to choice. We have been given the gift of free will. Simply put, we can choose to accept the notion we are all equally created with the ability to tap into His power and love, or not. Sometimes life seemed like it would have been a lot easier if I could have simply hit the switch and turned off the thinking mechanism in my head. I guess that's why people still hold on to their religions, it does the thinking for them.

BEATING AROUND THE BUSH

The war in Iraq had been going on for too long and sorry to say, it looked as if there was no way out of that nightmare. Every day, horrifying images of beheadings, suicide bombings, battle and bloodshed infiltrated their way into our relatively safe and secure households as the magic of television provided us with front row seats to the tragic events. I didn't believe in political parties any more than I believed in religious denominations. I didn't vote for George Bush Sr. or George Bush Jr. and when junior was up for re-election, I couldn't understand how this nation elected him to lead us down the road to ruin for another four long years. Sadly, John Kerry wasn't much of an opponent, but common sense led me to trust America would have wanted a change before more lives were lost. Ordinarily, Kerry wouldn't have been my candidate of choice either, but considering the mess we were in, Big Bird seemed like a better alternative than Bush. I also knew Bush wasn't smart enough to get the country into the mess it was in. He was just a puppet who was greatly compensated and undemocratically put into the hot seat while the "mysterious powers that be" ran the world.

My cousin Christopher made the unfortunate mistake of joining the army for the sole purpose of furthering his education, compliments of Uncle Sam. He never dreamed one day he'd be squatting over a hole in the hot sand with a semi-automatic weapon in his lap while trying to take a dump in an Iraqi desert. "Payback's a bitch," he said, "It was like signing a pact with the devil."

Fortunately, he returned from hell on earth with all of his limbs intact. One evening I had the opportunity to speak with him and heard first hand his terrifying tales from Baghdad. "Don't believe anything coming out of Washington!" he warned, "Don't let anybody fool you into thinking we're fighting for the freedom of the Iraqi people or looking for weapons of mass destruction!" He took a breath, pausing to see if he was going to get an argument from me, then carried on, "We're there for one reason and one reason only, and that's to protect the pipelines and our interests in oil!" His angry words continued to flow steadily. "From now until doomsday we could send a million troops and nothing is going to improve life in that fucking hell hole!" Once again, he paused, and as his voice seemed to tighten, he spoke slowly, "John, human beings were blown to bits right before my eyes…that's never going away!" Part of my daily morning ritual was checking the local weather and traffic. I now had the added pleasure of checking the daily terrorist threat level.

DREAM A LITTLE DREAM FOR ME

I'd always wished, in this day of technological wizardry, there was a contraption able to videotape or digitally record our dreams. Who knows, maybe in the very near future, some genius will be inspired enough to create a form of skullcap, wired with a bunch of electrodes, that will somehow transmit the images that crawl out from behind the walls of our subconscious while we sleep, onto tape or DVD for viewing the following day. Aside from the occasional pornographic ones with obvious explanations, I would love to be able to study my dreams and find the meaning of the many epics produced by my overactive imagination. Some of my slumber-land escapades made Fellini films seem like half-hour sitcoms. There had been many a night when I'd been catapulted out of a dead sleep by some disturbing dream or nightmare. I usually rolled over hoping my restlessness would cause Julianne to awaken. If and when she did, she'd ask me from a trance-like state if I was all right. Even though I knew she had absolutely no interest in what I was dreaming about, I attempted to tell her anyway. I think voicing out what I experienced in my sleep helped me to remember the dream the following morning. Her reaction was always the same, "I don't want to hear about your stupid dream, call Toni-Ann and tell her!"

Toni and I are like dream soul mates. We love listening to each other's dreams and trying to figure out just what the hell they mean. I'm pretty good at remembering the gist of most of my elaborate dreams, but every so often, it's not until sometime later on the very next day when an image will come into mind and I'll realize it was from the previous night's dream.

After a while, however, the details begin to fade and before long they get stored back into the files of my subconscious. That's why a mechanism for dream recording would be so cool!

I had two very vivid dreams I'd talked about so often, they remained pretty fresh in my memory. The first one found me in what I can best describe as a waiting room or green room. The walls of the room were almost colorless and alongside one wall was a wooden bench. There were several strangers milling about with me, and for the most part, I had no idea why any of us were there. Most of the people appeared to be much older than I was and they all showed signs of distress on their aging faces. I was not feeling the least bit of fear or anxiety, but not knowing the reason why I was there baffled me, so I asked if any of them knew what the purpose of this odd gathering was. A woman, who I guessed to be in her mid to late sixties, dressed very modestly, almost puritanical, broke the silence, "The end of the world is at hand and we are awaiting the Lord's return! He should be coming momentarily!"

The others in the room looked as if they were meditating or praying. Some sat on the bench with their heads bowed and some paced the floor in circles. There was a small window in the corner of the room and occasionally someone would stand on the bench and peer out at the skies. My curiosity had the best of me, so I too would sporadically glance out the window looking for any sign of impending doom. I wasn't able to calculate just how long I had been cooped up in this room and I couldn't understand why it never even occurred to me to just leave.

After what felt like centuries of waiting, I spoke out to the entire group and asked, "What makes you so sure the end is near and so certain He's coming back? Did you ever think maybe everything you're hoping for is based upon stories conjured up by men to help in finding a purpose to our existence?"

Everyone in the room stopped what they were doing. The pacing, the praying, the chanting all came to a dead stop. They all turned to look at each other then simultaneously gazed at me. Their expressions shifted from ones of exasperation to ones of confusion and dread, making me wonder if maybe I shouldn't have said anything. Trying to comfort them I continued to speak, "Maybe it's not like we'd been taught. Maybe when it's our time, we simply return to the place from where we came..."

Just then an incredible transformation took place. It was as if I had suddenly vaporized and became a thought. I was weightless and could envision myself drifting about inside a large bubble. My personality was still intact but I no longer possessed any of my human features, no arms, legs, or organs of any kind. I could think very clearly but all that remained of me was light and thought. I seemed to be floating about the same room I was just in, but all the people were gone. "I was right!" I thought, but remember feeling disappointed and frustrated not being able to function any longer as a human being.

No longer could I walk on the beach, touch, play my guitar, make love to my wife, drink wine, hug my kids or talk to my friends. Feeling as if my mental circuits were on overload and about ready to snap, I suddenly broke free from the dream. Springing from a restless sleep, it felt as if I were being launched out from my bed. I was quite shaken and breathing heavily. As I walked towards the bathroom, the images I just experienced in my dream wouldn't leave my head. I splashed cold water on my face and mumbled some kind of prayer, "Please let it go away, please let it go away..."

Grateful I was still me, I crawled back into bed and snuggled up close to Julianne. "Are you all right?" she asked.

"I just had the most screwed up dream!" I said.

"Go to sleep!" she answered, "You can tell Toni all about it tomorrow!"

Just about a week later right in the middle of what I hoped would be a deep, uninterrupted peaceful sleep, the on-switch to my dream engine was activated and another full blown late night saga was in full production, starring yours truly. I sprang out from my sleep the next morning like a clown from a jack-in-the-box wondering what the heck I had eaten the night before that caused me to dream what I dreamt. The adventure began with Julianne asking me to please go back to church. I told her she was wasting her breath and there was no chance of me ever returning. After a while, I started feeling bad about my stubbornness and decided that just to make her happy, I'd give it a shot and go back. It was a Sunday morning and just like I did in the days when I was attending church and playing with the praise and worship team, I headed off to church by myself an hour or so before service began. When I pulled into the parking lot I noticed the building didn't look quite the same. It seemed more like a very large trailer home than the ultra modern construction I used to patronize. I cautiously entered through the front doors and glanced inside a small room to my left where Brett and the church band were rehearsing. Brett turned his attention from the music for a brief second, gave me a cross look, then resumed playing. The sound of the music irritated me and I thought to myself, "Nothing's changed. It's the same old bullshit!"

I walked a little further down the corridor and came to another room where someone with an unfamiliar face, who was wearing a long black robe, seemed to be teaching Sunday school to a captive group of twenty or so people. One male member of the group turned when he heard my steps and gave me the same cross look as Brett did. From another room I could hear the distinct sound of Pastor Ted's annoying voice and I told myself no matter how much I loved my wife and wanted to make her happy, I couldn't do this. I quickened my pace and darting out the doors I said under my breath, "How can she stomach this bullshit week after week?"

Suddenly I was determined that I needed to escape and my eyes became focused on a red pick-up truck parked at the very front of the church. Why I just didn't get back into my own car and go home, I don't know, remember, this was a dream! Walking alongside the red truck and coming towards me was a foreign couple. I couldn't really say what nationality they were, but their skin was dark, their hair jet black and they were no taller than five feet two inches. As they approached me, they smiled, nodded and said good morning with an unrecognizable accent. Just then I reached into my pocket and pulled out a revolver. I held it up to the little man's head and commanded both of them to get into the front of the pick-up. I climbed into the small back seat and demanded they drive off. I really had no idea where they were taking me, but according to the script of the dream, they were supposedly bringing me home. They pleaded with me not to shoot (which I had no intention of doing), started up the vehicle and drove off. At that point I realized the church was connected to the rear of the truck and we were dragging it along right behind us. As we pulled out of the parking lot, the church almost toppled as it bounced over the curb and I could hear the cries of the congregants inside. "Praise the Lord!" Pastor Ted shouted, "God will protect us!"

I motioned for the frightened driver to step on it and as the screams continued to stream from the building behind us, the red pick-up with the huge church trailer attached, raced through the narrow suburban streets off to who knows where. Dreams are so cool because anything can happen and there's no need to explain why. The landscape dramatically changed around us. From a neighborhood of cookie-cutter capes and ranches, we were suddenly transported to a stretch of mountain highway, where we raced by miles and miles of tall evergreens momentarily surrounding us. Peering out, we could see up ahead in the distance was a long black suspension bridge that appeared to go over a large body of water and led to a city.

The driver and his partner looked back at me as if to say, "You don't expect us to drive over that bridge do you?" and before they could utter a word, the sky before us displayed the most amazing array of colors I had ever seen.

The truck came to a full stop just before the entrance to the bridge. Each of us was stricken with awe as we watched the sky unfold a light show of colors I couldn't even begin to name or describe. Explosions sputtering bouquets of the most vivid colors decorated the heavens. The couple in the front seat, who should have despised me for abducting them and hijacking a vehicle, turned to me, and with looks of astonishment, thanked me over and over again. "If you didn't force us at gunpoint to take this journey we never would have seen the beauty we just experienced. Our lives are forever changed for which we can never repay you!"

I apologized for my thoughtless and forceful behavior and as the colors in the sky above us gradually faded back to its natural blue, we slowly drove across the bridge. Upon reaching the other side and entering a city-like setting, I exited the pick-up.

"This is where I get off!" I told the astounded hostages, even though the area was totally unfamiliar to me. "Will you find your way back?" I asked.

"We have found our way. How can we ever thank you?" they replied and sped away, no longer hauling the building that was trailing behind for the entire journey. I couldn't wait to tell Toni!

NEW FACE, SAME MESSAGE

It had been almost two years since I disassociated myself from Pastor Ted and the Full Gospel Church of Island Terrace. Julianne, who had never been one for change, hung in there, even though the general feeling going around was their dear pastor was losing his anointing. Although I shouldn't speak for her, I believe some of the Old Catholic indoctrinating like "missing Mass on Sundays is a sin," hadn't been thoroughly removed from her system. Like a loyal soldier, she attended service every Sunday and swore it was because she liked to go (although she'd always be at least thirty minutes late).

When I used to attend service and the pastor would cry out, "Who's glad they're in God's house this morning and not in the hospital?" the congregation would cry out, "Amen" and applaud wildly. I used to think, "Give us a better choice. Try asking where we'd rather be, in church or the Bahamas and then see what the response would be! If anyone was the least bit honest, shouts of 'Bahamas' would have rung out."

There were also Sunday mornings when Pastor Ted used to say, as he held his Bible way above his badly coiffed head, "If every word in this book is not true and Jesus is not who it says he is, then Christianity is the biggest hoax to ever hit the planet!" I used to sit there and wonder, "What if he's right about that?"

Although he's not the sole reason why I left the church, there was something about Pastor Ted that began rubbing me the wrong way. His words and his antics all seemed so contrived. Church was just another form of show business, cheap entertainment. Either he changed drastically from the hopeful day when he became the church's new shepherd, or the flock just wasn't able to see through the brilliant façade.

After Pastor Ralph fell from grace, the church was so desperate for a new leader, when Ted floated in through the doors of our modest little building, most of the assembly agreed he was God's answer to prayer. One would assume that matters pertaining to the work of the Lord wouldn't require contracts, attorneys and the like, but since the reality of life is nobody can be trusted, it did. The elders of the church were so sold on Ted that they presented him with an offer he couldn't refuse. He was to live rent free in a parsonage purchased and owned by the church. Ralph and the previous pastor owned their own houses, so for the first time in its history, the church had to get into the real estate business. The dwelling they bought to house their dear pastor and family was a mint, mother-daughter in a prime location, walking distance to a beautiful beach. He was also to be given a new car every three years, which was paid for and insured by the church. (His package also included medical insurance, a competitive salary and a pension equal to the difference of the value of the parsonage from the time of purchase to the day of retirement. Nobody ever dreamed real estate would sky rocket the way it did, except maybe for Ted!)

Wherever there are people there is drama. Remember, all the world's a stage and we are merely actors. The church had its fair share of drama during Pastor Ted's twelve-year dictatorship, and from what I could garner from Julianne's conversations with fellow church chums, it was time for Ted to throw in the towel. Although he preferred to label himself an evangelist, in lieu of the latest events, I must conclude my instincts were right when I labeled him a shrewd politician. An emergency business meeting was arranged for one Sunday evening when Pastor Ted made his greatly anticipated, much prepared and well rehearsed speech announcing he and his sidekick Greta were going to retire. From what I heard it was one of his better performances. Pastor Ted seemed to spit out from memory his farewell message while his mental calculator totaled up the four hundred fifty thousand dollars he knew was legally due him.

He promised the congregation he would remain on board throughout the holiday season and continue to do so until they elected a new pastor. Within days, I was told, his bags were packed and within weeks, he was headed south with a much negotiated retirement package of one hundred and fifty thousand dollars finally agreed upon! He probably could have won a legal battle for the full four fifty, but that would have left the church financially crippled, causing it to close its doors and go out of the soul saving business. Needless to say it also would have ruined Ted's reputation as a "man of God!"

So now Full Gospel Church of Island Terrace was facing the challenge of having to elect a new pastor. As to not make the same mistake twice, the Assemblies of God corporate office was contacted and an ad for "PASTOR WANTED" was listed in the AOG clergyman classifieds. The church elders selected five eligible candidates and drilled each of them mercilessly. If there were skeletons hiding in anyone's closet, the investigative committee was sure to dig them up. After all, if one's career choice is to preach the gospel, what better gig could one ask for than to pastor a church in a relatively well to do beach community? For some of these holy hillbillies, I'm sure landing this job could've been compared to leaving a cashier's position at Wal-Mart for that of a VP at Microsoft!

Julianne kept me up to date on all the activities surrounding the search for a new pastor. She informed me, that after weeks of extensive interviewing, the board members, certain the Holy Spirit had guided them in arriving at their decision, announced who they considered was the right man for the job. Now it was left up to the membership to vote on whether or not they agreed with the choice of their appointed officials.

Before the voting was to take place and the final decision be made, naturally the congregation had to meet the candidate. The church was all abuzz with sparks of anticipation when a decision was made to have the prospective pastor spend a three-day weekend at the church in order to get acquainted with the various ministries, from the youth group, to the ladies' fellowship. He would be criticized and scrutinized as he tried to win the membership's approval by jumping through holy hoops of fire. Activities scheduled for his audition would be to perform Sunday morning service, preach a message (of course from God) and teach Sunday school. He would have the opportunity to mingle with the members during a potluck dinner, and then be placed before the firing squad to answer a blitz of endless questions.

It was on the Saturday afternoon during the three-day meet the pastor weekend when Julianne called me from the church.

"John!" she said with a hint of excitement in her voice, "Guess what town the new pastor's from?"

NEW FACE, SAME MESSAGE

I don't know what led me to give Julianne the answer I did, but without pausing I replied as if I were absolutely certain, "College Point!"

Astonished I knew the answer to her question, she asked, "Who told you?"

"Nobody," I said, "I just had a feeling!"

Julianne went on to quiz me again, "John, you'll never guess whose cousin he is!"

I swear I have no notion at all as to why I responded like I did, but without batting an eyelash, I said confidently, "Johnny Samba, my old bass player!"

"Who told you?" she asked, "How could you possibly know that?"

I didn't understand it, but I wasn't the least bit surprised, when Julianne told me my guess was right. For some strange reason I just knew. Upon learning the new pastor was my old buddy's cousin, I thought it might be interesting to meet him. It was the first time I had stepped foot into the church in quite some time. Most of the old familiar faces welcomed me with open arms, kisses and hugs, pleading with me to come back. A couple of my ex-brothers in Christ totally ignored me. One of them actually snickered, "What's he doing here?" I maintain friendships with many people who have different religious preferences than mine, so why my presence should have irritated them was inexplicable.

It was easy picking out the potential new guy. He had the typical Pentecostal look, from his neatly parted haircut down to his conservative shoes. He appeared to be a little stiff, all dressed up in a neck tie and navy blue blazer, while juggling his paper plate full of home made goodies and cup of fruit juice. God knows how awkward he must have felt having to chat with all those strangers, knowing all the while he was being dissected and analyzed like a frog in a high school science lab. His face was vaguely familiar; after all it's been well over forty years since we'd crossed paths. I introduced myself and we then engaged in a friendly twenty-minute conversation about his cousin John and the old neighborhood. We discovered that we attended the same grammar school, good old St. Fidelis; we knew the same nuns, the same priests, the same neighborhood families and much of the same small town gossip. Mick (of Mick and Faith), who was one of the present board members of the church, and still considered me a friend, was explaining to my old schoolmate how I excommunicated myself from the church. I found it somewhat disconcerting how he didn't even inquire as to why I split. Wasn't he in the salvation business? I was hoping he would have said something, but I guess it was just bad timing. He had enough on his mind. He needed a job.

Even though Julianne wasn't totally sold on him at the end of the weekend tryouts, Phillip Colonna from College Point was voted in as new Pastor of Full Gospel Church of Island Terrace. Meeting and talking with him certainly proved this is indeed a small world. What were the chances of someone who was related to an old friend of mine, who probably passed me in the halls a thousand times in my old grammar school and lived just blocks away, becoming the pastor of the same church I left after attending for twenty years? Nothing in this world happens by coincidence. I was anxious to learn how it was all going to fit together.

CONFIRMATION OR PAYBACK?

When I was attending Full Gospel Church, I developed a friendship with a woman in the congregation named Jennifer. Jennifer was a family psychologist, a little eccentric I must admit, and probably for that reason alone we hit it off. We shared some inside jokes and had an unspoken understanding of each other. "Doctor," I would call out from across the church when I saw her walk in, "It's time for our session!" She would always crack up hysterically then humor me with a witty comeback.

"Your husband is nuts!" she would tell Julianne, "But you've got to love him!"

Julianne would roll her eyes and with an artificial grin respond, "He's a real riot!"

During the years I'd known Jennifer, her marriage had fallen apart and she'd gotten a divorce. Divorce was frowned upon by the church, so it wasn't an easy thing for her to do. She found her church family to be very consoling during that troubled time. Sometime later she began dating a man named Tristan. He was also a psychologist, as well as an ex-pastor of a Manhattan Christian church. Jennifer started bringing him to church with her on Sunday mornings and they eventually got married. I never got a chance to really know the new man in her life, because by that time, I had left the church.

On an occasional Sunday, Julianne would get home from service and say, "You should have been there this morning, Jennifer's husband Tristan preached and he was really good!"

"That's nice!" I'd remark, seemingly unimpressed.

Church had become an integral part of Jennifer's life and for a while she even led the women's ministry. I was glad to hear she was with a man with whom she shared common interests. She was a good person and she certainly deserved to be happy. One of the things I missed by leaving the church was the chance to talk and joke around with Jennifer every so often.

During the 2002 Memorial Day weekend, Julianne's church was having a yard sale in their parking lot. Our friend Sue was the person responsible for getting such events off the ground and Julianne thought it might be nice if we gave her a little support. It was a beautiful day; we had nothing better to do, so we went. While Julianne got right to work lending a hand, I milled about taking a gander at all the junk people were trying to unload. While looking through some old books, I looked up and to my surprise came face to face with Jennifer.

"Johnny! How the hell are you my friend!" she called out.

I told her how good it was to see her, then she asked me out of genuine concern, "So, what have you been up to?"

I told her why I had left the church and all about the spiritual maze I'd been trying to find my way through. She was grinning from ear to ear and it looked as if she was going to burst if she couldn't tell me what she was eager to say. I let her speak.

"My God!" she said excitedly, "You sound just like my husband! He thinks just like you do!"

"I thought he was preaching here from time to time," I questioned, "Julianne told me he's a wonderful preacher!"

Jennifer laughed and answered my question by saying, "Yeah, he's good at it, but he's been re-thinking everything. When the pastor asked him to preach, he felt bad turning him down, so he tried sneaking in some new ideas, whether the congregation picked up on it, who knows?"

She picked up a teapot from a vendor's table, held it up for me to see and sniggered, "What do you think Johnny? Is it worth three bucks? You have to come over one night and talk to him. The two of you guys will love each other!"

Running into Jennifer ignited a spark in me and reinforced my feelings about the synchronicity of the universe. The idea of talking to Tristan excited me. I couldn't help but speculate, that if Julianne loved his preaching so much, maybe she would eventually join in our discussions and he'd be instrumental in broadening her spiritual perspective, then possibly putting Julianne and I back on the same page.

A few weeks later, I went over to Jennifer and Tristan's place for what was the first of several get-togethers. The two of them had since left the church, so we had lots to talk about. We conversed until two in the morning engrossed in the most exhilarating discussions about religion, mythology and the church. It was encouraging to be able to fellowship with people who I felt believed what I believed. I was anxious to tell Julianne what Tristan and I had spoken about, and when I did, she was unmoved. As far as she was concerned, he was as lost as I was.

Many times I've had to accompany Julianne to parties or occasions affiliated with her circle of church friends and now it was payback time. Jennifer had sent us an invitation to attend a dinner party at her house to celebrate her birthday. Julianne wasn't the least bit thrilled about having to be there, but after just a little resistance, and knowing our friend Sue was also invited, she agreed to go.

It was a nice little gathering of close friends and family. The guests were all seated around the dining room table for a buffet dinner and it didn't take very long before almost everybody was on their way to getting smashed. The assortment of alcoholic beverage was plentiful. Julianne always seemed to know her limit and we could usually depend on her to be the designated driver. God knows we needed her that night.

With dinner and dessert out of the way, Tristan and I stood in the kitchen slurring our words making our best attempts at getting spiritually philosophical, while Sue hunted the cabinets for more Vodka. Jennifer was completely out of her head, as she seemed to be skating about from room to room, flaunting herself most suggestively.

I was in the middle of a drunken dissertation about the misconceptions in the Bible, when the night's hostess comes crashing into my side, causing me to spill my drink, and whispers into my ear, "Right now in my mind I'm making love to you!" The whole scene was quite bizarre. Tristan made his way into the living room where he made an inebriated attempt at giving a lesson in the Gnostic gospels to Julianne. Even in my intoxicated state I could read Julianne's face, it said, "Get me the hell out of here!"

It was a crazy night resulting with me waking up the next morning with one of the worst hangovers I'd ever had.

"You're an idiot!" Julianne chided, reminding me of the toxic combination of drinks I allowed to enter my bloodstream on the previous evening.

"You were drinking a water glass full of Anisette! What were you thinking?" she asked curiously and unsympathetically, as the thought of the syrupy sweet cordial nauseated me.

Once again it was payback time. Still hung over and deathly sick to my stomach, I had to accompany Julianne, Sue, Sue's mother and our friend Linda to a daytime New York Mets' baseball game that morning.

"What in the world went on last night?" Sue asked, while wondering if what she saw and heard the night before really happened.

"Shut up Sue!" I moaned as I reluctantly lowered myself into the passenger seat of her Toyota, "I don't want to talk about it!"

Not only did Tristan, Jennifer and I lose all credibility with Julianne, I had to sit through nine innings of the most boring game in the world, feeling like at any minute I was going to throw up. I hated baseball!

BONNIE'S BABY

There had to be a reason why Bonnie kept showing up in my life. The last time we corresponded I learned her trip to the Ukraine was cut short by tragedy and her good intentions of adopting a baby, which she was so certain was due to God's intervening, was not going to happen. Because of my cynical nature, I was thinking how could an undertaking like the one Bonnie set out to accomplish be of God, if it failed so miserably? When I sat down to check my e-mail one evening, I was curiously surprised to see there was one from my unaffordable ex-marriage counselor. I opened the mail to find she wrote me a letter of great length describing her recent trip to the Ukraine. She didn't abandon the idea of adopting a baby after all. In a heartwarming account she informed us about her latest adventures in what she depicted as the poorest disease-ridden spot on the planet. Her and her saintly husband Kevin traveled from orphanage to orphanage searching for the child who their instincts would tell them was the one. After visiting four orphanages, their hearts breaking for every child they saw, they felt their efforts were in vain because they knew they still hadn't found the child they were destined to meet. When both Bonnie and her husband got taken ill with dysentery and who knows what else, they surrendered. "Maybe this whole thing wasn't of God!" Bonnie sadly thought, "Maybe it's just my own wishful thinking and we made a mistake coming here!"

They informed their travel guide of their decision to give up the search and head back to the states. With all their belongings packed and their minds made up they were going home empty-handed, the travel guide told them she had to make one more stop at an orphanage near Chernobyl. Since they were at the mercy of the driver, what choice did they have

457 ‣

but to accompany her? As their weary legs dragged them into the lobby of the orphanage, they were greeted by the excited exclamations of the facility's director who thought there was a striking resemblance between a particular orphan and Bonnie's husband. As soon as Bonnie and Kevin saw the two-year old boy, they knew instantly their search was over. Although they made the decision to adopt the child, the law required they return to the US empty-handed. Weeks later, after all the necessary paperwork was complete, they were permitted to return to the Ukraine to claim him. Maybe God had His hand in this affair all the while. Maybe we become more appreciative when we have to work harder for something. Maybe our determination is God working inside us. Maybe, maybe, maybe!

Because of the extreme poverty in the Ukraine, it was mandatory for would-be parents to donate needed items to the orphanage each time they visited. Bonnie was told to bring one hundred pairs of baby shoes on her return trip. In her letter she asked if Julianne and I could help in any way. We put the word out. Julianne made an appeal to her fellow churchgoers and I asked some people on my route. In a matter of a few days we collected seventy-five pairs of shoes. I wrote Bonnie to tell her the news and she was overjoyed. One night after work we met up outside her office building where I delivered the goods. I could see how excited she was when her eyes beheld all those shoes. She hugged me, called me an angel and told me how good it was to see me. After I loaded the shoes into her car, Bonnie told me that when she returned she was going to give Julianne and me a free session. I told her Jule and I were doing all right even though I thought some occasional tuning up couldn't hurt. Jule may have disagreed, but the truth was, we couldn't afford Bonnie.

"I don't know about Julianne, but I've got a few things I'd like to talk to you about!" I said.

Bonnie gave me a look like she knew exactly what I was going to say and before I could continue, she said, "Spiritual stuff, huh?"

"Yeah, Bonnie," I answered, "I don't know what's happened to me in the last couple of years. Everything I once believed and stood for is gone. I'm not the same!"

Bonnie gave me a big smile. "I know!" she said reassuringly, "There's an army of us out there! We'll talk when I return!"

I wasn't quite sure if I liked the sound of that statement, "an army of us." As far as I was concerned I fled from an army and wasn't about to become part of another.

PARIS, NICOLE AND THE POPE

The cushions and the pillows of the couch in our den enveloped me as I sunk down into its calming softness. After another long workday and the two glasses of cabernet I consumed with dinner, I was exhausted. My concentration level was at a minimum, so an episode of "The Simple Life" was about all I could endure. It's funny how at one time I wouldn't be caught dead wasting life's precious hours watching any of the garbage reality programming offered by the Fox network. For a short period, my kids and I made it a practice to share some quality time glued to the TV for the teenage sexploitation of "The O.C." Julianne joined us as we gathered around our modest twenty-seven inch screen, all on the edge of our seats to see who would be eliminated in the next "American Idol." I'm ashamed to say we were hooked with millions of other Americans. Sometimes I wondered if the secret to world peace was to get our enemy nations, such as Iraq and Iran, captivated on the mindless trash Americans watch on a daily basis. Get those crazy Muslims addicted to reality television and predictable sit-coms, and they won't have time to blow up buildings or set out on suicide missions!

The entire world had the opportunity to watch Paris Hilton give her boyfriend oral sex via the Internet, and overnight, the heiress of a multi-million dollar hotel empire got her very own weekly program. The sickest thing is that I went from being such a harsh critic of celebrities such as Paris and Nicole, calling them everything from spoiled-rotten young sluts to no-talent airheads, to becoming one of their fans! I found them fascinating and funny. Who knows, maybe when all is said and done, I am just a simple idiot!

So one evening as I was mindlessly allowing Paris and Nicole to entertain me, Julianne dumped a basket of warm, just-out-of-the-dryer clothes onto the couch beside me. "John," she asked sweetly, as the blondes stole her attention for a moment, "Could you, uh, please fold these for me while you're watching?" So there I sat, a fifty-two year old man, who's usually driven by his quest for spiritual enlightenment, totally engrossed in "The Simple Life" as I folded pair after pair of my daughters' thong panties. "What the heck were they thinking when they bought these?"I wondered, as the cameras attempted to reveal as much as Paris Hilton's flesh as the FCC permitted.

It was April 2005, the week of Pope John Paul's death, and not since JFK's assassination do I remember a world event having such extensive news coverage. No matter where I tuned into, I could not escape the papal news. I'm not a fan of Catholicism. The more I delved into its history, the more enlightened I became on how the organization has been a disservice to its members, a stumbling block to attaining any degree of spiritual growth. One afternoon, during the period when I was obsessed with Torah teaching and the Hebrew roots of Christianity, I got into a heated discussion with my sister Virginia over some of our religious differences. Virginia had been studying very hard to earn herself a degree in Theology, so needless to say, she was a wealth of information and therefore much more knowledgeable in these matters than I was. I tried to explain my feelings that theology and spirituality had nothing to do with each other and then I went into my Catholic-bashing song and dance. Virginia was losing her patience with me and I was losing mine with her. Our voices got louder as we tried to drown out each other's opinions.

She kept repeating and repeating, almost as if to keep from hearing me, "Read Pope John the twenty-third's letters to the Ecumenical Council! Read Pope John XXIII's letters to the Ecumenical Council..."

I couldn't take it any more, so out of sheer frustration, I retorted by screaming, "Fuck the Pope and his Ecumenical Council! Why don't you just read the Old Testament?"

Immediately I realized I screwed up when she went storming out of my home, slamming the front door behind her. I heard the angry tone in my voice as I screamed appropriate scripture verses at her, giving them the same effect as hurtful obscenities. As she drove off I knew I had to apologize at once. Not a very good job of witnessing if I must say so myself! I called her and asked her forgiveness. As much as we disagreed, we knew we still loved each other. She forgave me!

Now back to the Pope! He seemed like a pretty nice guy and I felt bad that he died, but I felt worse about the way he had to live his last few months. The poor old fellow could hardly walk and barely speak. His roadies had him propped up behind some window high above the crowds. He was barely able to wave his arms and in a desperate attempt to please his loyal followers, he made a labored sign of the cross. I wouldn't have been the least bit shocked if I later found out he was wired up like a marionette while some ambitious cardinals pulled the strings.

All week long the networks ran programming about the life of John Paul and there's no questioning that he was indeed a very brilliant man, able to speak twelve languages fluently. He was known as a great communicator and underneath those crazy hats his mind must have been a storehouse of knowledge. This is what confused me. How could someone with such vast intelligence really have believed he was the Vicar of Christ on earth and try to uphold myths and traditions which are not even scriptural? For example, where does the Vatican come up with the notion that priests cannot marry? By twisting the words of Paul in the New Testament, that's how! It's unfortunate, but due to the archaic thinking of this religion's hierarchy, the priesthood has become a haven for gay men and child molesters. Furthermore, how could any of those pontifical people take themselves the least bit seriously adorned in those stupid looking hats? Vatican City along with all its gold, marble and splendor, is a far cry from the ways of Jesus, the central figure of the faith. Is it all just politics and big business disguised in the pomp and circumstance of religion? I wonder if in the privacy of the Pope's chambers, he may have tuned into an episode of "The Simple Life" now and then.

If there was a television turned on in anyone's household, watching the images coming out of Rome couldn't be avoided. Hundreds of thousands of people flocked to the "Holy City" (what a misnomer that is) and waited for days just to get a glimpse of a dead man. As I watched the news footage, the numbers of people crowding into the Italian city amazed me. It was sad to watch John Paul deteriorate during the last few months of his life, but for me it was much sadder to see so many blind people bound by the chains of a misleading religion and assuming even for a second, John

Paul was anything more than a mere misguided mortal.

As of this writing, the cardinals from the world over had gathered to elect a new Pope. Just like the words of Pete Townsend's anthem "We Won't Get Fooled Again," "*Meet the new boss, the same as the old boss...*" For almost two thousand years, nothing has changed, except maybe meatless Fridays, and the renouncing of the patron saint of travel, Christopher. What made anyone think things were going to change now?

THE GOSPEL ACCORDING TO DAD

One rare and memorable afternoon around the time just before my car accident, before the thought of writing this book even occurred to me, I was able to take some time off from my busy schedule to join my dad for lunch at a local diner. Because it's become the topic I enjoyed talking about the most, the conversation turned to one of religion and spirituality. Surprisingly, dad listened attentively as I rattled off bits and pieces of my newfound knowledge. I tried to gently point out how guilt, obligation and tradition make up the glue holding the Roman Catholic institution together. I don't believe my dad's ever read through the Bible, yet he strongly professed the following:

1. The Bible is all interpretation
2. Somewhere in the New Testament it clearly states, "Everything in moderation!" and
3. Loving your fellow man is the key!

If I were sitting in that diner with him today, I'd probably agree with almost everything he said, but at that time, I was quite dogmatic and on a mission. Whenever dad half-listened to me run through what little Bible knowledge I had (he was always a much better talker than a listener), he would tell me how he'd love to set up a debate between me and whoever he considered a Bible expert, such as our dearly departed friend Father Ghirlando, or the current pastor of his parish. For some strange reason, he found what I had to say interesting, admitted that he disagreed with most of Catholic doctrine, but just like most churchgoers, could not break away. I really could never figure out if he stayed just to keep my mom happy or because he'd been so conditioned, the routine has just become second nature, almost like breathing. It's much easier to listen and accept what the priest propagates week after week than to explore all the information that's readily available in the local library and come to your own conclusions. To paraphrase Scripture, I told my dad we were instructed to listen to no man and be led by the Spirit. Well much to my surprise, this time my dad did not suggest I debate the neighborhood scholars, instead he suggested I put all my thoughts and feelings down on paper and write a book. "People are very interested in these kinds of ideas!" he said encouragingly, "You're good with words, you really should do it!"

Even though my Bible expertise is infinitesimal, compared to my dad's understanding of Scripture, I seemed like a genius. So it was there in that very diner when my dear old dad encouraged me to take on the challenge of writing this book. From the moment I first put ink to paper well over five years ago, I'd seen my direction change. I can't remember who said it or where I read it, but the following words ring true, "*Great doubt, great awakening. Some doubt, some awakening. No doubt, no awakening.*"

A QUICK ANALOGY

In the very same way the demise of the oil and drug conglomerates could occur, should safe, sensible alternatives and natural remedies be introduced to the world, so too, would the walls of religious institution come crashing down should human beings get the incentive to search within to uncover truth and peace. Find yourself and chances are you will then find God. Spiritual awakening could eventually result in the extinction of mainstream organized religions.

IN RETROSPECT

Every so often I would think about my grandmother (still do) and the words she spoke to me just before her spirit left its earthly vessel. With ninety-six years of life experience showing in her eyes she sadly said, "Johnny, life is too short!"

There I was in my early fifties with retirement less than three years away and I was wondering where did the time go? Our children had all grown into young adults and I asked myself over and over again if I did the very best I could in raising them. Were their attitudes towards life a direct result of any mistakes I'd made? Had the inconsistencies in our seesaw marriage and the difference in opinions Julianne and I had towards child rearing had any effect on shaping their characters? Are we born with our personalities or do they gradually develop through the influence of our parents' behavior? I love all three of my kids very much and each of them have very different and unique personalities. I never surmised that any of us were here by our own choice. So in the same way I believe God provided all that is necessary to live satisfying and rewarding lives, I also want to be a good provider for my family. I can only hope and pray my words and actions did not and will not hinder them from achieving their goals and dreams.

When I was a youngster growing up in College Point, Leo and Grace Veccione along with their three children, Peter, Charles and Lynnette, were our next-door neighbors. Leo was a truly nice guy but he really loved to lay the bullshit on thick! He led people to believe he was a pharmacist when what he really did was sell convalescent aids in a neighborhood pharmacy.

Talking to Leo was always a game of "can you top this?" He lived vicariously through his doctor, lawyer and the professional acquaintances who he claimed were his "good friends." If you knew a guy who had five million in the bank, he knew someone with eight! I guess Mr. V needed people to think he was more than who he was, which was a shame because he was basically a really nice man.

One summer afternoon he treated a bunch of us kids to Jahn's, a very popular old-fashioned ice cream parlor. All the selections on the Jahn's dessert menu were listed by names such as "The Kitchen Sink" or "The Jim Dandy." Mr. V, assuming we were all just a bunch of gullible impressionable kids, told us in order to get a job in a Jahn's one was required to graduate from a special "Ice Cream School" and earn a degree! He was really shoveling it on that afternoon, trying to get us to swallow the idea, being a soda jerk or a waitress in an ice cream shop was comparable to being a nuclear physicist! As young and stupid as I may have been, I knew he was talking out of his ass. Raised to respect my elders, I kept it to myself.

Right from the time Peter, Charles (never Charlie or Chuck) and Lynnette were in diapers, Leo and Grace began programming their kids by telling them over and over again they were going to become professionals. I wasn't so sure if it was for the benefit of the kids or the false pride of the parents but by the time they started grade school, they believed it. "My son the doctor, my son the lawyer..." was how they were introduced. They saw to it their children socialized with the children of doctors and lawyers as often as they could. The Veccione kids were nurtured to financially succeed and it worked! Peter became a very wealthy plastic surgeon in an affluent New Jersey neighborhood. Charles turned out to be a very successful attorney. Lynnette opened up a dance studio, and then married a multi-millionaire who was old enough to be her grandfather. He died and left it all to Lynnette! Leo and Grace's "Groomed for Greatness" plan may have appeared to work out wonderfully, but just how much of a happy and fulfilling life each of them led is anybody's guess.

When Christiann told Julianne and me she wanted to go away to college to study fashion design, we thought, "Oh no, why not dentistry instead?" My dad supported my rock and roll dreams, but all of his encouragement and a college degree landed me in the driver's seat of a UPS truck for twenty-five years! It's an honest job but it sure couldn't meet the expense of putting three kids through college. Life is hard enough these days and having to pay off school loans equal to a mortgage was the last thing I wanted my kids to deal with. We were so afraid Christiann was going to end up in major debt and come out of school working as a clerk in the women's wear department of Bloomingdale's. She surprised us, however, and landed a good job as an associate designer for a well-known company. Samantha and Matthew, on the other hand, could possibly have benefited from the Veccione technique of pre-determining your child's career choice. Sam, so unsure of what she wanted to do with her life, was unhappily attending college with the hopes of finding out. Matthew was (and still remains) convinced he had been destined for fame and fortune by playing drums in a rock band! Sounds way too familiar! Like any teenager with rock and roll blood in his veins, Matt refused to take advantage of my wisdom or listen to the advice I'd acquired through experience.

My son is so much like me it's scary. His obsession with music and his rebellious streak make him a chip off the old block. I regret I didn't have a better relationship with him through the years, but I do have my reasons or at least bad excuses. Firstly, I blame it on the increasingly long hours of my job. Too much was left up to Julianne because of how late I got home every night. He was left to do a lot on his own without the companionship of his dad. I also blame it on my non-confrontational personality. I never really put my foot down to defend him when I felt he was right, only to try and keep the peace with his mom. I also never put my foot down when he was wrong, which didn't help to keep the peace between Julianne and me. Matt's occasional disrespect, especially with Julianne, got out of control and I didn't know how to stop it. I knew he was a great kid and I needed to be able to tell him. I picked up his high school yearbook and as I sat alone reading what his fellow classmates had to say about him, I got all choked up. He was genuinely loved and admired by all who know him. If there's one thing I needed to do, it was to bond with my son. If there's one thing Matthew needed to do, it was to let his mother know he loved her. I wrote a song few years ago with these words: "*Every generation seems to criticize its youth, I think it's only jealousy they feel. Burdened by the myths of who they think they have to be, what's forbidden never loses its appeal.*" Life and learning, young and old, it's a vicious cycle.

No matter what my children become, no matter what levels of success they achieve, the one thing I hope for is that they recognize their own spirituality. My desire is for each of them to discover there is much more to this life than the physical. My hopes are for each of them to understand the importance of loving themselves, of living in harmony with nature and to love and accept all people for who they are. I want them to recognize that each and every soul, along with every living thing, is connected through the Spirit of God, the Source of all, and by being connected to that Source nothing is impossible.

I don't know if it's because I've reached a time in my life, the mid fifties, or because I'd been enlightened to things it took me fifty years to realize, but for no apparent reason my thoughts drift back to a time that often seems like centuries ago. I've been able to time travel back to an era before the rise of shopping malls and mega-stores; back to a time before the Internet, when our lives included a cast of regular characters who, in my eyes, were like part of the family. The following list includes the names of all the people who visited our house on a regular basis: Carl the egg man, Murray the man who waxed the floors, Tony the dry cleaner, Chuck the mailman, the nameless Dugan's bread and breakfast treats man, and Vito the ice cream man. I could set my watch by Vito. Every weekday through spring, summer and early fall, like clockwork, Vito made his way down our street ringing his bells at three-thirty. Storm doors would bust open, as all the kids on the block would come running towards the white spotless truck screaming at the top of their lungs, "Vito! Wait!" as if he held a magic spell over them. Vito could have been my grandfather. He moved slow, had thinning soft wavy gray hair and always smiled. I remember always being fascinated by the change contraption he wore on his belt. Without looking he would tap the keys on the silver cylinders and out would slide the correct number of dimes, nickels or quarters producing exact change. As the neighborhood developed, other ice cream vendors tried to muscle in on Vito's territory. In the course of an afternoon, the Good Humor man, the Bungalow Bar man, Mister Softee and Freezer Fresh all took their turns cruising up and down our street competing for Vito's business. Even though the Good Humor man offered to give us rides on his truck in spite of the signs that read, "Absolutely No Riders," we remained loyal to Vito.

Before the age of the mall and the monster-sized supermarkets, there were the local mom and pop convenience stores. We were walking distance from Schwab's delicatessen, where old man Schwab and his ancient wife made a living selling sliced cold cuts, penny candy, newspapers and cigarettes. There were no scanners, adding machines or fancy cash registers. Mr. Schwab totaled all our items with his pencil right on our paper bag. If we didn't have the cash, he'd let us run a tab. With the same chewed up pencil he'd scribble our names down on a piece of scrap paper, make a note of how much we owed him and scotch taped it to the wall beside the counter. When we had the money, we paid him.

My folks never bought their meats from a grocery store. Every Saturday morning, my sister and I took a ride with mom and dad to Tony the butcher in Astoria. As we stood upon the sawdust covered floor, staring at the different cuts of meats in the showcase, getting grossed out by the sight of liver, Tony would offer us slices of bologna by dangling them over our heads. Like baby birds looking up to their mother for nourishment, we always reached up, accepted and ate. It was part of the weekly ritual.

Another regular in our lives was Charlie Weidel. He owned the shoe store in town, selling only quality products such as Buster Brown, Keds, PF Flyers, and Friedman. Long before the rise of Fayva, Payless and the plastic shoe, the shoe-storeowner got the same respect as a doctor. He was a professional who knew precisely how to measure our feet and be sure we were getting the proper size with just the right amount of room for growth!

Way back when in those days of innocence, we were ruled by tradition, routine or habit. Every Sunday morning found us standing, kneeling and genuflecting for an hour at the nine o'clock Mass, then taking a number and standing on line at Zach's bakery. When we got home from church, we'd all sit around the table as a family, share the Sunday newspaper and nosh on assorted buns, crullers and jelly donuts, while mom got the meatballs and sauce started for Sunday dinner. Our weekly obligation to attend Mass was complete. God checked our names off in His roll book and once again we were in good standing, ready to face another week. Yes, we were a good Catholic family, revering the words God, Jesus, Mary and Joseph and abhorring words like fuck and shit, completely oblivious to the fact, every syllable of the aforementioned names and expressions, were fashioned by man.

I grew up in an era when there was nothing better than going to the local record store and buying a new LP. There was such great joy in sliding the record out of its jacket, placing it on the turntable and hearing the crackle of the needle touching down onto the vinyl. As the music played, I held onto the album cover as if it was a sacred scroll. I read every liner note, every song lyric and studied every square inch of artwork. It was the era before microwave ovens, cell phones, cable T.V., computers, CD and DVD players were household words. When I got older and these newfangled items were introduced to the world, I tried my very best to hold out from owning them. Microwave cooking just didn't seem safe and natural to me. Cable programming would only result in my kids wasting more hours glued to a television set. The idea that a cell phone was meant only for emergencies turned out to be the greatest ploy of the telecommunications industry. Everybody's spending big money by talking, sending text messages and saying absolutely nothing!

No different than most Americans, I became a victim to technology. I own a microwave. I pay for cable. There are three working computers in my home with Internet access and we are a household of five cell phones. The latest addition to the list of society controlling gadgets to enter our lives was the I-Pod. This miniature hi-tech invention can store up to ten thousand songs in its memory and almost every high school and college student, including my own, has one permanently attached to his or her ear. No matter where it is I go these days, it's almost impossible to spot someone who's not wearing a headset, either yapping into the mouthpiece of a cell phone or bopping his head to the sound of I-tunes. In order to hear the voice of God, connect to our spiritual Source, or whatever one desires to call it, perhaps the phones and the music should be turned off. Be still and listen for it in the beautiful silence.

COME OUT OF THE BOX MY PEOPLE

Most of my life, thanks to Catholicism and Pentecostalism, I had such a limited understanding of the nature of God. Could He really be the tyrant they made Him out to be, sitting upon His heavenly thrown, demanding the blood sacrifice of His very own son as payment for our sins? Could He be the sadist who took pleasure in watching the walls come tumbling down to crush thousands of people; does He send plagues and cause earthquakes? Or did He just love us so much, and in order to prove it, He became one of us and allowed Himself to be crucified and take the fall for all of humanity? We attribute the soul-staining blemish we call sin, to the lurking of Satan and his legion of fallen angels, who will do everything in their limited power to tempt us, snatch us away from God and drag us into the eternal fires of hell. So indirectly we can say God Himself, since He created the angels, created the very evil that lures us into a sinful life. I can't help but feel that somehow, somewhere along the evolving course of civilization, a "mind virus" has infected humanity, contaminating our thought processes for generations. I seriously believe we've got it all wrong! Maybe my old church pals were right; I'm nuts and my salvation is in jeopardy. Maybe Artie and Sara were right and I'd gone off the deep end from reading too many thought provoking secular books! Not until the day when Pastor Ted's antics pushed me over the edge, did I truly begin seeking something deeper than the emotional fluff of a Sunday service. With my eyes shut tight and my head bowed down, I tried to get my thoughts to connect with My Maker, pleading for His divine direction. If you don't question, you don't grow! If the physical Jesus/Yehshua were walking about this planet today, preaching the message he preached two thousand years ago, he'd probably be labeled a "New Age" teacher and would most likely be silenced by the same people who fill the pews of Christian churches. When people hear new ideas they become threatened and uncomfortable, and as a result, have the need to put labels on them. The ideas I've come to embrace are not new. The very same concepts found in the Tao, dating 2500 years ago, are the same concepts Jesus taught five-hundred years later. Labels divide people; therefore, being separate from each other we are separating ourselves from God. When I was first able to let go of the concept of God I carried with me for so many years, I finally understood what the verse "The truth shall set you free" meant. At last I was free from tradition, ritual, guilt, obligation and all the myths and lies of religion. Sometimes it's a scary, lonely, insecure feeling to climb out of the box and acknowledge new visions so opposed to the teachings of the mainstream churches. Even though my spirit felt energized and alive after discovering this new freedom, my superstitious conditioning left me second-guessing and praying unceasingly for God to restore the beliefs I once held, "If it be Your will, Father, bring me back…" My prayers resulted in me deviating further from the box.

I traveled the causeway of superstition and guilt, better known as Catholicism. I exited onto the Born Again Pentecostal Bypass of self-righteousness, only to detour by way of the historical Hebrew Roots Highway, until I ventured down a fork in the road that brought me to the realization God is an all-encompassing divine Source of energy, with both a male and female nature, to which everything in the universe is connected. Each new revelation brought along with it much excitement and the burning desire to share it with others. I knew I had to be careful about with who I chose to disclose these new developments because most people were writing me off as nuts.

Abigail was another discontented member of Full Gospel Christianity. We met in the church years ago and probably because of our similar easy-going personalities, we hit it off. I had a way of making her laugh and she had a way of making me feel loved. Abigail's a widow with five kids who had been doing her best to keep it together. Her husband Roy became grossly overweight and his heart eventually gave out. She, being such a petite and fragile little thing, I often wondered how in the world the two of them ever connected to produce children. Only proves the theory "when there's a will there's a way!" When I started going through my spiritual changes, I felt compelled to talk to Abigail. She was attentive, most receptive to whatever I had to say and looked forward to any opportunity for us to get together. Whether it was while we walked along the boardwalk or had coffee at the diner, Abigail allowed me to monopolize our conversations with my unconventional way of thinking. The day I became perceptive to God's nature possessing both male and female characteristics, I couldn't wait to talk about it with Abigail. Unlike the male chauvinistic, lightning bolt tossing, pestilence loving God we were raised to know and fear, I discovered a nurturing, loving Creator of abundance and perfection. She asked me to drop by for coffee one evening knowing her oldest son Kevin would be around, who she thought would be very interested in what I had to say. I tried my very best to simply explain what I believed what "being created in God's image" meant. I delicately described how God is both male and female in nature, and how in two separate beings humans possess the very same distinct natures. Kevin had a very difficult time in grasping what I was trying to convey. Keep in mind, Kevin was no kid. He was a recently married young adult in his late twenties. He nervously swung his arms and shook his clean-shaven head. Taking long drags from an endless chain of cigarettes, confusion his only facial expression, he mumbled, "No fucking way man! I was taught God is a dude! Now you're trying to tell me He has tits AND a dick!"

From man's earliest attempts at defining the persona of God, he'd been describing the supernatural Source of all to think and act like a human. I knew it was time to finish my coffee, head home and save my talk with Abigail for another day.

THE JESUS DILEMMA

Whenever I tried to have an intellectual conversation with my Christian friends about God, creation, and man's place in the universe, I came up against the usual responses. If I questioned something I didn't feel represented a loving God, the comeback line was always, "God's ways are not man's ways...." When I asked why people didn't see results to prayer, the standard comeback was, "He answers all prayers, sometimes He just says no!" Another response to why many prayers don't come to fruition was because, "It's not His will!"

I don't know if it's because Christians have this uncanny ability to stop using their God-given brains or if it's because they're not able to fully let go of the superstitions of Catholicism. Encapsulating God by putting Him into a neat little box with limitations and rules seems to make most people a little more secure about the possibilities of getting into heaven. God fearing people have no problem acknowledging God is indeed everywhere, but when I dare to mention His presence is in every molecule, every grain of sand, every breath of air and that His love and power is so readily available and easily accessible, I'm looked upon as a new-age whack-o. Not until we are able to recognize that all things in the universe, including man, were designed to work together in harmony, will we begin to fully experience the awesome nature of God.

I have come to an understanding, no language known to man has been able to fully describe or clearly define the Creator and His limitless possibilities. The earliest Hebrew inscriptions would not even attempt to put God's name in writing, as they would leave the space blank. The

Scriptures relate an account of God instructing Moses to address Him as Yahweh, which we are taught, translates to "I am." Doesn't that simple statement imply how God is the "Eternal Present," existing in every form of his creation? Jesus taught that in order for us to love God we must love our neighbor. Doesn't that suggest God is undeniably part of every human being or every human being is part of God? In the same way, when Jesus commented, "When you see me, you see the Father," couldn't that have been His way of illustrating how the spirit of God dwells in each of us? Jesus the man fully recognized the living Spirit of God in him one hundred percent. I believe, although man has not yet been able to attain that fullness in spirit, we each have the potential. Someday, because attaining fullness in Spirit is His intention, I am fairly certain it will be achieved. An often-used analogy, attempting to illuminate our relationship to God, suggests we envision God as the ocean and each of us is but a thimble-full of that same ocean water. We could never attain to be the ocean, but would always be part of it.

When Christians quote Jesus as saying, "I have come so that you may have life and have it more abundantly," isn't it possible what He was proposing was for us to tap into the same Divine Spirit that lived in Him, and life would present us with endless possibilities?" When Jesus made the claim, "You too will perform works even greater than these," it is evident to me what He meant was, achieve God-realization and performing miracles could be a ordinary occurrence. His purpose was to raise our consciousness level, diminish our egos, take away our fears, put an end to judgment, and to basically reverse our way of thinking. By no means would I ever contemplate downsizing the role of Jesus in human history, He was the single most influential human being who has ever graced planet earth. Two thousand years ago, however, even His disciples looked upon Him as a political rebel. Initially failing to comprehend His true purpose, they depicted Jesus as someone who would free the Jews from Roman oppression. Anyone, however, who had the audacity to make the "blasphemous" claims Jesus made, and speaking out against the hierarchy, as He did, was surely going to be eliminated, thus His horrific crucifixion. Jesus taught about the importance of living in the Spirit, something He was positively certain about, and something He wanted to make mankind certain about. Gandhi, Buddha and the mystical priests who lived prior to Jesus' birth, also taught the same principles. Until we awaken to Spirit, the higher level of consciousness, we are truly asleep. One afternoon while discussing Christianity with one of my son's friends, he expressed how he was beginning to have doubts about its claims. "When a preacher told me even Gandhi was going to hell," he said without hesitation, "I realized I didn't want to serve that kind of God!"

Whenever I set my eyes upon any part of creation, I see God and His infinite unconditional love. The perfection of the cosmos leaves me in constant awe of my Creator. The stars have never left their place in the heavens. The sun has risen and set for what scientists believe to be millions upon millions of years. Creation is continuous…it is constant… it is never-ending and every unique human being plays a part in a divine unexplainable plan. My desire is to live up to my potential by learning how to keep in constant connection with His energy and His love. It's all around us; we just have to tap in. It is only by way of our foolish pride, our ego, that we separate ourselves from Him. The saying "Pride comes before a fall" speaks volumes. A man's pride gives him a false feeling of independence. It makes him believe he is able to accomplish most things on his own. If the plan of creation is for all things to work in harmony, then it only makes sense, pride will separate man from God along with the tremendous promises that exist for us. Simply put, pride cuts one off from the Source.

I was steadfast for over twenty years in attending church and listening to the many twists on "God's Word." I'd socialized with fellow Christians and established what I thought were some close friendships. When circumstances drew me away, some of my so-called friends snubbed me. It made me question how a denomination all about God's love can be a haven for so many arrogant, self-righteous, proud and miserable people. Our physical lives should reflect our spiritual lives and from the looks of what had been going on in the lives of so many people who have religiously attended church, including my own, something was definitely not right. Too many Pentecostals seem to direct so much of their attention to their dissatisfaction with their earthly existence and talk anxiously about being in Heaven with Jesus. I call these folks suicidal Christians. Where was this joy of the Lord they sang about? Where was this abundant life they preached? While conversing on the phone one afternoon with my old friend Randy, she was mentioning the terrible state of the school her daughter was teaching in. "Oh!" she sighed, "I truly pray Jesus is returning soon!" I'm sorry, but in my mind, that is simply a gloom and doom, defeatist attitude, implying there is no hope for humanity. Rather than trying to have a positive influence on society, pray for Jesus to hurry back and save all the Christians, before a wrathful God puts a gruesome end to His beautiful world! I am also hoping for the speedy return of Jesus, but not in the way Christians assume it's going to happen. I yearn for humanity to awaken. I long for the day when the same Spirit, once manifested through Jesus, and dwelling within the core of every man, will finally be fully recognized, a shift in consciousness will occur and the Kingdom will be established on earth once again.

Years ago, when I was immersed in the Born Again mindset, I was shooting the breeze about life, death and salvation with my friend Gino. Gino is a psychologist, and at the time, he approached spiritual matters much differently than I did. Unlike the hard sell of most unbending Pentecostals, who refuse to remove their blinders and even consider anybody else's point of view, Gino suggested the possibility that perhaps more logical explanations of the mysteries of faith do exist and are worth looking into. "Johnny," Gino gently explained, "Just maybe the crucifixion of Christ occurred as a means of teaching mankind not to fear death, that only through dying can our spirits return to God, the Source of all creation. If God is spirit and spirit is eternal, then the same spirit, which is the breath of life in each of us, is eternal. Our spirit has always been and will always be. Essentially, we never die. When these physical bodies decay and wither away (absent from the body, present with the Lord), we return to where we came from in the first place! It's like we're all part of the soup. Maybe we get to come back in another physical manifestation, maybe we don't! We'll find out when we get there, buddy!"

Although Gino's way of thinking made sense, at that point in time, it was much more comforting for me to believe the fantasy that I could actually escape death by being "raptured." Fooling myself to believe that one day Jesus would be swooping down from heaven to carry me off into the clouds of glory was encouraging. The Bible makes many references to marriage, where metaphorically speaking, Jesus, the groom, will come and take the church for His bride. The imagery of "…the two shall become one" makes perfect sense in representing an aligning of Spirit. I finally see what Gino was trying to say all those years ago.

ON A MISSION FROM GOD?

A line of Scripture I heard used so often is, "To whom much is given, much is required." I guess that could mean a number of things, but the most common explanation seems to be, whatever spiritual revelations one receives, he or she is obligated to share them. The Great Commission is to spread the gospel to the four corners of the earth because it is God's desire every man be saved. A question often asked is "What happens to someone who has not heard the gospel? Is he damned?" The standard answer to that question is, "No! He is excused!" Well then I would have to say it's probably better to remain ignorant and gain entrance to the Kingdom, than to have been exposed to the gospels, have questions and doubts, forever running the risk of being cast out! Ignorance is indeed bliss and a restless mind is torment.

The same verse could also apply to the physical, whether it is food, clothing, money or shelter. A few friends and acquaintances of ours have intentionally interrupted the comfort of their suburban lifestyles to venture out onto the mission fields in some of the world's most diseased and poverty-stricken countries, such as Haiti, Santo Domingo, and Kenya. The stories they returned with were heartbreaking. They described for us the encounters they've had with children who were on the brink of death due to starvation and malnutrition. One of my friends explained how deformity was commonplace along the streets of Santo Domingo. As rewarding as it may be for these "amateur Mother Theresas" to visit these countries, with the intention of delivering hope to these desperate souls, I'm sure it has to be greatly depressing as well. How do you tell starving children, "Jesus loves you," while listening to the hunger pangs echo from within their empty stomachs? People whose lives hold for them nothing but despair are probably open to anyone or anything representing the slightest glimmer of hope. When the interpreters translate the salvation message to these emaciated victims of circumstance, wouldn't they be thinking, "Okay, if Jesus is as wonderful as you claim He is, why are we still starving? Show us the loaves and the fishes!"

The salvation message is one of eternal life in heaven, where hunger, fear and pain are non-existent. If these unfortunate people never heard the Gospels, God's mercy would not hold them accountable and Heaven would be in their future anyway. Do the hopeful words of the mission workers, describing a future paradise, really mean anything to folks who walk the tightrope between life and death daily? A loaf of bread and a bottle of Poland Spring would probably mean a lot more to them than words about a place they can go to after they die.

Every living creature (except maybe a suicide bomber) is built with a survival mechanism. Nobody wants to die no matter how wonderful Heaven promises to be. When the weekend missionaries leave the battlefields and return to the modern conveniences of home, the hunger and famine remain. It's easy to thank God for His great blessings from the warm massaging waters of a bubbling Jacuzzi. Busboys from the over-priced New York City restaurants alone, toss food enough into the trash that could easily provide banquets for the starving people of third world countries.

How was I so fortunate, as to enter this world as someone who was born into a loving family in a country of great wealth, rather than someone who wasn't dealt as good a hand?" I have asked myself this question over and over, yet never seem to arrive at a satisfactory answer. Where's the reality? Here in the suburbs of Long Island where the roadways are jammed with forty thousand dollar luxury cars or in the ghettos of Haiti where a glass of clean water is a rarity?

The world was created whereby everything was designed to replenish itself. God is a creator and a provider of great abundance. There is no need, whatsoever, for anyone anywhere on this earth to go hungry. Missionaries should be honored and admired for their efforts and we should thank God for these caring souls. The truth of the matter, however, is feeding the world should not be left up to them. It is every human being's responsibility to care for one another ("Whatever you do for the least of them you do for me"). When I witness the plentiful yield of our little backyard garden, I am in tremendous awe and extremely grateful to a loving Creator who intended life to continually flourish. I hope for the day when the human race will rise up against the tremendous wastefulness and greed of world government. The planet is not in need of any more atomic weapons, space programs, and advancements in technological entertainment. We need to put those energies into living or lives according to the ways instituted by our Maker so that we may have life more abundantly. Our efforts should be spent being "good stewards of the earth," providing ways to protect our environment and insuring no one goes hungry.

NOT SO SECRET ADMIRERS

When I began dating Julianne in college I used to think I was part of an experiment in a psychology class of hers. I must say, she ranked high on the list of beautiful girls and I couldn't believe she was actually romantically involved with the likes of me. I imagined that part of her grade was based upon how long she could string me along. I was just waiting for her to break my heart, tell me the news she got an "A" in the course and was no longer in need of my services. I pictured a scene in which I am standing alone, watching her walk off into the distance, arm in arm with some hard-bodied jock. I'm not suggesting I was so undesirable; I'm just implying, at the time, I thought she could have done a lot better than me. I was scrawny with long straggly hair and by no means the Robert Redford type. (Now I'm absolutely certain she couldn't have found a better man than me.)

My suspicions were all wrong. I wasn't part of a cruel experiment in human behavior. Julianne and I have been together now for almost thirty-seven years, not all of them happy ones, nevertheless, still together. She's still beautiful and it's become obvious to me, I'm not the only man who sees it. One Valentine's day a few years ago, Julianne came home from work with two bottles of red wine and what looked like a very large homemade greeting card. She told me one of her customers gave it to her, but before she let me see the card, she warned me about its content. There are not many things I find offensive, so I could only imagine what was in the big brown manila envelope. Upon opening up the card, I immediately saw, whoever took the time to create it definitely had a fixation on my wife! On the face of the card was some handwritten text explaining why the profits had been soaring at the CVS pharmacy recently. When I opened it up to take a peek at the centerfold, my eyes were treated to a rather provocative drawing of my Julianne. She was clad in a white lab coat with her shirt open just enough to expose what he depicted as some very shapely breasts. I wasn't quite sure how to react, so I said, "Wow he certainly did a good job of enhancing those, didn't he?" Wrong thing to say!!! Julianne told me any normal husband would demand to know who this not-so-secret admirer was and punch his lights out. I just didn't see it that way. I trust Julianne with my life and if this guy was hot for her that was his problem. Besides, I got two bottles of my favorite beverage so how could I be pissed off?

Knowing there was another man who desired my wife didn't concern me too much. The truth of the matter is, she is an attractive woman who works with the public, so it's anybody's guess how many guys are having Julianne fantasies. Anyone who's honest has to admit they've had fantasies about someone other than their spouse at one time or another. This fellow just happened to be bold enough to take action and let her know. That doesn't necessarily make him a bad guy!

Every so often, Julianne would come home with stories about how this relentless fan of hers would come into the pharmacy and flaunt his wealth by inviting her to join him on trips to Las Vegas or Europe. He was completely aware of the fact she was married but it didn't stop him from pursuing her. I would think it had to be somewhat of an ego boost knowing someone other than me had a thing for her! One day my daughter told me one of her college friends thought I was hot. Once I heard that piece of ego-boosting news, I couldn't fit my head through the doorway for weeks!

On Valentine's Day the following year, Julianne received what had to be a true sign of admiration from her infatuated devotee. He presented her with, not one, but six bottles of his homemade wine neatly arranged in a rose-adorned wicker basket and another provocative custom-made greeting card. The bizarre thing about this gift was the labels attached to each bottle. Every one of them had a picture of a woman bearing a striking resemblance to Julianne. He even named the wine, "Kiss of the Princess," from the "Cellars of Armando" describing its flavor by comparing it to the seductive kiss of a beautiful princess. Armando was most definitely obsessed with Julianne. Knowing Julianne as well as I do, however, I knew this was all just harmless flirtation.

We were having a yard sale one Saturday afternoon when a bright red truck pulled up in front of the house. The expression on Julianne's face immediately turned to one of dismay when she saw Armando exit the truck and make his way up our driveway. "Oh shit!" she said under her breath, "Now he knows where I live!" I could understand her feeling a little uncomfortable in this situation, so Jule did the only thing she could do. She introduced him to me. I gave him the once over and as this average sized fellow of about fifty or so, with thinning hair, clad in 1970's polyester, approached me, she said, "Armando, this is my husband John!"

I extended my hand and as we shook he said as honestly as one could, "Nice to meet you John, I'm the guy who's in love with your wife!"

Immediately I saw he was definitely not Julianne's type, so there was absolutely no need to stir up any confrontation. I answered by saying, "Well, you certainly have good taste!"

Most people can't believe I didn't deck the guy, but I must admit he seemed like a nice person…a little eccentric, but nice. He asked me if I liked the wine and not wanting to hurt his feelings, I told him it was pretty good. Two hours later he returned with three cases. How could you hit a guy like that?

Armando eventually befriended my family. He took a liking to my son Matt, hired him and started giving him pointers on how to make a lot of money. He also admired Samantha and helped her to make a few bucks by doing some simple catalog modeling. Sometimes I wondered if he had ulterior motives, that is, get to the mom by befriending the kids! Nevertheless, Armando has become just another in the cast of characters to enter our lives. He continues to try to coax Julianne into going away with him. I have to laugh because the fantasy far surpasses the reality!

The latest admirer of Julianne's, who I know of, was a frail little man from Latvia. He had a mild stroke, making his Latvian accent even harder to understand. He's divorced, lives alone, and would visit the pharmacy two and three times a day, every day, to carry on conversations with her. He wrote her letters about his life and would bring along endless tokens of his fondness for her, including Latvian newspapers and homemade copies of Abba cassette tapes. During one of their daily conferences, the topic of conversation must have been gardening. We have a small vegetable garden and her new friend Uldis mentioned he too had a thriving garden, so this became a common point of interest for them. Day after day Uldis was bringing Julianne containers full of blackberries, raspberries, strawberries and gooseberries. He told her he wanted to give her some cuttings so she could begin to grow her own. So of course Julianne, being the overly-friendly type, accepted his offer and agreed to visit his home to see his garden. Julianne, however, doesn't venture out into these journeys alone, she drags me along. There we were on a gorgeous Saturday afternoon, following this little foreign guy all around his property as he stuttered the names of all the fruits and vegetables growing on almost every square inch of available soil. Now I don't understand how Julianne can't get this through her thick head, but men are not nice to women just for the hell of it. I don't care if a man is twenty or eighty, if there is blood flowing through his veins and he's not gay, there's something of a sexual nature going on in his mind, even if there's absolutely no chance of something happening. When Uldis looked at Julianne, I am certain he saw a beautiful woman, and just by Julianne giving him the attention she did, was turn-on enough for him. Stroke or no stroke, men enjoy the company of pretty women!

I wonder just how attentive a woman would be to a man's casual conversation if she could read his mind. Although we may be talking about the weather, in our heads we have women contorting in every possible position just to satisfy our twisted desires, and in our fantasies, they love it!!! Sorry to say ladies, but that's just the nature of the beast. We're not always as innocent as we pretend to be. There had been many a time during the course of my day when I lingered about the desk of a pretty receptionist a little longer than I needed to. Some days the imagination appreciates a little treat. Is what's good for the goose really what's good for the gander, or are we all just nuts? I do believe, however, the better the sex life is at home, the less likely it is the imagination will stray. If I can paraphrase Scripture, somewhere it makes a point about keeping a husband sexually content so he doesn't feel driven to find it elsewhere. And vice versa, I suppose.

It was intended by Our Maker, the sexes be attracted to and desire each other. Sometimes it may seem like a cruel joke. In a world full of billions of mating possibilities and with a thirst for variety, how does a man fool himself into thinking he found Miss Right (and vice versa) and commit to loving, honoring and obeying the same human being until the day one of them dies? During the early stages of most relationships, couples are thinking purely with their genitals, secondly with their hearts and lastly with their brains! For a brief period, they truly believe theirs is a match made in heaven and they will live happily ever after. It's only a matter of time before many starry-eyed lovers realize how very different they are from one another. A strong resentment soon sets in and staying together becomes one of the most difficult tasks imaginable! There is usually a breakdown in communication and eventually the game of who can hold out from sex the longest begins. Before they know it, the gap has widened so much, it becomes almost impossible to reconcile. Why is anyone baffled about the divorce rate climbing to nearly sixty percent and why marriage counselors are in such high demand? If the average person could afford a divorce, I'm sure the number would be closer to ninety percent! I used to think it was just Julianne and me, but it seems almost every married couple I meet experiences the same frustrations and disappointments (except maybe Wesley and Toni). It's crazy to observe how even after realizing wedded bliss is practically impossible, and how it is not feasible for a man and a woman to live together forever without the use of chemicals, the fantasy and the chase go on. Knowing we will ultimately only make each other miserable, why do we still desire each other so much?

The old sayings go, "The grass is always greener," "The anticipation is always better than the actual event," and "The fantasy is much better than the reality." So to Armando and Uldis I say, "Enjoy the fantasy because I live the reality!"

ONLY HALFWAY THERE

I'd been on a journey for fifty-five years, spending most of that time with the automatic pilot engaged, not paying much attention to where I was headed, and as a result missed out on a lot of the scenery. During the last three years or so of this journey, I decided it was finally time to pay more attention and exhort a little control as to where I was going. There are millions of us out there on the highways and byways, unknowingly cruising towards the same final destination, missing countless opportunities to experience the miraculous beauty that envelops us. As we run in dizzying circles, we pass up innumerable occasions to communicate and learn with each other. We all share in a similar quest to know our purpose, seeking a connection to a Higher Intelligence. As I've come to visualize myself as a part in a Divine plan of Creation, designed to live harmoniously with all things in the universe, my perception has changed greatly. It has become almost impossible for me to walk past a tree in bloom or a garden of flowers and not be filled with gratitude and awe. The sky has never appeared more blue, the sun more bright, and the grass more green. I've developed a keener sense and a deeper appreciation for all living things. I've learned to perceive God as a loving, kind, and endless Creative force present in every form of life, rather than an unbending overseer of the galaxies who scrutinizes and punishes.

What astonishes me is the way people who share very similar thoughts to mine have suddenly appeared in my life. By someone's mannerisms, the look in their eyes (the eyes are the windows to the soul), and the sound of their voice, I can sense the bond. They just show up! One morning while making a delivery I happened to catch Elise at home. We got engaged in one of our conversations concerning the higher things. We could have talked for hours but I had to get back to work. Our words seemed to energize each other. We were experiencing a very powerful spiritual union and when she reached out to hold my arm, I understood how necessary it was to make physical contact. I told her most of my family and friends thought I went off the deep end.

That evening Elise sent me an e-mail which read, "There are no coincidences; we've certainly crossed paths for a reason. Remember for every person who thinks you've gone off the deep end, there will be you and your knowledge of yourself and the world, and an occasional light that you recognize in someone's eyes when you are sharing what you believe, and can see they hear you and are willing to let it in. I have come to recognize my sanity in the way most people think I've lost it!"

Should the magician's secrets be revealed, the fascination of the audience would disappear along with their desire to attend any future performances. The lure is gone. In pretty much the same way, I don't believe I can ever again belong to a church. I've seen through the façade. I feel a tie to God I've never sensed before, a feeling I'm sorry to say I wasn't able to attain from a lifetime of attending church. What I've been experiencing as of late is something very real, a gentle force guiding me along, placing me in circumstances where I am crossing paths with people who understand and encourage. This part of my journey has become very exciting and I am looking forward with confidence to a time when Julianne and my children will be able to share in the experience. Together through the Spirit of our Maker, who has already seen the results, all things are truly possible.

WHO ARE THESE PEOPLE?

Sometimes I wonder, do things ever really change or is it just our perception of things that changes? Julianne felt it was once again time to visit her parents because of her dad's declining health and her brother Joe felt obligated to do the same. To save us all from being bored out of our minds, he came up with a great suggestion. Rather than all of us congregating in Homosassa, Joe thought it would be a great idea to get his folks to take a drive down to his new place where there was room enough for all of us to stay. My in-laws agreed, we settled on a date, so Jule and I booked our flights. It didn't come as much of a surprise, when on the night prior to our departure, we got a call from my mother-in-law informing us dad was very sick and they wouldn't be coming. Joe and Corinne arranged their very busy lives to be available that week so there was no way they would even consider us canceling.

Julianne was feeling pretty bad about visiting Florida and not being able to see her folks, but we figured maybe in a day or two her dad would feel better and decide to make the trip. He didn't. Joe and Corinne's house was magnificent and Julianne and I were treated like royalty. Whether we were floating in the pool, soaking in the hot tub, watching a movie in their in-home theater, or feasting on one of Corinne's many gourmet meals, we had a really nice time. One day, however, Julianne suggested maybe we should get up early and take a drive to Homosassa to visit mom and dad. Joe and Corinne graciously offered us their car but said in no uncertain terms were they about to join us in the four-hour ride. We took them up on their offer and as much as I wasn't looking forward to driving eight hours in one day to visit the two people who I knew were going to make me crazy, to make Julianne happy, I did.

My father-in-law was feeling much better when we arrived. After the warm welcome and the "how was your trip" chatter, we sat around the kitchen table to have lunch. My mother-in-law had known me for over thirty-five years and was extremely aware of my finicky eating habits. When she unsealed a package of vacuum-packed, extra-slimy "could-be-turkey-breast," I thought to myself, "How in the world could they eat this crap never mind offer it to us?"

I made up my mind not to bring any subject I thought would trigger a political or religious debate with my father-in-law. As we sat having lunch, the television in the adjacent room was blaring. From the corner of my eye I could see Ellen interviewing Britney Spears, and thinking there was no way this could spark an argument, I made the grave mistake of simply mentioning how I thought Britney was a very pretty girl.

"You think she's pretty?" my father-in-law snapped, "I see no beauty in her at all!" That was it. I pressed his button. From that minute, until the four or five hours later when we finally escaped, I was lectured to death. "Would you want your daughters emulating her?" he asked with an angry holler, "she should be ashamed of herself and so should anybody who finds beauty in her!"

He was relentless. He kept hitting me over the head with his strong-headed but narrow views on Catholicism, politics, immorality, death, and the Pope. I really wasn't in the mood to get into a debate with him, so I basically just nodded. Now that he was approaching his late seventies and with his health failing, he seemed to be pre-occupied with dying and getting into heaven. To hear him talk about regretting many of the things he did during his lifetime because they either "stained his soul" or "drew him away from God" was rather sad. He ignored common sense just to defend the pointless traditions of his religion. He felt so threatened by his own children's knowledge of the Bible and their zest in what they believed, he refused to even discuss it with them any longer. He was right and that's all there was to it! Since moving to Florida my mother-in-law no longer had a mind of her own. She either went along with everything he said or swore by whatever she heard from Oprah, Dr. Phil or Regis.

Right in the middle of one of my father-in-law's senseless sermons on how suffering gets one closer to the Lord, my brother-in-law Gregory dropped in for a visit. Gregory wasn't in the house for even a minute when the conversation quickly segued into a full-blown argument over Gregory's poor driving skills.

"Julianne," he lectured, "if you saw the way he was tailgating and changing lanes, you'd wonder where the hell he got his license." Raising his voice while trying to verbally re-enact Gregory's driving maneuvers, he tried to drag Julianne and me into the argument by asking what we thought. At the same time, Gregory began mumbling something in his defense, which only got his father more agitated. "People like you cause accidents!" he shouted pointing at his son. Gregory shrugged his shoulders, his eyes teeming with frustration, looked at us briefly for sympathy, and then continued his losing battle. The two of them were screaming at each other as if the house were on fire. It was crazy. I couldn't make up stuff this bizarre.

On the Mother's Day 2004, before we left for Florida, Julianne, the kids, and I were at my parent's house for our annual Mother's Day visit. Right after dinner, my dad got a call from my Aunt Jean. She wasn't feeling very well and asked if he could swing by. My brother Jim and I tagged along with Dad. As we walked into my aunt's sixth floor apartment, I was overcome by a stale odor and greeted by a pile of cat droppings. Aunt Jean looked frighteningly bad. She could hardly breathe. I suggested to my dad we call her doctor and get her over to the hospital immediately.

I sat beside her on the living room couch and as her fear-filled eyes locked glances with mine, she struggled to whisper, "Johnny, I have to beat this. I have to get better!"

With my arms around her shivering frail body, I encouraged her that she was going to be fine. "Aunt Jean!" I said confidently, "You can't go anywhere. You have to edit my book first!"

My aunt still had lots to do. She was not ready to die.

Somewhere in the middle of another of my father-in-law's never-ending speeches about the infallibility of the feeble Pope, my cell phone rang. It was my brother Bill to gently inform me Aunt Jean had passed away. Even as I write these words my eyes are filling with tears. As much as I expected it, I still couldn't believe it. Minutes later, my dad called to confirm what I just heard from Bill. Joe and Corinne were waiting for us to have dinner, so it was time for us to bid our farewells and hit the highway.

As Jule and I were cruising along the town roads making our way towards the Florida turnpike, the screaming of a siren and the flashing of a red light interrupted our conversation. Looking into my rear view mirror, I couldn't help but notice an unmarked police car right on my tail and a cop motioning me to pull over. When the officer told me I was clocked doing seventy in a fifty-five mile per hour zone, I was shocked. I tried to explain to him how I had my eye on the speedometer and there was no way I was travelling at the speed he accused me of. I also tried using the sympathy method of avoiding a ticket by explaining how I just received the bad news of my aunt's death and I had to get a plane back to New York. He was unmoved and slapped me with a two hundred dollar ticket. Needless to say, I was extremely pissed off.

"Between gas, tolls and this lousy ticket," I cried to Julianne, "It cost us three hundred dollars to visit your parents! That's more than it cost us to fly!"

"I'm sorry!" was all she could say.

I was right after all! When I told Joe about the ticket, he suddenly remembered that the car had been recalled for faulty gauges, including the speedometer. Even though I went through the trouble of contacting my attorney, getting all the proper documents to prove my innocence, the redneck Florida judge denied this Yankee's plea!

I've attended many wakes and many funerals in my lifetime and was always pretty good about coping with death. Seeing my Aunt Jean's body lying so still in a coffin had the strangest effect on me. I had the hardest time accepting she was gone. Aunt Jean goes way back to my earliest childhood memories. She was always a part of my life and now that very important part of my life is no longer around. As friends and family stopped by the funeral parlor to pay their respects, I felt as if I were playing a part in a scene that wasn't for real. I guess in a way Aunt Jean's death made me come to grips with the fact that when they say, "Life is but a vapor," they aren't kidding. My dad is now the only remaining sibling and I'm sure the thought weighed heavily on his mind. The presiding priest asked if any friends or family would care to eulogize my aunt.

After my siblings directed a few sarcastic comments towards me like,

"You were her favorite," I knew I had to say something. I relayed how she had always been a permanent fixture in my life and just how much I was going to miss her. I did mention how she always told me I was her favorite and how she would unceasingly encourage me to write, but something prompted me to close with this thought. I spoke confidently, "If we could all just take a minute to restructure our way of thinking. Instead of regarding ourselves as human beings who have had an occasional spiritual experience, why not think of us as eternal spirits who have lived a temporary human experience. I believe Aunt Jean had a wonderful and rewarding human experience!" To this day, my brother Jim goofs on me for my attempt at the metaphysical.

The huge task of cleaning out Aunt Jean's apartment was the next order of business. Sometimes the death of a loved one has a way of bringing about the worst in people. My aunt had a piano that had been in her apartment for as long as I can remember. As a kid I used to sit and bang on the keys until my uncle Hank couldn't take it any more. "For crying out loud, take some lessons!!" he would say with a hint of annoyance in his voice. He didn't realize he was hurting my feelings. I thought I sounded pretty good! Years later, after Uncle Hank passed away, my kids would sit on the same piano bench banging away on those keys until I would screech, "That's enough, take some lessons!!!"

According to my dad, one of my aunt's last wishes was for my sister, my brothers and I go through her apartment and take anything we wanted. Since all of us had a piano, except for my overly-sentimental brother Bill, he expressed interest in taking Aunt Jean's. None of us had any problem with Bill taking the piano, except for my dad and my sister Virginia, who in their undying allegiance to their parish and the Catholic Church, took it upon themselves to donate it to the nuns. Of course my dad, in an attempt to protect Virginia from any antagonism, tried to convince us it was his decision to give away the piano, but I didn't believe it for a minute. This act of charity had my sister, the theologian, written all over it.

"What about my feelings?" Bill questioned, "I never ask for anything, why couldn't you politely tell the nuns we prefer to keep the piano in the family?"

"Aunt Jean, if she were alive, would want the nuns to have the piano," Dad interjected, "Besides, Bill, you don't even play the piano!"

"That's not the point!" Bill replied, "Doesn't sentiment count for something?"

"Suddenly everyone's getting sentimental!" Virginia chimed in sarcastically, "Where were all of you when Aunt Jean was sick?"

With that comment my brother Jim sprung from his seat and ripped into Virginia, "For years you never had a nice word to say about Aunt Jean and now after she's dead you come riding in like a hero..."

"Go fuck yourself!" Virginia yelled and before I knew it total pandemonium broke out among brothers, sister, mother and father.

I seriously thought my mom was going to have a nervous breakdown. Truthfully, I couldn't believe what I was witnessing. I was smack dab in the middle of another surreal situation watching people I've known my entire life playing characters I just couldn't relate to. What was most disconcerting to me was to see church-going, God-fearing people bickering so unreasonably. Where was the compassion, the forgiveness or the understanding?

Everything eventually settled down. Everyone cooled off; we hugged, kissed and apologized. My sister blamed her erratic behavior on the grounds she had to put my aunt's very sick cat to sleep. In my mind I was thinking, "She's more upset over the cat than her aunt!" To this day that piano remains an issue. Not a family gathering goes by without a sarcastic comment. On a future afternoon during a discussion about donating organs, Bill's wife asked the family if any one of them ever considered being a donor. I got the dirtiest looks when I chimed in, "No, they've already donated a piano!"

We all hung around for a while and over coffee and a fresh baked cake, some deep dark family secrets were revealed. My mom told us about how meddlesome and controlling my aunt was throughout the years. We learned about my Uncle Hank's secret drawer and his chronic gambling problem, something he kept hidden from my aunt for her entire life. After he died, my mom was giving Aunt Jean a hand getting rid of Hank's belongings. Jean refused to look inside the one drawer her husband requested she never open. When my mom went ahead and opened the mystery drawer, she learned of her brother-in-law's life threatening betting illness. My parents decided to keep it to themselves rather than shatter Aunt Jean's image of her late husband. Meanwhile, they just shattered my image of my favorite uncle! We couldn't help but wonder if some of his play money came from the collection baskets during his days as an usher at Aunt Jean's church. Little by little, more tidbits of family dysfunction, including one case of incest, came out into the light. Some I'm glad I know, some I wish I'd never heard. It was disheartening for me to see everyone acting so insane. Sometimes, some things are better left unsaid, because when you get down to it, nothing really matters. Right now Aunt Jean could care less about the stupid piano, Uncle Hank's gambling or the fact she drove my mom nuts for most of her life. Eventually we're all going to be where Aunt Jean is, wherever that may be! Life's too short! By the way, I heard the nuns opened up a piano lounge!

MY NEPHEW NICK

Very recently, my daughter Samantha was feeling nostalgic, and began viewing some VHS tapes of past family events and holidays. Because I was negligent about labeling each of the cassettes, it was anybody's guess as to what she was going to view next. "Oh my God, Daddy, it's Nick when he was a baby!" she cried out. We all came running into the den to watch the video of Julianne dressing her nephew Nicholas in his Baptismal outfit. That event took place over twenty-five years ago.

Nick was the first-born son of Julianne's sister Maryanne. Through the years we never did get to see very much of Maryanne and her family. Her husband was in the military, so home was usually an Air Force Base somewhere in the world. The marriage wound up in divorce and Maryanne and the kids eventually settled in Florida.

In a crazy family full of hardcore Catholics, fanatical Pentecostals, and who knows what, Nicholas became an agnostic, grew dreadlocks and moved to Alaska where he made music, rescued animals and communed with nature. Although I only got to see him on rare occasions, such as weddings and funerals, I thought he was a pretty cool kid.

In January of 2008, on his last visit from Alaska to see his mom and siblings in Florida, Nick had the misfortune of partying a little too much with some of his old chums and overdosed on a prescription pain killer. The news of his death was devastating to the entire family.

It's funny how people hold onto their religious doctrine so firmly until they are staring into a coffin at a loved one. "Nick looked so at peace, I know he's in a better place with God!" was a line often repeated by many who'd always held onto the conviction that only through Jesus does someone enter the kingdom of heaven. The one thing I did know about Nick was he did not believe in the conventional God most of his family did. He was anti-religion, anti-establishment and loved creation. Suddenly it didn't seem to matter; everyone agreed Nick was with God.

Were those who were present at the wake just say reassuring things to comfort Maryanne in her time of confusion and grief, even if they really didn't believe what they were saying? "Too bad Nick's not going to be in Heaven with Jesus because he didn't believe in him!" were words I'm sure crossed no one's lips. Nick's death didn't change anything. The family still argues over idiotic issues of doctrine. As for Nick and I, we know they're all crazy!

IN CONCLUSION

I have to wonder if thinking too much is a blessing or a curse. In some strange way, I really enjoy the eccentric workings of my mind, always asking a million unanswerable questions, always trying to explain the unexplainable. On the other hand, I've had episodes when my thoughts have spiraled, taking me so deep inside the rabbit hole, I got worried I might never come back out. Mild anxiety would sometimes set in and I would be overcome by the feeling I could possibly snap. I feared I could easily become one of those village freaks aimlessly walking the streets talking to himself. Up to now I'd been able to pull the reigns on my unruly thoughts and slip back into reality (whatever reality is) before going totally crazy. I would try to shift my focus to something mindless like sex. Thank goodness that's been a help. Maybe there are certain things we're just not supposed to know.

I wish I could nail down the hands of time because time truly does fly. I can't believe I've finally retired. I'd been on the same route at UPS for about twenty-two years and in my mind it seemed like almost everybody I came in contact with was growing old except for me. The secret to that trick was to not look into the mirror too often! Babies had grown into adults; countless familiar faces had disappeared due to what seemed like a cancer epidemic. I'd gotten so used to seeing and talking with so many kind people and in a flash, some of them were gone. What I find so amusingly odd was how I'd been able to detach myself from what I'd witnessed daily by saying, "This isn't going to happen to me!"

My children are adults. Christiann is a working girl living in Manhattan.

Matthew keeps himself quite busy attending his last semester in college, working a job and playing in a really good original rock band. It seems like he's never around anymore. Samantha recently completed college, is going to grad school and hopefully she'll find a rewarding job. She spends most of her time with her boyfriend. It's rare when we all sit down to share a meal together. I think I miss having them around all the time, especially since their frequent absences hasn't seemed to restore the "Julianne and John" I'd been longing for, for quite some time.

Conversely, I think Julianne seems to like the idea of the kids eventually being completely on their own. Since most of our arguments have been about the kids and the way they "mess" the house, she claims once they're gone, the two of us will become closer by there being less housework for her to do, therefore, allowing more time for us. I'm not so sure I agree. Once the kids all leave for good, I can only hope some of her obsessive energy will be directed towards "us" and not at the fading wallpaper, the chip in the tile, the stain on the carpet or the weeds in the lawn, or anything else that has continued to steal her attention from "our relationship" and her relationship to life. Although I continually try, I just can't understand the radical change from the daredevil, fun-loving woman I fell in love with years ago, to the sometimes despondent, discontented wife and mother, who I admit, I still love today. The years have been quite an emotional roller coaster ride for us. When it's good, it's good. The only problem being, it's just never been that good often enough.

I must confess I love retirement. Waking up on the first morning after my last day of work was reminiscent of rising on the first day of summer vacation when I was going to school. The only difference is, now I'm on a permanent vacation. Many people have asked me questions like, "Why are you retiring so young?" or "What are you going to do with yourself, aren't you going to be bored?" Truthfully, even though I answered them by saying, "What's so bad about doing nothing," I never dreamed I'd be so busy. I have the time now to do all the things working a full time job has kept me from doing for so many years. Call it "being in the right place at the right time" or call it "synchronicity," but things just seem to be working out. I was able to retire and retain all of my 401K earnings before the economy crashed. I have crossed paths with certain people who have presented me the opportunity to re-ignite my love for performing and be currently playing in two working rock bands. I have the time now to concentrate on writing, reading, and playing music, the things I'd always been passionate about, without the thought hanging over my head of having to spend ten hours a day at a job.

The only drawback about retired life is Julianne still works and I think she resents that I'm home and she's not. I don't have any guilt feelings. I earn a decent pension, the result of working my ass off for twenty-five years of my life. I have no problem helping around the house. I'll do the laundry, the food shopping and prepare dinners when I can. Although her salary helps to pay some bills, quite honestly, I would love her to be home with me if we could spend the bulk of our time together by sharing ideas and enjoying each other's company. With the kids rarely around anymore, there is no reason why we couldn't. My fear is, if and when that day comes, Julianne won't know how to relax and her obsession with cleaning and tidiness will drive me to go find a job!

I am far from an expert on human behavior, but Julianne's need for structure and order might explain why she remains loyal to the belief system I chose to run from years ago. In the same way she refuses to move a piece of furniture, once it has been situated, she refuses to even consider entertaining broader spiritual ideas. Up to now she has not deviated from the ritual of the Sunday morning comfort club and shows no sign she ever will. It frustrates me terribly to see her cling to an organization I look upon as debilitating and controlling, and it infuriates me to know she financially supports it. Even though it may bring her comfort and a sense of purpose, I wish she would realize the only reality and everlasting thing in this world is love; to be forever conscious that she comes from love, therefore, she is love. To be able to love herself and have the love of her husband, her children, family and friends is all that will ever matter. All structure, including organized religion, is illusion and will collapse. Some years ago, for reasons I can only hypothesize, she developed a negative mindset, which since then has only attracted more negativity. I can't be certain, but I would assume most of Julianne's recurrent aches and pains could very well be attributed to that. She has headaches more often than not. I just haven't seen her religious convictions facilitating her to bear "fruit" in her physical life. Because I do love her, I am saddened, not angry, that she hasn't been able to break free from the prison she creates for herself. Sadly, I know she puts the blame on me for most of her unhappiness.

More often than I find necessary, she has a broom, a sponge or a bottle of disinfectant in her hands. Somehow she has an eye for the most microscopic stain, piece of dust, or imperfection. She calls it a curse, but in today's world of marvelous medications, there is a cure. She's quite perceptive in seeing the shortcomings, faults and inadequacies in others, but is in extreme denial about herself. If only she adhered to the words of the Jesus she claims to worship, "Take the log out of your own eye before you point to the speck in another's." If only she paid as much attention to the deeper needs of her family and the "unseen," as much as she did to the cleaning, we might just have had a ridiculously happy household. She claims if we paid more attention to keeping the house in order, she'd have more time for us. The truth is, our eyes don't see what she sees. Sometimes I feel as if she uses cleaning as a tool to avoid living life; "I don't have time for you, I have to clean!" It's almost as if housekeeping has become her identity, her purpose.

The more aware I become of my spiritual self, the more I try to love, understand and forgive. The more I understand how all things were created in love, the less I seem to care about possessions and things. Trying to live life with the realization that the Creator has everything in control should ultimately eliminate stress. We create our own tension. The kids and I were talking one day about how tense and uneasy we feel when "mommy's home." I never admitted this to Julianne because firstly, I didn't want to hurt her. Secondly, she would've probably just denied it. I'm not suggesting my kids are angels and their mother's a tyrant, but I am saying we should count our blessings and learn to appreciate each other while we still have each other. When we were going for counseling, Bonnie tried to enlighten us that a home should be a safe haven for the family. I think perhaps we abandoned therapy too soon. Although we've been getting along better than we have in the past, in my heart I know there's room for much improvement. Whenever we travel things are pretty good. We enjoy each other's company and for the most part life is good. It's the familiar surroundings of the home that seems to bring out the worst in us. I don't understand it. Somewhere along the road we must have screwed up. I know she loves the kids and I know the kids love her, but sometimes love needs to be expressed with hugs, kisses and encouraging words, the very things lacking in Julianne's childhood. Out of frustration or anger, sometimes Samantha would tell me, "I can't stand mom," when deep down inside what she really can't stand is having a poor relationship with her mom.

Lack of communication is crippling to any relationship. I will admit, not being open with all my feelings has helped contribute to the breakdown. Somehow I wish we could all come to the place where we see the big picture. Julianne doesn't seem to remember, youth and rebellion go hand in hand. We all live and learn. When Matthew came home drunk after graduating high school, Julianne lectured me about being responsible for my kids' eternal lives. "Do you want your children going to hell?" she asked, "Because if they don't stop drinking that's where they're headed!" Little did she realize how she'd been creating our own personal hell right there in the living room as she chided us for crushing the fluffiness of the couch cushions.

No matter how diligently we search, I am convinced no man will ever know for certain the absolute meaning of life, the secrets of the universe and the mind of God until leaving these earthly vessels and entering the "other realm," the afterlife, or wherever the heck it is we're all headed! Until then, as much as some of us are getting closer, it's the pursuit of answers that makes life interesting and fun. One of the major disagreements between Julianne and me is that she believes Jesus is the only road to salvation. I believe Jesus was without a doubt the most influential being who ever lived, with a mission to shake up the planet and awaken humanity to the Oneness of creation. On one of our vacations to Prince Edward Island, Gino and I spent hours discussing religion, faith and the need to be saved. "Saved from what?" he asked. As I sat upon a grassy green hill in his yard, gazing out at the red cliffs engulfing the beautiful blue water of the Umberland Strait, a feeling of complete wonderment overtook me. "Saved from what?" I thought. As far as I was concerned, I was in the presence of the Creator. The very essence of who I am became one with all the beauty surrounding me.

There's no doubt I have been richly blessed just by knowing most of the people I know and by having the friends and family I have. Old hippie I am, I believe love is the only hope for the world and I try to spread that love around to the best of my ability. Up to now my human experience has basically been a good one. I wouldn't be honest if I said I didn't have any regrets. I regret Julianne and I didn't have the blissful marriage I'd always thought we'd have. There was a time we started to drift apart and we waited far too long before deciding to seek help. I regret I didn't spend enough quality time with Matt while he was growing up. I'm not too happy about being SO laid back, I allowed Julianne to have so much control in the ruling of the roost. Sometimes avoiding confrontation is not the wisest move. I found consolation in my songwriting rather than being straightforward and expressing my desires and disappointments to my life partner. It is what it is. Regrets serve no purpose. We have to move on.

The world isn't in the very best shape at the present. War and unrest never seem to go away, both usually stemming from religious and political differences, along with everyone's desire to be right. The way I see it, as long as human beings remain trapped in their little boxes of self-righteousness, where they continue to fuel their egos, the condition of this planet can't possibly mend. Sometimes I wonder if we're actually going to have to be on the brink of annihilation before a spiritual awakening will consume mankind and elevate us to become the creatures God intended us to be. The earth is a playground lovingly designed by God where all His children should be able to freely roam about. It really doesn't take a radical mind to figure out we all come from the same place. We all consist of the same elements, compounds and chemicals readily found in trees, the earth's soil and her mighty oceans. (In a sense, Mother Earth is truly our mother.) We all need the nurturing of a parent, the nourishment of food. We all need to laugh, to love and be loved. We exist to express ourselves and to continue the creation process. Every last one of us has a purpose. We were made in the Creator's image, in other words, in His nature. We share in His Spirit and until we're able to recognize His Spirit in ourselves and in each other, our journeys will be futile and the blind spots will prevent us from freely changing lanes and moving forward.

AFTERWORD: JUST SOME THOUGHTS BEFORE I GO

I have not lost my sense of humor! Far too many of us take ourselves too seriously. That could be the very reason why the world is in the sad shape it's in. To quote something I read in an underground 60's magazine in my hippie days, "*To those who think, life is a comedy, to those who feel, a tragedy.*" With all the thinking I've done lately, I should have laughed myself into oblivion by now. If laughter is the best medicine (which quantum physics proves to be true), then maybe what we all need to do is sharpen up on our joke telling skills and spread some laughter around!

There's nothing I would enjoy more than knowing I had a hand in helping to tear down the walls of the religious institutions dividing us. A house divided cannot stand! Therefore, how will Christianity prevail when it has been separated into 20,000 different sects? Karl Marx once stated that religion is the opiate of the masses. I'm certain it's safe to assume a very large percentage of the people flocking to church every Sunday morning are not only in disagreement with most of the doctrine being preached to them, but couldn't tell you the first thing about their faith. I'm opposed to fences, denominations, borders, political parties and anything else separating human beings. Perhaps the secret to world peace is to drop all the labels and simply consider ourselves as Earthlings, with the hope we don't make contact with extra-terrestrials, because then we'd only find something to fight about with them!

Lenny Bruce once made a statement I thought was rather profound. He said, "If Jesus happened to be put to death by means of electrocution, would Christians be wearing miniature fourteen-karat gold electric chairs around their necks?" It seems as though marketing and making a buck finds its way into everything. It's easier to wear a cross, slap a Jesus fish or a zany bumper sticker on your car than to actually love your neighbor.

People, through the help of Madison Ave. and the fashion industry, have turned themselves into human billboards. It's rather funny how so many folks have this need to show their individuality by sporting tee shirts displaying the names of their favorite stores, designers, athletes or rock bands. Abercrombie sells a torn and tattered shirt with their logo on it for thirty bucks. The garment, usually made in a poverty stricken country like Sri-Lanka, isn't worth seventy-five cents, yet young people have no problem forking over their money, and then turning themselves into living advertisements. In some way everyone conforms to the trends of the fashion industry. Conform to be an individual! Why haven't they caught on to oneness in spirit? Somehow I get the feeling, when someone expresses his likes or dislikes across his chest, it is done simply to antagonize someone with opposing views. I can't count the number of conversations I've heard between sports fans that went something like this:

"The Yankees suck!"

"You suck, Boston's going to kick Yankee butt!"

"You're an asshole and the Red Sox are assholes!"

"Fuck You! You Yankee sack of shit!"

"Fuck You!"

I could never understand why people would fight over their preference of professional sports teams. What difference does it make? Athletes are getting paid millions while fans are ready to kill each other over meaningless, trivial issues that have absolutely no effect on their personal lives! The truth of the matter is we should all learn to agree to disagree. We can't all possibly like the same things!

One thing I've come to understand, after living a little more than a half century in this human shell, life is indeed crazy! To quote the words of John Lennon again, "All I want is SOME truth…just give me SOME truth!" He doesn't even suggest he could ever attain one hundred percent unadulterated truth, all he's asking for is SOME. Throughout civilizations, man has been on a quest for the truth, after all, everyone wants to be free and if the truth sets one free why wouldn't we want to know the whole truth? It seems as though every time someone thought they found the truth, a religion sprang up. Some joined, some kept searching. We have developed ideas about what is good and what is bad. We've all been taught, at one time or other, certain acts are sinful. As far as I'm concerned, God is way beyond what we define as sin. Sin is something conceived by man so he could make judgments. If God, however, could be displeased by anything, I would have to say judgment and non-belief are close contenders. By non-belief, I simply mean being able to witness the perfection in the universe, the wonder of life, and still not be confident that a supernatural creative entity with power and intelligence far beyond what our human minds can comprehend is responsible. Stemming from this non-belief comes what I feel are the two things detrimental to humankind...pride and greed. Judgment is equally destructive, creating the illusion one man is better than the next. To believe in God is to believe in love. Love goes hand in hand with compassion and forgiveness. Love and greed cannot co-exist. Pride and forgiveness cannot co-exist. Love will mend the world; greed and judgment will cripple it.

Imagine a world where everyone could travel anywhere and feel welcome. Imagine going through a day without fear or anxiety. Imagine unconditional love between a man and a woman with no jealousy, no strings attached, no judgment and no disagreement. Just think about what it might be like if every human being could recognize the presence of God's spirit in each other. Imagine being able to move mountains because doubt has finally been eliminated. How wonderful it would be to have the confidence that our children and our children's children are going to experience that kind of world. If there is a Supreme Being in control of the universe, which I'm certain there is, then I am hopeful, one day peace will finally reign, the lamb will lay down with the lion and all will live as one. The truth will finally set man free...as it was intended!

EPILOGUE

"Just tap your heels three times and repeat after me, 'There's no place like home, there's no place like home...'"

Dorothy took quite a journey before she finally realized what she really yearned for was the place where she began. The trouble is, without the journey she never would have come to that realization. There are numerous accounts in literature, both old and recent, where characters have traveled far and wide only to end up where they started...at the very beginning.

Some of us go through our daily lives not even conscious that every breath and every step we take is all part of a journey. Sometimes, some things happen in our lives that trigger feelings in our hearts and make us suddenly aware there's more to the picture than meets the eye. It wasn't up until about five years ago when questions about faith and religion began to nag at me. It was only then I became mindful that I'd been traveling an overcrowded path and it was now up to me to continue on this journey by myself.

Along the way, I mysteriously started meeting many interesting people, folks I probably never would have stopped to talk with if I hadn't wandered off alone. We shared ideas, stories and philosophies and each time I walked away, something of theirs became part of me and vice versa I'm sure. Many of the people who knew me and loved me were wondering, "What in the world could he possibly be looking for?" There were times in my life when I thought I knew God, I thought I knew myself, and I thought I knew, not quite everything, but a lot! As I traveled onward, I kept glancing back to see the things I once stood for crumbling. There was no turning back.

Spirit has no beginning and no end. It always was, and will always be, one with God, the eternal spirit, the breath of life. At one time, before becoming physical beings, we all must have known God. At one time we all knew the Truth. Life is the path back to re-knowing that Truth.

It took me a very long time, fifty-five years in fact, to begin piecing together the puzzle parts. It took all the folks I've met along the way. It took the struggles, the heartache, the good times and the laughter. It took disease, a car accident, a rocky marriage and years of religious confusion to come full circle. I think I can safely say the sole purpose of our existence is to be Christ-like, which is, to come to the full realization of "Who" has been present within us from the beginning. Find God and you may find yourself, find yourself and you may find God.

I appreciate everyone I've bumped into along my journey. They were all instrumental in helping me find my way back to Kansas, so to speak. Sometimes I feel just like Dorothy after she spinning down from the sky to land safely in her bed. She was relieved to be back in the company of all her close friends. She promised she would never leave them again and told them all how much they were loved. No matter how far off the beaten path I've roamed, no matter how many new acquaintances I've made, no one holds a place in my heart like my old friends from the Bummers. From time to time when our busy schedules allow us the chance to get together, it's like going back home.

Joe and I were inseparable all through high school and college. People used to say when we died they were going to bury us side by side. Due to the course of events that shaped our lives, I hadn't been able to see Joe in years. He moved out of state and getting together just became too difficult. I think about him a lot and so one day I said, "Screw it! I'm going to call him and make some plans to go visit!"

We finally got together sometime ago and when we saw each other it was like a day hadn't passed since we were traipsing along the college campus looking for girls. We were catching up on whatever music we'd been listening to or movies we'd seen, and it was amazing to find out our tastes were identical.

Joe pulled out this obscure record from his vast collection and said, "Bet you haven't heard this one yet!"

I couldn't believe it. "Joe!" I shrieked excitedly, "I bought that one the very same day it was released!"

It doesn't matter how the miles may separate us or how much time elapses between our meetings, there's a connection between my old friends and I that will remain throughout eternity. Like a song I wrote says, "Nobody knows me like my old friends…I'd do anything to go back again and piss away the time with my old friends."

Well one thing I'm grateful for is being able to occasionally see the big picture. Each of us plays a part in the Grand Design, so in the scheme of things my little problems don't add up to squat. Compared to eternity, my life here on this planet is but a blink of an eye. I know just as my ashes return to the earth, my spirit will return from where it came, and who knows what new adventures await me. My son Matthew has been asking me a lot of questions lately. He's growing restless and I can tell he's about to step out on a journey of his own. My only advice to him has been to be alert and enjoy the ride. If I told him where I thought he was going to end up, he might not believe me.

Julianne is uncompromising in her faith. I'm not quite certain if her unwavering stance is based upon faith or conditioning. I know I can't make her believe what I believe or think what I think. I do know she has a good heart. I also know she is a fairly intelligent woman and deep within has had to question many of the mysteries and doctrines of her so-called faith. Somehow she's comfortable believing what she believes and chooses not to even read or discuss anything with opposing ideas or views. It hasn't been easy, not being able to share and discuss the topics and ideas I am so passionate about with my lifetime partner. I'm sure that it hasn't been easy for Julianne either, witnessing me abandon what was once something we may have had in common. The funny thing is our views really aren't so far off from each other's, and in the end, it's not going to make a difference. We just have different takes on the same God! What's been a bit frustrating for me, however, is being able to know how much richer life can be when two souls connect.

We're all on a journey. We all travel at different speeds. Many of us stand at the various forks and crossroads and are led to follow new paths. Many of us continue in the same direction and many of us choose to stay put. Sooner or later, one way or another, we will all arrive at the same destination. We just don't arrive at the same time. Some of us are well on the way, while some of us need refining and may need to live through another lifetime. Once we all get there, it's going to be interesting to see how much we didn't know!

THE LAST WORD: CLOSING REMARKS

In April of 2008, Julianne and I took another trip out west to visit her brother Art and to experience the Grand Canyon again. This time, however, when word got out, a few of Julianne's siblings decided to join us on our vacation. The old saying holds true, "The more the merrier!" We had a fun-filled week, but aside from the sightseeing and the fabulous weather, some of the best times occurred while we were sitting around the patio and over a few beers, listening to or engaging in family conversation.

Julianne and I, along with her two sisters, couldn't get a word in edge wise as Art, Joseph and Bobby argued over who got treated worse by their parents. As comical as it was, it was also depressing. "Dad fucked me up the most!" Bobby claimed almost proudly, as if he were going to win a prize. "He forbade me to pick up my date for the prom until I was done helping him on one of his fucking projects. I was so embarrassed," he continued bitterly, "I almost missed the fucking prom!" The brothers went on and on like old soldiers telling "Who Can Top This" war stories, although missing a prom and doing some demolition work was a far cry from some of the child abuse stories in the headlines today! Not being able to relate at all, I still felt sorry for them.

My father-in-law always put his father on a pedestal. In fact, I've never heard him utter anything but praise for both his parents. Ironically, what I did learn from Julianne and her sisters was how his dad treated him even more unfairly than my brothers-in-law claimed they were treated. Legend has it that my father-in-law, one of nine siblings, was his father's personal slave. He had to make himself readily available to tend to all of the household chores, including painting and janitorial work. Unlike the joyous childhood memories of his brothers and sisters, his weren't pleasant. Julianne's dad apparently couldn't take the mistreatment and in order to escape his father's iron fist, he left to join the merchant marine at fifteen years old. He vehemently denies he was ever treated unfairly. Oddly enough, both his parents died in a tragic car accident several years later. It's strangely curious what human beings choose to remember and choose to forget. It's also sad to see how people are often affected by the mistakes of prior generations and never learn to overcome them. I'd have to assume, as far as child rearing goes, they all did the best they could. Forgiving them doesn't mean forgetting what they did, it means understanding why.

Just recently my dad was given a copy of "A New Earth." Because he had heard so much about it and because it was an Oprah recommendation, he decided to read it. He called me on the phone one afternoon and asked me if I had read it. I told him I was looking forward to checking it out, even though it was Oprah endorsed, and perhaps I could borrow it when he was done. (I could only hope for Oprah endorsing my book!) "John," he said with a slight tone of perplexity in his voice, "I will gladly lend it to you because I want to see what you think. I don't get it! I think the world's gone stir crazy...what is it lacking in peoples' lives that they devour books like this?" I couldn't answer him right on the spot because, obviously, I hadn't yet read it.

Whenever my dad and I talk about the afterlife, he always brings up a movie we saw at the Mormon Pavilion at the 1965 World's Fair. The film dealt with the topic of life after death and portrayed the passing away of a loved one who was entering the pearly gates of heaven. Back on earth, while the family of the dearly departed was grieving, Grandma was filled with unspeakable joy as she strolled along the streets of gold meeting all the friends and loved ones who had passed on before her.

"That's the way I think it's going to be, John," Dad said with a sense of unconvincing confidence, "when I die I'm going to see my mother and father again!"

"Dad," I asked matter-of-factly, "and just how is grandma going to look when you get there? Like the weak and feeble ninety-year woman old she was when she died or the young and virile twenty-year old she was before you were even in her thoughts?"

Dad was comfortable in his beliefs, so rather than get tangled up in a clutter of metaphysical chatter, I didn't push for an answer.

I loved the message of "A New Earth." He didn't get it. He believes what suits his tailor-made world. He prefers to keep things simple. Heaven is up and hell is down. God is God, no need to address Him as the Source, Creator, the Maker, or Yahweh. Like he says, "Everybody's crazy!" To some limited extent, he's right. He's made it this far...

THE END FOR NOW

Breinigsville, PA USA
12 October 2010
247226BV00002B/27/P

9 781432 747374